Group Performance and Interaction

Group Performance and Interaction

Craig D. Parks
and
Lawrence J. Sanna

Washington State University

Westview Press
A Member of the Perseus Books Group

Copyright © 1999 by Westview Press, A Member of the Perseus Books Group

Published in 1999 in the United States of America by Westview Press, 5500 Central Avenue, Boulder, Colorado 80301-2877, and in the United Kingdom by Westview Press, 12 Hid's Copse Road, Cumnor Hill, Oxford OX2 9JJ

Library of Congress Cataloging-in-Publication Data
Parks, Craig D.
  Group performance and interaction / Craig D. Parks, Lawrence J. Sanna.
    p. cm.
  Includes bibliographical references and index.
  ISBN 0-8133-3319-9 (hc). — ISBN 0-8133-3320-2 (pb)
  1. Small groups.   2. Social groups.   3. Group decisionmaking.
4. Social interaction.   5. Social psychology.   I. Sanna, Lawrence
J. II. Title.
HM133.P35   1999
302.3'4—dc21   98-27911
                                     `   CIP

The paper used in this publication meets the requirements of the American National Standard for Permanence of Paper for Printed Library Materials Z39.48-1984.

10   9   8   7   6   5   4   3   2   1

Contents

List of Tables and Illustrations   ix
Preface   xi

1   Introduction and Overview   1

PART ONE
BASIC GROUP PROCESSES

2   The Experience of Group Membership   9

    Group Formation and Development, 10
    Being a Group Member, 17
    Chapter Summary, 20

3   Group Influence   21

    Mathematical Models of Group Influence, 22
    Dual Process Models of Influence, 35
    Chapter Summary, 41

PART TWO
GROUP PERFORMANCE AND INTERACTION

4   Group Decisionmaking   45

    Group Discussion, 46
    Combination of Preferences, 51
    Groupthink, 54
    Problemsolving Groups, 56
    Chapter Summary, 59

5   Social Facilitation   61

    Social Facilitation: Performing Alone or with
      Others Present, 62
    Drive Theories: Arousal and Activation as
      Motivating Forces, 64

Self Theories: Thoughts and Feelings About
  Yourself and Others as a Motivating Force, 71
Resource Theories: Physical and Psychological
  Capacity Limits on Performance, 76
Chapter Summary, 77

6 Social Motivation Losses   79

Steiner's Topology of Productivity, Resources,
  and Tasks, 79
Social Loafing: Performing Individually or Collectively, 82
Free Riders and Suckers: Taking Advantage of
  Others Without Their Taking Advantage of You, 90
What to Do About Free-Riding, Sucker, and Social-
  Loafing Effects? 93
Social Compensation: Making Up for Others'
  Inadequacies, 94
Group Performance: Some Possibly Integrative
  Views, 96
Chapter Summary, 97

7 Social Dilemmas   99

The Prisoner's Dilemma, 100
The Public Goods Game, 102
The Resource Dilemma, 113
Chapter Summary, 124

PART THREE
SPECIFIC TYPES OF GROUPS

8 Groups in the Workplace   127

Leadership, 127
Equity Theory, 131
Relative Deprivation, 135
Social Comparison, 142
Negotiation, 146
Teamwork, 151
Organizational Culture, 153
Chapter Summary, 155

9 Juries   157

Mock Jury Methodology, 158
Jury Decision Processes, 159

Procedural Influences on the Jury, 162
Scientific Jury Selection, 167
Chapter Summary, 168

10 Computer-Based Groups   169

Group Software, 169
Dynamics of Computer-Based Groups, 170
Computer Group Performance, 175
Simulated Groups, 177
Chapter Summary, 179

11 Unique Groups   181

Military Groups, 181
Flight Crews: Groups in the Cockpit, 183
Hospital Teams, 187
Sports Teams: There's No Place Like Home . . . Or
    Is There? 190
Sports Fans as Groups: Affiliating and Dissociating
    with Teams, 197
Chapter Summary, 201

12 Future Directions in Group Research   203

The Dynamic Nature of Groups, 203
Group Information Processing, 204
Groups and Social Cognition, 205
Electronic Performance Monitoring, 206
Evaluation of Group Improvement Interventions, 207
Concluding Thoughts, 208

Appendix: Methodological Issues in Groups Research   209
References   219
Index   267

Tables and Illustrations

Tables

6.1   Number of uses generated by coworker effort
         and condition   96

7.1   A prisoner's dilemma outcome matrix   101
7.2   The decision to contribute to a charity   104

8.1   Fiedler's (1967) eight different work situations, placed
         on a favorability continuum   129
8.2   Predictions from Carnevale's (1986) Model of
         Mediator Behavior   150

A.1   Bales's (1950) Interaction Process Analysis (IPA)
         coding system   214

Figures

1.1   Overview of the book   3

3.1   Effects of strength, immediacy, and number:
         Multiplicative and divisive social impact   24
3.2   Marginally increasing effects of passersby
         craning and gawking   26
3.3   Experimental setting for testing personal space boundaries   32
3.4   Gompertz growth functions   34

5.1   Social facilitation effects   63
5.2   Easy and difficult cockroach mazes   66
5.3   The distraction/conflict model   70
5.4   Self-efficacy and outcome expectancies   75

6.1   Sound production   85
6.2   Effects of evaluation on social loafing   87

6.3   Effects of mood and goals on social loafing   90
6.4   Free-rider and sucker effects   93

8.1   Referent cognitions theory   139

Photos

6.1   Social loafing: Working hard, and hardly working   84

11.1 Basking in the reflected glory of favorite sports teams   198

Preface

Group performance and interaction has been of great interest as a subject of research and theory for the past century. This is likely due in no small part to the fact that human beings are essentially social creatures. Interacting in groups deeply affects all of us, whether it is with our families, in our leisure activities, or at our workplace. Research on groups has been a growing, dynamic, and exciting area of study. Our purpose in writing this book is to convey some of this excitement to readers and to those who may have an interest in working with or understanding groups.

We have chosen to organize this book in three main sections. The chapters within each section present theoretical expositions of the various group topics and descriptions of existing research. As the title of our book suggests, these discussions emphasize performance and interaction issues. Our primary objective is to give readers a flavor for the variety of theoretical perspectives proposed by group researchers and to lend a greater understanding of group phenomena.

As with any project of this magnitude, there are several people who assisted in making this book possible. We would like to thank our editor, Cathy Murphy, and the people at Westview Press for their encouragement and support of this project, as well as Michelle Baxter, under whose guidance the book was initiated. We would also like to thank our anonymous reviewers. In addition, we are grateful to Stefanie Miller for her assistance in conducting some of the literature searches and for her help in constructing the subject index, and to John Burick, Jim Davis, Bob Gifford, and Paul Whitney, who provided input on various topics.

Craig D. Parks
Lawrence J. Sanna

Chapter One

Introduction and Overview

Groups are all around us. We all belong to groups—be it work groups, family groups, play groups, political groups, and so on. It is our good fortune that the publication of this book coincides with the 100-year anniversary of the beginning of group research. In 1898, Norman Triplett initiated this subject of research with his study of bicycle racers (see Chapter 5), and since that time research on groups has been a growing, dynamic, and exciting area of study. The focus of this volume is on group performance and interaction. Of course, as with any topic as extensive as group performance and interaction, we have by no means exhausted the range of issues that could potentially fit under this umbrella. However, we have tried to focus on some of the major topics and on some exciting new developments that we believe have not received adequate coverage in previous volumes.

Group performance and interaction is an interesting and fundamental area of study, with an unabashedly "social" flavor. Over the years, the specific topics of focal interest to group researchers have waxed and waned. Steiner (1974, 1983, 1986), for instance, has written several interesting analyses of factors related to the activity level in the area of group research. Moreland, Hogg, and Hains (1994) have suggested that an interest in group research is in fact on the increase in recent years, and Sanna and Parks (1997) have pointed out that interest in group research has taken hold within many areas of psychology. Because of this, we would venture to speculate that the study of groups will never become a dormant interest to psychologists and researchers and theorists in other areas. It deals with a whole range of intriguing questions about how people are influenced by the groups to which they belong, or with whom they are interacting, and how these groups in turn might be influenced by their members. What is the experience of being in a group? What types of influences might groups have? What are the influences of groups on decisionmaking and performance?

What are the implications of being in groups for applied settings, such as workplaces, juries, or airline cockpits? These are just a few examples of some of the many issues that are represented in *Group Performance and Interaction*. Thus, although the specific topics of focal interest to group researchers may have changed as the years have passed and will likely continue to do so, we believe that the general enthusiasm for group performance and interaction issues will remain constant.

Although undoubtedly there are many other ways in which we could have organized this book, we have chosen to do so in the context of three main sections or parts; these are depicted in Figure 1.1. In Part One, we focus on some basic group processes. These include the experience of group membership (Chapter 2) and group influence (Chapter 3). Group members are often subject to several forces that affect their formation and development, in both natural and experimental settings. Such factors as affinity or similarity, for instance, seem to have an ubiquitous influence on the choice to join and maintain belonging to a group (Simpson & Harris, 1994). This feeling of "closeness" to other human beings appears to be at the heart of our existence. When interacting in groups, people develop a sense of affinity with the group to which they belong, their "ingroup," and they have a tendency to differentiate this from other, outside groups, or "outgroups" (Brewer, 1979). This differentiation, at least at times, can be an important source of status (Berger, Webster, Ridgeway, & Rosenholtz, 1986) or social identity (Tajfel, 1982; Turner, Oakes, Haslam, & McGarty, 1994). In Chapter 3, we focus on some basic influence processes that may occur when people are part of, or are interacting with, a group. This chapter is divided into two main parts, each dealing with a description of how people can influence, and can be influenced by, other group members. Several models of group influence have been proposed, which focus variously on group members as both sources and targets of influence (e.g., Knowles, 1978; Latané, 1981; Mullen, 1983; Tanford & Penrod, 1984). Each of these models focuses on the influence of the number of present group members, their closeness, and their strength, either individually or in some combination. In the second part of this chapter, we focus on some dual process models of group influence, which attempt to address the relationships between majority and minority influence. In groups, there is a push for consensus, information can be shared and categorized, and so on (e.g., Crano, 1994; Thibaut & Kelley, 1959). We have chosen to include these topics at the beginning of our book because these issues are relevant to virtually all aspects of group life and thus are presumed to be operative in behaviors discussed in each of our following chapters.

Part Two represents what is perhaps the real heart of our book. Here we discuss and describe some primary topics of group performance and interaction. We begin with a discussion of the fascinating topic of group deci-

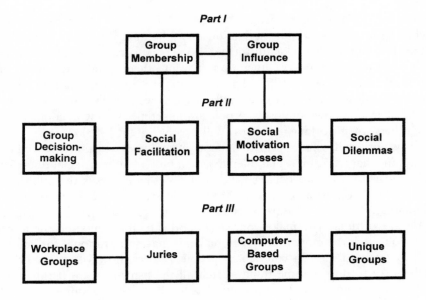

FIGURE 1.1   Overview of the book

sionmaking (Chapter 4). On the surface, the assumption is often made that groups make better decisions than individuals. In Chapter 4, however, we see that this is not always the case. We discuss issues such as brainstorming in groups (e.g., Diehl & Stroebe, 1987), conflict within groups (e.g., Mc-Grath, 1984), group discussion (Stasser & Titus, 1987), groupthink (Janis, 1982), and many other issues critical to group decisionmaking. An assumption of much of the group decisionmaking literature is that the outcomes of a successful or unsuccessful decision represent a particular type of performance. Building on this notion, in Chapter 5, we begin to examine specific performance issues. The "social facilitation effect," as it has come to be known, represents an important group phenomenon, as it tests the effects of perhaps the most minimal of social conditions. Social facilitation researchers have tried to assess a contrast between performances when alone versus performances when audiences or coworkers are present. We describe and discuss several intriguing theories on this issue as well as research that has been designed to test performance differences (e.g., Baron, 1986; Cottrell, 1972; Zajonc, 1965).

In Chapter 6, we describe social motivation losses. Many investigators had noticed that group members do not always seem to perform up to their individual potential. For example, when people work in groups, they sometimes "loaf" because they believe that others cannot identify or evaluate their individual performances (e.g., Williams, Harkins, & Latané, 1981; Harkins &

Jackson, 1985). In short, people "slack off." However, sometimes people working in groups exhibit motivation losses because they can "free ride" (they believe they can take advantage of others' efforts) or because they do not want to be a "sucker" (they do not want others to take advantage of their efforts) (e.g., Kerr, 1983). Each of these processes can result in social motivation losses, albeit for different reasons, as we describe. At times, however, far from motivation losses, people are sometimes willing to compensate for others when working in groups (Williams & Karau, 1993).

This notion of what appear to be motivation losses or gains is picked up again in Chapter 7, on social dilemmas. An individual in a social dilemma is faced with a choice between individual self-gain versus the collective good (e.g., Komorita & Parks, 1995). A classic example, is a "resource dilemma." Suppose you are a fisher and you are faced with a potential shortage of tuna. You make your livelihood catching tuna, and the more fish you catch the more money you make. It may seem rational for you to try to catch all the fish you can. A problem arises, however, if the other fishers try to do the same thing—catch all the fish they can. If this happened, there would soon be no tuna left at all, the fish population could not replenish itself, and no one would have a job catching fish (to say nothing of the loss of a species). Chapter 7 focuses on many variables that influence peoples' decisions in social dilemmas (e.g., group size, Kerr, 1989; trust, Yamagishi, 1986), a primary interactive context for studying group behaviors.

In Part Three, we discuss some specific groups, many of which are in applied areas. Our final section includes a discussion of workplace groups, juries, computer-based groups, and other unique groups. In our discussion of workplace groups (Chapter 8), we discuss topics such as leadership (e.g., Ayman, Chemers, & Fiedler, 1995), equity (e.g., Adams, 1965), relative deprivation (e.g., Folger, 1986b), and negotiation (e.g., Pruitt & Carnevale, 1993), among others. The types of leaders that we have, as well as our perceptions of how we compare to others, most certainly affects our performances and interactions in the workplace. Juries, of course, are another interesting group. How do juries interact and make decisions? In Chapter 9, we explore some relevant variables. Research suggests that such things as the jury's preferences for decision rules (e.g., Davis, 1980), deliberation style (e.g., Kaplan & Schersching, 1981), and a number of other variables are critical in this regard. In Chapter 10 we deal with an emerging topic in group performance and interaction—that of computer-based groups. Here we deal with such intriguing topics as feelings of anonymity or "deindividuation" (Diener, 1980), "flaming" (Lea, O'Shea, Fung, & Spears, 1992), and other processes that affect groups when working on computers. In Chapter 11, we focus on a variety of group settings, from military groups to flight crews, to sports groups, to hospital teams. In Part Three, we borrow heavily and refer frequently to material covered in our previous chapters, but we also take the liberty to greatly move beyond these prior chapters by discussing much unique material that is particularly pertinent to the topics at hand.

We provide here an introduction and overview of a diversity of group performance and interaction topics that have not as yet been available within any single volume. Because of this breadth, we believe that our book will be of interest not only to psychologists but also to those with interests in many other areas. We have geared our book to the advanced undergraduate and graduate level. However, our primary objective is to expose readers to the variety of theoretical perspectives proposed by group researchers. In short, this book should be of interest to anyone who wishes to gain a greater understanding of group performance and interaction phenomena.

Part One

Basic Group Processes

Chapter Two

The Experience of Group Membership

We begin our examination of groups by asking some of the most basic questions about groups: How do they form? How do they stay together? What is it like to be a member of a group? For some types of groups, the answers to some of these questions are obvious. For example, there is no mystery as to how a jury is formed. It is done through a careful selection process, the goal being to identify a set of people who are impartial, yet capable of processing the evidence and rendering a legal decision. How does the jury stay together? In fact, jurors have no choice about whether they should continue their membership. Only the presiding judge can decide whether a juror should leave the group, and he or she will remove a juror only under extraordinary circumstances: The juror may be very ill, or the judge may feel that the juror's impartiality has been compromised by outside forces (e.g., a biased news commentary).

Most groups in our society, however, are not so easily analyzed. It is the rare group indeed for which we can easily answer all three of the questions that we have posed. Note that we did not discuss the final question—what is it like to be a member of a group—in the jury example above. This is because it is not clear exactly what impact serving as a juror has on people. You will see in Chapter 8, devoted exclusively to juries, that we have some ideas about how to answer the question of impact, but there are far too many unanswered questions for us to confidently describe the jury experience in every detail.

In this chapter we discuss some basic ideas regarding group assembly, continuation, and impact. The ideas that we introduce appear in other chapters as well, because they are fundamental features of every group.

Group Formation and Development

Let us start with the most basic group issue: How do groups form and stay together? As we alluded to in our jury example, many groups are purposely formed to accomplish a specific goal. A committee is another good example. We refer to such groups as *ad hoc* groups. This type of group remains together only as long as it takes to accomplish the goal, and then it disbands. By contrast, a second type of group, which we refer to as a *natural* group, comes together without outside impetus. A good example of a natural group is a group of friends. Groups of friends arise and evolve over time; they are not carefully constructed to achieve a goal. In the following text, we will see how natural groups form.

Regardless of how the group was assembled, all groups develop sets of behavioral rules. These rules address such things as acceptable behavior within the group, rules of procedure, and roles. The rules may also touch upon issues such as which attitude about a topic is considered appropriate for group members to hold; how group members should present themselves in terms of dress and appearance; and even what constitutes morality. Where do these rules come from? How are they learned and transmitted? We will discuss these questions also.

Finally, we need to understand how groups survive. As with the jury, some groups are prohibited from breaking apart until the goal is accomplished, but even an ad hoc group is not guaranteed of surviving until the goal is met. We will look at what factors determine group survival.

Formation of Natural Groups

How do natural groups develop? The strongest factor is *attraction*. Quite simply, natural groups will not form if their members are not attracted to one another. (It is important to understand that, to a researcher, the term attraction refers to a general sense of wanting to be with other people. Many people equate attraction with romantic attraction and assume that if two people are attracted to each other, they are romantically linked. When we talk about attraction, we are using the general term.) There are many factors that determine whether people are attracted to one another.

Rewards.   We like to associate with people who provide us with rewards (Aronson & Linder, 1965). All else being equal, we are most attracted to groups that, by mere membership in the group, convey upon us social rewards. For example, a particular group might be very prestigious, and to be a member of that group is considered a great honor. We can also get rewards from the other group members, most often in the form of praise and a sense of self-worth. In fact, it has been argued that a major reason that adolescents join gangs is because of the rewards gang membership conveys, rewards that its members cannot receive elsewhere: Being in a gang provides status and prestige (at least in certain communities), money and material goods, and gang members provide support to each other (Burden, Miller, & Boozer, 1996).

When we think about the rewards of group membership, we actually think in terms of a *cost/benefit ratio:* We identify the rewards that we can receive from the group (benefits), but we also think about what we must do in order to join and remain in the group (costs) (Thibaut & Kelley, 1959). We prefer groups for which the benefits exceed the costs; that is, we get more out of the group than we put in. We have seen some of the rewards associated with gang membership, but consider the costs: almost continual danger, with the very real threat of early death; frequent run-ins with law enforcement; and engagement in activities that most people consider morally wrong (e.g., drug selling, killing). Most of us would like to have status, wealth, and social support, but acquisition of those things is not worth subjecting ourselves to danger, possible death, and violation of our morals. In other words, the costs of gang membership are greater than the benefits. However, for some people these rewards are so important that they will put up with the threat of death and will violate moral standards in order to acquire them.

Another aspect of group rewards is association with people who are socially desirable; that is, they possess characteristics that society as a whole values. Some examples of these characteristics are truthfulness, honesty, friendliness, happiness, responsibility, and loyalty; some examples of undesirable characteristics are rudeness, conceit, cruelty, and hostility (Anderson, 1968a; Leary, Rogers, Canfield, & Coe, 1986; Lott, Lott, Reed, & Crow, 1970; Lydon, Jamieson, & Zanna, 1988). Association with groups of socially desirable people is rewarding because the interactions are typically pleasant and because these groups usually have prestige due to their skills. In fact, this association can be so desirable that it is not unusual for members of such groups to call attention to the fact that they are members. Think, for example, of the behavior of a person whose favorite sports team has just won the championship. This person will probably trumpet the fact that his or her team won, perhaps by wearing team-related clothing, hanging posters (or framed magazine covers) of the team, or displaying team-related memorabilia. Such behavior is known as basking in reflected glory, or *BIRGing* (Cialdini, Borden, Thorne, Walker, Freeman, & Sloane, 1976). By contrast, association with undesirable groups (e.g., a very bad sports team) is unlikely to produce any rewards and may actually produce some negative outcomes, such as ridicule or embarrassment, so that people often deny such an association. This is known as cutting off reflected failure, or *CORFing* (Snyder, Lassegard, & Ford, 1986).

Similarity.   We are most attracted to groups that contain members who are similar to us at a very basic level on such aspects as beliefs, interests, personal background, and values (Simpson & Harris, 1994). If you think about your circle of friends, for example, it is likely that you all share many of the same beliefs and like to engage in the same types of activities.

There are many explanations for the power of similarity in attraction. First, interacting with similar others is typically more pleasant than interacting with dissimilar others because the dissimilar others may well question and criticize our beliefs and interests (Rosenbaum, 1986). Attraction to similar others is also logical from a cognitive consistency standpoint—why would you dislike people who have most of the qualities that you have? Finally, for reasons that are still unclear, when people are similar to each other, they tend to develop a *unit relationship,* or a feeling that they "belong together" (Arkin & Burger, 1980).

Proximity.   People who are separated by great distances do not often coalesce. Think about your friends and how you first met them. In all likelihood, you were in some situation in which you were in close physical proximity to one another: You lived in the same neighborhood, shared the same classes, or worked at the same job. It is very unlikely that you met your best friend by randomly dialing a phone number for a different city, and bonded with the person who answered the phone. Physical closeness is an important precursor of attraction. One reason is familiarity: The more physically close people are, the more frequently they encounter one another. It is known that repeated exposure to an object typically increases our liking for that object. This is known as the *mere exposure* effect (Zajonc, 1968). Frequent contact also leads us to anticipate future interaction with the person, and when we expect to interact with a person in the future, we tend to focus on the person's positive features and to downplay his or her negative features, so as to make the future interaction more pleasant (Tyler & Sears, 1977).

Comparison Levels

We now know that attraction to a group is primarily determined by rewards, similarity, and proximity. We most prefer groups that provide us with rewards, that contain group members who are similar to us, and that are in the same physical area. But is it necessarily the case that we will want to join *any* group that meets these criteria? In fact, the decision is not this simple. When we are deciding whether to join (or remain in) a group, we consider not only these three factors but also how the group's cost/benefit ratio compares both to other similar groups to which we have previously belonged and to other groups that we could possibly join right now. The use of past groups as a standard for comparison is referred to as a *comparison level* (or CL), and the use of current other groups is known as *comparison level for alternatives* (or CLalt) (Thibaut & Kelley, 1959). In general, CLalt determines whether we will join the group, and CL determines our reaction to membership in the group. We will join a group whenever CLalt is high, which means that there is no other current group that can offer us a better cost/benefit ratio. We will enjoy being part of the group when CL is high because the group's cost/benefit ratio is better than what we have previously experienced. This theory makes some predictions about group membership that may surprise you. First, if CLalt is high, but CL is low, this means that the group is not attractive, but there is no better group currently available; hence, we will join an unattractive group. Second if CLalt is low, but CL is high, then the group is very attractive, but there is a better group currently available; hence, we will not join an attractive group. Thibaut and Kelley's basic ideas have been clearly supported by empirical research and are considered to be fundamental principles of group dynamics.

Group Development

Research on group formation describes how individuals come to be associated with one another. But a mere assemblage of people is not automatically defined as a "group." Group researchers distinguish between a "collective," which is generally defined as a large, unorganized, and temporary set of individuals (e.g., the audience at a baseball game), and a "group," which is smaller, more permanent, and has a definite infrastructure (Turner & Killian, 1987). Researchers who study group development are interested in this infrastructure. In this section, we look at some of the major factors that separate a group from a collective.

Norms. All groups have associated with them "norms," or standards of behavior. Norms tell us what actions will and will not be tolerated by other group members. Of course, even when we are part of a collective much of our behavior is driven by social norms. You would not, for example, remove all of your clothes at a baseball game because doing so is not tolerated by society at large. But most groups also have associated with them particular standards that are peculiar to that group. Society has no particular position regarding what brand of clothes you should wear, but it may be the case that, within your circle of friends, the expectation is that members wear clothing made by certain designers. Norms are transmitted to new group members via *socialization,* which can be thought of as the process of learning about a recently entered group. Just as children are socialized into the ways of their culture, so are new group members taught about the expectations within the group. Besides norms, another very important piece of information that is conveyed during the socialization process concerns the roles within the group.

Roles and Status. As social beings, all of us have roles that we must fill. In fact, most of us must fill multiple roles. For example, at various times of the day a male professor can be either a husband, father, teacher, colleague, or friend. Quite often he plays a number of these roles at the same time. Under certain circumstances he may fill more unusual roles, such as patient or shopper. Roles are a part of almost every group to which we belong, and the assignment of roles to group members is a key factor that distinguishes a group from a collective. In fact, each of the roles that we have listed for the professor correspond to his membership in a group. Husband and father correspond to his family group; teacher and colleague to his work group; and friend to his friendship group. Roles are important for group members because associated with the roles are rules of behavior. To "fill a role" means to perform the behaviors that are connected to the role. To be a teacher the professor must engage in certain behaviors; further, they are not behaviors that he would perform when he is with his family.

Associated with the roles that we fill are particular levels of *status,* or standing within the group. Status provides prestige. When we describe a person as having high status, we mean that the person is considered by other group members to be prestigious. Typically, high-status individuals also have considerable influence within the group, although status does not necessarily empower a person. Status is generally determined by one's ability to help the group achieve its goals (Berger, Webster, Ridgeway, & Rosenholtz, 1986). Hence, status is most closely associated with ability, in that those with high status typically have some unusual level of ability. Doctors have high status in most cultures because they are most able to help society achieve the goal of universal health.

Status can also be conveyed upon a person for reasons that are unrelated to group goals. For example, some people have high status simply because they possess desirable characteristics, even though those characteristics are irrelevant to the group's goals. The best example of this is physical beauty. Attractive people typically have elevated status, at least in our society, even though it is difficult to conceive of a group goal that can most easily be accomplished simply by having a large number of beautiful members. Some people acquire status through the process of *status generalization* (Molm, 1986), which occurs when group members assume that a person with high ability in one area is capable in other, unrelated areas. One of your authors can relate a personal experience that is a good example of this. He was recently asked to head up a search committee to find and hire a new chief administrator for his son's preschool. When he pointed out that he knew nothing about school administration skills, particularly at the preschool level, he was told that he would nonetheless be an effective committee leader because he had a Ph.D. In other words, the assumption was being made that his having an extensive education automatically made him a skilled group leader, even though the task at hand was outside his range of expertise. In fact, he would have been a useless addition to the search committee because he had no clue what skills to focus on in evaluating candidates for preschool administrator. (As you can probably tell, he turned down the offer.)

Status generalization is pervasive. In the work world, industrial/organizational psychologists deal with a problem called "halo error," which occurs during performance appraisal. Basically, a performance judge commits a halo error when he or she observes that a worker is highly skilled at one task and concludes that the person is skilled at all tasks, without actually having seen the worker perform those other tasks (Nisbett & Wilson, 1977). People who are in the business of influencing others (e.g., advertisers) often employ status generalization to their advantage by having highly skilled individuals, such as athletes, endorse products. When Michael Jordan tells you that no pain reliever is more effective at fighting headaches than Brand X, he is implying that he has made a careful study of all available pain relievers and has concluded that Brand X is superior to anything else available. This is unlikely to have happened, to say the least. The advertiser is hoping that you will engage in status generalization and conclude that Jordan's skill on the basketball court transfers to comparative judgments of pain relievers.

Cohesion.   Once the group is formed, what holds it together? For many groups, the binding force is simply some common goal. For example, jurors work toward the goal of a verdict in a court case until one is reached or the jury is hung (i.e., cannot reach agreement). At that point, the jury breaks apart. It would be very surprising if a jury requested that the judge dismiss them, even though they were making progress toward a verdict. (In fact, it would be so surprising that the judge would probably deny the request.) But few groups are assembled for such an explicit and narrow purpose. Groups of friends, clubs, and intramural sports teams, for example, typically exist for a myriad of reasons. What holds these groups together? The major factor is *cohesiveness.* We define cohesion as a general sense of community and attraction to the group and its members. More informally, a group is cohesive if its members want to be together. Many factors determine the amount of cohesion within a group: the extent to which group members like each other; satisfaction with the group's performance; the extent to which personal and group goals match; and external forces that discourage leaving, to name a few (Cota, Evans, Dion, Kilik, & Longman, 1995). Cohesion increases as these factors become stronger. Consider a business administration club at a university. If the club was very cohesive, we might see that (a) the members like each other; (b) the group's reason for existence—to disseminate information about careers in business administration—is congruent with members' interests; (c) the members believe that the club does a good job at disseminating information; and (d) the club has employment contacts with industry that the members could not access if they were not members of the club.

Communication.   Communication between group members is essential. Without it, coordination of activities and integration of information is extremely difficult, sometimes impossible (Maznevski, 1994). It is thus important for the group members to establish some type of communication system, or *network,* early in the group's existence. There are two types of communication networks: formal and informal.

Formal Networks.   A formal communication network is one that describes how group members are "supposed" to interact with one another. The formality may be explicitly stated or implied. There are two types of formal networks. A *decentralized* network is any network in which group members can speak freely with one another. A group of friends is an excellent example of a decentralized communication network. You can speak with any of your friends whenever you want. By contrast, under a *centralized* communication network certain group members are prohibited from direct interaction with one another. If one person wants to speak to another, he or she must send a message through at least one other person. Centralized networks are characteristic of the workplace (Zahn, 1991). If a factory worker at General Motors wants to communicate with the president of the company, the worker probably cannot simply call the president on the phone. Instead, the worker likely needs to prepare a message, give it to his or her shift supervisor, who will give it to the plant foreman, and so on up the chain of command until the message reaches the president.

   Considerable research has been conducted on the nature of communication in centralized networks. For example, it is known that downward communication is often flawed both because superiors (those high up in the network) tend to underestimate how much information subordinates (those low in the network) need (Likert, 1961) and because superiors overestimate the clarity of their communications (Callan, 1993). These flaws are important as there seems to be a direct connection between quality and frequency of network communications and group productivity (Clampitt & Downs, 1993). It is also the case that a message is increasingly likely to become distorted, either through omission or exaggeration of details, as it passes through more and more "links" in the network (Gaines, 1980). This is especially likely to occur if the message is a negative one (Lee, 1993; O'Reilly, 1978; Tesser & Rosen, 1975).

Informal Networks.   Many groups, especially those that operate under a centralized communication network, also have informal lines of communication. These informal lines, typically called *grapevines,* operate much like a decentralized network: Conceivably, anybody can talk to anybody, although in practice grapevine interaction is almost always between friends (Baird, 1977). Grapevines actually serve many important functions within a group, such as maintenance of social relations between members and reinforcement of messages that are sent over the formal network. However, superiors within a formal network are often negative about grapevines because of the fairly common perception that grapevines foster transmission of false information. This presumption is not supported by research, however (Mishra, 1990).

Being a Group Member

Group membership exerts a strong influence over much of our daily lives. It affects how we interact with others and how we think about ourselves. Let us look more closely at this influence.

Interactions with Others

In essence, there are two types of groups: those to which we belong and those to which we do not. Any group to which we belong is called an *ingroup*, and any group to which we do not belong is an *outgroup*. The manner in which we interact with another person is often affected by whether that person is an ingroup member or an outgroup member. In some cultures, sharp distinctions are drawn between how one acts toward an ingroup or outgroup member, although in the United States ingroup versus outgroup interaction is less strongly delineated (Triandis, McCusker, & Hui, 1990). However, even if ingroup-outgroup interaction is behaviorally similar to ingroup-ingroup interaction, the nature of ingroup-outgroup interaction differs considerably from the interaction that occurs between ingroup members. For example, an ingroup member will share resources fairly equally with other ingroup members but will give outgroup members only a small portion of the resources (Messe, Hymes, & MacCoun, 1986). In fact, ingroup members are generally more concerned with "beating" the outgroup than with maximizing the ingroup's total payoff (Tajfel & Turner, 1986). This means that if given a choice between gaining $50 while the outgroup gains $40, or gaining $30 while the outgroup gains $10, ingroup members will generally favor the second set of outcomes. They will pass up the chance to get the largest possible payoff ($50) in order to maximize the difference between their outcome and the outgroup's outcome. In the workplace, leaders tend to form an ingroup and an outgroup of subordinates, based upon the worker's commitment to the organization, with committed workers forming the ingroup. Ingroup workers are given considerable autonomy and influence, but outgroup workers have their activities highly structured and have little influence (Scandura & Graen, 1984).

Ingroup-outgroup differences also influence how we perceive others. Ingroup members tend to be more critical of an outgroup member's performance than of an ingroup member's performance (Hinkle & Schopler, 1986; Wayne & Ferris, 1990). Ingroup members generally perceive their fellow members as being very diverse, whereas the outgroup is seen as being very homogeneous (Mullen & Hu, 1989). These perceptions of outgroup member similarity apply not only to psychological characteristics but also to physical features; in other words, ingroup members tend to believe that members of outgroups all look alike (Anthony, Cooper, & Mullen, 1992). The outgroup is also more likely to be perceived in terms of stereotypes than is the ingroup (Judd, Ryan, & Park, 1991).

The conclusion, then, is that the manner in which we interact with and perceive people is often influenced by whether we share membership in the same groups as those people. One should not underestimate the pervasiveness of this ingroup-outgroup effect. For example, it is generally considered to be one of the major factors that underlie prejudice. Brewer and Miller (1996) provide an excellent overview of the many different facets of ingroup-outgroup behavior, and the interested reader should consult their book.

Self-Perceptions

Group membership also influences how we perceive ourselves. To demonstrate this, ask yourself the question "Who am I?" and try to come up with a number of different answers to the question, perhaps twenty or so. At some point, you will probably start answering the question in terms of group membership (e.g., "I am a member of Beta Theta Pi sorority"). Although the extent to which we think of ourselves as members of groups, rather than in individualistic terms, is culturally influenced (Triandis, 1989), group membership is nonetheless an important component of self-perception.

The role of groups in determining one's self-concept is most often described by *social identity theory* (Tajfel, 1982; Turner, Oakes, Haslam, & McGarty, 1994). This theory argues that we organize the world into ingroups and outgroups and that our membership in ingroups influences our self-esteem, specifically through our evaluation of our ingroup relative to outgroups. If, for example, your intramural softball team is the worst in the league, social identity theory predicts that you will experience low self-esteem because, compared to outgroups (i.e., the other teams in the league), your group is not very capable or desirable. The group that we most commonly reference in self-perception is our ethnic group (Phinney, 1991), although a host of other personal and societal groups factor into self-perception as well (Deaux, Reid, Mizrahi, & Ethier, 1995).

The connection between group membership and self-esteem is still being investigated by researchers. Some predictions of social identity theory have been supported, but others have not. For example, social identity theory predicts that being in a low-status group will lead to low self-esteem in its members. Some researchers have indeed observed this (e.g., Bat-Chava, 1994), but others have not (e.g., Crocker & Major, 1989). Social identity theory also predicts that when one's membership in a group is not secure, one will be most likely to show ingroup and outgroup biases, and this has been observed (Noel, Wann, & Branscombe, 1995). The person is trying to bolster self-esteem by building up the ingroup and derogating the outgroup. However, it should also be the case that a person with low self-esteem will demonstrate ingroup-outgroup biases regardless of the security of their in-group membership, again so as to increase self-esteem, but this does not seem to happen (Wills, 1981). We may be able to explain this discrepancy by arguing that there are different types of self-esteem: that connected to personal accomplishment ("private self-esteem"), and that connected to group accomplishment ("collective self-esteem") (Tajfel & Turner, 1986). Little research has been conducted on private versus collective self-esteem, but what has been done seems to support the notion (Crocker & Luhtanen, 1990).

The *group value model* argues that self-perceptions are affected by two factors: pride, which refers to how we evaluate the group as a whole, and respect, which refers to our relative standing within the group (Tyler, Degoey, & Smith, 1996; Tyler & Lind, 1992). This model makes many predictions about how pride and respect influence both self-esteem and behavior within the group. For example, it predicts that a person who has high standing in a low-status group will prefer to remain in the group and work toward bettering its status rather than accept a low-standing position in a high-status group. Although this is a very new model, some research exists to support the notion that both pride and respect affect self-evaluation and group-related behaviors (Smith & Tyler, 1997).

Group-to-Individual Transfer

Of course, not all of our behaviors take place within the context of a group. There are many tasks that we complete, and problems that we tackle, by ourselves. But perhaps the experiences that we have in the group affect our subsequent individual behavior. That is, maybe we take away from the group general behavioral strategies that we then apply to individual-level tasks. This notion is referred to as *group-to-individual transfer,* and although it is an attractive and intuitively compelling notion, the actual research evidence is mixed as to whether group experiences influence later individual behavior. Transfer research sometimes focuses on how the group environment affects its members. For example, it is known that individuals who have been in very cohesive groups have an easier time adjusting to societal changes than do individuals who have not experienced such cohesion (Hoyle & Crawford, 1994). However, most group-to-individual transfer research looks at decisionmaking and how specific group decisionmaking strategies influence individual members, and it is here where the pattern of results becomes less consistent. Transfer is typically observed when the group is working on "intellective" tasks, or tasks that have a clearly right answer (Gabbert, Johnson, & Johnson, 1986; Johnson, Johnson, Ortiz, & Stanne, 1991; Stasson, Kameda, Parks, Zimmerman, & Davis, 1991). A good example of such a task is solution of math problems. However, when the group is faced with a "judgmental" task, which does not have a clearly correct answer (e.g., deciding in which of three stock portfolios to invest), the research evidence is much less clear: Some researchers have observed transfer (Stasson & Hawkes, 1995), but others have not (Laughlin & Barth, 1981; Laughlin & Sweeney, 1977). Clearly, more work is necessary to clarify under what conditions the experiences of group membership affect later individual performance on various tasks.

Chapter Summary

In this chapter we have focused on the "basics" of a group—how it forms, how it stays together, and what impact group membership has on members. We looked at the various factors related to attraction, and we saw that such factors as norms and roles distinguish a "group" from a mere collection of people. We also saw that being a group member influences how we interact with others. Specifically, we interact quite differently with a person depending upon whether the person shares membership in the same group. Group membership also affects how we think about ourselves and plays an important role in our self-concept. Finally, we saw that it is not clear whether the experiences one has in a group affect subsequent individual performance.

Chapter Three

Group Influence

Consider each of the following situations:

- Members of a small campus group that is opposed to the use of animals in laboratory research stand in a busy pedestrian mall every day, regardless of the weather, to distribute informational leaflets to passersby.
- A student who has just joined a fraternity feels very self-conscious because he seems to be the only member of his house who does not wear a particular style of clothing.
- Antiabortion protesters continue to surround abortion clinics and use aggressive tactics, despite arrests and physical harassment.

Although each of these situations may at first seem to be quite different, they are in fact all examples of a single psychological phenomenon, *group influence*. In general, when we talk about group influence we are discussing an attempt by one social unit to change the behaviors, attitudes, beliefs, and cognitions of another social unit.

Influence has become an increasingly popular topic among psychologists, sociologists, marketing researchers, and political scientists, and it is a broad area of study. For instance, many researchers are interested in persuasion, or the situation in which one person tries to influence another person (Cialdini, 1993). In this chapter, we focus on group influence, or how a group of people brings about changes in a single person or another group. Although some of what is known about individual influence processes may also apply to group influence (e.g., persuasion), there are several theories that have been developed specifically to account for group influence. These are the theories that we discuss in this chapter.

There are two major schools of thought in the group influence field. Researchers who subscribe to *mathematical models* of group influence propose that group influence can be viewed as a function of several physical characteristics of groups, for instance, the number or importance of people who constitute the group. The relationship between these physical characteristics is often expressed in mathematical equations by these researchers. However, it is important to note that it is not the mathematical equations per se that are critical to an understanding of group influence; rather, what is important are the variables that have been identified by these researchers as being relevant to the influence process. The equations have become merely a convenient way to represent the relationships among the variables of interest. By contrast, *dual process* theorists argue that different types of group influence involve distinctly different types of processes.

We will examine each of these positions in turn, and we will also discuss some strengths and weaknesses of each. We will also refer to examples of group processes in later chapters where it is possible that these group influence theories can help one to understand what is going on in a particular group situation. We chose to present these basic group influence theories early in this book because they may have broad applicability to a variety of group situations, which we will discuss in later chapters.

Mathematical Models of Group Influence

There are four models of group influence: social impact theory, self-attention theory, social physics, and the social influence model. Each of these theories of group influence assumes "force field" type influences, in which other people are presumed to exert their effects in ways analogous to physical stimuli (e.g., light, sound, gravity, and so on). We describe each of these four models and discuss research evidence in support of each model's assumptions. Again, important here are the variables that have been identified by researchers as being significant to the group influence process. The relationships among these important variables are represented in terms of mathematical equations.

Social Impact Theory

Multiplicative and Divisive Impact.   Perhaps the most heavily researched model of group influence is social impact theory (Latané, 1981; Latané & Wolf, 1981). This model has been successfully used to describe social influence in a variety of areas, such as helping behavior (Jackson & Latané, 1987; Latané, 1981; Mishra & Das, 1983; Williams & Williams, 1983), persuasion (Williams & Williams, 1989) and social performance (Beatty & Payne, 1983; Jackson & Latané, 1981; Singh & Singh, 1989).

According to social impact theory, social forces (e.g., other people) affect a person in a manner similar to physical forces such as light, sound, or gravity. To use Latané's (1981) analogy, the amount of light that falls on a surface is a function of the strength of the light, the light's distance from the surface, and the number of lights. In a similar fashion, the amount of social impact (*SI*) that is felt by a person is assumed to be a function of the strength (*S*), immediacy (*I*), and number (*N*) of source persons. For instance, suppose a group of people are trying to influence your attitude toward the use of animals in laboratory research, as in the example we presented at the beginning of this chapter. Social impact theory would predict that the potential magnitude of influence that this group could have on your attitude would depend upon their strength (e.g., their status or power), their immediacy (e.g., how physically close they are to you), and the number of group members.

Another easy way of expressing this relationship is in terms of a mathematical equation. From the perspective of sources of influence (e.g., the animal rights group), these three elements are hypothesized to be multiplicatively related in the form $SI = f(SIN)$, where *SI* is the amount of social impact that is felt, and *S*, *I*, and *N*, represent the strength, immediacy, and number of sources. This equation simply states that the amount of group influence that you experience depends on the strength of the source group, the source group's immediacy to you, and the number of source group members. The greater the strength, immediacy, and number of sources, the more influence is predicted to be felt, with each element being multiplicatively related to total social impact. This relationship is presented graphically in Figure 3.1.

Another important proposal of social impact theory, however, is that of divisive social influence (or divisive force fields). This is, in effect, the inverse of the multiplicative group influence that we just described. To use another of Latané's (1981) analogies, the amount of force or impact on a particular tree bending in the wind is lessened in accordance with the size of the surrounding trees, the proximity of the trees, and the number of trees.

From the perspective of targets of influence (e.g., you as a target of influence by the animal rights group), this can be represented by the simple mathematical equation, $SI = f(1/SIN)$. This equation is similar to the one that we presented above for sources of influence, except that it represents the opposite relationship. Here we are looking at things from the perspective of the target of influence. This relationship is also represented diagrammatically in Figure 3.1.

Suppose we again have an animal rights group that is trying to influence your attitude toward laboratory research. Here, however, the social impact of any one particular group member on you would be diffused to the extent that there are other, strong, and immediate targets of impact along with you. The amount of influence that each source has on you is lessened in this case. That is, each source has less weight. The first source of influence has the most social impact, with other sources adding only marginally to the total influence that is experienced by you.

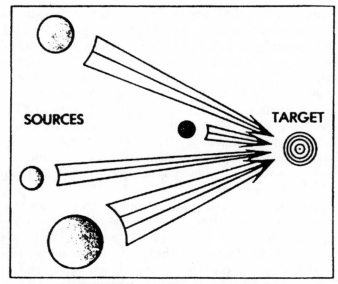

Multiplication of impact: $I = f(SIN)$

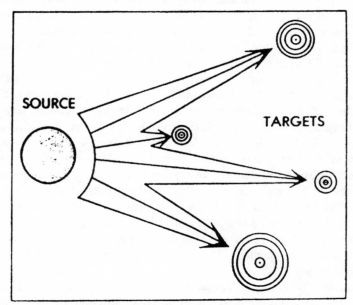

Division of impact: $I = f(1/SIN)$

FIGURE 3.1.   Effects of strength, immediacy, and number: Multiplicative and divisive social impact

Source: Latané, B. (1981). The psychology of social impact. *American Psychologist, 36*, 344 & 349. © American Psychological Association. Reprinted with permission.

Exponential Impact. The marginally increasing effect that sources of influence have on targets (or the marginally decreasing way that targets are affected by sources) is presumed to conform to a power function (Latané, 1981; Latané & Nida, 1980; Wolf & Latané, 1981). That is, each additional element (e.g., a fourth person) contributes to impact less than the addition of a previous element (e.g., a third person). Other people therefore have a great influence with increasing numbers, but this effect levels out as more and more people are added. One way of looking at this is by using an economic analogy. For example, the move from $0 to $1 has more impact (is more consequential) for a person than does the move from $99 to $100. This marginally increasing impact of each additional element is hypothesized to take the form of a power function; for example, for the number of others, the power function is represented by $SI = sN^{-t}$ (Latané & Nida, 1980).

From the perspective of targets of influence, SI represents the amount of social impact experienced, s represents a scaling constant (e.g., equal to individual reactions in the particular situation), N represents the number of others, and $-t$ represents an exponential power function that can range from 0 to −1 (see Latané, 1981; Latané & Nida, 1980; Wolf & Latané, 1981). Alternatively, from the perspective of sources of influence, again for the social impact of the number of others, the equation is identical to that just described except that the exponent is assumed to be simply t, which can range from 0 to 1 (i.e., $SI = sN^{t}$).

Evidence for Social Impact Theory. There is a good deal of evidence for social impact theory. Latané (1981) presented some initial evidence for social impact theory from a re-analysis of areas such as conformity, helping behavior, and social performance. For example, a well-known "craning and gawking" study (Milgram, Bickman, & Berkowitz, 1969), in which groups (confederates) would stop and stare up at a window while being unobtrusively filmed, found that increasing the number of confederates who were craning and gawking led to increases in passersby craning and gawking, but only at a marginally increasing rate in accordance with social impact's power function predictions (see Figure 3.2). In Figure 3.2, we can see how social impact theory and the power function works. The more people there were staring and looking up at a window, the more likely that passersby would stop and also look up at a window. However, although the first few group members had a large impact, the addition of more group members had less and less influence on passersby. In Asch's (1951; see also Gerard, Wilhelmy, & Conolly, 1968) classic research, conformity similarly grew with increases in group size, but only in a marginally increasing manner (with the major changes coming with increases in sizes from one to three).

Research on helping behavior and diffusion of responsibility (e.g., Darley & Latané, 1968) has been similarly interpreted. A well-established finding

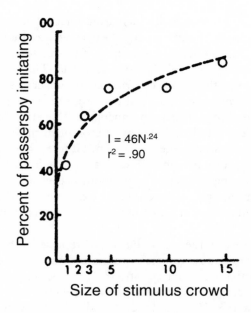

FIGURE 3.2.   Marginally increasing effects of passersby craning and gawking
    Source: Data from Migram, Bickman, & Berkowitz (1969); figure from Latané,
B. (1981). The psychology of social impact. *American Psychologist, 36,* 345. ©
American Psychological Association. Reprinted with permission.

in helping research is that the more people there are who potentially can offer assistance, the less likely any one person is to offer assistance, with the
biggest increase coming when moving from one to two people and marginally increasing (according to a power function) with each additional person
(see Latané & Darley, 1970). In a more explicit test of social impact theory's relation to helping, Williams and Williams (1983) found that time to
help was significantly longer as the number of potential helpers increased
and marginally longer as the strength (expertise) of potential helpers increased; the effects of immediacy were in the predicted direction, though
not significant, providing at least partial support for predictions derived
from social impact theory applied to helping (see also Jackson, 1987;
Mishra & Das, 1983).
    Social performance areas, particularly social loafing (Latané, Williams, &
Harkins, 1979; see Chapter 5), have also been interpreted as being related to
diffusion of responsibility and have been related to social impact theory. In
social loafing, the more people there are working collectively at a task, the
more likely each person is to work less hard than would be expected on the
basis of a person's individual performance, conforming to a marginally decreasing power function of about 0.20 (Harkins & Jackson, 1985). Social
loafing appears to be due in part to the decreased identifiability or evaluabil-

ity of individual outputs that occurs when working collectively (Harkins & Jackson, 1985; Sanna, 1992). In helping research, diffusion of responsibility should occur simply because of a perception that "someone else will do it," irrespective of evaluation potential (Latané, 1981). However, social loafing and diffusion of responsibility are related from the perspective of social impact in that the influence of others can be explained by a power function.

Finally, a study conducted by Jackson and Latané (1981) provides more direct evidence in support of social impact theory. These researchers used a cross-modality matching technique in which participants drew lines of various lengths on a grid that were to correspond to the imagined felt tension in response to an audience. Participants were shown slides that were used to manipulate the perception of high-status (professors) and low-status (students) people and the strength and number of source persons. In addition, the strength and number of targets were manipulated by showing slides that were supposed to represent coworkers of high and low status and of varying numbers. Results were consistent with social impact theory. High-status audiences of a large size had greater impact, but this impact was reduced when participants were asked to imagine working with high-status coworkers in a large group. Beatty and Payne (1983) also reported that the strength and number of people present is useful in explaining the magnitude of anxiety that is experienced by public speakers.

Summary of Social Impact Theory. There is a lot of evidence supporting social impact theory. The theory proposes that group influence is a function of the strength, immediacy, and number of others. This is true both from the perspective of sources of impact (multiplicative impact) and from the perspective of targets of impact (divisive impact). Social impact theory has been successfully applied to a variety of topics, from conformity to social performance, and even restaurant preferences (Wolf & Latané, 1983) and responses of courtroom witnesses (Wolf & Bugaj, 1990).

As with many theories, however, some additional questions remain. For instance, some have questioned the social impact theory's predictive utility (e.g., Mullen, 1983). Although predictions are that social impact will have a marginally increasing (or decreasing) effect, the exponents are calculated in a post hoc manner, with the only specification being that they should be between -1 and 1. In addition, two components of social impact theory—strength and immediacy—have received relatively little research attention, and what has been done has met with some mixed results (Mullen, 1985; but see also Jackson, 1986, and Mullen, 1986c). This is unfortunate because these two elements are defining characteristics that help to distinguish social impact theory from other theories of group influence. Further research has been aimed at assessing the effects of immediacy and strength, as well as number, variables (e.g., Latané, Liu, Nowak, Bonevento, & Zheng, 1995; Sedikides & Jackson, 1990).

Finally, the mathematical equation for social impact becomes a bit more complex when both the target and source of impact are simultaneously taken into account along with their respective marginally increasing effects (Jackson, 1987). The full hypothesis of social impact theory (see Jackson, 1987) is represented by the equation $SI = k(S^a I^b N^c_{sources}/S^x I^y N^z_{targets})$. These assumptions have yet to be examined within a single study.

Self-Attention Theory

Other-Total Ratio.   In contrast to the power functions of social impact theory, self-attention theory represents the social influence of groups on an individual by a ratio of self (or subgroup) to the total group (Mullen, 1983, 1987). Thus, group influence is viewed as resulting from the relationship (ratio) between the number of own group members to other group members. For example, if you are with a small group of fellow Republicans in a large room full of Democrats, then self-attention theory predicts that you would be more influenced when your group (Republicans) is smaller relative to the size of the other group (Democrats). Conversely, you will be less influenced as the number of people in your group increases relative to the other group.

The relationship of own group to other group is represented by what is known as the Other-Total Ratio (OTR), which is somewhat simpler than the equation for social impact theory. The OTR is $O/(O + S)$, where O is the number of people in the other subgroup and S is the number of people in the person's own subgroup. Again, as with all mathematical models of group influence, keep in mind that what are most important are the variables that have been identified by these researchers. The relationships between the proposed variables are most easily expressed in equation form.

Self-attention theory proposes that people become more self-attentive (cf. Carver & Scheier, 1981b) the more the relative size of their subgroup decreases because their subgroup becomes figural against the ground of the group total (Mullen, 1983, 1987). This results in subgroup members focusing greater attention on themselves, leading them to become more conscious about meeting salient behavioral standards (à la Carver & Scheier, 1981b). In contrast, taken from the perspective of members of the larger subgroup, less self-attention and less concern with matching salient behavioral standards should result.

We can come back to the example of our group trying to influence your attitude toward the use of animals in laboratory research, represented in Figure 3.1. If there were four animal rights activists trying to influence your opinion, the OTR for the predicted influence on you would be $4/(4 + 1) = 0.80$. Conversely, if there were a group of you and three friends and one animal rights activist, then the predicted influence on you would be

$1/(1 + 4) = 0.20$. In short, the predicted influence would be greater for one target (you) and four activists (sources) than four targets (you and three friends) and one activist. Additional *OTRs* can be calculated in a similar fashion (see Mullen, 1987). The larger the *OTR*, the greater the predicted group influence.

Evidence for Self-Attention Theory.   Research on self-attention theory began with an analysis of areas such as conformity, helping, and social loafing (Mullen, 1983), which makes its initial applications very similar to those of social impact theory. The essence of self-attention theory is to analyze the relationship between various dependent measures of interest (e.g., conformity or group performance) and the *OTR* to assess how well these dependent measures can be predicted by the *OTR*.

In a test of the relationship between *OTR* and conformity, for example, Mullen identified twelve studies that examined the effects of group contexts on some aspect of conformity (see Mullen, 1983, for the specific studies). The basic research strategy was a two-step process. First, effect sizes (measures of the statistical magnitude of the research findings) for each study were calculated. Effect sizes are a measure of the strength of an effect, with larger effect sizes indicating strong effects and small effect sizes (those near zero) indicating small effects. After the effect sizes were obtained, the correlations between the effect sizes and *OTRs* were assessed. Once these correlations were known, they could be combined to yield a mean correlation, using a statistical technique called meta-analysis. Meta-analysis is a tool that allows a researcher to statistically combine the results of many studies in order to arrive at some general conclusions (e.g., Rosenthal, 1984).

For the conformity studies, the mean coefficient of regression was 0.88, and the mean coefficient of determination was 0.78, indicating that the *OTR* could predict conformity in these studies quite well (see Mullen, 1983). Similar analysis strategies were used in areas such as helping (Mean $R = 0.99$; Mean $R^2 = 0.98$) and social loafing (Mean $R = 0.97$; Mean $R^2 = 0.95$); these results suggest that the effects of groups in these areas can be predicted by *OTRs* (Mullen, 1983). Looking at past research, then, the *OTR* seems to be a good predictor of research findings in these areas.

Further evidence in support of self-attention theory was obtained with more direct experimental research. For example, Mullen (1986b) tested the effect of audience size on stutterers. Results indicated that the *OTR* was significantly able to account for the effects of audience size on stuttering; that is, amount of stuttering increased as a function of audience size in a negatively decelerating manner (see Figure 3.2). The *OTRs* that were calculated by Mullen in this research were obtained in the exact same way that we have described. The *OTRs* were simply related to the amount of stuttering.

In a similar fashion, the *OTR* has been shown to be related to organizational productivity (Mullen, Johnson, & Drake, 1987) and even to atrocities in lynch mobs (Mullen, 1986a). In this research, productivity increased as the number of subordinates decreased relative to the number of supervisors, suggesting attentiveness to standards (Mullen, Johnson, & Drake, 1987), and transgressive behaviors coded from newspaper accounts were shown to be more severe as the number of lynchers increased relative to the number of victims, suggesting decreased self-attentiveness (Mullen, 1986a). We discuss organizational issues in more detail in a later chapter (see Chapter 7).

The *OTR* has also been used to predict harvesting behaviors in a commons dilemma (Chapman, 1991), a topic that we cover in more detail in Chapter 6. In this study, undergraduates took part in a resource use task in groups ranging in size from two to six. Before the harvesting trials, participants predicted the number of others that they expected to overharvest and to underharvest and indicated to which of these groups they assigned themselves. The *OTR* was able to predict matching-to-standard behavior in a commons dilemma from a self-attention perspective. As the *OTR* increased, indexing an increase in self-attention, those participants who expressed an intention to overharvest became more conservative in their resource use (Chapman, 1991).

Summary of Self-Attention Theory.   As with social impact theory, there is a lot of evidence in support of self-attention theory, and this evidence comes from a variety of areas in both field and lab settings. One strength of self-attention theory is that it does propose a process of group influence, namely, self-attention (Mullen, 1983, 1987). Another positive feature of self-attention theory is that it is easy to calculate the *OTR*, which makes it readily accessible to many group researchers, and it may be as good a predictor of group influence as the more complex power functions of other models. For example, in Mullen's (1983) analysis, studies were obtained in which the *OTR* explained an average of 90 percent of the variance across group research areas. Thus, in many instances, the relationship between the *OTR* and dependent measures seems to be good.

However, more research documenting the exact nature of self-attention is needed, since there are few studies in which self-attention is actually measured directly (but see Mullen, 1983); rather it is normally just inferred (e.g., Mullen, 1986a; Mullen et al., 1987; Chapman, 1991). A weakness of self-attention theory may be that it only focuses on the number variable in accounts of group influence. There is no treatment of variables such as strength and immediacy. If strength and immediacy are truly important variables, then some acknowledgment of these variables should be made to account for a fuller range of group phenomena (Jackson, 1986; cf. Mullen, 1986a, 1986b).

Social Physics

A third model of group influence, known as social physics (Knowles, 1978, 1989), has received relatively little research attention. Nevertheless, it suggests some interesting possibilities and implications for models of group influence. Social physics specifically presumes that gravity can serve as an analog for human interactions. It is argued that other people exert effects on a target as a function of their number and distance. In other words, other people or groups have an increasing effect on you the greater their numbers and the closer they are to you.

As with our previous two theories, group influence according to social physics is most easily represented by an equation that encompasses the relationships between the important variables in the model. Specifically, the mathematical equation for social influence according to social physics is $E = kN^n/D^d$ (Knowles, 1978, 1989). In this equation, the potential influence of other people (E) is viewed as a function (k) of the number of people (N) raised to some power (n) divided by their distance (D) also raised to some power (d).

Knowles (1983) has suggested that the most likely values for the exponents n and d are 0.5, and research bears this out. Reactions to others are predicted to increase as a function of the square root of their number and to decrease as a function of the square root of their distance (Knowles, 1983).

Evidence for Social Physics. Thus far, the social physics model has been applied primarily to research on the effects of proximity and crowding, although it may also have applicability to other areas. Initial evidence supportive of social physics comes from a review of crowding research in which the number of others, as well as their distance, has been shown to affect people's thoughts and behaviors (Knowles, 1978, 1989).

In one set of studies using the social physics analog, Knowles, Kreuser, Hass, Hyde, and Schuchart (1976) investigated the effect of group size on the distances at which pedestrians passed the group. In a field study, one, two, three, or four confederates were seated on a bench that was receded into a hallway alcove. In a paper-and-pencil replication, two, four, six, or eight figures were represented in a hallway alcove either in a circle or straight-line arrangement. In both studies, the more confederates that were seated on the bench (in either arrangement), the more passersby would distance themselves when walking past, as though they were being "deflected" by a gravitational force field (Figure 3.3 depicts the experimental setting).

The more confederates there were seated on the bench, the greater distances passersby walked around them (Knowles et al., 1976).

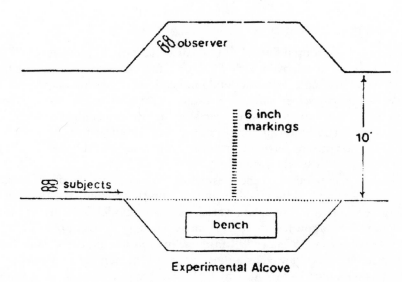

FIGURE 3.3.   Experimental setting for testing personal space boundaries
    Source: Knowles, E.S., Kreuser, B., Haas, S., Hyde, M., & Schuchart, G.E.
(1976). Group size and the extension of personal space boundaries. *Journal of Personality and Social Psychology, 33,* 649. © American Psychological Association.
Reprinted with permission.

In another series of studies, Knowles (1983) asked participants to provide judgments of crowding in reaction to slides that varied the number and distance of an audience. In two studies, perceptions of crowding conformed closely to the square root of the audience's number divided by distance. A third study investigated judgments of crowding and social facilitation (see Chapter 6) in a between-subjects design in which participants learned a simple maze alone or in front of an audience that varied in size (two, four, or eight people) and closeness (0.9, 3.1, or 7.3 meters). In front of the largest audience, participants learned more slowly, forgot more during retests, and recalled fewer peripheral aspects of the experiment, providing at least some support for social physics assumptions. However, closeness did not affect task performance in this study, contrary to what had been expected.

Summary of Social Physics.   The social physics model has thus far been applied mainly to research on proximity and crowding. However, it has received support in this area. Social physics, like self-attention theory, focuses mostly on the number variable, although like social impact theory, it also takes closeness (i.e., immediacy) into account as well. In fact, Knowles's (1978) distance variable, *D,* appears to be very consistent with the inverse of social impact's immediacy variable. Important here, however, is that again we have a model of group influence that proposes that the number of group members has an effect in social contexts. Immediacy may also be relevant. The strength of sources, however, receives very little attention in social physics, although a "mass" variable (Knowles, 1978) has been suggested, which may in some sense be related to importance or strength.

Perhaps the major drawback to social physics, at this time, is its limited application to the areas of proximity and crowding. Although it can be useful to limit a theory to a restricted range of topics, given that the variables proposed by social physics are similar to those of other theories of group influence, we might expect that the theory would have good explanatory power in other areas as well (e.g., conformity, helping, and so on). We believe that this is the case, and so we feel that it is useful to outline what is known about social physics at this time. However, this potential is only speculative; future research could directly test this proposal.

Social Influence Model

Tanford and Penrod's (1984) social influence model is a fourth mathematical theory of group influence. This model has been applied to areas such as conformity, minority influence, and deviate rejection. The social influence model was derived from computer simulation results (Penrod & Hastie, 1980). The social influence model was developed as an attempt to explain the group influence process in terms of a mathematical combination of the number of sources and the number of targets, taking into account both minority and majority influences (e.g., in juries; see Chapter 12).

This is a mathematically complex model. However, as with the others, it is important to keep in mind that the identified variables and the relationships between them is what is most important for present discussion. We suggest that those who are truly interested in calculating the different functions, which is not necessary for the present discussion, consult the original sources.

The general social influence model, with parameter estimates obtained by Tanford and Penrod (1984), is $I = 1 * e^{-4e-(s1.75)/T}$. In this equation, I represents the amount of social influence (normally represented as a percentage); S represents the number of sources, raised to an exponent of -1.75; T represents the number of targets; and e is the natural antilog of 1 (2.7183 . . .). The results of this equation are a series of Gompertz ("S-shaped") growth curves that account for majority and minority influence within a single power function. The group influence curves bear some similarity to those of some of the other models (e.g., social impact theory); however, they are S-shaped to account for both increasing and decreasing influences at different points in the curve.

SIM COMPUTER SIMULATION RESULTS

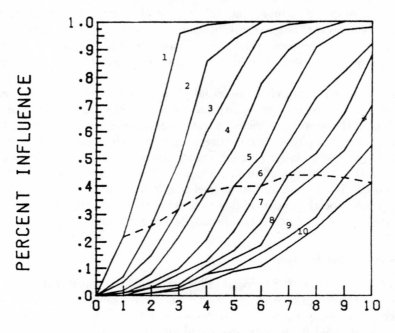

NUMBER OF INFLUENCE SOURCES

FIGURE 3.4.   Gompertz growth functions
   Source: Tanford, S., & Penrod, S. (1984). Social influence model: A formal integration of research on majority and minority influence processes. *Psychological Bulletin, 95,* 198. © American Psychological Association. Reprinted with permission.

Evidence for Social Influence Model.   Thus far, Tanford and Penrod's (1984) social influence model has received very little research attention. Evidence for the model is based primarily on computer simulations. The general strategy employed by Tanford and Penrod was to use computer-simulated groups to assess the impact of varying numbers of targets and sources on the magnitude of social influence. The social influence represented by the model builds upon both majority and minority influence effects, predicting that as a faction size increases, its impact will increase, whereas as faction size decreases, so will its impact.

The results of Tanford and Penrod's (1984) computer simulations are presented graphically in Figure 3.4. The top portion of the figure represents situations in which the influence is the majority. The bottom portion represents situations in which the influence is a minority. The horizontal dotted line crossing the curves represents situations in which the group is evenly split. As can be seen, the curves produced by the social influence model are S-shaped. Influence begins as a positively accelerating function of the number of sources and reaches a point of inflection after the addition of the first few sources. At that point, the amount of influence accelerates negatively until it reaches an asymptote at 1.0 (perfect consensus). In other words, in comparison to social impact theory, the main difference here is that the first few sources are assumed to have a marginally increasing impact, whereas the next sources are assumed to have a marginally decreasing impact.

Summary of Social Influence Model. The social influence model has been developed to account for minority and majority influence within a single Gompertz growth function. In contrast to the other models, the social influence model predicts the greatest influence for the second or third added source rather than for the first. Explorations of this model have been done with computer simulations. The model has some potentially important implications because it tries to account for both minority and majority influences in ongoing dynamic interactions, which none of the other group influence models do. For example, in decisionmaking tasks (e.g., juries) it has been shown that single minorities exert little influence on majority decisions. However, in contrast to other models, Tanford and Penrod (1984) attempt to address reciprocal influences; for example, sometimes minorities can have influence if they are consistent in their arguments. Weaknesses of the model, however, may lie in the fact that so far it is based primarily on computer simulations and that it is somewhat esoteric, relying on lots of relatively complex S-shaped growth curve predictions.

Clearly, all of the models of group influence offer some interesting insights into the social influence process. More research that attempts to empirically compare and contrast these theories (e.g., Tindale, Davis, Vollrath, Nagao, & Hinsz, 1990) and that attempts to determine the conditions under which each model can make unique or complementary predictions would be most useful.

Dual Process Models of Influence

In contrast to the mathematical models of influence, there is a second class of theories that propose that majority and minority influence work in fundamentally different ways to bring about change. "Dual process" theorists argue that the mathematical models of influence only examine change at a surface level, by concentrating only on explanation of overt behavioral change and description of how a minority can induce behavioral change in the majority. Weapons of influence, however, can work on attitudes as well as on behavior. That is, when we attempt to influence someone, we may bring about attitudinal as well as behavioral change. Group influence theorists who take the dual process approach argue that majority and minority influence processes differ in the extent to which they bring about cognitive, as well as behavioral, change. The exact nature of those differences is the subject of some debate, and in this section we explore those different positions, as well as examine recent research on the different processes.

Conversion Model

The first theoretical position that we examine was proposed by Moscovici (1980). Moscovici's argument is based on the notions of *normative* and *informational* influence (Thibaut & Kelley, 1959). Normative influence is influence that changes behavior only, whereas informational influence changes attitude as well as behavior. Moscovici argues that majority influence is equivalent to normative influence, and minority to informational influence. The majority works by appealing to numbers and the seemingly widely held assumption that "the majority rules" or is always correct. Hence, a majority can bring about behavioral change by simply arguing that this is a behavior that most people are performing, and for that reason it must be valid. An important point to recognize is that the target of influence changes *without thinking about* the new behavior; he or she simply makes the assumption that if the majority of people are doing it, it must be correct. As a result, the target of influence may adopt a new behavior without necessarily believing that it is the most appropriate behavior to perform.

The minority has no such numbers to appeal to and must bring about change through different means. The minority does this by trying to explain why its position should be adopted. In other words, the minority provides information about its position and gets members of the majority to think about *why* they are engaging in the current behavior and why they should adopt a new behavior. The end result of this informational influence is not only adoption of the new behavior but also attitudinal change. The information allows the target to evaluate the new behavior in light of his or her existing beliefs and to see that the new behavior is truly the more appropriate one to perform. If the target reaches this conclusion, it follows that he or she would modify his or her beliefs accordingly. Hence, successful minority influence leads to changes in behavior *and* attitudes.

It is important to note that the change resulting from minority influence is typically not immediate but delayed. The minority often convincingly states its case but sees no results until after a period of time has elapsed. This is primarily because attitude change is a time-consuming process. This lack of immediate results can make it frustrating to be a member of a minority, but, as we shall see, it is very important that the minority persevere and maintain a consistent message despite a lack of immediate gratification.

The attitude change element of minority influence is important because it means that the behavior change will endure. If you believe that a behavior is appropriate, then you will continually perform it. By contrast, behavior that is the result of normative (majority) influence lasts only until the majority decides that the behavior is no longer appropriate. The world of fashion provides an excellent example of this. Many people adopt clothing styles that they do not like simply because the style is "in" and gladly discard the clothes when the style falls out of favor. When was the last time you saw someone wearing a leisure suit? Sometimes, however, we do see someone whose dress is seriously outmoded. Why might this happen? Because the person truly believes that the style is the best one to wear, which is a textbook example of the enduring quality of informational influence. The implications of this should be obvious. Majority influence, because of its sole emphasis on norms, brings about short-term behavior change, whereas minority influence, with its emphasis on information, brings about long-term change. This is why this theoretical position is referred to as "conversion"; minority influence acts to convert others to a new way of thinking.

Our description of conversion theory makes it sound amazingly easy for the minority to prevail. Simply explain why you do what you do, and you will triumph. In fact, it is very difficult for minorities to succeed. What can minority members do to maximize the probability that they will successfully convert the majority? The means by which the information is presented is crucial. Specifically, the minority needs to present its argument in a forceful manner and not deviate from its basic message (Moscovici & Paicheler, 1983; Wood, Lundgren, Ouellette, Busceme, & Blackstone, 1994). Such forcefulness and consistency is necessary to overcome the initial perception that the minority's position is incorrect (a perception that must exist if the majority is initially seen as being in the right). A forceful and consistent presentation leads majority members to ask why people who are so obviously wrong advocate their beliefs so strongly. The majority members conclude that perhaps there is some substance to the minority position and begin to process the information presented by the minority. An argument that is weakly presented, or the content of which is continually shifting, does not lead majority members to question the correctness of the majority. Forcefulness and consistency are in turn facilitated by the minority members being very committed to and serious about their cause and by the minority being quite homogeneous (Gerard, 1985).

Objective-Consensus Model

Our second dual process model of influence was proposed by Nemeth (1986; Peterson & Nemeth, 1996; see also Mackie, 1987). Termed the "objective-consensus" model, it follows the same basic logic as the conversion model. In fact, it is seemingly so similar to the conversion model that researchers often mistakenly assume that the objective-consensus model is just an extension of the conversion model. In fact, there are important differences between the two theories, which we shall delineate as we outline the objective-consensus model.

The basic idea behind the objective-consensus model is that which underlies the conversion model, namely, successful minority influence is informational in nature, and majority influence involves some appeal to norms. There are, however, two crucial differences between the two models. First, objective-consensus argues that majorities also provide some informational influence. The majority appeals to sheer numbers *and* explains itself. Hence, rather than mindlessly accepting the majority point of view, targets of majority influence think about the majority position. However, the majority position is the *only* one that is considered; majority informational influence thus leads to what is termed "convergent thought." The second difference between the objective-consensus and conversion models lies in the cognitions that result from minority informational influence. The conversion model suggests that the targets think only about the minority's position, whereas objective-consensus argues that the targets think about multiple points of view ("divergent thought"). Thus, the target considers not only what this particular minority advocates but also the positions that other minorities might advocate. The products of these two types of influence can differ markedly. Group decisions that result from majority influence have broad popular appeal but little depth, whereas decisions that result from minority influence are well considered and of high quality (Nemeth, 1986). A number of studies have demonstrated the convergent-divergent thought patterns predicted by this model (de Dreu & de Vries, 1993; Trost, Maass, & Kenrick, 1992), as well as the high-quality products of minority influence (Mucchi-Faina, Maass, & Volpato, 1991; Nemeth & Kwan, 1985, 1987; Nemeth, Mayseless, Sherman, & Brown, 1990; Nemeth & Wachtler, 1983).

At this point, it is tempting to infer that minority influence is "good" and majority influence is "bad." However, we must be very careful not to draw that conclusion. Quite often, a majority advocates the best point of view. In such instances, we do not want to experience successful minority influence. Further, there are instances in which we do not want divergence; instead, we want everyone to converge upon and work from a single perspective (Brandstatter et al., 1991; Nemeth, Mosier, & Chiles, 1992; Peterson & Nemeth, 1996). Hence, we should not automatically conclude that minorities are "better" than majorities. This research is largely directed at those situations in which creative solutions to tasks are desirable (Legrenzi, Butera, Mugny, & Perez, 1991), or the minority position is the objectively better one to hold. A real life example of this is the movement toward equal rights for women, a position long held by a minority of people yet difficult to argue against (Mucchi-Faina, 1987).

Context/Categorization Model

The final theoretical position that we consider takes a quite different approach to minority influence. Crano (1994; Crano & Hannula-Bral, 1994) has argued that research on minority influence has focused exclusively on attitude *change* and has largely ignored the effects of minorities on attitude *formation*. Thus, we know how minorities can lead people to stop driving Chevrolets and start driving Volvos (a car driven by only a small minority of people in the United States), but we don't know how the minority convinces a person with no preexisting car preference to start with a Volvo. Crano's "context/categorization" model of influence attempts to explain the latter process.

The basic model is readily stated. Formation of attitudes requires information, and we have seen that minority influence is based completely upon informational influence. It follows that the minority should thus be a stronger source of new attitudes than the majority, which relies less upon informational influence. However, this basic effect is moderated by task type. Research has shown that people desire objective information when confronted with a task that has a clearly correct answer, such as a math problem, and subjective information (i.e., data on what others think) when performing a task that has no correct answer, such as choosing one of three stocks in which to invest (Kaplan, 1989; Laughlin & Ellis, 1986; Rugs & Kaplan, 1993). As a result, minority influence should be stronger with objective tasks than with subjective tasks, and vice versa for majority influence. Crano and Hannula-Bral (1994) were able to support these predictions. Because this model is so new, we cannot yet evaluate it in the same light as the conversion and objective-consensus models, but it seems to be quite promising.

Research on Dual Process Phenomena

The general dual process approach to influence, irrespective of theoretical bent, has attracted considerable research attention, and it is not hard to see why. This approach is decidedly cognitive in nature, which fits nicely into the current emphasis on cognitive processes in many areas of psychology and other fields. Also, this approach has considerable empirical support. We noted in our discussion of the objective-consensus model that its basic tenets are well supported, and we also saw that the mathematical models of influence have generally not been subjected to rigorous testing and hence are much sketchier.

The bulk of the research has concentrated on identifying factors that can help the minority succeed. One such factor is attractiveness, or the extent to which a person would want to be a member of the group. If the minority is unattractive, the target will not want to be associated with it, and the minority will have little ability to gain supporters (Perez & Mugny, 1987). An example here would be an owner of a timber logging company who encounters members of a small, radical environmental group who are trying to win supporters for restrictions on hunting. The logger may be willing to hear arguments for hunting restrictions, but it would be damaging (from a business point of view) for the logger to be associated with a group that opposes timber cutting. Hence, the environmentalists will not be able to obtain the logger's support, even if they present a forceful and consistent message. However, unattractive groups do seem to stimulate divergent thought (Mucchi-Faina, 1994) and can instigate some type of change in targets. Thus, the logger may well decide to join a more mainstream environmental group that supports some restrictions on hunting and advocates responsible economic use of natural resources.

Another major factor pertains to whether the minority contains members who are in the same ingroup as the majority members. Many studies have shown that minorities are more likely to have influence over majority members if the minority and majority are members of the same group (Gaffie, 1992; Kozakai, Moscovici, & Personnaz, 1994; Martin, 1988, 1992; Volpato, Maass, Mucchi-Faina, & Vitti, 1990). So, for example, a majority of women is more likely to be influenced by a minority of females than by a minority of males.

The content of the minority's argument is another important factor in success. The likelihood of success is enhanced if the minority can explicitly refute elements of the majority position (Clark, 1990). Related to our earlier discussion of the forcefulness of the minority's argument, the minority will have greater success if its statements are strong and definite ("It is absolutely necessary that we impose restrictions on hunting right now") as opposed to weak and qualified ("It would not be a bad idea to consider the restriction of hunting in the future") (Garlick & Mongeau, 1993). If the majority position is substantially different from the minority position, minority influence is more likely if the minority presents an objective argument (Papastamou & Mugny, 1990). Interestingly, the minority is more likely to be successful when its message content has been heavily censored (Clark, 1994), at first glance a counterintuitive finding. Censorship seems to invoke feelings of reactance in the target; that is, someone else is deciding that you should not hear this message. It is well known that reactance can lead people to do something other than what they had planned on doing; hence, a person who otherwise would not have attended to the minority message may now do so, simply because someone else does not want him or her to hear it.

There also seems to be some type of "critical mass" perception of minorities among majority members, in that a minority position is not credible unless it has certain critical number of supporters (Lortie-Lussier, Lemieux, & Godbout, 1989). There is probably no one single critical mass cutoff, in that any minority that has passed the cutoff is automatically deemed credible; rather, it likely varies from issue to issue. It should be noted that the endorsement of a prestigious person obviates the critical mass effect. In fact, very small minorities can be successful if its position is endorsed by a well-respected individual (Lortie-Lussier et al., 1989). The implication for minorities is clear: Do not attempt widespread influence of majority members until the minority group size is noticeably large or until a prestigious member has been recruited.

Finally, it is important to note a factor that hinders minority influence, namely, the importance of the issue. Minority influence is extremely unlikely to succeed if the issue in question is one that people consider to be of fundamental importance (Krosnick et al., 1993). Issues such as abortion, religious beliefs, and the death penalty are ones for which holders of the minority viewpoint will have great difficulty in winning converts from the majority because the beliefs that people hold about these issues tend to run deep and form a central part of most persons' belief systems.

Unresolved Issues

In contrast to the description-oriented mathematical models, the dual process models give us some insight into how influence works—the minority stimulates divergent thought, for example. But there are many more questions pertaining to the actual process by which a person is influenced that are yet to be answered. For example, where do divergent thoughts come from? We saw that the objective-consensus model states that minorities lead majority members to consider a broad range of positions, but how do majority members become aware of these positions? How does the person decide which of these positions to adopt? The next step in the process seems to be an understanding of how each *person* reacts to the influence process.

Chapter Summary

We first looked at four mathematical models of group influence: social impact theory, self-attention theory, social physics, and the social influence model. We saw that each theory offers some interesting insights into the influence process. However, we also noted that there are further issues that these theories must address, especially with regard to their ability to make predictions about, rather than simply describe, behavior. We looked next at three dual process models of influence: conversion, objective-consensus, and context/categorization. The first two of these models have been heavily researched, with clear support for the objective-consensus model. The third is a new model that has not yet received research attention. Finally, we saw that influence researchers have not yet gained insight into the role of individual differences in the influence process.

Part Two

Group Performance and Interaction

Chapter Four

Group Decisionmaking

We turn our attention now to a topic that is of primary importance to our society, namely, group decisionmaking. In our culture, most important decisions are made not by single individuals but rather by groups. Juries decide the ultimate fate of a defendant; Congress, not the president, makes the final decision regarding whether a bill becomes law; school boards, not the superintendent, make decisions about curriculum. In short, decisionmaking groups are pervasive throughout our society.

Their pervasiveness raises an obvious question: Why are they so popular? The answer seems simple: Groups bring more resources to the decision task than are available to any one person. Through discussion, group members can pool their knowledge sets and make a decision that is based upon more information than is known to any single group member. Groups have more man-hours available for working on a task than does a single person. The range of skills within a group is broader than is found in one person, and so on. The point is, groups have a much greater capacity for producing a high-quality decision than does one person.

The true state of affairs, however, is almost never as simple as one thinks. Marjorie Shaw (1932) was the first person to empirically test the assertion that groups are "better" at decisionmaking than are individuals. She gave individuals and four-person groups a number of word puzzle problems (e.g., tanner: cowhide as chandler: ?) and compared the number of correct solutions generated by each. She found that groups came up with more correct answers than did the isolated individuals. Her explanation for the group's superiority was that group members serve an error-checking function: If one person proposes an incorrect solution or has made an error in interpreting information, another person will spot the error, and it will be corrected. These results seem to confirm our hunch:

Groups really are better decisionmakers than are individuals. For about twenty years, Shaw's findings were considered definitive evidence for group superiority.

In the 1950s, however, researchers began to raise questions about her study (Marquart, 1955; Taylor & Faust, 1952). The primary concern was that when the number of correct answers produced by Shaw's groups were compared to the solution rate for individuals, the improvement because of grouping really did not seem all that impressive. In other words, one would have thought that the groups could have produced even more correct answers than they actually did. In 1955, Lorge and Solomon reanalyzed a portion of Shaw's data using a mathematical modeling technique and discovered that when the amount of available resources was taken into account, the groups really did not perform very well. In fact, the groups could actually be described as having been quite inefficient, in that the members did not make good use of their resources. The Lorge-Solomon finding was quickly replicated (Steiner & Rajaratnam, 1961), and the notion that groups are inefficient decisionmaking units has since become one of the most widely accepted in the groups field.

The obvious question is, why are groups such poor consumers of resources? Steiner (1972) provided a general answer: Groups often suffer from *process loss.* He suggested that when group members begin to combine their efforts, they use combination strategies that are inefficient. For example, assume that a jury is allowed to take notes during a trial. Note taking is a fairly arduous and unpopular task, so assume that no one volunteers to be the group's note taker. Finally, one juror agrees to do it, not because she is a good stenographer, but just because she realizes that the deadlock needs to be broken and the trial started. At one level, her actions were beneficial for the group because the notes can help the jury, but in the larger sense, this was a poor strategy on the part of the jurors because the note taker will probably not do a very good job. It would have been much more productive for the jurors to identify the best stenographer within the group and assign the task to that person. This would have guaranteed the highest-quality notes and hence made the jury's deliberation process that much more thorough.

Steiner's theorizing led groups researchers away from conceptions of groups as input-output devices (i.e., put information in, and a decision comes out) and toward a focus on the process by which groups reach decisions. In this chapter, we look at a number of factors that contribute to the group's achievement of consensus.

Group Discussion

Perhaps the most heavily studied aspect of decisionmaking groups, at least with regard to process, has been discussion. We mentioned earlier that one presumed advantage of grouping is the ability of group members to share information with one another, and hence broaden the pool of available facts that can be used for making a decision. But what actually gets discussed within groups?

Brainstorming

The first person to pose this question was Osborn (1957), who argued that group members spend too little discussion time generating ideas and solutions and too much time evaluating and criticizing what others say. Osborn suggested that groups can be maximally productive if the members concentrate completely on idea generation. He designed an intervention called *brainstorming* that was supposed to do exactly this: discourage criticism, and encourage creativity.

"Brainstorming" is one of those terms in our culture that has become generic and describes a wide array of phenomena. Many people are familiar with the term, but few conceive of brainstorming as Osborn described it. Indeed, Osborn would likely be horrified by some of the group interventions that are labeled "brainstorming." For him, a brainstorming session consisted of a set of specific procedural rules:

- Each group member is to generate as many ideas as he or she can, regardless of how silly the ideas may seem.
- No one is allowed to offer an opinion on the quality of an idea, even one that was self-generated.
- A group member may, however, take an idea and expand upon it. This is known as "idea building" or "piggybacking."
- The group is not to reach any conclusions as to which idea should be adopted. Selection of an idea as the group's choice is to be done at a later time.

Osborn's ideas became an immediate sensation, particularly in the workplace. But does brainstorming work? Do brainstorming groups really make better use of their resources? Researchers quickly tested brainstorming (Dunnette, Campbell, & Jaastad, 1963; Taylor, Berry, & Block, 1958) and found no support for it. Later tests of specific elements of brainstorming found that groups do not generate as many ideas as one would expect (Diehl & Stroebe, 1987, 1990) and that the ideas that are proposed are usually of lesser quality than those generated by individuals (Diehl & Stroebe, 1987). Reviews of the brainstorming literature conducted almost twenty years apart (Lamm & Trommsdorf, 1973; Mullen, Johnson, & Salas, 1991) each concluded that, in fact, brainstorming simply does not work, at least not under conditions in which this research has been conducted. The most likely explanation for the failure of brainstorming is "production blocking" (Diehl & Stroebe, 1987). Group members cannot simultaneously attend to messages from others and generate ideas. Because brainstorming demands interaction, group members are forced to emphasize attention to others over idea generation. This explains not only the low rate of productivity in brainstorming groups but also the poor quality of ideas—people cannot devote the mental resources needed for improvement of others' ideas.

Despite this overwhelming empirical evidence, brainstorming remains a very popular technique in the management sciences (see Thaima & Woods, 1984, for an example of such enthusiasm). There seem to be two major reasons for this. First, the belief that interaction with others stimulates individual creativity is intuitively compelling to many people; this is known as the illusion of group effectivity (Stroebe, Diehl, & Abakoumkin, 1992). In fact, people who expect to brainstorm with others believe that they will be more productive than if they were to work alone (Paulus, Dzindolet, Poletes, & Camacho, 1993). The second reason involves personal experience. People who have participated in brainstorming sessions perceive their personal performance as having been more productive than it actually was (Larey & Paulus, 1995; Paulus & Dzindolet, 1993; Paulus et al., 1993). Hence, someone who has experienced a brainstorming session goes into it expecting to be productive and comes away believing that he or she *was* productive, when in fact he or she was not. Given these positive reactions, it is perhaps not surprising that people continue to advocate brainstorming. In fact, its popularity is still so strong that researchers have begun asking whether the procedure could be modified so as to make it a useful technique. Some progress has been made on this front, with the development of electronic brainstorming, or brainstorming over a computer network. We discuss electronic brainstorming in depth in Chapter 10; for now, understand that it seems to hold promise in terms of enhancing group productivity.

Delphi and Nominal Groups

A key aspect of brainstorming is that group members spend some valuable discussion time on irrelevant topics. Supporters of the Delphi and nominal group (NGT) techniques (Dalkey, 1969) take this argument one step further—they assume that *all* of group discussion is misused. Group members socialize, exert influence on one another, refuse to let some members talk, and avoid controversy. The purpose of Delphi and NGT is to eliminate these "bad" aspects of discussion, leaving only task-oriented communication. Delphi accomplishes this by prohibiting all verbal interaction—all communications are in written form—and NGT requires each group member to generate ideas in isolation and then interact only to choose from among the individual ideas. One team of researchers has been able to show impressive gains in group productivity for both techniques (Delbecq, Van de Ven, & Gustafson, 1975; Van de Ven, 1974; Van de Ven & Delbecq, 1971). However, other researchers have not been able to replicate their findings (Gallupe, Bastianutti, & Cooper, 1991; Green, 1975; Rohrbaugh, 1979). Still other researchers (McGrath, 1984) have questioned the assumption that socialization, unequal participation, and so forth, are necessarily damaging to the group process. Currently, research on Delphi and NGT approaches to group interaction has ground to a halt, but the question of exactly how useful these techniques are is far from settled.

Conflict

Yet another position on the content of group discussion suggests that groups spend their discussion time devising a single decision option and then search exclusively for evidence that confirms the validity of that option. The presumed reason that groups take such a "confirmation bias" approach is because addition of a second option adds both uncertainty and conflict to the task, factors that group members prefer to avoid (Brodwin & Bourgeois, 1984). However, an exclusive search for confirming evidence hides flaws in the option; as a result, groups often advocate a solution despite the fact that it contains obvious drawbacks. Theorists who take this position on group discussion argue that the very conflict that the group seeks to avoid is beneficial and leads to higher-quality decisions. To that end, two different methods for introducing conflict into the discussion process have been created. *Devil's advocacy* involves subjecting the proposed decision to a rigorous critique. *Dialectical inquiry* requires the group to create a second decision option that is fundamentally different from the first, yet still viable, and then debate the merits of each option. The common idea underlying each approach is that the group is to take the original option and argue against its adoption. If it can survive such a critique, it should be advocated; if not, it should be abandoned.

Mason (1969), who first proposed the two approaches, predicted that dialectical inquiry would produce better-quality decisions than devil's advocacy because with dialectical inquiry the group immediately has a better decision to fall back on if the original one is found to be faulty. By contrast, if devil's advocacy reveals an option to be poor, the group must start from scratch and create another one. However, he predicted that each would be superior to conflict-free discussion. A considerable amount of research, primarily done by management scientists, has been devoted to the two approaches, and interestingly, Mason's predictions overall have not been supported. Devil's advocacy is indeed generally superior to conflict-free discussion, but dialectical inquiry is not. Devil's advocacy also seems to be superior to dialectical inquiry (Schwenk, 1990; Schwenk & Valacich, 1994). Finally, there are certain decision situations in which the two approaches actually seem to impair effective group decisionmaking (Schwenk, 1990). The best explanation for this pattern of results is that dialectical inquiry is an unusual and difficult approach to decisionmaking, and group members either cannot or do not want to master it (Mitroff, 1982; Schwenk, 1990).

It should be noted that both devil's advocacy and dialectical inquiry may introduce some undesirable side effects into the group experience. Research has shown that, compared to those who experience conflict-free discussion, group members who experience either approach are less satisfied with their experience (Schweiger, Sandberg, & Ragan, 1986); less accepting of the group decision (Schweiger et al., 1986; Schweiger, Sandberg, & Rechner, 1989); and less interested in continued interaction with the other group members (Schweiger et al., 1986; Schwenk & Cosier, 1993). Overall, then, the question of how beneficial the introduction of conflict into discussion is very much an open one.

The Content of Discussion

Thus far, we have been making assumptions about what is (and is not) discussed during group interaction. But what do groups actually talk about? Surprisingly little research has actually been conducted on the content of group discussion. There is a simple explanation for this: It is very difficult to classify every utterance that occurs during group interaction. Attempts have been made to develop comprehensive coding systems (Bales, 1950; Futoran, Kelly, & McGrath, 1989), but these systems have generally been too subjective for most researchers, in that they require the experimenter to interpret an utterance and then classify based upon his or her interpretation. The problem with such subjectivity is obvious: Two researchers might interpret the same utterance as reflecting two different intentions and hence place it into two different categories. Largely for this reason, the content of group interaction has been seriously understudied.

However, in the mid-1980s, Garold Stasser took a different approach to the issue. Rather than try to study every single utterance, he decided to focus solely on task-related discussion. He gave group members a set of information to discuss. Some pieces of information were given to everybody (common information), and each person in the group was also given some information that no one else received (unique information). (It should be noted that group members knew that both common and unique information existed, but they did not know which specific items were common or unique.) By audiotaping the group conversations, he was able to determine which pieces of his information appeared during discussion and how often each piece was mentioned. He ignored any statement that did not directly address one of his facts. In a series of studies (Stasser & Stewart, 1992; Stasser, Taylor, & Hanna, 1989; Stasser & Titus, 1985, 1987), he observed what he termed the "biased sampling" effect: Group members tend to concentrate discussion on common facts and largely ignore unique facts. Unique information would be introduced and then never repeated again. By contrast, common information was repeated many times. To see why this is troubling, recall why discussion is beneficial in the first place. By talking, group members can teach each other new facts. In other words, people can introduce each other to unique information. But Stasser's research showed that group members do not use discussion for teaching. They simply rehash what everyone already knows. As a result, groups make decisions using basically the same set of information that any one individual had at his or her disposal, which could explain why group decisions are not that much better than individual decisions. Subsequent research using Stasser's paradigm has shown that discussion content, both in terms of what and how much is discussed, is affected by elements of the group decision process such as time limits, the number of options under consideration (Parks & Cowlin, 1995), and the number of people who know the fact (Gigone & Hastie, 1993; Parks & Cowlin, 1996). It has also been demonstrated in real groups (Larson, Christensen, Abbott, & Franz, 1996). At this point, we can definitely say that group discussion of task-relevant information is influenced by many factors (and hence is probably a prime cause of process loss), but much more research on discussion content needs to be conducted.

Combination of Preferences

In our discussion of group versus individual decisionmakers, we briefly reviewed the work of Lorge and Solomon. Besides clarifying the question of group superiority, Lorge and Solomon introduced a new question into the groups field: How do individual group members combine their preferences to produce a single group decision? In other words, how do group members know when they have reached consensus? Lorge and Solomon argued that the process by which group members turn a distribution of individual preferences into a single group choice can be modeled mathematically. Their emphasis was on the probability with which a group member with the correct answer would voice his or her favored solution (recall that the groups under study, Shaw's groups, had been asked to solve word puzzles), and they developed some simple mathematical rules that, given the range of individual preferences within a group, could predict what the group's choice would likely be. When compared against the data on what the groups actually chose, Lorge and Solomon's models were very accurate in their predictions, and their predictive ability was later confirmed by other researchers (Steiner & Rajaratnam, 1961).

The formal model that the group uses to achieve consensus became known as a "decision rule" (Steiner, 1966). It is important to note that group members do not conduct a formal mathematical analysis of their situation when they apply a decision rule. Rather, the argument is that a decision rule can be expressed in explicit mathematical terms that allow researchers to make predictions about what the group will choose. In fact, many decision rules are readily stated and quite familiar. An excellent example is "majority wins." We all know what it means if the majority rules: The group will do what most members want to do. However, we can also express this rule more formally: The group will do what $(N / 2) + 1$ members want to do, where N stands for the total number of group members. Stating the majority rule in this way lets researchers make an explicit prediction about what the group's choice will be. We will not work through the mathematical process here, for it is often quite complex. However, Davis (1973) provides a careful demonstration of the entire procedure, and interested readers would be well advised to look at his examples.

Research on group decision rules has concentrated almost exclusively on "discrete" choice tasks, or tasks for which there are only a few possible choice options. An excellent example of a discrete task, and one that has been heavily studied by researchers, is the one faced by a criminal jury. (We examine jury research in detail in Chapter 9.) A criminal jury must decide a defendant's guilt or innocence. The jurors must consider three possible choice options: (1) The defendant is guilty; (2) the defendant is innocent; or (3) it is impossible to reach a verdict (i.e., the jury is "hung"). No other decision is possible. When a group is faced with a discrete task, many simple decision rules (or "social decision schemes" [Davis, 1973]) can be applied. We have already mentioned majority wins. Another simple one is unanimity, under which every group member must agree on the same option. We could split the difference between majority and unanimity and apply a 2/3-majority rule, under which 2/3 of the group members must agree. There are many other such rules, and a concise summary of a number of them is provided by Laughlin (1980).

Much less is known about "continuous" choice tasks, under which there are many plausible options. Returning to the legal arena, a civil jury is usually faced with a continuous decision task. The civil jury is less concerned with guilt or innocence and more concerned with damage awards. A civil trial is instituted when one party claims that it has been wronged by another party and demands that the wrongdoer pay restitution. The civil jury must decide how much restitution the wrongdoer must pay. The plaintiff may ask for a specific dollar amount, but the jury is not bound to consider only that amount—they may award any amount that they deem appropriate. Hence, there are typically a large number of choices that the jurors may consider. Because of this vast number of choice options, it is very unlikely that a majority of jurors will favor the exact same award amount. What is more likely is that each juror will prefer a different amount. How do group members integrate different preferences (and more specifically, preferences that sometimes differ widely) into a single group decision?

Social decision scheme analysis, which was originally designed for analysis of discrete decision tasks, does not describe continuous choice very well (Davis, Stasson, Parks, Hulbert, Kameda, Zimmerman, & Ono, 1993). Two related approaches have been taken to the continuous choice problem. The approaches are related in that both operate under the assumption that the *distance* between members' personal preferences affects how influential any one member is on another, in terms of one member convincing another to change his or her preference. Specifically, the farther apart personal preferences are, the less influence the two people will have on one another. So, if you prefer a civil trial award of $500,000, the person who favors $600,000 will probably be more persuasive to you than the person who favors $100,000. James Davis (1996) has outlined a variant of social decision scheme theory called "social judgment schemes." This approach relies on a mathematical model in which each member's preference is weighted by his or her "centrality," or the extent to which his or her preference is close to the preferences of others. The logic is that a person whose preference is centralized will be able to exert more influence on the others than will a person whose preference is extreme, and hence, the final group choice should be closest to the most central personal preferences. This model is very new, but Davis (1996) presents some data that support the predictions of the social judgment scheme model.

Helmut Crott and his colleagues have investigated decision rules that are based on a series of paired comparisons that group members can make (Crott, Szilvas, & Zuber, 1991; Crott & Werner, 1994; Crott, Zuber, & Schermer, 1986; Zuber, Crott, & Werner, 1992). Group members systematically compare the preference of one group member against the preference of another and decide which is more desirable. The more desirable option is then compared against another person's preference, and so on until only one option is left. This becomes the group choice. To illustrate, assume that the members of a four-person group favor the following monetary awards: $100, $300, $400, and $650. The group might first compare $100 against $300 and decide that $300 is the more appropriate choice. Next, $300 is compared against $400, and it is decided that $400 is the better of the two. Finally, $400 is compared against $650, and once again $400 is preferred. The group's choice, then, is $400.

Regardless of which approach one finds more appealing, the key idea here is that, in a continuous choice situation, group members engage in some type of member-by-member comparison of preferences. The approaches differ in terms of what is done with that comparison information.

Groupthink

In 1987, Burger King was in the midst of a financial downturn. Sales had fallen throughout much of the 1980s, and something needed to be done. Burger King executives decided to launch a major promotional effort built around the slogan "We Do It Like You'd Do It," the goal being to convince the public that Burger King was in touch with the preferences of its customers (Winters, 1987). Eighteen months later, the campaign was abandoned, with Burger King's sales actually having *declined* 0.6 percent, a large amount in retail, over those eighteen months (Landler, 1990). The slogan was replaced with another one: "Sometimes You Gotta Break the Rules." Almost immediately, owners of Burger King franchises were upset. Customers had no idea what the slogan was supposed to mean. Some thought it meant that Burger King had changed their recipes or their menu; some thought it meant that Burger King was giving away free food (Hume, 1990a; Landler, 1990). To deal with the problem, Burger King sank more money into the campaign, including addition of a Bart Simpson promotion, under which customers could buy Bart Simpson dolls, the presumption being that the general public thinks of Bart Simpson as a rule breaker. Just over one year after it was initiated, Burger King ended the "Break the Rules" campaign, in the process losing almost $200 million, experiencing a further decline in sales, and sticking its franchise owners with hundreds of unsold Bart Simpson dolls (Hume, 1990b, 1991).

The Burger King executives were, it is safe to assume, quite intelligent people—so how could they have made such bad decisions on their promotions? Although we do not know for certain, one very plausible explanation is that they succumbed to *groupthink*. Irving Janis (1982) described groupthink as the result of a set of phenomena acting in such a way upon the group as to lead group members, who are actually quite capable people, to advocate a poor choice. Those phenomena can be grouped into three major categories.

Structural Faults.   The group contains some inherent flaws that affect the decisionmaking process. Specifically, those flaws are ignorance of input from outsiders (insulation); lack of diversity in viewpoints and approaches to problems (homogeneity); tolerance of decisions that have not been first methodically analyzed; and a history of leaders who have failed to be impartial and have instead actively advocated solutions. Although we do not know if all of these faults were present in the Burger King situation, it is known that Burger King executives kept the two ad campaigns a secret and that the CEO favored each campaign (Landler, 1990; Winters, 1987).

Group Cohesiveness. We introduced the notion of group cohesiveness in Chapter 2. It contributes to groupthink by providing an atmosphere in which internal dissension and criticism is suppressed. Of course, if there is little tolerance of criticism, it is difficult for poor solutions to be rejected. We do not know how cohesive the Burger King executives were, so it is impossible to say whether cohesiveness was a factor in their decisions.

External Stress. Considerable pressure on the group to act is being exerted by an external agent. This pressure may preclude taking time to carefully analyze all possible courses of action and instead may lead the group to quickly advocate the first plausible option just so that something can be done. The Burger King executives were clearly under pressure from many outside agents to boost sales: its stockholders; its parent company in 1987, Pillsbury, which was trying to sell Burger King; and its parent company in 1989, Global Met, which had to justify having acquired it.

When groupthink occurs (and it should be noted that the presence of these phenomena do not guarantee the occurrence of groupthink—they simply provide the necessary conditions), group members exhibit particular traits: feelings of invulnerability, ostracism of dissenters, rationalization, false perceptions of unanimity within the group, and self-censorship, to name just a few examples. These traits in turn produce faulty decisionmaking processes, characterized by such things as failure to identify all possible choices; poor information search; failure to be objective about the available information; failure to assess the risks of the preferred choice; and failure to develop a contingency plan, which would be implemented if the choice failed. As a result of the faulty decisionmaking, the group adopts a choice that is poor.

The groupthink model is appealing to many theorists. However, hard data that can be used to test the model are sparse. Much of the work that has been done relies on after-the-fact analysis of real situations, a technique that can be revealing but does not really provide conclusive evidence that one's explanation is entirely accurate (see Tetlock, 1979). The vast majority of studies that have been done in controlled settings have examined only portions of the groupthink model (Park, 1990). In general, this research has shown that

1. it is not clear whether group cohesiveness has an effect on groupthink (Bernthal & Insko, 1993; Callaway & Esser, 1984; Leana, 1985; Turner, Pratkanis, Probasco, & Leve, 1992);

2. insulation does lead to consideration of fewer alternatives (Moor head & Montanari, 1986);
3. group acceptance of decisions that have not been methodically analyzed does not contribute to groupthink (Callaway, Marriott, & Esser, 1985); and
4. it is not clear whether biased leaders contribute to groupthink (Park, 1990).

You can see that there are many aspects of groupthink about which we know nothing and that the available evidence does not really support the basic groupthink model. Despite this, groupthink remains a popular model for explaining real-world decision blunders. For example, in recent years groupthink has been used to explain the Challenger space shuttle disaster (Esser & Lindoerfer, 1989; Moorhead, Ference, & Neck, 1991), errors in diagnosis among geriatric health care teams (Heinemann, Farrell, & Schmitt, 1994), and the Iran-Contra political scandal ('t Hart, 1991). Because of the seeming lack of empirical support for groupthink, many researchers have proposed modified versions of the groupthink model, incorporating such factors as time pressure (Heinemann et al., 1994; Neck & Moorhead, 1995), availability of group decision support systems (Barnes & Greller, 1994; Miranda, 1994), and collective self-esteem (Turner et al., 1992). However, as yet none of these models has been subjected to thorough testing. At this point, then, we still do not really understand how capable groups can make bad decisions, although there are many promising leads.

Problemsolving Groups

To this point, we have concentrated exclusively on groups that must make decisions about problems that have no clearly right answer. We cannot consult an answer key to determine if a group has chosen the "correct" marketing strategy, investment plan, dollar amount to be awarded, or guilt verdict. (Technically, there is a "correct" answer to a criminal trial because in truth the accused did or did not commit the crime. But if we had a means of determining with certainty the correct verdict, there would be no need for a trial.) Tasks for which there are no single correct answers are called *judgmental* tasks (Laughlin & Ellis, 1986). However, there is a second class of tasks for which there are single right answers, and the job of the group is to uncover that answer. In other words, the group needs to solve a problem rather than make a decision. Examples of such situations range from fairly mundane ones, such as a group of students working on homework problems, to ones of high importance, such as a group of doctors trying to determine what is ailing a patient. These tasks are called *intellective* tasks (Laughlin & Ellis, 1986), and we now turn our attention to them.

The current focus in the group problemsolving research is on rule induction, which asks the question, "How do groups derive general explanations from specific pieces of evidence?" Let us give an example of an induction process. Suppose that you are given some letters in a specific order and are told that there is a rule that governs the ordering of the letters. It is your task to figure out what the rule is. Here is the sequence:

J F M A M

You are allowed to collect additional information about the rule by trying to guess what the next letter in the sequence will be. An experimenter will tell you whether your guess is correct. This collection of additional information is a form of hypothesis testing. What you will likely do is develop a "theory" of what the rule is, figure out what the next letter should be if your "theory" is correct, and then actually see whether that is the next letter. If you are wrong, that is proof that your "theory" is incorrect. If you are right, then you will probably test some more letters and continue doing so until either your "theory" is disproven or you are convinced that it is correct. So, for example, you might theorize that the rule governing the letter sequence is some type of reflection rule, under which there is a short series of letters that occur, reverse, and then repeat. If you are right, then the above sequence of letters might extend out to

J F M A M F J F M A M F J F M A M F J.

To test this hypothesis, you would guess that the next letter in the sequence is "F." In fact, it is not "F," a fact that disproves the reflection theory. You must now devise a new hypothesis, with the additional knowledge that "F" is not the next letter. The actual rule is given later in the chapter.

This example is a fairly trivial one. But imagine now that instead of trying to induce a rule governing letter sequences, a team of doctors is given a set of symptoms of a sick patient and must induce what illness is producing this pattern of symptoms. The doctors will likely use the same approach that we described above: They will formulate an initial diagnosis, test the diagnosis, perhaps by administering drugs that should make the symptoms disappear if the diagnosis is correct, and then observe whether their diagnosis was right. If the drugs have no effect, then this disproves the original diagnosis, and the doctors must come up with a new one. If the drugs do work, then the doctors will probably initiate further treatment that is consistent with their hunch and continue treating in this manner until (a) the patient recovers, which is proof that the diagnosis was right, or (b) the patient suffers a relapse, which means that the diagnosis was not right.

Again, the question is, "How do group members formulate solutions?" This question has been studied most thoroughly by Patrick Laughlin and his colleagues. He has proposed a general theory that explains the group induction process (Laughlin, Chandler, Shupe, Magley, & Hulbert, 1995; Laughlin & Hollingshead, 1995; Laughlin, VanderStoep, & Hollingshead, 1991). This theory suggests that group members derive solutions for the problem by using certain rules. In general, a group may use one of five selection rules:

1. Select one solution at random.
2. Vote for the best solution.
3. Take turns inducing the solution, with each person proposing his or her own solution on succeeding information-gathering trials.
4. Clearly demonstrate that one specific solution is correct.
5. Invent a new solution that was not previously proposed by anyone.

Assuming that the group members have enough information to induce a correct solution, can recognize an incorrect solution, and have the ability and desire to demonstrate a correct solution, then they will select the solution that represents the group choice by first identifying all plausible hypotheses (that is, all hypotheses that are not violated by the available information). If a majority of members advocate the same hypothesis, then that one is adopted, but if there is no majority, then the turn-taking approach is used, and the group adopts the solution that eventually emerges during the turn-taking process.

To demonstrate how this process might work, let us return to the letter problem that we introduced earlier. Recall that the sequence of letters is

J F M A M

and you have learned that "F" is *not* the next letter. Hence, the solution "reflection rule" is not plausible because it is clearly violated by the available information. Assume that someone in our group next presents the hypothesis "alternating consonants and vowels." We can conclude that this hypothesis is implausible without gathering additional information because we all have the ability to immediately recognize that it is not consistent with the available information. Another person proposes converting the letters to numbers, corresponding to each letter's position in the alphabet. Doing so gives the number sequence

10, 6, 13, 1, 13.

Maybe the solution is "subtract 4, add 7, subtract 12, add 12." Strange, to be sure, but definitely plausible given the available information (including the knowledge that "F" is not the next letter, because going from "M" to "F" would require subtracting 7, not 4). If this hypothesis is correct, then the next letter should be in the 13 − 4 = 9th position in the alphabet, which is "I." On the next information-gathering trial, then, the group will ask whether "I" is indeed the next letter. In fact, it is not, which makes the "add-subtract" hypothesis implausible. This demonstrates the turn-taking process: Different solutions are posed, and each is tested by gathering of information.

Let us now assume that a member hits upon the correct solution. If he or she can demonstrate its correctness, then Laughlin's model predicts that it will be adopted by the group. The person first predicts that the next letter in the sequence is "J," which it is. He or she then describes the rule as being "first letters in the names of the calendar months" and demonstrates by elaborating the sequence:

January, February, March, April, May

and showing that his or her rule correctly predicted that the next letter would be "J." Given this demonstration, it is very doubtful that anyone would quarrel with the solution. Laughlin's model thus offers a very concise explanation of how the group problemsolving process works. Indeed, he has demonstrated its accuracy in a number of experiments (Laughlin et al., 1995; Laughlin & Hollingshead, 1995).

Chapter Summary

There are many factors that affect the group decisionmaking process. The bulk of the chapter was devoted to research on judgmental tasks, or tasks that have no single correct answers. We saw that a considerable amount of research has been devoted to group discussion—what types of things are and are not discussed, techniques for improving the quality of group discussion, and so on. Despite this research, there is still much that is not known about group discussion processes. We addressed the question of how group members integrate individual preferences into a single group decision, with the focus being on various decision rules that groups might use. We defined groupthink and saw that empirical research, though scant, casts doubt on some of the major propositions of the groupthink model. Finally, we looked at group solutions of intellective tasks, and examined how collective induction theory models this process.

Chapter Five

Social Facilitation

Would you ride a bicycle faster when someone else is riding along with you or when you are by yourself? This seemingly simple question was the starting point for one of the most extensively researched areas in group performance, an area that has become known as *social facilitation*. Norman Triplett, an American psychologist and bicycling enthusiast, noticed that bicycle racers always raced faster when they were competing against someone else than when they raced by themselves (even when the solo performances were timed). It thus appeared that the presence of other people (e.g., other bicycle racers in this case) would spur people on to even greater performances; that is, performances seemed to be *socially facilitated* in some way. Triplett (1898) took these initial observations back to his laboratory and subsequently found that on a variety of tasks such as winding fishing reels, people would work more quickly when others were present than when they worked by themselves.

From this initial research, the area of group performance had begun. In fact, Triplett's (1898) studies are generally regarded as the first social psychology experiments of any kind. As the first studies in social psychology and in group performance, this research became important for several reasons. First, Triplett's performance groups represented very elemental social units; that is, research on social facilitation focuses attention on the most minimal social conditions: a comparison of how being alone versus having someone else present affects our behaviors. Second, even from the earliest reports, social facilitation had been demonstrated on a variety of tasks and with a wide range of species (e.g., dogs, ants, and chickens) in addition to people. Finally, social facilitation had also been demonstrated with *audiences* (spectators who were watching a performance) and with *coactors* (coworkers who were independently performing an identical task as the subject).

Perhaps not surprisingly, given its early beginnings, research on social facilitation is now fairly extensive, with well over 300 studies published to date (for reviews, see Bond & Titus, 1983; Geen, 1989; Guerin, 1993). Many of these studies demonstrated that performances are improved in the presence of others, in comparison to when working alone, as Triplett had found. However, as in many cases, results were not always so straightforward. It quickly became apparent, even early on (e.g., Allport, 1920), that sometimes other people had the opposite effect on performance; that is, another person's presence sometimes produced a *poorer* performance than when working alone. For example, Allport (1924) found that social facilitation occurred on some tasks (e.g., simple multiplication problems), but on others (e.g., refuting Greek epigrams) a worse performance was found in the presence of others. In other words, a social performance *impairment* was obtained.

Results such as these at first produced a good deal of confusion. On the one hand, the presence of others seemed to produce improved performance over that when performing alone. On the other hand, the presence of others seemed to produce impaired performance in comparison to performing alone. What can be made of these apparently contradictory findings? In this chapter, we describe some theories of group performance that have been proposed to account for these apparent discrepancies. As we shall see, the sometimes improved and sometimes impaired performances when others are present may not be contradictory at all. In discussing social facilitation, it is important to keep in mind that researchers have come to use the term social facilitation to refer to *both* social facilitation (better performance) and social impairment (worse performance) effects. In other words, although it is somewhat of a misnomer, researchers refer to both improved *and* impaired performance in the presence of others inclusively as "social facilitation effects."

Because research on social facilitation has such broad and wide-ranging implications—it is potentially relevant whenever people perform in the presence of others (and is therefore applicable to many other topics discussed throughout this book)—it has been an exciting and dynamic area of study for almost a century.

Social Facilitation: Performing Alone or with Others Present

There are several theories of social facilitation. However, one thing to keep in mind is that all theories have come to focus on *task difficulty* as the main variable that is important in predicting whether performance is improved or impaired in the presence of other people. The social facilitation effects (both improved and impaired performances) are illustrated in Figure 5.1. If the task is *simple* (easy or well-learned), performance is improved when

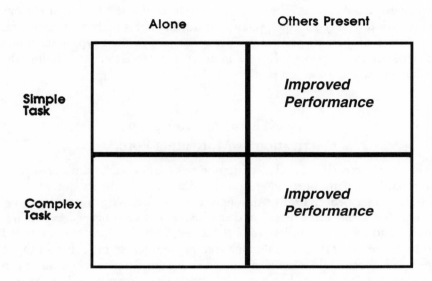

FIGURE 5.1. Social facilitation effects

others are present in comparison to performers who are alone. In contrast, if the task is *complex* (difficult or not well-learned), performance is impaired in the presence of others in comparison to performers who are alone. Task difficulty is therefore viewed as the key to resolving the apparently contradictory findings that we previously mentioned. For example, on simple or well-learned tasks, such as Triplett's (1898) bicycle racers or Allport's (1924) simple multiplication problems, performance is improved when others are present. However, on complex or not well-learned tasks, such as refuting Greek epigrams (Allport, 1924), performance is impaired when others are present in comparison with performance alone.

However, task difficulty is only part of the answer. Although most theories of social facilitation propose that task difficulty determines whether performance is improved or impaired in another's presence, many of the theories differ in their proposed reasons *why* task difficulty affects social performance. In addition, many social facilitation theorists disagree on *why* the presence of others affects performance. That is, theorists disagree on the processes that are involved in producing group performance effects, both in terms of why task difficulty affects performance and in why the presence of others affects performance. In other words, the various theories of social facilitation that we discuss differ in their proposed *mediating mechanisms* (presumed processes) of performance.

Although there may be other ways to classify them, we assign social facilitation theories to three different categories: drive theories, self-theories, and resource theories. These perspectives differ in their proposed reasons why task difficulty and the presence of others affects performance. We review each of these theoretical perspectives and give some typical examples of research that support each view in order to provide some insight into the different theories of group performance.

Drive Theories: Arousal and Activation as Motivating Forces

Most of the theories of social facilitation rely on notions of drive or arousal and habit strength, borrowing from classical learning theory notions (e.g., Hull, 1943; Spence, 1956). Although it is not necessary for present purposes to describe drive theory in detail, there are two concepts that are important to social facilitation: (a) *habit strength or dominant response;* and (b) *drive or arousal.* First, a dominant response refers to the behavior that a person is most likely to emit in a given situation. Dominant responses can be due to such things as habit, training, personal preference, or innate capabilities. Second, drive or arousal refers to the physical excitation or motivation of the performer. Under conditions of high drive, we are generally more likely to respond more quickly and more strongly.

Zajonc (1965) was the first to resolve the findings of previous social facilitation researchers. In a clever application of drive theory, he proposed that social facilitation effects depend on (a) task difficulty; and (b) the drive level of the performer. Zajonc proposed that on simple tasks, correct responses would be dominant. For example, one of the authors of this book frequently finds himself trying to play guitar in his spare time. The types of actions required (e.g., notes or chords played) can be viewed as specific sets of responses or habits. On simple tasks, such as playing relatively easy A, D, E chord patterns (basic chord patterns for guitar), your author is quite good. In other words, the correct responses are dominant and are likely to be emitted. However, on complex tasks, such as when your author tries to emulate his favorite guitarist (who happens to be Jimi Hendrix), he is not so good. In fact, he has a tendency to make many mistakes. In other words, on more complex tasks, more incorrect responses predominate and are likely to be emitted.

In addition to dominant responses is the notion of drive. Here, Zajonc (1965) proposed that the presence of other species mates would increase arousal or drive. Arousal or drive, in turn, would increase the tendency of emitting dominant responses. Because dominant responses are likely to be correct on simple tasks (such as the relatively easy A, D, E guitar chord patterns), performance should be improved in the presence of others since arousal or drive is higher relative to when a performer is alone. That is, more dominant *correct* responses are emitted. In contrast, on relatively complex tasks (such as trying to emulate a favorite accomplished guitarist) performance should be impaired in the presence of others, since arousal or drive is higher, relative to performance when alone; that is, more dominant *incorrect* responses are emitted. Thus, according to Zajonc, this is the reason why performances are sometimes improved and sometimes impaired when others are present. If dominant responses are correct (as they normally are on simple tasks), then performances will be improved in the presence of others. However, if dominant responses are incorrect (as they normally are on complex tasks), then performances will be impaired in the presence of others.

Mere Presence

But Zajonc (1965; see also Zajonc, 1980) went even further than this. He proposed that it was the *mere presence* of species mates that produced increases in the performer's level of arousal. In other words, in Zajonc's view, just the sheer physical presence of someone else (a species mate)—by itself—increases arousal or drive, in the absence of any other concerns that the present other might have for the performer (e.g., in the absence of such things as evaluation potential or modeling). Zajonc's "mere presence" proposal has actually been one of the most controversial parts of his theory.

Initial direct tests of Zajonc's (1965, 1980) proposals were generally supportive (e.g., see Geen & Gange, 1977). For example, in what is perhaps one of the most intriguing social facilitation studies, Zajonc, Heingartner, and Herman (1969) used cockroaches as "subjects." Two versions of a maze were constructed: In one version, a cockroach could run straight to escape a light source; in a second version, a turn was necessary to escape a light source (see Figure 5.2). For cockroaches, running straight is a dominant response; when faced with an aversive cue such as light they will run straight and as fast as they can to escape possible danger. In contrast, making a turn is a nondominant response for cockroaches. In addition, half of the cockroaches ran mazes with an "audience" of onlooking fellow cockroaches (who were placed on the sides of the mazes in Plexiglass cubicles), whereas the other half of cockroaches ran the maze alone. Interestingly, when cockroaches could escape the light by exhibiting a dominant response (running straight) the presence of other cockroaches induced them to run faster than when alone. However, when cockroaches were required to make a turn (nondominant response), the presence of other cockroaches induced them to run slower. In other words, the presence of species mates facilitated and impaired the cockroaches' maze running, depending upon whether a dominant or nondominant response was re-

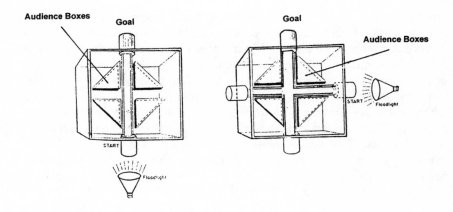

FIGURE 5.2   Easy and difficult cockroach mazes
Source: Zajonc, R.B., Heingartner, A., & Herman, E.M. (1969). Social enhancement and impairment of performance in the cockroach. *Journal of Personality and Social Psychology, 13,* 85. © American Psychological Association. Reprinted with permission.

quired. (See Guerin, 1993, for a review of other social facilitation research with nonhumans.)

Schmitt, Gilovich, Goore, and Joseph (1986) found similar results with people. These researchers varied task difficulty while having subjects type their names into a computer in two different ways: regularly (easy task) and then backward with numbers interspersed among the letters (difficult task). What is important here is that subjects did this before they believed that the actual experiment had even begun; that is, subjects thought that they were just providing a means of identification before performing a task of interest, which should have minimized or eliminated concerns over possible evaluation. Some subjects performed this action alone, and some subjects performed this action with an attentive onlooker present. In addition, another group of subjects performed this action in the presence of another person who was wearing a blindfold and a headset (so they could not see nor hear the performer); subjects in this condition were told that the other person was preparing for an upcoming study on sensory perception. In other words, this other person, from the subject's perspective, was "merely present." Easy typing was improved and difficult typing was impaired in the presence of others in comparison to performance alone; importantly, the "mere presence" and attentive onlooker (audience) conditions did not differ from each other, suggesting that mere presence may be enough to produce social facilitation effects. Several other studies are supportive of the mere presence position to varying degrees (e.g., Innes & Young, 1975; Markus, 1978; Rajecki, Ickes, Corcoran, & Lenerz, 1977).

There is thus some evidence that the mere presence of a species mate may produce social facilitation effects. But why? Zajonc (1980) proposed that the mere presence of other people (or other species mates) is an antecedent to social drive, which is due to the fact that the presence of others leads to feelings of *uncertainty* for the performer. That is, when others are present, performers may be more alert and sensitive to changes in their environment (Cacioppo, Rourke, Tassinary, Marshall-Goodall, & Baron, 1990), producing drive increases. In a related view, Guerin and Innes (1982; see also Guerin, 1983) proposed that the mere presence of others leads to uncertainty and increased drive, but only when the present others cannot be monitored by the performer. In other words, the presence of other people who are sitting behind the performer, who cannot be seen, should have more of an effect on drive than others sitting in front of the performer and who could be monitored. Therefore, according to the mere presence/uncertainty view, other people who are merely physically present (especially those who cannot be monitored) should produce social facilitation effects.

By far, the most heavily emphasized set of social facilitation theories have been the drive theories, following Zajonc (1965, 1980). All drive theories have in common the assumption that the presence of other people increases drive, which in turn enhances dominant responses. However, the various drive theories that we discuss differ with respect to their proposed antecedents of social drive. To illustrate this point, we examine two other drive theories of social facilitation: evaluation apprehension and distraction/conflict. There is some evidence in support of each of these theoretical perspectives.

Evaluation Apprehension

In one of the first departures from Zajonc's (1965, 1980) mere presence hypothesis, Cottrell (1972; see also Cottrell, 1968) proposed that *evaluation apprehension* is necessary to produce social facilitation effects. In other words, according to Cottrell, it is not mere presence per se that produces social facilitation effects. Rather, it was argued that the presence of others increases arousal or drive because we have learned to *associate* them with rewards and/or punishments (e.g., praise or blame). According to this learned drive view, through conditioning, we often experience a heightened state of activation at the sheer awareness of another's presence while we are performing, provided that we are reminded of either pleasant or unpleasant past experiences. An example of this process is having a supervisor arrive at your workplace (see Chapter 8), and the mere sight of that person activates thoughts of evaluations that have occurred in the past.

Cottrell's (1968, 1972) proposals are interesting because, like Zajonc's (1965, 1980), they can account for both human and nonhuman social facilitation. In particular, with people, Cottrell predicted that social facilitation effects should occur primarily when the situation is *evaluative* or *competitive*. That is, when performing in front of others, people should become concerned about doing well and should become concerned about potential evaluation because evaluative settings should have some of the strongest associations with rewards and punishments. With nonhumans, species mates might also have become associated with a variety of rewards (e.g., sexual satisfaction) and punishments (e.g., competition for shelter), producing social facilitation effects (although concerns over evaluation may be negligible).

There are several studies that are supportive of the evaluation apprehension viewpoint. For example, Cottrell, Wack, Sekerak, and Rittle (1968) had subjects perform one of two verbal learning tasks. One of these tasks was an easy paired-associates list in which subjects learned lists of words that were highly associated (e.g., mother-father). Subjects were given one word (e.g., mother) and were asked to come up with its associate (i.e., father); on this task correct responses (e.g., father) should be dominant. On another list, a difficult task, correct responses were not dominant (e.g., jacket-road). Subjects learned these lists while alone, in the presence of an audience, or in the presence of a nonattentive onlooker who could neither see nor hear the performer (a person "merely present"). Cottrell et al. found that easy lists were learned more quickly and difficult lists were learned more slowly when an audience was present, a person who could potentially evaluate the performer's progress. The mere presence and alone conditions did not differ, indicating that evaluation apprehension, and not mere presence per se, may be necessary to produce social facilitation effects. There are a number of other studies that support the evaluation apprehension viewpoint (e.g., Henchy & Glass, 1968; Paulus & Murdoch, 1971). For example, Strube, Miles, and Finch (1981) and Worringham and Messick (1983) found that onlookers increased the speed of joggers, but only if those onlookers were attentive to the joggers' actions.

At this point, despite the area's long history, whether mere presence or evaluation apprehension produces social facilitation effects is still somewhat controversial. For example, in one major review of the area, Bond and Titus (1983) found little evidence that evaluation apprehension significantly increased social facilitation effects over that of mere presence. However, it is extremely difficult to construct a condition in which others are "merely present" and cannot be evaluated. In fact, in the majority of studies, even subjects performing "alone" were asked to perform with an experimenter or someone else present, so they were not really alone (see Guerin, 1993). In other words, there are few studies that actually include appropriate alone and mere presence comparisons. Also, if one assumes that other people serve as a cue for evaluation *whenever* they are present, then it becomes even more difficult to disentangle mere presence from evaluation apprehension positions. Therefore, perhaps the best conclusion to date is that mere presence may produce social facilitation and that evaluation apprehension further contributes to social facilitation, especially when human beings are involved (Baron, 1986; Geen, 1989, 1991).

Distraction/Conflict

Another drive-based attempt at accounting for social facilitation effects is *distraction/conflict* theory (Baron, Moore, & Sanders, 1978; Sanders, Baron, & Moore, 1978; see Baron, 1986). According to this view, the presence of others produces an attentional conflict for a performer. The performer becomes torn between paying attention to the task at hand and paying attention to the audience or coactor. This attentional conflict increases drive or arousal, which then results in the social facilitation effects that we described earlier (see Figure 5.3). Having others present can be distracting for several reasons. However, in performance settings, one of the main reasons seems to be because people like to *compare* their performances with others or because they like to *monitor* the audiences reactions to their performances (e.g., Sanders et al., 1978). In nonhumans, distraction may occur because of such things as fear of attack, competition over resources, and so on. Because attentional conflict is a well-established source of drive, the distraction/conflict view can account for social facilitation in human and nonhuman species.

In a test of this theory, Sanders et al. (1978) required subjects to perform either an easy or difficult copying task under one of several conditions: (a) alone; (b) with a coactor performing an identical task; and (c) with a coactor performing a different task. It was argued that only when the coactor was performing an identical task as the subject was social comparison possible, and therefore only that condition would lead to distraction and social facilitation effects. In fact, this is exactly what was found. Only when subjects were performing an identical task as the coactor was simple task performance facilitated and complex task performance impaired in the presence of others. Interestingly, social facilitation effects have been demonstrated with nonsocial sources of distraction (e.g., listening to bells or watching flashing lights; see Sanders & Baron, 1975), further supporting this view.

Groff, Baron, and Moore (1983) reasoned that one way to prevent an attentional conflict from occurring on a performance task is to give the subjects the task of attending to the audience; in this way, the usual conflict between attending to the task and the audience is eliminated! To do this, the researchers constructed an ingenious experiment in which the subjects' pri-

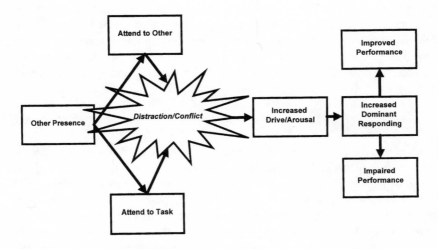

FIGURE 5.3.   The distraction/conflict model

mary task was to monitor whether a face on a TV screen was reacting positively or negatively. In a low-conflict condition, on the TV screen was a *live
image* of a person sitting near by, presumably evaluating the performance.
Thus, as subjects monitored the TV screen they were monitoring the audience as well. In a high-conflict condition, the face on the TV was not that of
the audience. Therefore, if subjects wished to monitor the audience in this
case, they would have to *look away* from their primary task (likely to cause
an attentional conflict). In a third condition, subjects performed the rating
task without an audience. All subjects were asked to squeeze a plastic bottle
whenever they made ratings. As predicted, Groff et al. found evidence of
social facilitation on the squeeze response only in the high-conflict condition. This study, and others (see Sanders, 1981), indicates that attentional
conflict may contribute to social facilitation effects (cf. Geen, 1981;
Markus, 1981).

Summary of Drive Theories

Without question the drive theories of social facilitation have had a major
influence on how researchers think about group performance. Many of the
theories are either modifications of a drive approach, or as we shall see, departures from drive theory proposals. It is important to emphasize that all
of the theories of social facilitation that we have described to this point assume that the presence of others increases drive or arousal, which then enhances the tendency to emit dominant responses. However, the theories differ in their proposed antecedents of social drive—mere presence, evaluation

apprehension, or distraction/conflict. It is also important to recognize that, as we described, there is some research support for each of the theories. However, some theorists have questioned the drive view (e.g., see Manstead & Semin, 1980; Glaser, 1982; Geen, 1989). These researchers have argued that drive and dominant responses may not be the best way to conceptualize social facilitation effects, and they often point to some findings that are not so easily explained by drive theory. Next we describe some of these alternative perspectives.

Self Theories: Thoughts and Feelings About Yourself and Others as a Motivating Force

A second set of explanations for social facilitation effects can be classified as "self-theories." Although the self-theories of group performance differ in their specifics, they have in common the assumption that the presence of others creates demands on the performer to behave in some way. In the following sections, we discuss several examples of this view of social facilitation: self-attention, self-presentation, and self-efficacy.

Self-Attention

Perhaps one of the most developed self-theories of group performance is self-attention theory (e.g., Carver & Scheier, 1981a; see also Carver & Scheier, 1981b, for a review). This theory is based on a control systems model of self-attention (e.g., Carver, 1979). According to self-attention theory, the presence of others increases the salience of behavioral standards (i.e., to be successful). If these standards are being met, as would be expected on a simple task, then performance would be improved due to increased effort at the task. However, if behavioral standards are not being met (e.g., through failure at a complex task), then performance would be impaired due to decreased effort and withdrawal. Many of these assumptions are analogous to those made by self-awareness theory (e.g., Duval & Wicklund, 1972), a related approach, which assumes that the presence of other people make a performer self-aware of meeting standards. In other words, according to this view, increased self-attention is presumed to make performers more aware of any discrepancies between their current performance level and some idealized standard, which in turn leads to either improved (social facilitation) or impaired (social impairment) performance depending on whether these standards are being realized.

Interestingly, Carver and Scheier (1981a) proposed that the performance standards could come from either the self or from others. For example, suppose you set a standard of doing fifty sit-ups every morning before breakfast.

According to self-attention theory, you would periodically check your performance against this standard. If, for a few mornings in a row, you found that you were doing thirty-five sit-ups, then the discrepancy should trigger you again to try to match your standard—and therefore you may try harder to reach your goal the next morning. This would result in a social facilitation effect, if the performer believed that the standards *could be met* (as might normally occur on simple tasks). However, a performer might also come to think that standards *could not be met* (as on more complex tasks). For example, repeated attempts at doing fifty sit-ups with little success could lead a performer to actually decrease his or her efforts—to "give up" or withdraw—resulting in social impairment effects. In a similar fashion, standards of performance can come from other people; for example, a physician suggests an exercise routine to you that includes fifty sit-ups every morning, or as in many social facilitation studies, performance standards are suggested or implied by the experimental context (e.g., to be successful at a task).

Self-attention theorists make the intriguing prediction that anything that increases self-awareness should increase attempts at matching-to-standard (see Carver & Scheier, 1981b; Duval & Wicklund, 1972). Having an audience or coactor present is thus only one way to increase self-awareness and standard matching. Having a mirror in front of a performer is another way. Seeing oneself in a mirror also apparently induces people to become self-aware. Audiences or coactors and mirrors should therefore produce similar effects; the mirror conditions in research might therefore be viewed as a type of "mirror presence." Carver and Scheier (1981a) provided support for their view by demonstrating that both the presence of an audience and the presence of a mirror produced similar effects: Task performance was facilitated in both conditions in comparison to subjects who worked alone. The task in this study involved a simple copying of German prose. In this way, Carver and Scheier argued that explanations for social facilitation effects need not rely on notions of drive and dominant responses. The self-attention view was thus one of the first departures from drive theory explanations for social facilitation, and it was one of the first to suggest that processes other than those proposed by the drive account may be producing social facilitation effects.

Self-Presentation

A second very influential self-theory of social facilitation is self-presentation theory (Bond, 1982). According to self-presentation theory, audiences or coactors affect a performer by increasing his or her concerns about maintaining a favorable impression when in the presence of others. In other words, self-presentation is a motive to look good, competent, and to be viewed positively by others (e.g., Baumeister, 1982; Schlenker, 1980, for reviews). For example, you might try to present yourself as a nice person in order to have others view you favorably, or you might act knowledgeable about a topic in order to try to convey a sense of competence. In a similar fashion, you can also convey a sense of competence by performing well at a task, if you are able.

The self-presentational view of social facilitation (Bond, 1982) proposes that the improved performance on simple tasks that occurs in the presence of others results from performers believing they can maintain an *image of competence* because they put more effort into task performance. In other words, because you may be able to perform well at simple tasks, you may come to believe that others may view you favorably (e.g., that you are successful). However, social impairment may occur when performing complex tasks because making errors may make you look bad and may be *embarrassing,* which then disrupts performance. You may notice some similarities here between the self-attention and self-presentation viewpoints. They both emphasize a need to "look good." However, self-attention theory (Carver & Scheier, 1981a) emphasizes a need to reduce discrepancies and to look good to oneself (although standards can come from the self or from others), whereas self-presentation theory (Bond, 1982) emphasizes a need to look good to others. Despite these differences, however, both the self-attention and self-presentation viewpoints see the performer's perceptions of successful or unsuccessful task performance as playing a key role in producing social facilitation and impairment effects.

In a test of self-presentation theory, Bond (1982) had subjects perform either of two types of paired-associates tasks: (a) a list with mostly simple items but that also included a few complex items; and (b) a list with mostly complex items but that included a few simple items. The tasks used in Bond's research were similar to the paired-associates lists that we previously described when we talked about evaluation apprehension theory. Bond's construction of tasks provided a good opportunity to contrast self-presentation theory with drive theory approaches.

According to drive theories, the difficulty of the *items* on the paired-associates lists should matter. The presence of others should lead to improved performance on simple items and impaired performance on complex items. This should occur irrespective of whether the simple items appeared on an otherwise mostly complex list, or whether the complex items appeared on the otherwise mostly simple list. In contrast, according to self-presentation theory, the task *context* should matter. That is, the presence of others should facilitate performance on the list with predominantly simple items and impair performance on the list with predominantly complex items. This is exactly what was found. Even the complex items were facilitated when embedded in an otherwise simple list, and even the simple items were impaired when embedded in an otherwise complex list, which is not easily explained by drive theory. Thus, it was argued, when performers can maintain an image of competence, as when working on simple tasks, performance may be improved in the presence of an audience. When performers cannot maintain an image of competence, as when working on complex tasks, performance may be impaired in the presence of others, due to such things as embarrassment.

Self-Efficacy

The final self-theory of social facilitation that we discuss explicitly acknowledges the role of expectations in the group performance process. In this way, it builds on some of the findings of self-attention and self-presentation researchers. The self-efficacy viewpoint (Sanna, 1992; Sanna & Shotland, 1990; Sanna & Pusecker, 1994) proposes that task difficulty affects performance only insofar as it affects a performer's expectations of success or failure. On simple tasks, performers would most likely develop expectations that they are doing well. On complex tasks, performers would most likely develop expectations that they are doing poorly. Expectations of success ("I can do it") can be referred to as *high self-efficacy*, whereas expectations of failure ("I cannot do it") can be referred to as *low self-efficacy* (see Bandura, 1986, for a review). The self-efficacy view might therefore account not only for research in which task difficulty was manipulated (by proposing that self-efficacy will be spontaneously influenced during the course of performing) but also research that shows that performance can be affected by direct success or failure feedback, even if this performance feedback is false (e.g., Geen, 1979; Good, 1973; Seta & Hassan, 1980).

But self-efficacy is only one type of expectation that a person may have. Bandura (1986), in his general theory of human behavior, proposed that people may have *outcome expectancies*. Whereas self-efficacy expectancies refer to a person's beliefs about successfully executing courses of action, outcome expectancies refer to a person's beliefs about the likely consequences of those actions (see Figure 5.4). For example, you may hold the belief that you can or cannot execute fifty sit-ups (self-efficacy expectation) and that your doing fifty sit-ups will result in various consequences (outcome expectations) such as praise or reproach from others, or greater or lesser self-satisfaction, better health, and so on. In the context of social facilitation research, one major type of outcome expectation may be beliefs about possible evaluation from others (e.g., audience, coactors, experimenter) or possible self-evaluation. Thus, self-efficacy theory provides a different explanation of why task difficulty and the presence of others may produce social facilitation and social impairment effects: Task difficulty affects self-efficacy expectancies and possible evaluation affects outcome expectancies (e.g., Sanna, 1992; Sanna & Shotland, 1990; Sanna & Pusecker, 1994).

According to the self-efficacy view of social facilitation, the combination of self-efficacy and outcome expectancies is also important. If a performer

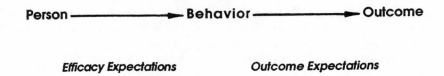

FIGURE 5.4   Self-efficacy and outcome expectancies

believes he or she can perform successfully (high self-efficacy expectancy) and believes that he or she could be evaluated (high outcome expectancy), then a *positive evaluation* should be expected (e.g., a performer may expect praise by an audience). However, if a performer believes that he or she cannot perform successfully (low self-efficacy expectancy) and believes that he or she can be evaluated (high outcome expectancy), then a *negative evaluation* should be expected (e.g., a performer may expect blame or reproach by an audience). It is proposed that expected positive evaluation should produce socially facilitated performances, whereas expected negative evaluation should produce socially impaired performances. This is exactly what was found in a series of experiments. These experiments used both task difficulty and false feedback to manipulate self-efficacy expectancies and used both social (e.g., audience or experimenter) and self-evaluation to manipulate outcome expectancies (Sanna, 1992; Sanna & Shotland, 1990; Sanna & Pusecker, 1994). In addition, it seems that expected evaluation may work through multiple mediational processes (e.g., attention, effort, self-presentation) (Sanna & Mark, 1991) and that performers may actively try to manipulate the experimental context in order to attempt to receive the most positive social or self-evaluation (Sanna & Mark, 1995).

Summary of Self-Theories

The self-theories of group performance represent a major departure from drive theory explanations of social facilitation effects. Although the self-theories differ in their specifics, there are some commonalities among these viewpoints. First, the theories propose that task difficulty affects performance through a subject's perceptions of how well he or she is doing at the task (e.g., reducing behavioral discrepancies or influencing specific expectations). Second, the theories propose that the presence of others places demands on a performer to behave in some way (e.g., through self-attention or expected evaluation). A performer may also be motivated to be viewed positively by the present others. These accounts differ from drive theory in that social performance is not viewed as a result of arousal or drive and dominant responses. As with the drive approaches, there is some research support for each of the self-theories that we have described. More research is needed that directly compares the drive and self-theories, determining which theories are more viable explanations of social performance and under which conditions (e.g., Sanders, 1984).

Resource Theories: Physical and Psychological Capacity Limits on Performance

Other explanations for social facilitation effects rely on notions of attentional overload (see Baron, 1986). These theoretical perspectives were proposed as alternatives to drive theory and focus on how the presence of other people might affect information processing and attention. Attentional overload may result when a performer tries to pay attention to too many things at the same time and no longer has the resources available to process information about the task. This can happen in a couple of ways.

One effect of having others present can be *physical* and/or *cognitive* distraction. For example, a performer may be overloaded because he or she is trying to attend to more things (e.g., the audience and the task) than he or she has the capacity to process. An example of this would be driving while attending to the radio, family members who are riding along with you, and oncoming traffic. In trying to manage all of these activities, at least some time will be spent away from the task at hand—driving! Depending upon the particular activity involved, the physical and/or cognitive distraction of turning the head and body away could be detrimental or beneficial (Baron, 1986).

The key to understanding the resource explanations is that when we are bombarded with lots of information, our attentional focus actually shrinks (e.g., Geen, 1980; see also Blank, 1980; Easterbrook, 1959). Under such conditions, people attend to a narrower range of stimuli. This can lead to a facilitation of performance in cases where the task at hand requires only a narrow range of responses, as would normally be the case on simple tasks. In these cases, a narrow focus of attention actually allows performers to screen out lots of irrelevant information. In contrast, a narrowing of attentional focus could lead to an impairment of performance in cases where the task at hand requires a wider range of responses, as would normally be the case on complex tasks (such as driving). Here, a narrow attentional focus screens out cues that could be essential to successful task completion. Manstead and Semin (1980) similarly suggested that social facilitation occurs only on tasks that require a processing of a narrow range of cues. On more complex tasks, narrow attention screens out needed cues (see also Geen, 1989).

There is less research directly relating to the resource explanations of social facilitation effects than to the other theories of social facilitation described in this chapter. However, the resource theories have the potential to integrate a number of theoretical positions. For example, social uncertainty, self-attention, and distraction/conflict may all provoke resource overload because they absorb attentional capacity (Baron, 1986; Geen, 1989). More research, however, is needed on these issues.

Chapter Summary

For almost a century, social facilitation has proven to be an exciting and dynamic area of study for group researchers. We have reviewed some of the major theories of social facilitation, which we classified as drive theories (mere presence, evaluation apprehension, and distraction/conflict), self-theories (self-attention, self-presentation, and self-efficacy), and resource theories (physical or cognitive distraction). Each of these theories provides an interesting perspective on group performance. Because performance in groups has such wide-ranging implications and is such a major part of our lives (the chapters in this book testify to this), it is important to fully understand the processes involved in performance settings. The theories of social facilitation that we have described all attempt to do this. However, because there are so many theories of social facilitation, there is an increasing need for integration (see Guerin, 1993). On the one hand, all of the theories view task difficulty and the presence of others as important variables in producing social performance effects. There is common agreement here. On the other hand, the theories differ in their proposed reasons for these effects—in their mediational processes. There is little agreement here. At this point, it is intriguing to speculate that each of the theories is correct to some degree and in some contexts. The key is finding out where and when. Without question, social facilitation will continue to be of primary interest to researchers of group performance.

Chapter Six

Social Motivation Losses

In the previous chapter, we discussed how the presence of other people can affect a person's performance. The majority of this research was concerned with how the social environment or group influences individual people. However, in most instances there is more to group influence than simply other people's presence. For example, on many occasions, we work together as *part* of a group—whether it be completing a proposal for a supervisor or instructor, planning a social event such as a party or wedding, or playing together on an office or intramural softball team. Typically, when working in such groups, members perceive themselves to be part of some larger collective in which they attempt to accomplish a shared objective and in which they share a common fate. In this chapter, we focus on people's performances when working as part of a group and on the social motivation losses that can sometimes result. Research on how people function when working together as part of a group has raised several intriguing questions: What are the variables and processes that produce social motivation losses? What are the characteristics of group members and of the social environment that produce such losses? And finally, if social motivation losses can occur when working in groups, then how can they be reduced or eliminated? We discuss some answers to these questions for a variety of distinct types of social motivation losses. Underlying our discussion is attention to the nature of the type of task performed by the group. Finally, we end this chapter by discussing some integrative models of social performance, which build on the theories of social facilitation (Chapter 5) and those of this chapter.

Steiner's Topology of Productivity, Resources, and Tasks

In some ways, research on social motivation losses paralleled the research on social facilitation, although until recently few connections had been made between the two areas (we describe some possible connections later in this chapter). In both cases, these two research traditions started with what seemed like a simple initial question. For social motivation loss researchers, the question was, which is more productive, people working individually or as part of a group? However, as we described for social facilitation, the answer to what seems like a simple question is often not so straightforward. If you think about it for a while, you will probably arrive at an answer similar to that of group researchers: It depends.

In attempting to provide answers to "it depends," Steiner (1966, 1972) proposed an extremely influential topology that outlined the conditions under which people are likely to perform well or poorly when working as part of a group. One of the main concepts in Steiner's topology is the notion of *potential productivity,* or the group's maximum possible level of productivity at a task. According to Steiner, potential productivity depends upon two factors: *member resources* and *task demands.* Member resources refers to such things as the group members' knowledge, abilities, or other tools that are available when performing a task. What makes a resource relevant is the particular task at hand. For example, physical strength may be a resource when moving heavy furniture but not when solving a series of arithmetic problems. Task demands encompass several features, one of the most basic being the performance criterion. For example, one can focus on either speed or accuracy when assessing performance. Steiner argued that if you know the group's resources and task demands, then you can estimate the group's potential productivity.

However, rarely do groups achieve their full potential—and this is where social motivation losses come in to play. Steiner (1966, 1972) called this failure to achieve full potential *process loss,* and he went on to propose that Actual Productivity = Potential Productivity − Process Loss. Process loss therefore reflects the fact that a group's actual productivity rarely reaches 100 percent of potential. For instance, again using the example of moving heavy furniture, if you know how much weight each person can lift individually, then the potential productivity of the group is a simple sum of each member's strength. However, Steiner argued that this potential would probably not be reached because of two types of process loss. The first of these is *coordination loss,* which occurs when group members do not optimally organize their efforts. For example, if members of the group lift at slightly different times, the weight that they can lift is greatly diminished. The second type of process loss is *motivation loss,* and it occurs when group members fail to be optimally motivated. For example, if members of the group do not try as hard when lifting together as when lifting individually, motivation losses would contribute to a diminished lifted weight. Whereas coordination losses are due primarily to the mechanics of task performance, motivation losses are due primarily to the psychological processes of group members. As such, motivation losses are the predominant focus of this chapter.

An additional important feature of Steiner's topology is a classification of types of tasks. Steiner argued that the type of task on which the group is working is critical to understanding group performance. In this regard, Steiner proposed that there are three general dimensions on which to classify tasks. The first dimension involves potential task divisibility. *Divisible* tasks can be divided into subtasks, each of which can be performed by different individuals; *unitary* tasks cannot be subdivided. For example, building an automobile is a divisible task, as many individual tasks contribute to the final product, whereas downhill skiing is a unitary task, in that one person's skills alone contribute to his or her safely reaching the bottom. A second dimension is the performance criterion. Tasks that are *maximizing* identify success as a function of how rapidly they are completed; our skier, if racing, is a good example of this. Other tasks, however, are *optimizing,* which require some correct or optimal solution for successful performance; our previous example of a person solving a mathematical problem serves here as well.

The final dimension proposed by Steiner deals with how task demands link member resources to potential group productivity. In essence, Steiner proposed that there are four types of unitary tasks. On *additive* tasks, the final group product is a sum of individual group member contributions; our now familiar furniture-moving task is an example. On *disjunctive* tasks, performance is based on the best or most proficient member's contributions. For example, when solving a math problem, a group's final solution is determined by its most capable member. In contrast, with *conjunctive* tasks, a group's final product is determined by its worst or least proficient member; a mountain-climbing team who are all tied to each other, for example, can go no faster than its least capable member. Finally, on *discretionary* tasks, individual contributions are combined in any manner that the group chooses. In a jazz band, for example, the various musicians combine their talents in any way that they choose. To better understand this topology, consider a set of three gymnastic vaulting teams, each with four members. Their scores are as follows: Team A—8.5, 8.6, 9.0, and 9.8; Team B—8.7, 8.9, 9.3, and 9.7; Team C—8.9, 8.9, 9.0, and 9.3. Who wins the event? It depends upon how performance is defined. Team B wins if the task is additive (highest average score); Team A wins if the task is disjunctive (highest individual score); Team C wins if the task is conjunctive (highest low score). Although many real-life tasks do not always conform neatly to this topology, Steiner's ideas have guided much of the research on group performance and social motivation losses, and in one form or another they come up throughout this chapter.

Steiner (1966, 1972) proposed several dimensions that are important to understanding people's performances when working as part of a group and social motivation losses. According to Steiner, potential group productivity is a function of member resources and task demands. However, groups rarely realize their full potential, which Steiner referred to as process loss. There are two types of process loss: coordination loss and motivation loss. In addition, Steiner proposed that there are two task dimensions that aid in an understanding of group functioning: divisibility (divisible versus unitary) and performance criterion (maximizing versus optimizing). In addition, there are four types of unitary tasks (additive, disjunctive, conjunctive, and discretionary), which refer to the linkages between member resources and potential group productivity. Steiner's topology has had a profound influence on research within the area of group performance and social motivation losses.

Social Loafing: Performing Individually or Collectively

One of the most heavily researched topics within the area of social motivation losses is *social loafing,* which also has its roots in some of the earliest experiments within social psychology. Social loafing refers to the reduced efforts that are often exhibited by individual group members when they work collectively at a task. For example, in academic settings, we all have probably had the experience of an instructor assigning a group project, and some group members seemed to work hard whereas other group members hardly worked. The reduced efforts when working collectively (when only one measure of output is available for all group members) is typical of social loafing. As with social facilitation, the study of social loafing has a long history. In an initial study, Ringelmann (1913; see Kravitz & Martin, 1986) had individuals and groups of two, three, and eight people pull on a rope as hard as they could. The average force (in kilograms) was 63 kg for individuals, 118 kg for two-person groups, 160 kg for three-person groups, and 248 kg for eight-person groups. Clearly, the amount of force exerted by the addition of each new group member was less than that due to the previous person added to the group. To date, there are about eighty studies related to social loafing (see Karau & Williams, 1993). Social loafing has been observed on a variety of physical tasks in addition to rope pulling (e.g., pumping air, Kerr & Bruun, 1981; clapping and shouting, Latané, Williams, & Harkins, 1979; and folding papers, Zaccaro, 1984), and on a variety of cognitive tasks (e.g., reacting to proposals, Brickner, Harkins, & Ostrom, 1986; brainstorming and vigilance, Harkins & Petty, 1982; solving mazes, Jackson & Williams, 1985; and evaluating essays, Petty, Harkins, & Williams, 1980). It has also been observed in a many different cultures, including Japan (Shirakashi, 1985), and China and Taiwan (Gabrenya, Latané, & Wang, 1983). Researchers have focused on a number of variables that seem to produce, and reduce, social loafing. We discuss some of the main variables below.

Identifiability

When considering Ringelmann's (1913) findings, we can see that as group size increased, the amount of force exerted on the rope did not also increase in a linear fashion. That is, the amount of force exerted by eight-person groups (248 kg) was not simply four times that of two-person groups (118 kg); in fact, it was only just a little more than twice as much. If there had been no process loss, of course, then the amount of force pulled on the rope should have increased linearly with group size. However, an unanswered question is, which type of process loss is at work, coordination loss or motivation loss? Both Ringelmann (1913) and Steiner (1972) speculated that coordination losses were probably responsible for the reduced performances when working together as a group.

To examine this possibility empirically, Ingham, Levinger, Graves, and Peckham (1974) decided to try to disentangle the potential contribution of coordination losses from motivation losses. After essentially replicating Ringelmann's rope-pulling experiment in a first study, Ingham et al. conducted a second study in which they tried to estimate motivation losses by eliminating the possibility of coordination losses. As in Ringelmann's study, participants came into the laboratory and, on different trials, one to six participants were instructed to pull on a rope as hard as possible (see Photo 6.1). However, a key feature of Ingham et al.'s ingenious study was that seven of the persons were confederates of the experimenter and did not actually pull on the rope. The real participant was positioned first in the line, closest to the measurement gauge. Also, all persons were blindfolded, supposedly to eliminate distractions. Imagine yourself as a participant in this study. On certain trials, you are asked to pull on a rope as hard as possible. Sometimes you think that from one to six other people are actually pulling with you—but they're not! You just think that they are (these were called "pseudogroup" trials because participants merely thought they were pulling with a group). These pseudogroup trials, of course, provided no opportunities for coordination losses since only one person was pulling. Ingham et al. found that as perceived group size increased, performance fell; this was particularly true for changes from one to three persons. Thus, findings such as Ringelmann's appear to be at least partly due to motivation losses: As group size increases, the amount of effort put forth decreases.

Several years later, Latané et al. (1979) replicated Ringelmann's and Ingham et al.'s findings, using clapping and shouting tasks. In addition, Latané et al. provided further evidence that performance decrements were due at least partly to motivation losses (they were the first to use the term "social loafing") and not just to coordination losses. Their design was similar to

PHOTO 6.1   Social loafing: Working hard, and hardly working (photos by Collin Evans).

Ingham et al.'s. For example, in one study, participants on certain trials each shouted alone, in actual groups of two and six, and in pseudogroups of two and six. Participants wore blindfolds and headsets over which they were given instructions. Individual motivation (sound output) decreased with both actual and apparent group size; see Figure 6.1, which presents the intensity of sound produced per person. Across the top of the figure, potential productivity (recall our previous discussion of Steiner's topology) is represented by the dashed line; it is an estimate of the maximum potential output per person and is indexed here by sound intensity when performing alone. The lower solid line in the figure indicates sound output when shouting in actual groups of two and six, whereas the upper solid line indicates sound output when shouting in pseudogroups of two and six.

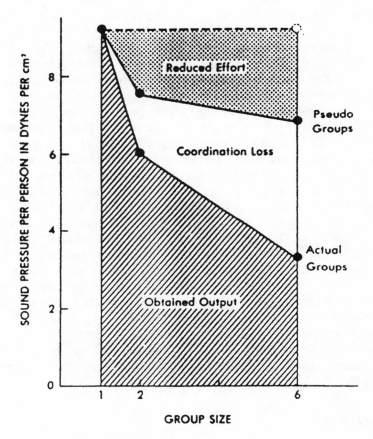

FIGURE 6.1.   Sound production
Source: Latané, B., Williams, K., & Harkins, S. (1979). Many hands make light
the work: The causes and consequences of social loafing. *Journal of Personality
and Social Psychology, 37,* 827. © American Psychological Association. Reprinted
with permission.

Note that there are two types of process loss taking place. The difference
between potential productivity (performance alone) and performance in
pseudogroups represents reduced effort or motivation loss—social loafing
(cf. Harkins, Latané, & Williams, 1980). The additional difference between
pseudogroup performance and actual group performance represents coordination loss. What is also interesting about Figure 6.1 is that performance
per person in both actual and pseudogroups decreased in approximation to
a power function, as predicted by social impact and other theories of group
influence, as we discussed in Chapter 3 (see also Petty, Harkins, Williams,
& Latané, 1977; Sanna & Mark, 1991).

But why does social loafing occur? The studies that we have just described suggested that *identifiability* of member outputs may be the underlying cause of social loafing. When a person is part of a group that is rope pulling or clapping and shouting, he or she may feel less identifiable. These tasks are additive tasks that combine all individual member outputs into a single group product. Thus, no individual member's contributions can be identified (at least from the participant's perspective)—they are *information reducing* (Davis, 1969). In support of these proposals, Williams, Harkins, and Latané (1981) used variations on Latané et al.'s (1979) cheering task. In the first stage of one study, participants shouted alone, in actual groups of two and six, and in pseudogroups of two and six. The basic social loafing effect of Latané et al. was replicated. However, in a second stage of the study, Williams et al. led all participants to believe that their individual shouts would be identifiable even when they worked in groups. When this was the case, social loafing was eliminated. In a second study, Williams et al. further demonstrated that when individual shouts were *always* identifiable (even when working in groups) social loafing was eliminated, and when individual shouts were *never* identifiable (even when working alone), social loafing occurred. Kerr and Bruun (1981) obtained essentially similar results using an air-pumping task. Together, the results of these studies suggest that identifiability (or lack thereof) has an important influence on social loafing. If people believe that individual contributions cannot be identified, they socially loaf. If people believe that their individual contributions can be identified, they do not socially loaf.

Evaluability

Although initial studies pointed to identifiability as a cause of social loafing, some later research has suggested that it may not be identifiability per se that is the relevant variable, but rather it is the potential for *evaluation* that identifiability makes possible. In other words, if you thought that your contribution to the group could be identified, you might still loaf if you thought that no one could evaluate your performance.

An ingenious study by Harkins and Jackson (1985) provided evidence that evaluability, not just identifiability, is necessary to eliminate social loafing. Four-person groups performed a brainstorming task in which members generated uses for objects (e.g., a knife). These uses were written on slips of paper and were to be deposited into a box. Half of the participants were led to think they were identifiable; their uses were collected individually into four separate compartments within the box. The other half of the participants were led to think they were not identifiable; their uses were collected into a box that had no divider so they were combined with those of other group members. However, critical to Harkins and Jackson's study, half of

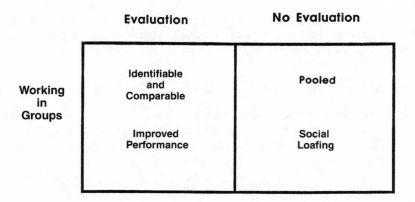

FIGURE 6.2   Effects of evaluation on social loafing

the participants were also led to believe that they would be generating uses for the *same* object, whereas the other half of the participants were led to believe that they would be generating uses for *different* objects. Only when both identifiability (separate compartments) and a comparison (same objects) are present should evaluation be possible. Consider performance on an exam, for example. Suppose you were told that you scored a 254. What does this mean? In order to evaluate your performance, one would need to know not only your score (identifiability) but some standard of comparison (e.g., the performances of other participants). Note that in the prior social loafing research that we described (e.g., rope pulling and shouting) all participants were performing the same tasks. Thus, according to Harkins and Jackson, not only was identifiability possible but so was evaluation. Consistent with their arguments for evaluation, Harkins and Jackson found that social loafing was eliminated only when uses were identifiable and comparable—when evaluation was possible. When uses were not comparable, even though they could be identified, social loafing occurred (see Figure 6.2).

Much subsequent research has supported the proposal that lack of evaluation may be a cause of social loafing. This research has also found that self-evaluation (not just evaluation from external sources) and evaluation with different standards (Harkins & Szymanski, 1988; Szymanski & Harkins, 1987, 1993), and evaluation at the group level (Harkins & Szymanski, 1989) can eliminate social loafing. That evaluation, in particular, may be relevant to social loafing also has the potential to directly connect it with social facilitation research (Harkins, 1987; Harkins & Szymanski, 1987; Sanna, 1992; Sanna & Pusecker, 1994), which we discuss in more detail below. Moreover, participants in such settings have been shown to engage in various strategies (e.g., self-handicapping) in an attempt to increase the possibility of positive evaluations and decrease the possibility of negative evaluations (Sanna & Mark, 1995).

Personal Motives and Goals

In addition to identifiability and evaluability, there are several other variables that have been found to be relevant to social loafing. This research has generally shown that social loafing can be decreased irrespective of the possibility of identification or evaluation. For example, Brickner et al. (1986) have demonstrated that when tasks are *personally involving,* social loafing is eliminated even when evaluation is not possible. Personally involving tasks are those that have intrinsic importance, personal meaning, or significant consequences for one's life (e.g., Petty & Cacioppo, 1981). Participants, all of whom were college students, were instructed to list their thoughts about the implementation of general comprehensive exams as a requirement for graduation. A high level of involvement was created in half of the participants by telling them that these exams were planned for their school for the coming semester; other participants were told that the exams would be started later or that they were planned for another school. Evaluation potential was also manipulated through pooling of responses as had been done in prior research. Participants socially loafed (generated fewer thoughts) more when evaluation was not possible than when it was, but only when the task was not highly involving. When the task was highly involving, participants did not loaf (they generated a high number of thoughts) even when they could not be evaluated. In a similar manner, Bartis, Szymanski, and Harkins (1988; see also Szymanski & Harkins, 1992) found that participants would not loaf when they were asked to be "creative." It therefore appears that if people have some additional incentives, such as some intrinsic interest or personal involvement in a task, they will not socially loaf irrespective of the possibility of identification or evaluation (e.g., Harkins & Petty, 1982; Price, 1987; Shepperd & Wright, 1989; Zaccaro, 1984). Conversely, the threat of punishments can also directly deter social loafing (Miles & Greenberg, 1993).

Setting personal performance *goals* (e.g., Locke & Latham, 1990) for people has also been shown to influence social loafing. White, Kjelgaard, and Harkins (1995) argued that goals may eliminate social loafing because they serve as standards for self-evaluation. In one study, for example, participants were either asked to "do your best" or told that previous participants were able to generate thirty or forty uses for a knife. These conditions were crossed with those of evaluation versus no evaluation by the experimenter. Participants generated more uses when they were evaluated than when they were not in the do-your-best condition (replicating prior research) and in the forty-goal condition. In the thirty-goal condition, evaluation did not matter. White et al. explained these results by proposing that goals served as attainable standards in the thirty-goal condition (participants in past research had generated an average of about thirty uses) but that forty uses was seen as an unattainable standard, so loafing still occurred. It seems that goals need to be viewed as attainable in order for them to have any effect on social loafing.

People's moods may further interact with goals, however. A good deal of research has shown that people feel good when they are meeting or have met their goals, but they feel bad when they are not meeting or have not met their goals (e.g., Carver & Scheier, 1990). However, an alternative possibility has been raised by mood-as-input researchers (e.g., Martin, Ward, Achee, & Wyer, 1993): People may construe an already existing good mood as meaning they have met set goals, whereas they may construe an already existing bad mood as meaning they have not met set goals. Applying this reasoning to social loafing, Sanna, Turley, & Mark (1996) directly manipulated people's moods by using a series of happy or sad film clips, and they included a no-manipulated-mood control condition. Critical to Sanna et al.'s study, half of the participants were told to ask themselves, "Have I generated as many uses as I can?" (a typical social loafing goal), whereas the remaining participants were told to ask themselves, "Do I feel like continuing with this task?" Goals interacted with moods as predicted (see Figure 6.3). In the control-mood condition, participants generated fewer uses when they could not be evaluated than when they could be evaluated irrespective of goal—a social loafing effect. However, for participants who were asked to generate as many uses as they could, a negative mood was construed as meaning they had not met their goal (they had not generated as many uses as they could), whereas a positive mood was construed as meaning they had met their goal. In the former case, participants continued to generate uses, eliminating loafing (evaluation and no-evaluation conditions did not differ), whereas in the latter case participants discontinued generating uses and loafed. In contrast, for participants who were asked to generate uses until they no longer felt like it, a positive mood was construed as meaning they had not met their goal (they still felt like generating uses), whereas a negative mood was construed as meaning they had met their goal. Here, in the former case, participants continued to generate uses, eliminating loafing (evaluation and no-evaluation conditions did not differ), whereas in the latter case participants discontinued generating uses and loafed. Thus, although goals may influence loafing, they may depend further on people's moods, interacting with them to determine performance.

Summary of Social Loafing

Social loafing is by far one of the most heavily researched areas of social motivation losses, and it has had a long and illustrious history. Over the

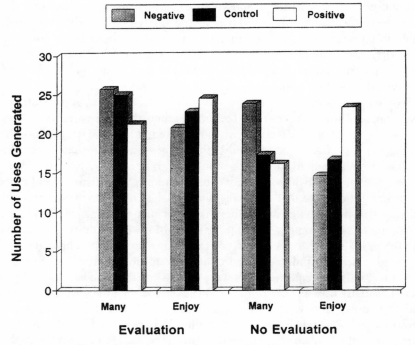

FIGURE 6.3   Effects of mood and goals on social loafing
Source: Sanna, L.J., Turley, K.J., & Mark, M.M. (1996). Expected evaluation, goals, and performance: Mood as input. *Personality and Social Psychology Bulletin, 22,* 329. © Sage Publications, Inc. Reprinted with permission.

years, researchers have determined a number of variables that appear to produce, and reduce, social loafing. Identifiability and evaluability of individual outputs have been the two most heavily researched variables. Having individual performances identifiable and evaluable seems to eliminate loafing. Social loafing has been demonstrated on a variety of physical and cognitive tasks in a wide array of settings. Personal motives and goals have also been shown to eliminate social loafing, even when evaluation is not present. Obviously, there are many personal and situational variables at work, and future research is needed to determine how these interact to produce and reduce loafing.

Free Riders and Suckers: Taking Advantage of Others Without Their Taking Advantage of You

Social loafing is similar in some respects to two other phenomena found in the social motivation loss literature: *free-rider* and *sucker* effects. When the term "social loafing" is used in the generic sense to mean any social motivation losses, then free-rider and sucker effects might reasonably be viewed as a type of social loafing. However, free-rider and sucker phenomena differ in some very distinct ways from social loafing. First, free-rider and sucker effects may occur whether or not individual contributions can be identified or evaluated. It will be recalled that the nonevaluability of individual contributions seems to be one key cause of social loafing. Second, social loafing and free-rider and sucker effects appear to occur under very different task circumstances. As we described previously, social loafing occurs primarily on additive tasks, whereas free-rider and sucker effects occur most often on disjunctive and conjunctive tasks.

For many group tasks there exists the possibility that only some members are necessary to do all or most of the work that is required for the group to succeed. Consider the following example of a group of construction workers paving sidewalks (a real-life "concrete" example from one of your author's summer jobs while in high school). If I am working to pave sidewalks, I could exert little or no effort at all and still be part of a successful work group that gets its required amount of sidewalk paved, that is, as long as one or more group members (not me) paves sidewalk. In situations such as this, people may be less willing to exert themselves when they can free ride (Olson, 1965). I get all of the benefits, such as the sidewalk being paved and a paycheck, without any cost, such as putting in very little effort and no lower back pain—as long as I can get away with it. In other words, I would be "riding" on the contributions of others and getting the benefits for "free." But now consider an alternative view of this situation: Other workers could free ride on *my* contributions! Now what would I do? Research on the sucker effect suggests that I might find this situation aversive and reduce my own efforts. In other words, I would likely not want to "play the sucker" by being exploited by the other free riders. Note that, in the case of both the free-rider and the sucker effects, the response is reduced effort at the task—and thus we have social motivation losses—albeit for somewhat different reasons.

In tests of these ideas, Kerr and colleagues (Kerr, 1983; Kerr & Bruun, 1983) proposed that group members are sensitive to the *dispensability* of their efforts (see also Harkins & Petty, 1982). Dispensibility of efforts simply refers to the extent to which a group member perceives his or her contributions to be critical to completing the group task. For example, if I believe that my efforts are critical to getting a sidewalk paved, I might work hard. However, if I believe that my efforts are not critical, especially when that effort is costly (paving sidewalks is very hard work), then I might not work as hard to contribute to the task.

Participants in Kerr's (1983) research worked in dyads or individually. Their task was to pump air using a sphygmograph bulb. If participants reached a certain level of performance, they succeeded. For participants working individually, this meant earning 25¢ per trial (with a potential for $2.25 total for the nine trials in the study). The group (dyad) tasks were defined disjunctively; that is, if either group member succeeded, then each member would receive 25¢. In addition, before performing the air-pumping task, participants were given information about their partner's ability level (actually this information was manipulated by false feedback): Participants were led to believe that their partner had either high or low ability at the task. There were five conditions in Kerr's study. In the Control condition, participants performed individually. There were also four group conditions: (a) Able-Succeed; (b) Able-Fail; (c) Unable-Fail; and (d) Individual-Model. In the Able conditions, participants thought they had a capable partner; in the Unable condition, participants thought their partner was incapable of success at the air-pumping task. In the Succeed condition, participants' partners succeeded at the air-pumping task; in the Fail condition, the partners did not. For example, in the Able-Fail condition, participants thought they had a capable partner who was failing. In the Individual-Model condition, the partner was able and failed, but participants were told that performances were independent (i.e., participants could earn 25¢ per trial if they succeeded irrespective of what the other person did).

Kerr's (1983) results turned out to be very interesting (see Figure 6.4). In comparison with the Control condition, participants in the Able-Succeed condition were successful on a significantly lower percentage of trials. Once participants learned that their partners were succeeding, they quickly realized that they could take advantage of this by free riding on their partners' efforts (their efforts were dispensable), since the partner apparently was willing to carry the load of the dyad by putting work into air pumping to ensure the group's success. Also in comparison with the Control condition, participants in the Able-Fail condition similarly reduced their efforts. Here, it will be recalled, participants had what they thought was a capable partner, but the partner was failing. This left the participant to carry the weight of the group. In other words, the partner seemed to be free riding on them! To not be taken advantage of, participants reduced their efforts so they would not play the role of a sucker—and this occurred even at the expense of the participant's own success (since the task was disjunctive). It seems that playing the sucker may be so aversive that people are willing to take the whole group down (including themselves) in order to avoid having others free ride on their efforts. In contrast, the remaining conditions did not differ from the Control condition. It was only when participants could free ride on the efforts of others (Able-Succeed) or when they wanted to avoid being the sucker (Able-Fail) that social motivation losses occurred. Importantly, these free-rider and sucker effects are different from the social loafing effects that we described previously, as all group members in Kerr's study were always individually identifiable and evaluable by the experimenter across conditions (see also Kerr & Bruun, 1983).

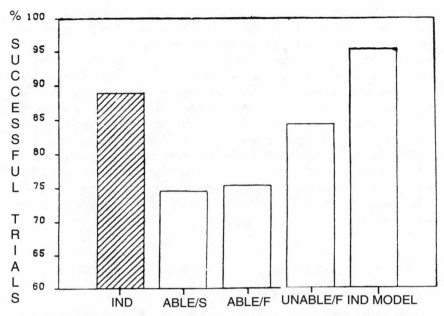

FIGURE 6.4 Free-rider and sucker effects. (IND = Individual; S = Succeed; F = Fail)
Source: Kerr, N.L. (1983). Motivation losses in small groups: A social dilemma analysis. *Journal of Personality and Social Psychology, 45,* 824. © American Psychological Association. Reprinted with permission.

What to Do About Free-Riding, Sucker, and Social-Loafing Effects?

As we have discussed throughout this chapter, social motivation losses can result in huge deficits in productivity. It is not hard to imagine how this could have tremendous consequences for entities such as organizations (e.g., Latané, 1986) and the like. The question is, can anything be done about it? We have talked about some variables that may eliminate social loafing (e.g., evaluation) already. But what about free-rider and sucker effects? Shepperd (1993) has provided an interesting analysis of productivity losses in groups that may provide at least part of the answer. This analysis borrows heavily from expectancy-based theories and from work on social dilemmas (we discuss social dilemmas more in Chapter 7). According to Shepperd, proposed solutions to social motivation losses depend on the nature of the problem. He argues persuasively that the main problem for social loafing is that individual contributions go unrewarded (or punished) when working collectively. Therefore, in order to effectively eliminate social loafing, one needs to provide incentives for contributing. These incentives may be external (e.g., economic rewards or sanctions—or external evaluation) or internal (e.g., pride, duty—or personal involvement) and can occur on either individual or collective levels. For free riding, the main problem is that people perceive their contributions to be unneeded or dispensable. To eliminate free riding, then, one must make contributions seem indispensable, such as making contributions appear critical, unique, or essential. Finally, the main problem for suckers is that they perceive their contributions as too costly. One can therefore decrease the physical (e.g., time, energy, or other resources) or psychological (e.g., inequity or other feelings of dissatisfaction) costs to eliminate the sucker effect. Although all solutions do not always fit so simply into this framework, Shepperd's proposals hold a lot of promise in helping people to think about and to deal with social loafing, free-riding, and sucker effects, and social motivational losses.

Social Compensation: Making Up for Others' Inadequacies

Thus far we have focused a great deal on how individual members lose motivation and put forth little effort when working in groups—they socially loaf, free ride, and otherwise avoid being a sucker. Let's face it: All of this seems to present a fairly cynical picture of people when performing in groups. However, probably all of us can think of situations where we were extremely motivated when working together. In fact, we have maybe even performed more than our "fair share" of the workload to make up for other member's shortcomings. This may have been particularly true, for instance, if other group members were relatives or friends. There may be a positive side to it all. Research on *social compensation* has begun to address some of these issues. When people socially compensate, they actually work harder collectively than individually because they expect their coworkers to perform poorly on important or meaningful tasks. This is quite the opposite of the phenomena that we have discussed so far in this chapter.

Expectations of what we think our coworker might do appear to be important to the social compensation effect. Consider Kerr's (1983) research, which we have already discussed. There is another interesting aspect to that study: Participants in the *Unable*-Fail condition performed at a level essentially equivalent to the Control condition. Could participants in the Unable-Fail condition have tried to compensate for their partners' lack of ability? In other words, if together we have a certain amount of sidewalk to pave, but I am a poor paver, would you be willing to make up for my paving inadequacies? Williams and Karau (1991) provided some direct tests of social compensation ideas. In one study, for example, these researchers manipulated expectations of coworkers' efforts. Dyads worked on a brainstorming task in which they generated uses for a knife, similar to what we described previously (Harkins & Jackson, 1985). Uses were placed in a box individually (coactively) or collectively. Participants were told that they *shared the responsibility* for use generation, although they were instructed to generate uses independently and without communicating. Critical to Williams and Karau's research, however, one member of the group was actually a confederate who exclaimed his or her intended effort at the task before performing. In one condition the confederate stated that he or she would put forth low effort ("I don't think I'm going to work very hard"), whereas in another condition the confederate stated that he or she would put forth high effort ("I think I'm going to work really hard") (Williams & Karau, 1991, p. 575).

The results of Williams and Karau's (1991) study are presented in Table 6.1. When participants worked coactively, they "matched" the level of their coworkers' efforts (see also Harkins & Jackson, 1985), generating fewer uses under low-effort than high-effort conditions. In addition, when participants thought their coworker was going to work hard (high-effort condition), they generated more uses coactively than collectively; in other words, they socially loafed. Most interesting, however, Williams and Karau additionally found that when participants thought that their coworker was not going to work hard (low-effort condition), no loafing occurred. In fact, quite the contrary, participants generated greater numbers of uses as an attempt to overcome the low level of intended effort of their partners. It therefore appears that, at least when there is some shared responsibility for a task or some possible affinity with coworkers, people may be willing to work hard to compensate for a poor performing other. This finding is potentially very interesting and in stark contrast to the social motivation loss phenomena that we have discussed earlier in this chapter (see also Williams & Sommer, 1997). It remains to be determined by future research, however, how long and under what conditions people are willing to engage in social compensation.

Free-rider and sucker effects are two additional social motivation loss phenomena that have been studied by group researchers. By free riding, one is taking advantage of others' efforts, whereas by not wanting to be a sucker, one is trying to avoid having others take advantage of one's own efforts. Both free-rider and sucker effects differ from social loafing in that they appear to occur even when evaluation is possible; they also seem to occur primarily on disjunctive and conjunctive (rather than additive) tasks. What to do about social loafing, free-rider, and sucker effects differs depending on the nature of their underlying causes. In contrast to motivation losses when working in groups, there also may be circumstances under which people are willing to socially compensate for a poorly performing coworker.

TABLE 6.1   Number of Uses Generated by Coworker Effort and Condition

	Condition	
Coworker Effort	Coaction	Collective
High	24.45	29.20
Low	31.30	22.61

SOURCE: Williams, K.D., & Karau, S.J. (1991). Social loafing and social compensation: The effects of expectations of coworker performance. *Journal of Personality and Social Psychology, 61,* p. 576.

Group Performance: Some Possibly Integrative Views

We end this chapter by briefly mentioning some possibly integrative views of group performance. As we have seen in this chapter and in Chapter 5, performance issues and potential motivation losses have captured the attention of group researchers for at least one hundred years. There are many different phenomena that we have discussed. Although each of these phenomena is important in its own right, at this point, you may be asking yourself is there any way to put all of this knowledge together? Perhaps not too surprisingly, some researchers have attempted to do just that, and this is the focus of this section. What may be surprising, however, given such a long history of group research, is that theorists have really only recently tried to integrate different group performance phenomena. Therefore, although we mention some of what is known at this point, more work on integrating different social performance issues will probably be a strong focus in the foreseeable future.

Several theorists have attempted to integrate social facilitation and social loafing phenomena. It will be recalled from Chapter 5 that one proposed cause of social facilitation is feelings of evaluation. In this chapter, we have also seen that evaluation (specifically, a lack thereof) is linked to social loafing. It is on the basis of evaluation potential that Harkins (1987; Harkins & Szymanski, 1987) has tried to combine social facilitation and social loafing effects. Viewed in this way, there are three conditions present in social facilitation and social loafing research: (a) *alone,* in which participants work on a task by themselves; (b) *coaction,* in which participants work on a task with present others and performances can be evaluated; (c) *collective,* in which participants work with present others and performances are pooled. Alone versus coaction comparisons have been part of social facilitation research, whereas coaction versus collective comparisons have been part of social loafing research (see also Yamaguchi, Okamoto, & Oka, 1985). If we add task difficulty to the equation, we may then predict that persons will perform simple tasks better when working coactively than when working alone or collectively because only when working coactively can performances be evaluated. In contrast, when performing difficult tasks, for similar reasons based on the potential for evaluation, persons should perform worse when working coactively than when working alone or collectively. Jackson and Williams (1985) obtained results consistent with these predictions using easy and difficult maze tasks, indicating that social facilitation and social loafing may in fact be two sides of the same coin.

But why might these effects occur, and what are the processes involved? There are several possibilities, many of which are based on the theories of social facilitation that we discussed in Chapter 5. Some examples are self-efficacy and outcome expectancies (e.g., Sanna, 1992; Sanna & Pusecker, 1994), arousal and worry (e.g., Paulus, 1983; see also Griffith, Fichman, & Moreland, 1989), self-attention (e.g., Mullen & Baumeister, 1987), or self-presentation and social anxiety (e.g., Geen, 1989, 1991). All of these variables may hold some promise for integrating various group performance areas, and all have found some support in one form or another in the existing literature. But what about other effects, such as free-rider and sucker? Here there is thus far even less work on possible integrations. However, we have already mentioned some of Shepperd's (1993) proposals, based on expectancies and social dilemmas, which may prove to be relevant in this regard. In one of the more elaborate models of social performance, Karau and Williams (1993) have also proposed that performers' expectations may provide at least part of the answer. In addition, other cognitive and emotional factors such as attributions and mood may help to explain group performance. For instance, if persons can attribute a partner's poor performance to uncontrollable factors such as low ability or task constraints, they may be willing to socially compensate (Sanna, 1996b). Clearly, there is much room for future research. Possible integrations of various group performance phenomena represent perhaps one of the most intriguing questions in these areas.

Chapter Summary

In this chapter, we focused on various social motivation losses that occur when people work in groups. We began the chapter by describing Steiner's topology of productivity, resources, and tasks, which has formed the basis of much of the work on social motivation losses. We reviewed some of the major group motivation loss phenomena—social loafing and free-rider and sucker effects. Each of these phenomena may have different causes and consequences, as we described, and therefore each may require a unique solution. The common theme among them, of course, is that people seem to work less hard in groups than when they are by themselves. In some cases, however, people have been shown to socially compensate for another's poor performance when working in groups. There is a great deal of interesting research on the causes and consequences of these phenomena. Research may be directed toward further specifying the possible interrelationships between them. In a similar manner the interrelationships between social motivation losses and those of social facilitation are some of the most intriguing as yet unanswered questions in the areas of group performance.

Chapter Seven

Social Dilemmas

To this point, we have looked at the various tasks that groups can perform, and we have asked how group performance compares to the performance of an individual engaged in the same task. There are many situations in society, however, that involve *only* groups. We would never expect a single individual to completely fund a charity or public television. One person could not clean up the air in Los Angeles. One citizen does not have a water table all to himself. In each of these situations, people are going to be working together, and in fact, in order for the group to be successful at any of these tasks, group members are going to have to cooperate with each other. In order for a charity or public television station to survive, it needs to receive contributions from a large number of people. The air can be cleaned up only if all persons cut back on their use of automobiles. If a water table is to be managed successfully, all users will need to be careful of the rate at which they consume water.

Inherent in each of these situations, however, is a potentially destructive temptation that is presented to all group members. If everyone else in Los Angeles did reduce their driving, what difference would it make if you continued to drive as often as you wish? If the charity has a large number of contributors, what difference does it make if you fail to give money? If everyone else conserves water, what harm will it do if you water your lawn every day? The answer to each of these questions is, none. Your one car will not appreciably increase smog. Your failure to give $50 will not cause the charity to go bankrupt. Your lawn sprinkler will not quickly drain the water table. In fact, it would be *individually rational* for you to perform each of these behaviors. The problem is this: Every other member of the group is tempted to act in exactly the same way. If every person did indeed succumb to this temptation, what would happen? The air would be foul; the charity would cease to exist; the water table would quickly dry up. In other words, the group as a whole would be worse off. From the group's standpoint, it would have been better if no one would have given in to temptation. This is referred to as *collective rationality*.

Each of these situations is described by the general term *mixed-motive situation*. It is called a "mixed-motive" situation because there are two conflicting motives present, one of which must be ignored in order to satisfy the other. There are many types of mixed-motive situations, and in Chapter 8 we talk about one such situation, negotiation. In this chapter, we focus on perhaps the largest class of mixed-motive situations, the social dilemma. A *social dilemma* can be defined as any situation in which, regardless of what other group members do, it is always better (in terms of personal gain) to be selfish. However, if all persons act in this way, everyone is worse off than if everyone had acted for the good of the group (Komorita & Parks, 1995). Each of the examples given above are social dilemmas. Regardless of what other people are doing, it is personally better (more convenient, etc.) to drive your car than to use alternate modes of transportation. However, if everyone drives, then everyone must breathe filthy air, which would not have happened if everyone had taken the bus.

The continued attractiveness of the social dilemma, and of mixed-motive situations in general, is due in part to its many parallels to the real world. We would hazard a guess that none of the situations described above were unfamiliar to you. The goal of the groups researcher is to learn how to make people more willing to work for the good of the group, which is referred to as "cooperative" behavior. (Acting for selfish gain is called "competitive" behavior.)

The Prisoner's Dilemma

Social dilemmas have historically been studied with the prisoner's dilemma game (PDG) and its many variants. The basic PDG, which is shown in Table 7.1, works as follows. Imagine that two convicts have been arrested for committing a crime. They are separated and not allowed to communicate with each other. The police know that both were involved in the crime, and they have enough evidence to convict both, but they are not sure who planned the crime. Each prisoner is given the choice of confessing or not confessing to having planned the crime. If neither confesses, then the state will conduct a trial and present the incriminating evidence, and each will be sentenced to three years in jail. If both confess, then the state will be saved the expense of a trial and in gratitude will reduce the sentence to two years. However, if one prisoner confesses and the other does not, the state will conclude that the confessor is a dangerous criminal and impose a harsh sentence of four years in jail, and that the nonconfessor is simply an accomplice who deserves only one year in jail. The dilemma is this: Regardless of

TABLE 7.1   A Prisoner's Dilemma Outcome Matrix

	Other's choice	
	Cooperation	*Noncooperation*
Your choice		
Cooperation	3,3	1,4
Noncooperation	4,1	2,2

what the other prisoner does, it is always best for a prisoner not to confess. A one-year jail sentence is more desirable than a two-year sentence, and a three-year sentence is more desirable than a four-year sentence. However, this is also true for the other prisoner. This suggests that neither prisoner will confess, and each will get a three-year sentence, which is worse than the two-year sentence each would have received if both had confessed. Hence should one make the "obvious" choice and not cooperate, or gamble on confessing and hoping that the other will do the same?

Since its development in the 1950s, there have been literally hundreds of studies of the PDG. An entire book would be necessary just to summarize this body of research (and, in fact, entire books have been written on PDG research; see, for example, Rapoport & Chammah, 1965). The current focus among PDG researchers is on the role of strategic choice in the prisoner's dilemma, specifically, the use of a reciprocal, or tit-for-tat (TFT), strategy. Tit-for-tat is a simple rule to use: Be cooperative the first time you encounter the dilemma, and then ever after imitate what someone else did during the previous encounter. Continuing with our air pollution example, one could use the TFT strategy by taking the bus during the first week at a new job, observing a coworker's commuting behavior during that same week, and then ever after doing what the coworker had done the previous week. So, if your coworker always drove her car during your first week on the job, you would drive your car during your second week. If she switched to the bus during your fifteenth week, you would take the bus during your sixteenth week, and so on.

Both computer simulations (Axelrod, 1984) and empirical research (Komorita, Chan, & Parks, 1993; Komorita, Hilty, & Parks, 1991; Komorita, Parks, & Hulbert, 1992) have shown TFT to be an effective strategy for convincing others to engage in long-term cooperation. This is because the TFT user cannot be consistently exploited. *Exploitation* occurs when you take advantage of the cooperative efforts of others in order to achieve a large personal payoff (e.g., everyone else takes the bus, so I'll drive. I get convenience and an empty freeway). Tit-for-tat cannot be consistently exploited because, if no one else is cooperating, TFT requires that you immediately stop cooperating, and you begin cooperating again only after others have done so. This effectively reduces the dilemma to two possible states of affairs: Everyone is cooperating, or no one is cooperating. Recall that, in a social dilemma, mutual cooperation produces better payoffs than mutual competition. It follows that others should start cooperating, and this is what often happens. There is one drawback to TFT: It is quite ineffective in large groups, because it becomes very difficult to track the behavior of a specific person (Komorita et al., 1992). However, we can solve this problem by reciprocating not just one person but rather the majority of other group members. So, you might take the bus if most of your coworkers do so. Computer simulations of this approach suggest that it is very effective at inducing cooperation (Parks & Komorita, 1997).

Prisoner's dilemma research has tailed off somewhat in recent years, perhaps because of a debate regarding the external validity of the PDG that arose in the 1970s. To what extent does it accurately represent real-world situations? In other words, in how many real situations do you have just two possible courses of action, everyone else has the same two choices, and everyone's payoffs are exactly the same? (See van Lange, Liebrand, Messick, & Wilke, 1992, for a summary of the criticisms). Response to these criticisms came in two forms: an argument that questions of external validity pertain to conflict theory, not research paradigms (Schlenker & Bonoma, 1978), and an argument that the PDG was never intended to closely model real-world processes (Mook, 1983). (On this latter point, it is interesting to note that in other social science disciplines, the PDG and its variants are more widely accepted as realistic models of behavioral processes. For an example in political science, see Downs, Rocke, & Siverson, 1985.) Today the matter has not been resolved to anyone's satisfaction. There are those who continue to believe that the prisoner's dilemma is too artificial to serve much purpose and those who believe that it is a useful research tool. However, the debate did produce a beneficial side effect. As a result of the criticisms of the PDG, researchers began to look for social dilemma paradigms that more closely mimic real mixed-motive situations. Two such paradigms were devised: The public goods game, and the resource dilemma.

The Public Goods Game

Consider a charitable organization, such as the Muscular Dystrophy Association (MDA). Because it is a charitable organization, all of its funding comes from private donations, and every year the MDA conducts a television marathon (hosted by Jerry Lewis) to raise money. However, if you should ever require the services of the MDA, they would not first check to see if you had given them money before they helped you. This truism raises an interesting question: Should you send money to the MDA if contributing is not necessary in order to use their services?

On the face of it, the smart thing to do is not to contribute. You get the service without having to give up something (money) to obtain it. But suppose that everyone else acted similarly. In fact, suppose that of all the people who could contribute, only a few actually did. As a result, total contributions fall far short of what is needed to continue to offer basic services, and the MDA ceases to exist. Now there is no organization to help those who suffer from a terrible disease, and society as a whole is worse off than it was before the marathon began.

This situation is an example of a *public goods* social dilemma. A public good is some product that can be "consumed" by members of a group, the provision of which is almost entirely dependent on some form of contribution by group members. A public good is distinguished from other types of consumer goods by two properties. First, the good has *jointness of supply;* it cannot be "used up" no matter how many group members consume it. Charities do not "run out." If you called upon the MDA, you would never be told that they had run out of charity. Second, a public good has *impossibility of exclusion.* This means that it is very difficult to restrict noncontributors from consuming the good. The MDA could conceivably do this, by checking a computerized list of people who had ever given them money, for example, but this would be a very costly solution (and run counter to the philosophy of a charity). It is much easier to simply hope that people who must use the charity's services would find it in their hearts to give something back to the organization.

Recall that the defining characteristic of a social dilemma is the conflict between individual and collective rationality. The principles of jointness of supply and impossibility of exclusion make it clear what the individually rational choice concerning public goods is: Since your consumption of the good will not affect the amounts that other members can consume (jointness of supply) and since you cannot be prohibited from consumption (impossibility of exclusion), the individually rational thing for you to do is to not contribute to the good's provision. This is illustrated in Table 7.2. Regardless of whether the MDA receives enough donations to continue to exist, your personal outcome is better if you do not give any money. (The upper-left cell has an outcome of "– money" because it is very unlikely that the MDA would send you your money back if it went out of business.)

The conflict between individual and collective rationality lies in the method by which the public good is provided. Since the good's provision is almost entirely dependent on individual contributions and since the good is one that all group members can use, it is thus collectively rational to contribute. In fact, if the good is not provided, *all* members will be worse off than if the good were provided. This fact can be seen in Table 7.2. Assuming that the value to you of the charity is more than your contribution (a

TABLE 7.2   The Decision to Contribute to a Charity

	Did the MDA get enough money?	
	No	Yes
Did you contribute?		
Yes	– money	services – money
No	0	services

safe assumption because you would not normally pay more for something than it is worth to you), the upper-right cell (services – money) is greater than the lower-left cell (0). A public good, then, meets our definition of a social dilemma.

Types of Public Goods

Researchers talk about two types of public goods. A *discrete* or *step-level* public good is one that can be provided only in its entirety: It is not practical to provide a lesser amount of the good. Further, a certain minimum amount of money (or number of contributors) is needed to provide the good. An example of a discrete public good is a park. Let us assume that a city wants to build a new park. The cost of building the park will be covered by a temporary increase in the city sales tax. The park meets our definition of a public good: It is being provided by contributions from citizens (the tax); use of the park could not easily be limited to city residents; and a park cannot be "used up." What happens, however, if the sales tax generates only enough money to cover half of the cost of the park? It is useless to build only half of a park; consequently, the park will probably not be built at all. For this reason, the park is a discrete public good. Most psychological experimental studies of public goods examine discrete goods.

By contrast, a second type of public good can be provided at any level, and the level of provision is determined by the rate or amount of contribution. These are known as *continuous* goods. Public television is an example of a continuous public good. Public television subsists primarily on viewer donations. However, one can easily free ride on such donations simply because the station cannot prevent you from watching any of its shows. We can also logically assume that the value of the good is greater than the cost of contribution. In other words, the television shows are likely worth more to you than the money that you contribute. This is a continuous public good because it can be provided in some degree regardless of how many contributors there are. Even if just one person gives some money, the station can air at least one show. As more people contribute, the range of shows grows.

Economists have been interested in public goods-related issues since at least the 1930s, but psychologists first became interested in them after the 1965 publication of *The Logic of Collective Action* by Mancur Olson. In this book, Olson introduced the concept of "free riding," which we discussed in Chapter 6. Free riding occurs when a person does not contribute to the provision of the good. Free riding became a central concept of interest to psychologists and also suggested some larger psychological questions. First, why would someone ever act in a manner other than a self-interested one? Second, how can free riding be minimized and the provision of public goods increased? To state these questions a little more informally, why do people cooperate, and how can we make people more cooperative? Most psychological research on public goods has concentrated on these two questions.

When Will People Cooperate?

Let us start with the first question: Under what conditions will people go against their own best interests to help the group as a whole? On the face of it, this seems a fairly simple question to answer, but in truth the answer is very complex, involving many factors. Across a wide variety of studies, five such variables have consistently appeared as factors in the decision to help the group rather than oneself: Self-efficacy, expectations, group size, the "sucker effect," and trust. We discuss each of these in turn.

Self-Efficacy. Self-efficacy is a concept that appears in many different areas of psychology. Self-efficacy can be defined as the belief that your actions will affect your eventual outcome. In other words, your actions will make a difference (Bandura, 1986). Self-efficacy has long been thought to be an important variable in public goods behavior (Messick, 1973; Olson, 1965), and feelings of self-efficacy have been shown to exert a strong influence on a person's tendency to free ride. Norbert Kerr and his research associates have studied self-efficacy and free riding in great detail. Kerr and Bruun (1983) found that feelings of self-efficacy are affected by the method of provision of the good. In their study, whether a group received the public good (money) was determined by performance of a physical task (blowing air into a pulmonary testing device). For some of the groups, the criterion for receiving the good was the performance of their *worst* group member, or the person achieving the lowest pulmonary test score (a conjunctive task); for other groups provision was determined by their *best* member, or highest test score (a disjunctive task). Each subject performed a pretest with the device, ostensibly to establish their ability; however, Kerr and Bruun actually gave each subject false feedback. Some subjects were told that their "ability" was high—their pretest score was better than 75 percent of all other subjects. The rest of the subjects were told that they had done poorly—75 percent of all other subjects had performed better than they had. These subjects had low "ability." Subjects then learned of the "abilities" of their fellow "group members" (in actuality, there were no groups) and completed a number of trials with the pulmonary device. Kerr and Bruun found that, in the "worst member" condition, those group members who thought they had high ability had a low sense of self-efficacy. In other words, the high-ability members felt there was little that they could do to affect the group's chances of receiving the good. Conversely, in the "best member" condition, those with perceived low ability felt low self-efficacy. Low self-efficacy consequently produced a decline in cooperation in both conditions. Finally, everyone's feelings of self-efficacy tended to decline as group size increased, a finding replicated by Kerr (1989).

Related to the issue of self-efficacy is the notion of criticalness. How do people behave when their actions will absolutely determine whether the good is provided? The research on this question is quite clear: People are extremely likely to cooperate if they know, with certainty, that cooperation will have a positive effect (Rapoport, Bornstein, & Erev, 1989; van de Kragt, Dawes, Orbell, Braver, & Wilson, 1986; van de Kragt, Orbell, & Dawes, 1983).

Expectations.   A second important factor in public goods behavior is beliefs about how others will act. Why should you contribute if you don't think anyone else will? Your contribution would just be wasted. In most public goods situations, you probably know little about your fellow group members, so how can you make predictions about their behavior? According to Amnon Rapoport (1987), one method you might use is to make a *homogeneity assumption*. You might just assume that all of the other group members have an equal probability of contributing to the public good. Although this assumption is simple, in some situations it may be unrealistic. It is not unreasonable, for example, to assume that some people are more likely to give money to a charity than others, even though you know very little about the entire group of potential contributors. Rapoport thus proposed a second method of forming expectations, the *heterogeneity assumption*. Under the heterogeneity assumption, you would select some probability values at random and assume that some people will contribute with each of those probabilities. For example, you might assume that some people are almost certain to contribute to the MDA (say, 90 percent), some people very unlikely (5 percent), and most people moderately likely (50 percent). Experimentally, Rapoport (1988) has found the heterogeneity assumption to be an accurate description of how expectations are initially formed.

Even in the most anonymous public good situations, however, you will usually possess at least some information about your fellow group members, and this basic information has been shown to have effects on your expectations about what others will do. For example, it is logical to assume that some group members have more *resources* (e.g., money, time) than others. Rapoport (1988) and Rapoport, Bornstein, and Erev (1989) have shown that your expectations can be based in part on these differences in resources. In their studies, individuals received a small, medium, or large endowment, which they could keep or contribute toward a public good. The researchers found that those with small endowments were perceived to be more likely to contribute than those with large endowments. Rapoport argued that this was because those with small endowments had less to lose if the good were not provided, and proportionately more to gain if it were provided, than those with large endowments.

Another piece of information that you have, of course, is your own behavior. Do your own preferences affect what you think others will do? Rapoport and Eshed-Levy (1989) suggest that they do. They showed that there is a generally strong positive relationship between whether you contribute and whether you think others will contribute (though as we will see a bit later, there is a situation where this does not occur). To put it simply, you will usually expect others to act as you do. This type of estimation strategy—to assume that others are like you—is actually not uncommon (Dawes, 1988). In fact, Orbell and Dawes (1991) have proposed a formal explanation of cooperation based on this strategy. In their theory, defectors expect others to defect as well; hence, defectors will not participate in the dilemma because they expect to end up in the "all-D" cell of the payoff matrix. By contrast, cooperators expect others to cooperate and as a result do play the game. Since defectors are not participating, a cooperator will end up interacting with other cooperators and receive the large "all-C" payoff.

Group Size.　Underlying our discussions of both self-efficacy and expectations is the issue of group size. How likely is it that you will be a critical member, or have any influence at all on the outcome, in a group containing thousands of members? How can you hope to predict what others will do in such a large group? In fact, group size seems to be a critical factor in public goods behavior. Kerr (1989; Kerr & Bruun, 1983) found that people generally believe they make less of a difference in larger groups and that large groups are generally perceived to be less effective at providing public goods than small groups. Researchers have also observed behavioral effects of group size, in that cooperation tends to decline as groups grow (Kerr & Bruun, 1983; Komorita, Parks, & Hulbert, 1992). Given these results, how do public goods get provided at all? After all, real-world groups working toward a public good are much larger than laboratory groups, which typically contain three to five members. If people work less hard in a five-person group than in a three-person group, how can a group of hundreds get *anything* accomplished?

The answer is that group size *by itself* does not seem to affect individual behavior, at least in social dilemma situations. Many researchers (e.g., Isaac & Walker, 1988b; Marwell & Ames, 1979; Stroebe & Frey, 1982) have shown that changing only group size has minimal effect on a person's public goods behavior. Individual contributions seem to be affected only when something else changes *along with* group size. For example, Isaac and Walker (1988b) showed that people will decrease their contributions to a good when increasing group size causes their enjoyment of the good to go down (e.g., a park becomes overcrowded). However, if enjoyment is not affected by group size, then people in large and small groups contribute at about equal rates. Another factor is criticalness. Rapoport (1988) has argued that one factor that changes with group size is the probability that a group member will be critical; as group size increases, the likelihood that any one member's contribution will be critical to the group's success declines. We have already seen that self-efficacy and criticalness can play a large part in people's decisions to contribute. If a particular group member will contribute to a good only when the contribution will "make a difference," then it would be quite unlikely that the person would contribute if the group were large.

One factor that almost always increases with group size is anonymity. The larger the group is, the more able you are to "hide in the crowd"; in other words, your actions become less noticeable (Kerr & Bruun, 1981). If your actions are hard to detect, then you can free ride and very few others (if any) will know. If this sounds similar to our discussion of social loafing in Chapter 6, it should; as we mentioned in that chapter, free riding can be thought of generically as a type of social loafing. Free riders are not expending "effort" (contribution) to help produce the group "product" (public good). To date, researchers have only just begun to attempt to integrate social loafing and social dilemma research.

The "Sucker Effect."   Another factor that seems to figure into the contribution decision is an unwillingness to let noncontributors benefit from your largesse. This aversion to "carrying" free riders is known as the *sucker effect* (Kerr, 1983; Orbell & Dawes, 1981), which we described in Chapter 6. Kerr (1983) has argued that people are aversive to being a sucker because it violates some social norms, like equity (the greater your contribution, the greater your reward should be), social responsibility (everyone should give something to their group), or reciprocity. The sucker effect was demonstrated in Kerr's experiment, which we previously described. If the "equity" and "social responsibility" explanations are accurate, then subjects in Able-Fail and Unable-Fail should perform much worse than in the Control because their "partner" is not contributing to the group. It can be recalled that Kerr found subjects in both the Unable-Fail and Individual Model conditions performed *at least as well* as those in the Control. Subjects in the Able-Fail condition performed worse than the Control. His subjects avoided playing the sucker only when they thought their partner was not working as hard as he or she could. Kerr explained these results by suggesting that people will support others unless the others are *exploiting* their contributions; people would rather see a good go unprovided than be taken advantage of.

Trust. Finally, there is an individual difference factor that affects public good choice behavior. Known as interpersonal trust, it is, like self-efficacy, a concept that appears in many different areas of psychology. However, unlike self-efficacy, trust is a slippery concept that can be defined in many ways. Social dilemma researchers define it as the belief that others will work for the benefit of the group (Komorita & Carnevale, 1992; Yamagishi, 1986). Thus, a low-trust individual believes that others will be selfish. One's degree of trust in others is quite predictive of rate of contribution toward a public good. Simply put, the more trusting you are in others, the more frequently you will contribute (Parks, 1994; Yamagishi, 1986, 1988).

How Can We Make People More Cooperative?

We now have a good idea of why people act in their own, or the collective's, best interests. Our second research question asks, are there steps that we can take to make people more cooperative when they prefer not to be? One obvious method is to alter the voluntary nature of the dilemma and compel people to contribute. Governments often use this technique; for example, there are stiff penalties for cheating on one's income tax. However, this solution is often difficult to implement, as well as being impractical, for private institutions. For example, there is almost nothing the Muscular Dystrophy Association could do to force you to contribute. For this reason, researchers look for remedies that are practical and easily implemented in real-world situations. Many solutions have been proposed, but there are three that have garnered most of the attention: discussion of the dilemma, removal of fear or greed, and social sanctioning on noncooperators.

Discussion. One possible solution is to have group members discuss the dilemma before acting. Laboratory research has shown discussion to be very effective at promoting high rates of contribution to a public good. For example, van de Kragt and his colleagues (1983, 1986) found that groups that were allowed to talk about the dilemma provided the public good over 95 percent of the time. Other researchers have reported similar strong effects of predecision interaction (e.g., Braver & Wilson, 1986; Isaac &

Walker, 1988a; Liebrand, 1984). Communication, then, seems to be an effective method of enhancing cooperation, at least in public goods situations. Further, it is a "naturally occurring" technique, in that people very frequently discuss public goods-type issues (e.g., political candidates, favorite programs on public television), and is thus both practical and easily implemented. The obvious question to ask is, *why* is discussion so effective? Researchers have differing viewpoints on the answer to this question. Some possible explanations for discussion's effectiveness are as follows:

- Discussion invokes conformity pressure. Discussion reveals the prevailing preference within the group, and others feel pressured to go along with that preference (Messick & Brewer, 1983).
- Discussion fosters mutual trust (Messick & Brewer, 1983).
- Discussion allows group members to coordinate their efforts (Bornstein & Rapoport, 1988).
- Discussion triggers a general "norm of cooperation" within the group. All individuals believe cooperative behavior to be a "good" course of action, and discussion makes this norm salient (Kerr, 1992).
- Discussion promotes *group identity*, or a substitution of group regard for individual concern (Orbell, van de Kragt, & Dawes, 1988).
- Discussion allows group members to make explicit promises as to how they will behave, and such promises can act as a binding "contract" (Orbell et al., 1988).

Relatively little research has been conducted that compares these various propositions. The most wide-ranging study was done by Orbell and colleagues (1988), who examined the last three arguments and found data to support both the group identity and promise-making explanations.

Fear and Greed.   Earlier we discussed Kerr's (1983) "sucker effect" as an explanation for motivation losses: Group members free ride because they fear being taken advantage of. Another way to conceive of fear in public goods is the fear that one's efforts will go to waste. If we are the only ones who contribute, and we cannot meet the critical level of contribution by ourselves, then our efforts have been for naught. The converse of this type of fear is greed. Greed occurs because people want to "have their cake and eat it too"; that is, group members desire the good *as well as* their contribution (the lower-right cell of Table 7.2). Theoretically, if we could guarantee that individual efforts will not be wasted and remove the element of greed, contribution rates should greatly improve.

The effects of removing fear and greed are typically studied with No Fear (NF) and No Greed (NG) paradigms, developed simultaneously by Dawes,

Orbell, Simmons, and van de Kragt (1986) and Rapoport (1987). Each paradigm makes a simple change in the basic dilemma. The NF game works by employing a "money-back guarantee": Group members are informed that if the good is not provided, contributors will get their contribution back. The NG game enforces a "fair share" rule: Group members are told that if the good is provided, noncontributors must give up their endowments. (Note that NG is not the same thing as coercion because each member may freely choose at the outset whether to contribute.)

Dawes et al. (1986) and Rapoport and Eshed-Levy (1989) have used the NF and NG games to examine the relative roles of fear and greed. Both sets of researchers found that greed is the stronger instigator of free riding. That is, the primary reason that people free ride is because they are trying to get something for nothing. Less clear is how fear factors into the process. Dawes and colleagues could not get any increases in contribution by offering a money-back guarantee, but Rapoport and Eshed-Levy did. It is difficult to say why this difference occurred. It may have a methodological basis: The studies were conducted in different cultures (America and Israel respectively) and involved a different number of trials (one for Dawes et al., twenty-five for Rapoport & Eshed-Levy). Alternately, there may be something more complex at work that we haven't yet untangled. For example, Yamagishi and Sato (1986) have shown that the relative importance of fear and greed is dependent on whether a good's provision is determined by the performance of the group's best or worst member. When provision is dependent on the best member (e.g., the quality of a school system that is paid for through property taxes will be heavily dependent on the largest landowner in the district), many people will realize that they themselves are not the group's best; as a result, these people should see no reason to exert effort (contribute). This is greedy behavior. Conversely, if the provision is determined by the worst member's actions (e.g., the ability to consume previously polluted water is totally dependent on the sewage treatment efforts of the "cheapest" polluter), it is possible that the person's performance will not be good enough to provide the good. All other contributions would thus be wasted. Group members that reason this way should thus withhold contribution out of fear.

Sanctions. The final major solution to free riding is the use of social sanctions. Both discussion and fear/greed elimination have been criticized as being impractical for use in the real world, in that both would be very hard to implement in real groups (Yamagishi, 1986). How could we get every person who watches the Muscular Dystrophy Association telethon to discuss the charity? How could the MDA discover that you had watched the telethon without donating money, and how could they force you to pay up? Given this, Yamagishi suggests that cooperation can be maximized in larger groups by means of a *sanctioning system*. Such a system consists of some form of punishment that has been provided by all group members. The punishment could be either tangible (e.g., restricted access to the good) or intangible (e.g., social stigmatization). For example, your friends that donate to the MDA might chastise and embarrass you for not contributing. To avoid such punishment, free riders will alter their behavior and begin to cooperate. Yamagishi (1986) found that such a system was very effective at inducing others to cooperate, especially when the group members had little trust in each other.

Group Competition for Public Goods

We conclude our discussion of public goods by noting a new line of research that addresses how individuals behave when they belong to a group that is competing with another group for a good. This research is especially important because it may be relevant to issues other than social dilemmas. Some researchers in the area of prejudice (e.g., Pettigrew, 1978; White, 1977; see also Hepworth & West, 1988) have argued that prejudicial attitudes occur because different categories of people are competing for the same scarce resources. An example would be male biases against female coworkers existing because the females took jobs away from other men. Since minimizing prejudice and discrimination involves fostering a sense of cooperation between various groups, the research on intergroup competition may suggest some useful approaches to the problem of prejudice.

The research has been conducted by Amnon Rapoport and his colleagues. It is quite recent, and as such little is yet known about the dynamics of intergroup competition for a public good. An obvious question to ask is whether a larger group will more often receive the good than a smaller group simply because it contains more potential contributors. To test this, Rapoport, Bornstein, and Erev (1989) pitted a three-person group against a five-person group. Surprisingly, the large group did not dominate the small group; the good went to the large group 60 percent of the time and to the small group 40 percent of the time (there were no ties). Further, the mean proportion of contributors in both groups was almost exactly the same (56 percent and 57 percent for large and small respectively).

A second variable that has been supposed to affect group competition for a public good is communication. How effective is communication within a group when that group is competing with another for the good? Two studies (Bornstein & Rapoport, 1988; Rapoport & Bornstein, 1989) showed that, consistent with previous research, preplay discussion within each group substantially improved contribution rates. In the 1988 study, contribution increased from 46 percent to 83 percent; in the 1989 study, it went from 47 percent to 82 percent. In addition, Bornstein, Rapoport, Kerpel, and Katz (1989) observed an 87 percent contribution rate when within-group discussion was allowed. Within-group discussion would thus seem to be beneficial. However, Bornstein (1992) recently discovered that within-group communication is only effective for step-level goods. When the groups are competing for a continuous good, between-group communication is more effective at producing high rates of cooperation.

Summary

The public goods social dilemma is turning out to be a fairly complex type of group situation. We have seen that at least five factors, namely self-efficacy, expectations, group size, the sucker effect, and trust, can influence the decision to contribute. As yet, we know little about how these factors interact to produce behavior. We have also identified three interventions—discussion, removal of fear and greed, and social sanctions—that seem to encourage people to be more cooperative. Clearly, much more work needs to be done on the public goods dilemma in order for us to have a solid grasp on the mechanics of the public goods situation.

The Resource Dilemma

The second major innovation in social dilemma research is the resource dilemma. First discussed by Hardin (1968), the resource dilemma models those real-world situations in which members of a group harvest from a common source that is replenished at some rate. An excellent example of a resource dilemma is a water table. Tens of millions of Americans regularly consume vast amounts of water for their personal benefit (not only drinking but also washing cars, watering lawns, etc.). Groundwater is regularly replenished by rainfall and snowmelt, though typically at a slower rate than the water is consumed. This means that the water table is slowly declining. Nobody can stop you from using as much water as you want, but if everyone does this, then use will far exceed replenishment, and eventually the water table will dry up. If this happens, an entire city will suffer grave consequences. Hence the dilemma: It is best to use a lot of water in the short run, but in the long run it is better to conserve. In a resource dilemma, conservation is defined as the cooperative behavior because it leads to long-term benefit for the group, and excessive harvesting is defined as the noncooperative behavior because such actions will cause the resource to eventually disappear.

David Messick and colleagues devised the resource dilemma paradigm that allows researchers to study resource dilemma behavior in the laboratory (Messick, Wilke, Brewer, Kramer, Zemke, & Lui, 1983). It is easily described. A group of subjects are given a pool of points from which they may take as many as they like, up to a certain maximum amount. (This cap exists in real life as well. There is only so much water that you can use in any given day because you do not have the machinery necessary to take more. Hence, you might like to consume 1000 gallons of water a day, but you don't have the ability to get that much.) After everyone has taken what he or she likes from the point pool, it is partially replenished by adding back into the pool an amount of points equal to a percentage of the remaining pool size. So, for example, if there were 300 points left after everyone had sampled, and our replenishment rate is 10 percent, we would add 10 percent of 300, or 30, points back into the pool. The next trial would thus start with 330 points. This process continues until the end of the game is reached or the pool gets so low that it becomes impossible to fulfill all possible requests. As an example of this latter situation, let's say that a group of four people may each take up to 20 points from a pool on any given trial. When the pool falls below 80 points, the game must stop because it is impossible to satisfy all persons if, say, each person wants 20 points on the next trial.

This paradigm simulates many real-world processes quite closely and is thus very attractive to researchers. (Admittedly, actual replenishment rates are seldom constant; if the researcher were concerned about this feature, he or she could simply vary the rate randomly, by sampling values from a mathematical distribution, etc.) A real-world example would be fishing waters. Fishermen can catch as many fish as they want because the population is partially replenished whenever the fish reproduce; but if the species becomes "endangered," the government might set catch limits or deny fishing rights to all but a few fishermen, or it may become unprofitable to attempt to catch so few fish. In other words, once the pool of fish gets too low, people may be prevented from taking any more fish.

This example makes obvious the nature of the dilemma in a social trap. How can one maximize reward *and* keep the pool from running out? In theory, there is an answer to this question. It is known as the concept of *optimal harvest level*. An optimal harvest level is an individual harvest value such that if everyone were to make a harvest of this value, the pool would always be replenished to its original size. Thus, the pool would never run out, and each group member could continue to use the pool for as long as necessary. Komorita and Parks (1996) showed that optimal harvest level can be calculated as follows:

$$\text{Optimal} = [(IPS)(r)] / [(N)(r + 1)] \quad (1)$$

where *IPS* denotes initial pool size, *N* denotes group size, and *r* denotes replenishment rate. For example, consider a four-person group that starts with 400 points and has a replenishment rate of 10 percent. Thus, *IPS* = 400, *N* = 4, and *r* = 0.1. The optimal harvest level for each subject is (400 x 0.1) / (4)(1.1) = 9.1 (rounded to 9) points per person per trial. If, on the very first trial, each person would have harvested 9 points, 364 points would have remained. Ten percent of 364 is 36.4, which rounds off to 36. Thirty-six added to 364 equals 400. As long as each person continues to take 9 points per trial, the resource pool will never change. As we shall see, it is relatively rare for individuals to harvest at the optimal level.

Behavior in a Resource Dilemma

What should a person do when faced with a resource dilemma? This is not an easy question to answer. Consider a water table. Some states have been plagued by droughts in recent years. Governments in these states have told their residents that they must cut back on their use of water or risk running out altogether. Most people would like to plan for the future, but most people also like a clean car, a green lawn, and long showers. On the other hand, important industries, such as farming, and popular diversions, such as golf courses, use tremendous amounts of water; maybe we should compensate for them by cutting our own use of water. Of course, if everyone else is using a lot of water, maybe we should also, so we don't get "cheated" out of our fair share.

Clearly, a member of a group faced with a resource dilemma has a number of factors to consider before deciding how to behave. Messick and his colleagues have studied in great detail how these factors affect one's behavior in a social trap. They hypothesize that an individual group member has at least three, often conflicting, motives in a resource dilemma (Messick et al., 1983). First, people want to act in their own best interests. It is most convenient to shower every day, so people should do so. This is the individually rational way to act, so it should not surprise you that this motive is present. Second, a person wants to use the resource pool wisely. An example of this behavior would be to "counteract" the choices of others. If most other people are overconsuming the resource, the smart thing to do would be to cut back on one's own usage so that the total amount of resource consumed remains the same. Thus, if two people each use 100 gallons of water a week, one should cut his or her consumption to 90 gallons if the other suddenly raises his or hers to 110. Finally, there are conformity pressures to make choices similar to those of other group members. In other words, if everyone else is conserving water, you should too. These motives frequently come into conflict, and the resolution of the conflict can be affected by a number of variables.

Responsible Harvesting. The motive to act responsibly is usually studied by showing subjects that their fellow group members are "overusing" or "underusing" the resource pool. Overuse, of course, means that the others are taking too much of the resource and it will soon be depleted. Underusing, or taking too little of a resource, means that individuals are not maximizing their own personal gain; in other words, their harvests are less than the optimal harvest level. Underuse can sometimes be as detrimental as overuse, especially if a resource is perishable. For example, grain in a food cooperative will rot if it is not consumed quickly enough. As we said earlier, a person who wants to act responsibly should make harvests that counteract, or are opposite to those of the others. That is, one should make small harvests if everyone else is overusing, and large harvests if everyone is underusing. In fact, this is exactly how subjects in resource dilemmas behave. Almost all studies of resource dilemmas show that when conformity pressure is held constant, overuse leads subjects to make smaller harvests than underuse (e.g., Rutte, Wilke, & Messick, 1987; Samuelson & Messick, 1986a, 1986b; Samuelson, Messick, Rutte, & Wilke, 1984). The desire to act responsibly seems to be well-established.

Conformity.   Conformity pressures can be studied by varying the range of harvests of the other group members. If conformity is a factor, the conformity pressures should increase as the range of harvests made by other group members narrows. This is because as the choices of other members become more similar, the person may come to perceive and develop a norm or standard for a "correct" amount to harvest, and he or she will be hesitant to deviate from that norm. By contrast, if choices vary widely, then there is probably no single harvest that the group "expects" each member to make. Individual choices do seem to be affected by the range of others' harvests, although the nature of the relationship is not exactly clear. Samuelson, Messick, Rutte, and Wilke (1984) showed that the range alone can sufficiently increase or decrease conformity pressure. In their studies, subjects believed that they were playing a resource dilemma with other subjects; in reality, the other "group members" were sets of choices that were predetermined by the experimenters. The range of harvests of the "group members" was either large or small. Subjects played for ten trials (though they did not know this exact figure) or until the pool ran out. At the end of the trials, there was a chance that the subjects' accumulated points would be converted into money at a five-cent-per-point rate. Samuelson and colleagues found that subjects whose fellow "group members" made a narrow range of choices showed harvest values much closer to the group average than did those who experienced a wide range. When variability was high, subjects tended to act in their own best interests and harvested at a rate higher than the average.

Other studies have shed further light on the range-conformity relation. Samuelson and Messick (1986a, 1986b) showed that variance interacts with use. In those studies, high variance led to large individual harvests only when others were using the pool responsibly; chronic overuse of the pool led subjects to make smaller-than-average harvests, even when variance was high. Samuelson and Messick (1986a) and Samuelson et al. (1984) found that variance interacts with trials. High variance produced individual harvests greater than the group norm, but only after a period of time. Taken together, these studies suggest that conformity pressure operates only when a resource is not overused. If the resource is being rapidly depleted, individuals tend to conserve, regardless of what others are doing.

Overuse or underuse of a resource is not necessarily caused by the individuals consuming it. The resource itself can sometimes produce over/underuse. For example, if six cooks are given 100 pounds of apples per month, it is likely the apples will go bad before they can all be used. The pool of apples has been underused but not because of any deficient behaviors on the part of the group members. Similarly, if the same six cooks are given only eight apples per month, the apple pool will probably be exhausted very quickly, though not through any fault of the individuals. It is possible that conformity pressures are affected by whether over/underuse is attributed to fellow group members or the resource itself. Rutte and colleagues (1987) examined this relation. They conducted a study using a procedure very similar to the one described earlier in this section, except that subjects played for money rather than points. Subjects believed they were part of a real group engaged in a resource dilemma. In reality, the behaviors of other "group members" were simulated by the experimenters. Subjects were led to believe that their "group" was either overusing or underusing the resource pool by receiving bogus feedback. This feedback indicated that other members were either harvesting a lot of money (overuse) or little money (underuse). Further, subjects were told that the over/underuse was caused by either the choices of their fellow "group members" (e.g., others were being greedy) or the initial pool size being too small/large (e.g., the pool was too small for so many people to use). Rutte et al. found that subjects tended to conform to the choices of others when over/underuse could be attributed to other group members but acted responsibly when over/underuse was believed to be the result of the environment (pool size).

Behavior over Time. All studies of resource dilemmas involve multitrial games. It is thus logical to ask whether behavior changes over time. Many studies show that harvests tend to increase over trials (e.g., Messick et al., 1983; Samuelson & Messick, 1986a; Samuelson et al., 1984). As the dilemma progresses, subjects act more for their own personal benefit (greed), and less for the group good, by taking larger portions of the pool. We have seen, however, that it is also very common for time and use to interact (e.g., Samuelson & Messick, 1986a, 1986b; Samuelson et al., 1984). In these studies, mean harvests increased over time only when others were not overusing the pool. People whose fellow group members repeatedly took near-maximum amounts of points tended to maintain a consistent level of harvesting or even decreased their harvests. Messick et al. (1983) found that time interacted with both use and variance; harvests increased only when the pool was not overused *and* the range of others' choices was high. The conclusion to be drawn here seems to be that individuals will increase their harvests as the game progresses, but only if others are not abusing the pool. (An exception to this, however, is Samuelson's (1991) study, in which subjects *decreased* their harvests as the game progressed.)

Complex Behavior in a Social Trap

We have seen that different, often conflicting, motives we face in a resource dilemma (own best interests, responsible pool use, conformity) can interact in many ways. It may seem that there is little consistency among the myriad of results we have discussed in this part of the chapter. In fact, the results do suggest one general conclusion: Prediction of harvesting behavior is extremely difficult to do without first analyzing the task confronting the group. In order to make predictions about a particular person's behavior, we would need to know whether that person was aware of the choices of others, whether he or she monitored the resource's changing size, and so on. In addition, researchers continue to test other social factors that may partially affect such behavior.

Solving Resource Dilemmas

A large portion of research on resource dilemmas has been devoted to how to "solve" them, that is, to identify techniques or interventions that will maintain the pool near its original or some viable, long-term level. Research has focused on two different types of solutions: *structural* solutions, or techniques that involve changing the structure of the dilemma in some way; and *individual* solutions, or attempts to alter individual choice behavior (Messick & Brewer, 1983).

Structural Solutions. Studies of structural alterations have mainly centered around two techniques: changing the methods in which group members choose their harvests, and partitioning the resource. The former has received much attention from researchers, whereas the latter is a new approach. The most commonly studied structural solution involves denying group members the opportunity to sample the resource at will and instead applying some type of resource distribution system. Specifically, Messick, Samuelson, and colleagues have investigated the efficiency and popularity of a "leader-based" means of harvesting. Under such a system, one member of the group is selected to act as the leader and harvests for each person in the group.

A very consistent finding is that subjects whose group overused the pool are much more likely to prefer to change the decision structure (Messick et al., 1983; Samuelson & Messick, 1986a, 1986b; Samuelson et al., 1984). Samuelson et al. (1984) argue that this is the result of an attributional process. Subjects believe that any system that allows others to overuse the pool must be a faulty one and therefore should be changed. Along these lines, it is interesting to note that subjects who experienced high variance in the choices of others expressed dissatisfaction with the game but were more likely to prefer to maintain the free-choice system. In this situation, subjects may be attributing fault not to the system but to a few greedy individuals and thus see no reason to change the system. Similarly, Samuelson (1991) found that subjects voted to change the decision structure (to a leader-based system) when they believed that depletion was caused by an inherent difficulty in maintaining the pool (they were told that almost no group had successfully managed the pool to that point) but not when they believed depletion was the result of many greedy group members. His results suggest that individuals desire a change not only when they believe the current system is inadequate but also when they believe a change will be effective at enforcing cooperation.

Interestingly, the popularity of the leader-based system among group members is mixed. Samuelson and Messick (1986a) had subjects play a standard resource dilemma game. After the session ended, subjects were told that they would play a second session and had the option of changing the decision structure. Some subjects had the option of switching to a leader system; some to a system in which all group members received an equal portion of the pool; and some to a proportional division system where point allotments were tied to one's first-session harvest total (i.e., the higher one's total harvest was, the larger one's second-session harvest would be). They found that subjects with the leader option most frequently voted to change the structure. In a second study in which all subjects considered all options, Samuelson and Messick (1986b) asked subjects to rank each of the above three alternatives in terms of preference; interestingly, the equal-division option, not the leader option, proved to be most popular. In fact, Rutte and Wilke (1985) showed that a leader-based system is very *unpopular* when members also have the option of having the group itself, rather than a single individual, decide the size of harvest allotments (e.g., majority or unanimity rules). It thus seems that leader selection is not a structural change preferred by many individuals.

The other major structural change is called partitioning, which involves division of the resource into discrete units. Allison and Messick (1990) have suggested that people often rely on decision heuristics, or simplification strategies, to help them decide how much to harvest. Specifically, they argue that these individuals use an "equality" heuristic, which prescribes that

Social Dilemmas

everyone should harvest the same amount. Since most people consider equal division to be a fair means of allocation (Messick & Sentis, 1979), it would seem to be preferable for group members to use this heuristic. There are some situations, however, where it is difficult to apply an equality rule. Allison, McQueen, and Schaerfl (1992) suggested that the partitionment of the resource is crucial to equality. If a four-person group has eight 20-gallon buckets of water, it is easy to apply the equality rule: Each person gets two buckets, or 40 gallons. But what if the group is given one 160-gallon bucket? Without a measuring device, it is virtually impossible to ensure that each person uses exactly 40 gallons. Further, in the former situation there is no way a group member can cheat without being caught, but in the latter instance it would be quite easy to be greedy. Who could tell if a person used 50, rather than 40, gallons? Allison and colleagues thus predicted that the equality rule would be applied less often when the resource is not easily divisible. To test this, they gave three- and twelve-person groups one of two resources to manage: A number of blocks (6 or 24 respectively) or a bucket of sand (6 or 24 pounds). It is easy to give all members an equal number of blocks but difficult (again, without a measuring device) to distribute equal amounts of sand. Allison and colleagues predicted that "block" groups would more often use the equality rule than "sand" groups. This is exactly what happened. Seventy-six percent of "block" groups used equality; only 40 percent of "sand" groups did. Further, members of twelve-person "sand" groups took on average more than 4.5 pounds of sand; equal division would give them 2 pounds. By contrast, members of three-person "sand" groups were very good at dividing the resource (1.8 pounds). As you might expect, both "block" groups harvested very close to the equal value—1.8 and 2.1 blocks respectively. Not all resources can be neatly divided, of course, but doing so for those resources with which it can be done would seem to help inhibit overconsumption, particularly in larger groups.

Individual Solutions. A second technique for "solving" resource dilemmas involves altering individual selection behavior rather than the resource structure itself. In contrast to structural solutions, a number of different *individual solutions* have been investigated. We review some of these solutions here.

We saw that allowing group members to discuss a public goods dilemma results in dramatic increases in cooperation. Could *communication* have similar effects in a social trap? Liebrand (1984) conducted a resource dilemma experiment in which half of the groups were allowed to discuss the task and the other half could not. The exact size of the pool (consisting of money) was unknown, but groups did know that the pool would fall within a certain specified range (from $95 to $115). Each subject requested some amount of money from the pool. After all members made a request, the requests were added to yield a total request. Pool size was randomly selected from within the specified range. If the pool was larger than the total request, all members got their harvests, but if the total request exceeded pool size, no payoffs were given. Liebrand found that discussion groups were much more effective pool managers than groups that had no verbal interaction. Collectively, the best course of action is to request individual amounts such that the total request is less than the range minimum of $95. That way, the pool will always exceed requests, and a payoff is guaranteed. In fact, 70 percent of Liebrand's communicating groups used exactly this strategy. The likelihood of *any* communicating group receiving a payoff was 94 percent. By contrast, none of the noncommunicating groups used this strategy; the likelihood of their receiving a payoff was only 54 percent. One group never received any payoffs. Messick, Allison, and Samuelson (1988) also found face-to-face discussion to be beneficial. Using a paradigm similar to the one employed by Liebrand, their subjects used free discussion to identify optimal behaviors and to coordinate their choices accordingly. Ninety percent of their communicating groups received payoffs; only 20 percent of noncommunicating groups did. Thus, discussion clearly seems to be effective at improving resource pool management.

A second important feature is experience. A common aspect of laboratory research is that the task is usually unfamiliar to all subjects. It is highly unlikely that any of the subjects had engaged in anything like an experimental resource dilemma before they entered the laboratory. In the real world, however, our encounters with real social traps are continual, and we may benefit from this experience by being able to make more informed decisions. The natural question to ask is, what if laboratory subjects had previous experience with an experimental resource dilemma?

Allison and Messick (1985) had subjects manage two consecutive sets of resource dilemmas. In the first session, subjects managed the pool either individually (i.e., they were the only person harvesting from the pool) or as part of a group. For the second session, all persons worked in groups: Groups from the first session were kept intact, while first-session individuals were grouped together. Allison and Messick found that groups composed of experienced individuals were significantly better at maintaining their pool in the second session than were experienced groups. Interestingly, experienced groups were no better than inexperienced groups at pool maintenance. Allison and Messick also showed that individual experience proved more beneficial as group size increased. Thus, people do seem to be able to learn efficient pool management strategies, but only by being solely responsible for the pool's maintenance. However, this individualized training seems to transfer to group management settings.

Stern (1976) tested the benefits of explicitly educating subjects about the likely consequences of their various choice options. His subjects received either basic pregame information regarding the nature of the game or a complete pregame description of how choices would affect the life of the pool. Not surprisingly, groups that had received the full information maintained their pool significantly longer than the basic-information groups. Stern also gave some subjects periodic "spot messages" that provided cues as to the optimal pattern of choices. Interestingly, such hints had no effect on individual harvests. Similarly, Orbell and Dawes (1981) observed increases in cooperative behavior when subjects were given a pregame lecture regarding the benefits of cooperation. Education thus seems to be effective only when it is fully and completely provided at the outset.

Taken together, these studies indicate that experience, either practical or formal, can produce positive results regarding resource conservation. However, not just any experience will suffice; attention must be paid to the type and form of experience given.

What if individual group members were punished for overconsumption? We have seen that punishment is a potentially effective technique for controlling free riding in public goods situations (Yamagishi, 1986). It is possible that punishment also inhibits individuals from harvesting excessive amounts of a resource. Bell, Petersen, and Hautaluoma (1989) tested this hypothesis. Subjects were told that if they accumulated an excessive amount of points, there was a probability (25 percent or 75 percent) that they would be penalized by having some points subtracted from their own accumulated total. Bell and colleagues found that, compared to subjects for whom there was no penalty, the presence of potential punishment significantly prolonged the life of the resource. Interestingly, the harsher (75 percent) penalty did not produce a longer resource life than the lenient (25 percent) penalty. This suggests that the mere threat of a penalty is sufficient to induce conservation; the severity of that threat is of little consequence. However, the presence of the threat had a negative side effect: Subjects became more willing to steal points from others. Conversely, attempting to inhibit stealing with punishment led to more frequent overharvesting. It is not clear what effect punishment would have on subjects for whom stealing is not an option; future research may address this issue.

Finally, there may be some individual difference factors that influence harvest behavior. For example, one's *social identity* may influence choice. Recall from Chapter 2 that an individual with a collective social identity places greater emphasis on group rather than individual gains, whereas the reverse is true for individual social identity. Many researchers (e.g., Dawes, 1990) believe that social identity is a crucial concept for understanding why people cooperate and how to improve cooperation. Brewer (1981) and Messick and Brewer (1983) have suggested that a group whose members feel a strong sense of collective identity should be much more efficient in maintaining a resource than a group whose members are individually oriented. Kramer and Brewer (1984) and Brewer and Kramer (1986) tested this hypothesis using both resource dilemma and public goods paradigms. In a series of studies, they systematically manipulated the level of social identity of subjects and compared the harvesting behaviors of collective-identity versus individual-identity subjects. Social identity was typically manipulated by taking advantage of naturally occurring categories. For example, in one study all subjects were psychology majors. The subjects were told that the other "group members" were economics majors. To instill a collective identity, some subjects were told that the purpose of the experiment was to compare the performance of university students against non-student groups. Subjects in the "individual identity" condition were told that the purpose of the experiment was to compare psychology majors and economics majors. Kramer and Brewer found that collective-identity individuals were significantly better at managing the resource than subordinate-identity subjects. This efficiency was independent of group size; collective-identity subjects were better than individual-identity subjects even when the "group" was as large as thirty-two members.

Another, more personality-based, individual difference that affects resource harvests is one's *social value orientation*. Simply put, your social value orientation reflects the extent to which you are a cooperative type of person. There seem to be three major classes of people: Cooperators, who want to maximize joint gain; Competitors, who want to maximize the difference between their personal payoff and the payoffs of others; and Individualists, who care only about their own outcomes and are indifferent to the outcomes of others. Social values have a long history in prisoner's dilemma research, and as you might suspect, the research shows that Cooperators are more cooperative than either of the other two types of people (see Komorita & Parks, 1996). The same pattern has been recently observed in resource dilemmas: Cooperators tend to take fewer points per trial than either Competitors or Individualists (Kramer, McClintock, & Messick, 1986; Parks, 1994; Parks & Hulbert, 1995).

Resource Dilemma Research and Real Problems

Although many areas of group research are related to real-world problems, resource dilemma research offers one of the clearest connections between the laboratory and real-world behavior. This connection is recognized by policymakers as well as by scientists. For example, in Canada the Minister of Environment recently published a paper in a top Canadian behavioral science journal calling for greater collaboration between resource dilemma researchers and lawmakers (Marchi, 1997). A similar appeal has not yet been made in the United States, but it seems safe to assume that American lawmakers would be responsive to such collaboration. Resource dilemma research thus affords psychologists a real opportunity to have an immediate impact on society.

Chapter Summary

In this chapter, we have provided a basic introduction to research on social dilemmas, or situations in which individuals face a conflict between doing what is best for themselves and what is best for the group as a whole. There are many real examples of social dilemmas, which is a major reason why they are an attractive research topic.

The prisoner's dilemma is the classic paradigm for studying social dilemmas, but controversy over its external validity has led to a substantial decline in its use. Prisoner's dilemma researchers currently focus on the effectiveness of strategic choice in inducing others to cooperate. Researchers have increasingly studied the public goods game and the resource dilemma, two very realistic analogues. Many factors seem to drive public goods behavior, and some interventions have been identified that seem to encourage greater rates of cooperation in group members. Behavior in a resource dilemma seems to be influenced by three major factors: conformity, responsibility, and personal gain. Exactly how these factors combine to affect behavior is not clear. Finally, there are some individual difference factors that are related to choice behavior in both types of dilemmas.

Part Three

Specific Types
of Groups

Chapter Eight

Groups in the Workplace

Group processes are an important component of the workplace. Be it group decisionmaking, work teams, or leadership, groups are vital to the functioning of many industries. Imagine, for example, trying to efficiently make cars without having organized sets of workers to perform various sets of tasks and a leadership structure that guides those sets of workers. For many years, groups were seen as a necessary evil in industry, and there were a number of common misconceptions about group performance in the workplace (Dipboye, Smith, & Howell, 1994; Schwartz, 1994). However, the study of groups is increasingly gaining prominence in industrial-organizational (I/O) psychology, the area of psychology that is directly concerned with workplace functioning (Sanna & Parks, 1997). In this chapter, we review the major group-related topics of interest in the workplace. For most of the chapter, we focus on factors that arise within the group—the need for leadership, perceptions of how one's outcomes compare to those of fellow group members and the impact of those perceptions on subsequent behavior, and the resolution of conflict within a group. We then finish with a consideration of more macro-level factors: teamwork and organizational culture.

Leadership

Leadership is the groups topic that has the longest history in I/O psychology. Its roots stretch back to at least the 1940s. Our discussion of leadership research is confined to group-oriented questions, but be aware that leadership researchers are also interested in more social cognitive-type questions, addressing topics such as leader prototypes and worker recall of effective leaders.

Leader Selection

The leadership question that has been most heavily studied has been, how can we identify the best leader for a work group? (By "best," we mean that the leader should be most able to help the work group to accomplish its tasks.) Probably the best known theory of leader selection, and certainly the one that has received the most research attention, is Fiedler's (1967) contingency model. This theory assumes that we each have one particular style of interacting with others that we most prefer to use. Fiedler proposed that there are two such styles: task orientation, under which we emphasize successful completion of tasks; and relationship orientation, under which we emphasize interpersonal harmony. Further, each work group has associated with it three characteristics: the leader's degree of power over subordinates; the quality of leader-subordinate relations; and the degree of structure inherent in the work group's task. Fiedler assumed that these characteristics are dichotomous; that is, a leader can have either strong or weak power; relations can be either good or bad; and the task is either structured or unstructured. The levels of these characteristics can be combined to form eight (2 x 2 x 2) different work situations. Fiedler then took these eight situations and organized them on a "favorability" continuum, where favorability is a general description of the conditions within the work group. The eight situations are shown in Table 8.1. The most favorable situation is one in which the leader has strong power, good relations with subordinates, and the task is structured; the least favorable is one in which the leader has no power, poor relations, and the task is unstructured.

Fiedler predicted that task-oriented individuals will be the best leaders when the situation is either favorable or unfavorable. In favorable situations, the group will be functioning at a high level, and the need is for a leader who can maintain that high level of functioning. In unfavorable situations, what is needed is someone who will inject some structure into the task and not worry about how subordinates will react; the relationship-oriented person can do neither of these. By contrast, relationship-oriented leaders will be most effective when the situation is moderate (in the center of the continuum) because here the leader must be most sensitive to interpersonal conflicts and increase worker satisfaction with the task. The task-oriented person will typically come across as being uncaring in these situations, and workers may react negatively to this.

The contingency model has been, and continues to be, hotly debated. Advocates tout the model's recognition that work groups are complex entities and that leadership is affected by a number of workplace factors (Ayman, Chemers, & Fiedler, 1995). Critics take exception with the model's reliance on a trait (task versus relationship orientation) that is not well-defined or studied (Rice, 1978; Schriesheim, Bannister, & Money, 1979) and point out that applications of the model to real work situations have not always strictly followed the model's predictions (Jago & Ragan, 1986). Reviews of the large body of research on the model do not help clarify the picture. Three meta-

TABLE 8.1   Fiedler's (1967) Eight Different Work Situations, Placed on a Favorability Continuum

	Leader Power	*Leader-Subordinate Relations*	*Task Structure*
Favorable	Strong	Good	Structured
	Weak	Good	Structured
	Strong	Good	Unstructured
	Weak	Good	Unstructured
	Strong	Poor	Structured
	Weak	Poor	Structured
	Strong	Poor	Unstructured
Unfavorable	Weak	Poor	Unstructured

analyses of the contingency model have been published. The first (Strube & Garcia, 1981) found good general support for the model; the second (Peters, Hartke, & Pohlmann, 1985) found that the model is more strongly supported by laboratory research than by research in real work settings; and the third (Schriesheim, Tepper, & Tetrault, 1994) found that the predictions for some of the eight work situations simply have no empirical support. Debate over the contingency model will likely continue for many years to come.

Leader-Subordinate Interaction

Leadership researchers have also looked inside the work group to study how leaders and subordinates interact with each other and whether those patterns of interaction affect worker performance. The theoretical perspective that dominates this area is the leader-member exchange (LMX) model, developed by Graen and colleagues, and originally called the vertical dyad linkage model (Dansereau, Graen, & Haga, 1975; Graen & Uhl-Bien, 1995). This model draws on the notion of ingroups and outgroups that we discussed in Chapter 2. The basic logic is that the leader maintains an ingroup and an outgroup of subordinates. Workers in the ingroup are generally treated better, receive considerable freedom on the job, and have good relationships with the leader, and the interactions between the leader and ingroup workers are of high quality. By contrast, outgroup workers are treated in a much more formal manner, have fairly highly structured tasks, and are not very close to the leader, and leader-worker interactions are of moderate or poor quality. Indeed, outgroup workers may rarely interact with the leader. It follows that ingroup workers tend to be more productive in, and satisfied with, their jobs than outgroup workers.

The LMX model has an impressive amount of empirical support. The major predictions of performance and satisfaction differences between ingroup and outgroup workers have been observed in a number of studies (e.g., Graen & Schiemann, 1978; Liden & Graen, 1980; Scandura & Graen, 1984). Research has also demonstrated that ingroup-outgroup assignment can happen very early in a worker's career, perhaps as early as the first week of work (Liden, Wayne, & Stilwell, 1993). Note, however, that this model is not without its problems. Specifically, concern has been raised about both accurate identification of the ingroup and the outgroup (Dienesch & Liden, 1986) and analysis of the quality of a leader-worker exchange episode (Dienesch & Liden, 1986; Fairhurst, 1993). These, however, are methodological rather than theoretical problems that can be worked out over time (and on which work has already begun; see Fairhurst, 1993; and Phillips & Bedian, 1994). The LMX model thus seems to be an important contribution to the understanding of within-group processes.

Leader Prototypes

An emerging factor that seems to play a role in leader-subordinate interaction is the leader prototype (sometimes called "implicit leadership theories"). The notion of a leader prototype draws on social cognitive theorizing about person perception. Basically, a leader prototype is the set of traits that an individual associates with effective leadership (Lord, 1985; Phillips & Lord, 1982; Rush, Thomas, & Lord, 1977). Workers maintain certain expectations regarding how a good leader should be, and the extent to which the leader meets these expectations can influence leader-subordinate relations, especially in terms of the leader's power and influence. Leaders who deviate considerably from subordinate prototypes can have difficulty exerting either power or influence over the workers (Cronshaw & Lord, 1987), presumably because a leader who does not fit the prototype is assumed by subordinates to be incompetent and hence unworthy of respect, whereas leaders who closely match the prototypes can gain a considerable amount of power (Foti & Luch, 1992).

Although specific prototypes vary from person to person, there seem to be some traits that are commonly associated with good leaders, and a number of researchers have tried to identify these common elements. Some examples of these common traits are intelligence, sensitivity, verbal skill, and dedication (Kenney, Blascovich, & Shaver, 1994; Lord, Foti, & DeVader, 1984;

Offermann, Kennedy, & Wirtz, 1994). However, recent research suggests that leader prototypes are actually quite diverse. For example, subordinates seem to maintain separate prototypes for new versus experienced leaders (Kenney et al., 1994). Much more work is needed on leader prototypes, but it seems clear that they have considerable influence over leader-worker interaction.

Transformational Versus Transactional Leadership

A relatively new approach to leadership that is garnering attention involves distinguishing between *transactional* and *transformational* leadership styles. As described by Bass (1985), transactional leadership involves rational analysis of a work situation in order to determine what must be done, how it should be done, and the benefits to workers of goal accomplishment. The transactional leader sees his or her job as one of clarifying the "what" and the "how" for workers so that they can best accomplish the goal. By contrast, transformational leadership is a complex, dynamic style of leadership in which the leader's job is to encourage workers to set and meet challenging goals. The leader does this by expanding the worker's set of job-related needs, so that the new goals are seen as desirable, and providing encouragement to the worker. To accomplish this, the leader can engage in such behaviors as articulation of a vision, promotion of worker cooperation, and provision of intellectual stimulation (Podsakoff, MacKenzie, Moorman, & Fetter, 1990). Perhaps the best way to fully understand the nature of transformational leadership is to consider some of the adjectives that Bass (1985) says are commonly applied to transformational leaders: inspiring, uplifting, evangelical, and exhorting. Because this is a new approach, there are as yet little data on the effectiveness of transformational leadership, although these data indicate that it is an effective approach to worker motivation (Hater & Bass, 1988).

Equity Theory

Equity theory has been extremely influential in analyzing people's reactions in the workplace. The equity concept focuses on a person's self-evaluation in comparison with other people. In this sense, it is a "groupy" theory because this self-evaluation occurs in comparison with other people, for example, other people at your workplace. However, this aspect of equity theory may not in and of itself make it relevant to group processes. In fact, some researchers argue that equity theory by itself focuses more on individual processes (e.g., individual reactions to inequities). Other researchers, however, have extended these concepts and have elaborated on their implications for group-level phenomena. It is in this context that we primarily focus our discussion of equity theory to applications in the workplace.

Ratio of Inputs to Outcomes

Equity theory is a cognitive consistency theory that has often been applied to reactions in the workplace. (Cognitive consistency theories propose that it is distasteful for people to hold inconsistent thoughts about things.) Some of the first formal statements of equity theory were made by Adams (1963, 1965; see also Walster, Berscheid, & Walster, 1973). In general, it was proposed that when people evaluate their transactions with others, their "inputs" and "outcomes" are carefully taken into consideration. Inputs are those things that one puts into his or her work and that the person thinks should earn some return on his or her investment—factors such as effort expended, time expended, or intrinsic talent. Outcomes are returns or rewards that one expects to obtain from his or her work, such as salary or fringe benefits.

According to equity theory, a person weighs the ratio of his or her inputs to outcomes and then compares this to the ratio of inputs to outcomes of other people. *Equity* is said to occur when the ratio of a person's inputs to outcomes equals that of another person's ratio of inputs to outcomes. This can be represented by the following equation:

$$\frac{O_{self}}{I_{self}} = \frac{O_{other}}{I_{other}}$$

In the above equation, O stands for the outcomes of self and other, and I stands for the inputs of self and other, respectively. An example of an equitable situation would be one in which you (self) work just as hard as a coworker (other), you both have equal inputs, you both receive equal pay, and you both have equal outcomes. In contrast, if the ratio of your inputs to outcomes is different from the ratio of your coworker's inputs to outcomes, then inequity exists.

Inequity is an interesting concept for several reasons. First, it seems to be an aversive situation. People, in general, do not like inequity; related to the notion of cognitive consistency, which we mentioned above, people find it distasteful to hold cognitions such as "I am working harder than she is" and "We are getting the same salary." This is interesting because people do several things to bring these discrepant cognitions back into balance, which we describe below. Second, it is assumed that inequity influences a person's reactions even when the direction of inequity seems favorable. That is, if a coworker has qualifications equal to your own and you both work equally hard, but the coworker is getting paid more than you are for the same work, inequity exists. However, inequity can also exist in the situation just described if the other person is getting paid *less* than you. In either case, the inequity may create tension, and this tension has motivating properties that impel a person to eliminate the inequity.

Ways to Reduce Inequity

If inequity is an aversive state and people strive to eliminate it, then how can this be accomplished? Researchers and theorists have proposed several ways to reduce inequity. We focus on some of the main ones. First, imagine that you feel that you are underpaid. One thing that you might do is change your own inputs by not putting so much effort into your work. This can be represented as the following (the size of the I's and O's represents the size of inputs and outcomes):

$$\frac{O_{self}}{I_{self}} \neq \frac{O_{other}}{I_{other}} \rightarrow \frac{O_{self}}{I_{self}} = \frac{O_{other}}{I_{other}}$$

In this situation, you may be putting as much effort into your work as a coworker, but the coworker is getting more outcomes, let's say salary. As we mentioned, equity theory would predict that this situation will be aversive to you. You are both working just as hard but your coworker is getting paid more! One thing you can do in this situation is not work so hard, which you believe will bring your work back in line with your salary and with the ratio of inputs to outcomes of your coworker.

A second thing that you can do, however, is try to increase your outcomes. For example, you might try to convince your boss that you deserve a pay raise. This can be represented as follows:

$$\frac{O_{self}}{I_{self}} \neq \frac{O_{other}}{I_{other}} \rightarrow \frac{O_{self}}{I_{self}} = \frac{O_{other}}{I_{other}}$$

Here, you are attempting to bring the relationship in line by boosting your outcomes (i.e., salary) to a level equal to that of your coworker. Note that in either case, equity is restored. Equity can also be restored in other ways as well. For example, if you have the power, you can ask the coworker to increase his or her input by doing extra work. You might also ask the coworker to reduce his or her outcomes, such as accepting lower pay or fewer fringe benefits. Alternatively, if none of these other means are available, you may quit comparing yourself to this coworker, or otherwise try to "restore" equity by distorting the situation (e.g., "being paid so little is really good for me because it builds character").

Evidence for Equity Theory

There are several studies that have tested equity theory predictions in work situations. In a study dealing with the effects of underpayment, Lawler and O'Gara (1967) hired undergraduates to conduct interviews. Some participants were paid 10¢ for each interview (underpayment condition), whereas other participants were paid 25¢ for each interview (equitably paid condition). Compared to equitably paid participants, underpaid participants spent less time on each interview, thereby decreasing their input. In addition, underpaid participants completed more interviews, thereby increasing their outcomes (i.e., pay). As an example, this situation can be represented as follows:

$$\frac{O_{10¢}}{I} \neq \frac{O_{25¢}}{I} \rightarrow \frac{O_{10¢}}{I} = \frac{O_{25¢}}{I}$$

Here, the 10¢ (underpaid) group decreases their inputs relative to outcomes, restoring equity.

That people will restore equity when they are underpaid is interesting; however, perhaps even more striking is that people will also restore equity when they are *overpaid*. In a demonstration of this, Adams and Jacobsen (1964) hired three groups of undergraduates to work on a proofreading task. One group of participants was told that, despite their inexperience, they would be paid the same rate as experienced proofreaders (30¢ per page). This group was thus the overpaid group because they were getting an outcome usually reserved for people with greater input (more experience). A second group of participants was told that, because of their inexperience, they would be paid only 20¢ per page. A third group was told that they *were* well-qualified and that they therefore would be paid 30¢ per page. This situation, representing the relationship of the three groups can be depicted as follows:

$$\frac{O_{30¢}}{I} \neq \frac{O_{20¢}}{I} = \frac{O_{10¢}}{I}$$

In this situation, according to Adams and Jacobsen, the first group (those who were overpaid) should be the only group to experience inequity—they were getting paid more than their experience warranted. Consistent with predictions, the overpaid group was found to spend more time on each page, increasing their inputs. As a result, the overpaid groups also received less pay (decreased outcomes). These things restored equity (see also Goodman & Friedman, 1971; Pritchard, 1969).

Evidence in support of equity theories has also been obtained in actual employment settings. For example, Pritchard, Dunnette, and Jorgenson (1972), when hiring 253 men to work as clerks for one week, promised a wage of about $2.00 per hour. Soon after they began working, some of the men were told they would be underpaid, others overpaid, and some paid the promised amount. On job-satisfaction questionnaires filled out during the work week, *both* underpaid and overpaid workers expressed less satisfaction than equitably paid workers (those who were promised $2 to begin with). As predicted by equity theory, inequity of either underpayment or overpayment was somewhat aversive (see also Brockner & Wisenfield, 1996; Milsap & Taylor, 1996; Platow, O'Connell, Shave, & Hanning, 1995; Schmitt & Marwell, 1972; van Dijk & Wilke, 1994).

In perhaps one of the more intriguing studies of equity in a real-world work setting, Lord and Hohenfeld (1979) studied the effects of free agency in major league baseball. In December of 1975, major league baseball abolished the "reserve clause" that had bound players to a specific team. When first implemented, star players tried to negotiate huge salary increases with the teams on which they were already playing. If these negotiations were not successful, then the players could "play out their option." This meant that a player could play with his current team for one year, usually at a reduced salary, and then become a "free agent," offering his services to the highest bidder. So what does this have to do with equity theory? Lord and Hohenfeld reasoned that playing out one's option would be particularly upsetting for the stars, who could see from newspapers and other sources how other stars were signing multimillion-dollar contracts. Those playing out their options at a reduced rate would feel grossly underpaid. As we have seen in our examples above, one way to restore equity is to decrease performance. This is exactly what was found: Baseball players who were playing out their options exhibited a drastic decrease in performance, just as equity theory would predict. It therefore seems clear that inequitable comparisons to other group members can have drastic effects on performance, satisfaction, and other reactions in a variety of laboratory and real-life work settings.

Relative Deprivation

Related to equity theory is the concept of relative deprivation. Relative deprivation theories are related to equity theories in that both sets of theories are concerned with people's reactions when they compare themselves with others. However, relative deprivation theories also bring up some other important issues. These additional aspects of theories of relative deprivation may help to further our understanding of people's reactions in the workplace when they are making comparisons with group members and coworkers.

Early History

Interest in relative deprivation began with a focus on people's reactions in the workplace in what has become a classic study of work performance and military personnel (Stouffer, Suchman, DeVinney, Star, & Williams, 1949). Among other aspects of their studies, Stouffer et al. found that the satisfaction of U.S. military personnel during World War II did not always seem to correspond with their objective job characteristics (e.g., opportunities for promotion). It was observed, for example, that airmen had a higher rate of promotion than did military police, but the airmen were more dissatisfied with their promotion system. To explain these apparently anomalous findings, the concept of *relative deprivation* was invoked. Stouffer et al. argued that the airmen's higher promotion rate led to higher expectations and thus to more dissatisfaction, even though the airmen had an objectively higher promotion rate than did the military police. In other words, people's satisfaction is related to how current outcomes are compared with some standard and *not* to the objective value of those outcomes.

In the Stouffer et al. (1949) studies, people who were objectively well-off (the airmen) experienced more dissatisfaction because they were comparing themselves with others who were even better off than they were. Imagine yourself working at a job, say a department store, in which you got promoted after a short time, and then you find out that your coworkers had gotten promoted even sooner or that a coworker is making even more money than you are. It no longer seems satisfying to know that someone else working at a different department store at the other end of the mall has not gotten promoted or is making less than you are. What matters now is that your coworkers seem to be reaping greater benefits than you. Your felt deprivation is *relative*. By the same token, objectively deprived persons can feel relatively satisfied with their position if they are comparing themselves to others in similar circumstances. For example, if coworkers at your store are being promoted at about the same rate as you, or if they are making about the same salary as you, then it may not matter so much that employees of a *different* store are being promoted faster and are making more money. Research has focused on various antecedent "preconditions" that may influence the experience of resentment about relative deprivation. We discuss some of these in the following sections.

Five- and Two-Factor Models of Relative Deprivation

Crosby (1976) proposed that relative deprivation could be understood through an examination of five factors, or preconditions—what has come to be known by some as the five-factor model of relative deprivation. According to Crosby, in order to experience relative deprivation, a person must (1) be aware that someone else possesses some object (X); (2) desire X; (3) feel entitled to X; (4) think it is feasible to obtain X; (5) lack a sense of personal responsibility for not having X. The object—"X"—could be virtually anything, such as position, pay, fringe benefits, and so on.

The first factor is related to *social comparison* processes more generally, which we describe later in this chapter. Here, it is argued that a person or group must be aware that another person or group has the object before relative deprivation is experienced. The second, "wanting," factor refers to the assumption that an object must be desired in order for relative deprivation to occur. For example, if you do not want a job that you do not have, why should you care? The third factor of entitlement makes the point that people or groups must think that they deserve some object before relative deprivation can occur. According to Crosby, for example, if you do not believe that you deserve a job that you do not have (because of lack of skills, qualifications, etc.) then no relative deprivation will occur. The fourth factor of feasibility refers to the fact that people or groups must view the possibility of obtaining the object as a realistic possibility before feeling relatively deprived. (Some theorists have additionally distinguished between *past* and *future* estimates of feasibility. Accordingly, relative deprivation may be greatest when past feasibility was high—you could have gotten the object at one time—and when future feasibility is low—you believe getting the object is now no longer possible: Cook, Crosby, & Hennigan, 1977.) The fifth and final factor, responsibility, proposes that people or groups will not experience relative deprivation if they blame themselves for not having the object. Several studies are supportive of Crosby's framework to varying degrees (e.g., Cook et al., 1977; Crosby, 1982; Crosby, Muehrer, & Loewenstein, 1986; Mark & Folger, 1984).

In one of the most complete tests of the five-factor model, Bernstein and Crosby (1980) gave participants vignettes describing situations in which all five factors were independently manipulated (e.g., wanting was sometimes high and sometimes low; responsibility was sometimes high and sometimes low, etc.). Participants rated the degree to which resentment and a variety of other emotions would characterize the experiences of the persons in the vignettes. For the most part, results provided some evidence for the importance of each of the hypothesized predictors. All of the factors affected relative deprivation in the predicted directions. What is perhaps most interesting about Crosby's (1976) formulation is that she suggested that the absence of any one of these preconditions precludes the experience of relative deprivation. You can certainly experience other reactions if one of these preconditions is lacking, but the experience will not be one of relative deprivation. For example, when wanting is lacking, a person or group may experience righteous indignation about not having the object. As another example, if a person or group accepts responsibility for not having the desired object, the experience may be one of envy or jealousy and not relative deprivation.

The five-factor model of relative deprivation has not gone unchallenged, however. Some researchers, including Crosby herself, tested whether the model could be simplified. One of the main issues was that many of the preconditions for relative deprivation may be interrelated; for example, people may want something that they know others possess. Recognizing these issues, in a study of women's dissatisfaction at home and in the workplace, Crosby (1982) found that the factors of wanting and deserving seemed to be the strongest predictors of relative deprivation. Thus, Crosby reasoned that people or groups will experience relative deprivation when they (1) lack an object that they want; and (2) feel entitled to have it. The other preconditions that were mentioned originally (e.g., responsibility) seem to remain important to predicting relative deprivation, but in perhaps a different relationship than was first proposed. Specifically, it seems that the other factors affect relative deprivation *through* their effects on wanting and entitlement. In other words, wanting and entitlement may be the two most important factors in predicting relative deprivation. The other factors may additionally influence the magnitude of experienced relative deprivation, but only indirectly through their effects on wanting and entitlement.

Referent Cognitions Theory

Another theory of relative deprivation, referent cognitions theory (RCT), takes a more explicitly social cognitive approach (e.g., Folger, 1986a, 1986b; Mark & Folger, 1984). Specifically, according to RCT, when people reflect upon their present outcomes it is assumed that their subjective evaluations of those outcomes will be affected by which simulated alternatives readily come to mind (e.g., Kahneman & Tversky, 1982). As we will see, this really involves a comparison between what a person can easily imagine having happened and what actually happened, and therefore RCT has much in common with equity theory and the two- and five-factor models that we described above. In RCT, however, these cognitive reconstructions provide a frame of reference, rather than just the known outcomes of others. Moreover, RCT goes further to propose that there are three main preconditions that may affect a person's experience of feeling relatively deprived. In the following sections, we discuss these three preconditions and

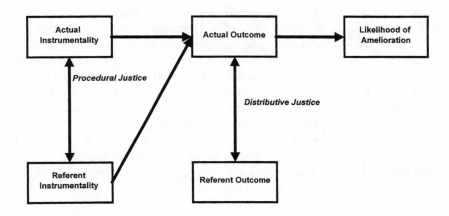

FIGURE 8.1   Referent cognitions theory

their implications for the experience of relative deprivation in the work-place.

Referent Outcomes.   The first precondition is that people must be able to easily imagine how better alternatives could have happened in the past, what is called a *referent outcome*. A referent outcome is a simulated alternative that is different from what actually happened; what actually happened is referred to as an *actual outcome*. Thus, according to RCT, the first precondition for relative deprivation to occur involves a comparison between actual outcomes (what actually happened) and referent outcomes (an alternative that might have happened); see Figure 8.1

High referent outcomes describe easily imagined alternatives that are hedonically better than the person's actual current state; *low* referent outcomes describe easily imagined alternatives that are hedonically worse than the person's actual current state. All else being equal, high referent outcomes lead to greater relative deprivation. An example of this in a workplace setting follows: Your current level of salary is lower than an alternative level of salary that you can easily imagine (e.g., "I am making $300 per week, but I might be making $450 per week").

At this point, you may notice some similarities with the "outcomes" mentioned in our discussion of equity theory. They are similar in that in each theory there is a comparison between two sets of outcomes. However, in RCT, the concept of outcomes is broadened to include outcomes that have as their bases a variety of sources (see Mark & Folger, 1984). First, in RCT, referent outcomes can have a *social* source as their basis (e.g., "I am making $300 per week but my coworker, John, is making $450 per week"); social sources of referent outcomes are most similar to the outcomes men-

tioned by equity theory in that they involve a comparison between your actual outcomes and the outcomes of others. Second, however, RCT also proposes that referent outcomes can have as their basis *expectancy* sources;
here a person compares his or her current actual outcomes with his or her
own outcomes at a previous time (e.g., "I am making $300 per week, but I
used to be making $450 per week"). Finally, RCT proposes that there
could be *theoretical* sources of referent outcomes (e.g., "I am making $300
per week, but I can theoretically imagine making $450 per week"); theoret-
ical sources are interesting because it is not necessary to know of others
who have the alternative outcome or to have had the alternative outcome
yourself in the past; rather they can be based on just some hypothetical
imagined alternative (Folger & Martin, 1986).

Justifications.   The notion of referent outcomes is focused on the concept
of "distributive fairness." That is, are the referent and actual outcomes
fairly allocated or distributed? However, in RCT this is not all there is.
RCT was also designed to account for the effects of "procedural fairness,"
which is something that had not been well articulated in equity theory. Procedural fairness refers to the fairness of the procedures that brought about
the outcomes (see also Austin, McGinn, & Susmilch, 1980; Brockner &
Wiesenfeld, 1996; Greenberg, 1980; van den Bos, Vermunt, & Wilke,
1997). In RCT, this is discussed in terms of *instrumentalities* (Folger
1986b). Instrumentalities refer to the "causal" circumstances that led up to
the outcomes. (You can view them as similar to "inputs," but they are
much broader as we shall see.)
     Instrumentalities can be evaluated comparatively just as can referent out-
comes. That is, the counterpart to comparisons between actual and referent
outcomes is a comparison between *actual instrumentalities* and *referent instrumentalities* (see Figure 8.1). Actual instrumentalities refer to the events,
circumstances, conditions, processes, or procedures that were responsible for
the outcomes actually received. Referent instrumentalities refer to the events,
circumstances, and so on, that can be alternatively imagined, that is, a mental
simulation of how things might have operated instead (e.g., if a different policy had been implemented or a different procedure had been followed). A
comparison between actual and referent instrumentalities determines *justification*. It asks the question, were the procedures that determined my current
outcomes just or fair? *Low* justification refers to a situation in which imagined referent instrumentalities are hedonically better than actual instrumentalities (e.g., having a promotion decision determined by a boss who is biased
against women may seem less just than the imagined alternative of an unbi-
ased boss). *High* justification exists if the circumstances leading up to actual
outcomes are hedonically better than referent instrumentalities. Therefore, all
else being equal, greater relative deprivation may be experienced under cases

of low justification than high justification. RCT thus incorporates both distributive and procedural justice principles.

Likelihood of Amelioration. The third and final determinant of whether a person or group will experience relative deprivation is termed *likelihood of amelioration,* or simply *likelihood.* Likelihood refers to whether the person believes his or her current life circumstances will get better in the future (see Figure 8.1). It is an assessment of what the future holds. The point here is that current outcomes may under some circumstances be considered transient, and thus less important, because there seems to be a strong chance that they will soon be replaced by much better outcomes (Folger, Rosenfield, Rheaume, & Martin, 1983; Folger, Rosenfield, & Robinson, 1983)— what has been called the "replacement effect." An example is a person who is somewhat dissatisfied with the fact that he or she is making $350 per week, but who also believes that he or she soon will be getting a raise in salary. In other words, why be upset with your current situation if tomorrow looks rosier?

Low likelihood refers to futures that are anticipated to be no better (or even worse) than the present. (Note that low likelihood does not refer to "unlikely" but to likely future outcomes that represent no amelioration of one's current state; see Folger, 1986a.) *High* likelihood refers to anticipated futures that are superior to one's current outcomes, that is, that things will get better. Therefore, all else being equal, a person will probably feel most relatively deprived when likelihood of amelioration is low rather than high.

Combining Preconditions

We have thus far separately discussed referent outcomes, justifications, and likelihood of amelioration. However, the key to RCT is that each of these preconditions combine to affect relative deprivation. At the extremes, according to RCT, the greatest relative deprivation will occur when referent outcomes are high, justifications are low, and likelihood of amelioration is low. Consider an example of a hypothetical employee, Sally, who is experiencing the following: "I am getting paid $350 per week instead of $450 per week like John" (high referent outcome); "I think it's unfair that I'm getting paid $350 and John is getting $450; my boss is biased against women" (low justification); "I don't think that my salary will be getting any better in the future" (low likelihood of amelioration). In contrast, at the other end of the continuum, the least relative deprivation should occur when referent outcomes are low, justification is high, and likelihood of amelioration is high. For example, from Sally's perspective John's pay is lower than hers; she thinks the way pay is determined is fair (e.g., she may have more experience); and further, she believes that she is due for a raise soon. The effects of other combinations of these three preconditions on relative deprivation may fall somewhere in between or may depend upon the particular aspects of the situation at hand (e.g., justifications may override other considerations in some situations; van den Bos, Lind, Vermunt & Wilke, 1997). Evidence in support of RCT has been obtained in several studies (e.g., see Folger, 1986a, 1986b; Mark & Folger, 1984; Olson & Hafer, 1996, for reviews).

Summary of Equity and Relative Deprivation

Equity and relative deprivation are two concepts that have been influential in analyzing people's reactions in the workplace. Each of these concepts focuses on a person's self-evaluation in comparison with other people, for example, coworkers. For equity theory, it is a comparison of the ratio of one's own inputs and outcomes to those of others. Equity occurs when these ratios are equal. Relative deprivation theories similarly focus on comparisons between oneself and some standard (e.g., a coworker); however, they also focus on other issues, such as feelings of entitlement or justification. RCT, for instance, was developed as an attempt to combine aspects of equity and relative deprivation theories into a single framework. There is a lot of evidence for the predictive utility of both equity and relative deprivation theories, which may further our understanding of reactions to other group members in the workplace.

Social Comparison

The issue of comparing oneself with other group members has received attention more generally in discussions of *social comparison* processes. The essence of social comparison is that people will compare themselves with others, which may fulfill a variety of motives (e.g., see Suls & Wills, 1981, for some reviews). Interest in social comparisons began with Festinger's (1954) now classic paper on the topic. Among other things, Festinger argued that (1) people will evaluate their opinions and abilities by comparing them with the opinions and abilities of other people; and (2) in order to do this they choose similar others with whom to compare. Social comparison, like the other topics in this chapter, is thus strongly rooted in interpersonal processes. As with our discussion of equity and relative deprivation, the implications for social comparisons to group processes in work settings is the focus of our current discussion.

Motives and Direction of Social Comparison in the Workplace

There are several diverse motives that have been used to explain why people engage in social comparisons. In initial statements of social comparison theory, a primary focus was placed on the motive of *self-assessment* (e.g., Festinger, 1954). Self-assessment refers to the fact that people often compare themselves with others in order to obtain an accurate appraisal of themselves. For example, by comparing your own performance with that of a coworker, you can learn how well you are doing. Social comparison in the service of self-assessment is used most often when "objective" standards do not already exist. For example, if you were told that you scored 71 points on a psychology exam, and you knew that scores were determined as a percentage of 100 points, then you would probably be less likely to use social comparison information to determine how well you performed. However, if you scored 71 points, and you did not know how grades were determined, one alternative way that you could assess how well you performed is to compare your score with the scores of others. Accurate self-assessment is argued to be best served by *lateral* social comparisons, comparisons with others who are at about the same level as oneself. Accurate self-assessment is thought to be essential to increasing self-knowledge (e.g., Festinger, 1954; Nisbett & Ross, 1980; Trope, 1983).

More recently, however, other motives for social comparison have been elaborated. In particular, many theorists have argued that social comparison processes can serve a motive of *self-improvement*. According to the self-improvement perspective, people are motivated to increase their abilities, skills, status, and so on. Recent research has emphasized the importance of *upward* social comparisons for meeting self-improvement needs (e.g., Collins, 1996; Taylor & Lobel, 1989; Taylor, Neter, & Wayment, 1995). Here, a person compares himself or herself to others who are better off. The notion is that by comparing yourself with a coworker who is better than you are, you can learn how you can also achieve that level. Upward comparisons are thought to be particularly useful for self-improvement both because these comparisons provide information about what a superior standing looks like and because they provide hope and inspiration and instill motivation (e.g., Collins, 1996; Markus & Nurius, 1986; Sedikides & Strube, 1995; Wood, 1989).

A third motive that can impel social comparisons is *self-enhancement*. By this it is meant that people may use social comparisons in order to feel good about themselves. Comparisons with others who are worse-off than yourself, what are known as *downward* social comparisons, may best serve this motive (e.g., Taylor & Brown, 1988; Tesser, 1988; Wills, 1981). If you were to compare your performance with that of a coworker who is doing worse than you are, you may feel better about your own work. According to the self-enhancement view, people are thus motivated to elevate the positivity of their self-concepts (or decrease the negativity of their self-concepts), thereby satisfying their self-enhancement needs. Self-assessment, self-improvement, and self-enhancement have been three of the most highly researched motives for social comparison (Sedikides & Strube, 1997;

Taylor, Wayment, & Carrillo, 1996; see also Helgeson & Mickelson, 1995, for other motives).

Relevance of Social Comparisons to Workplace Groups

Each of these motives has clear implications for understanding group processes, even though many of the tenets of social comparison theory have been developed with regard to individual processes (see Goethals & Darley, 1987; Levine & Moreland, 1987). In the following section, we further illustrate this by giving some specific examples of how social comparison theory can be more directly applied to group processes in the workplace. When possible, we also mention the concepts of equity and relative deprivation in our discussion, which we hope will further exemplify the applicability of these ideas to group phenomena.

For many years, the notion of *outcome comparisons* has been important when describing group processes in the workplace. These outcome comparisons may occur at the individual level or on the group level as a whole (e.g., Levine & Moreland, 1987). Our previous discussions of equity and relative deprivation further illustrated the importance of outcome comparisons, among other things, which help to determine people's reactions to group life. One of the specific approaches to social comparison in groups is *social identity theory* (e.g., Tajfel & Turner, 1986). Briefly, social identity theory is concerned with how individuals maintain self-esteem through comparison, or avoidance of comparison, with various other groups. A distinction is usually made between "ingroups" (groups that you are a part of) and "outgroups" (groups that you are not a part of); social identity theory was discussed in more detail in Chapter 2.

Social identity theory is interesting because it considers the importance of social comparisons on a between-group or intergroup basis rather than just on a within-group or interpersonal basis. For example, one way particular employees can maintain positive social identities is by drawing favorable comparisons with outgroup members. This might be done by making downward comparisons (e.g., "We are getting paid $350 per week working in shipping, but the secretarial staff is getting paid only $220 per week"). As we discussed previously, this type of comparison may best serve a self-enhancing function. Alternatively, employees may engage in upward comparisons with outgroup members (e.g., groups that are making more than their ingroup). In this case, of course, comparisons would be unfavorable, and the employees may be experiencing negative social identities. People experiencing negative social identities are predicted to attempt to leave their group or to make them better. For example, absenteeism has been shown to result from unfavorable outcome comparisons (Baron & Pfeffer, 1994; Geurts, Buunk, & Schaufeli, 1994; Steil & Hay, 1997). Finally, of course, employees can use social comparisons simply to assess how well their group compares with other groups, serving a self-assessment function.

Some other areas of interest to social comparisons and groups in the workplace are *group performance* and *group decisionmaking* (see also Chapters 4–6). Whether one is on an auto assembly line, in a sales office, or some other workplace, social comparison theory may help to inform what is known about group performance at work. For instance, if some employees are held up as a high standard (e.g., there are various "employee of the week" or "employee of the month" awards at a number of places), then it is possible that this may serve to motivate the rest of the workforce. Having this upward comparison information available and salient may thus serve as a type of "self-improvement" motive for workers. By the same token, having downward comparisons available may serve to make employees feel good.

This, however, brings up an interesting point about social comparisons. There actually may be a trade-off between upward and downward comparison directions. Specifically, upward comparisons may serve a preparative or self-improvement function but may make one feel bad in the meantime. For instance, knowing that some other group member is employee of the week may serve to motivate you to become employee of the week, but it will also make you feel bad by comparison (cf. Tesser, 1988). Having available downward social comparisons may make you feel good, but they may do little to motivate you to do any better. This possible trade-off between upward and downward comparisons and the different motives has recently become the subject of a good deal of research attention (e.g., Buunk, Collins, Taylor, VanYperen, & Dakof, 1990; Hemphill & Lehman, 1991; see also Roese, 1994; Sanna, 1996a, for related issues). Interestingly, the effects of social comparisons in the workplace may further depend on the type of task that is involved. For example, as we saw in our discussion of areas such as social loafing and social compensation, the effects of people doing worse than ourselves may depend upon whether the task is additive, conjunctive, or disjunctive. That is, under certain conditions, we will "loaf" when we are with others who are doing poorly; in other conditions, we may be willing to "compensate" for them (Harkins & Jackson, 1985; Karau & Williams, 1993; Kerr, 1983).

Finally, there are many areas of group decisionmaking in which social comparisons are applicable. However, we focus on one to illustrate our point—that of *groupthink*. People in work organizations are constantly asked to make decisions, whether it is how much of a product to buy, where to locate a new store, how much to pay employees, and so on. Research on groupthink (Janis, 1982) suggested that at least at times, people in groups make decisions very badly. This seems to result in part from the group's tendency to seek concurrence (*insulation* and *cohesiveness*) and to *disregard risk*.

Each of these things may be understood from a social comparison perspective. From this perspective, concurrence seeking reflects a tendency toward uniformity, stifling the expression of dissenting views, which results in an "illusion of unanimity." Because group members do not express their possible misgivings, they overestimate the degree to which there is agreement within the group. This can be understood from a social comparison perspective if one assumes that oftentimes there is no assured "correct" answer to a problem or at least none is known at the time of the decision (e.g., Burger King obviously did not know beforehand that the slogans "We do it like you'd do it," and "Sometimes you gotta break the rules," would be a bust). As we described above, one situation in which people are very likely to use social comparison information is when there is no objective standard. This in fact is the case in many decisionmaking settings. Pressures to self-validate or self-assess may be driving these pressures toward concurrence. In an analogous manner, social comparisons may help to explain the collective disregard for risk that contributes to groupthink. Research has shown that risk is a valued attribute in American culture (Brown, 1965), and higher risk may develop in group settings because members compete to try to compare favorably with others (e.g., Goethals & Zanna, 1979; Pruitt, 1971; Wallach, Kogan, & Bem, 1962), resulting in an escalation of risk—the "riskier" the better.

Summary of Social Comparison

Social comparison theory has been one of the preeminent theories in psychology. Recently, there has been renewed interest in the theory and its applications to group processes. Our focus in this chapter was on workplace groups. We described three major motives that may drive social comparisons—self-assessment, self-improvement, and self-enhancement. Next, we described some examples of how social comparison processes can help one to understand group reactions in the workplace. The field of social comparison processes with direct applications to the workplace, as well as the interrelationships between the different motives, certainly seems to be an extremely intriguing area for future exploration.

Negotiation

Of all of the group-related workplace topics, the study of conflict is growing the most quickly (Sanna & Parks, 1997). Conflict researchers are most strongly interested in the means by which conflict is resolved. In the workplace, this is often accomplished by means of negotiation. Negotiation is the process by which disputants resolve their differences and reach agreement on a common course of action. Negotiation typically involves, though is not limited to, two parties. It has been studied for many years, and the outcomes of negotiation research can fill an entire book. (In fact, such books do exist—an excellent one is by Pruitt and Carnevale [1993].) We simply want to provide an overview of negotiation, so that you have a basic feel for the kinds of questions negotiation researchers ask. In keeping with the theme of the book, we limit our discussion to group-process questions in negotiation, although researchers are also interested in more individual-based issues, such as negotiator cognition. Kramer and Messick (1995) provide excellent coverage of these individual-level topics.

Negotiation Strategy

How can negotiations be conducted such that you come away with the best possible deal for yourself? This is the classic question that has been studied for many years. In fact, there are two schools of thought on the issue. The first is based on the assumption that conflict can only be resolved through compromise. You are not going to get everything that you want, and your opponent is not going to get everything that he or she wants. The two of you are each going to need to modify your demands somewhat if you are to reach agreement. There are two theories of how compromise negotiations should be conducted. Level of aspiration (LOA) theory argues that toughness and firmness are important for successful negotiation. Basically, one should state one's position and then not budge from it (Siegel & Fouraker, 1960). According to LOA, a concession (which occurs whenever one modifies one's position by subtracting from it) will be interpreted by the opponent as a sign of weakness and will encourage the opponent to take advantage of you. It is better to hold firm to your original demand and force the opponent to make concessions. By contrast, GRIT theory suggests that not only should you make concessions, you should initiate them (Osgood, 1962). GRIT—which stands for Graduated Reciprocation In Tension-reduction—is based upon the principle of reciprocity that we discussed in Chapter 7. You should make an initial concession, invite your opponent to reciprocate your concession, and then continue conceding. Your concessions should be clear and unambiguous, and it should be easy for your opponent to see that they have been implemented. If your opponent does reciprocate, then the two of you should keep making concessions until common ground is reached. If he or she does not reciprocate, then eventually you will need to stop conceding and instead retaliate. The concessions and retaliations should be on a one-for-one basis: If your opponent concedes by $20, so should you.

A considerable amount of research has been conducted on LOA, and this research shows that LOA is an effective strategy when there is time pressure to reach agreement. If there is no time pressure, LOA frequently results in a *stalemate,* which occurs when negotiators cannot reach agreement. In a later section, we talk about the use of a third party to break a stalemate. A good example of LOA's effectiveness can be found in the 1994–1995 strike of Caterpillar Tractor in Peoria, Illinois, by the United Auto Workers. After months of fruitless negotiations, Caterpillar management made the union one final offer and refused to make any more concessions. The union rejected the offer, and discussions broke off. Although they were able to use salaried workers and strikebreakers to keep some production going, Caterpillar was losing a large amount of money because of the strike. However, management gambled that after the union's strike fund ran out, the striking workers would experience an increasingly severe economic pinch. They did, and after eighteen months of being on strike, workers accepted management's offer. Once the strike fund was depleted, there was strong time pressure on union leaders to reach agreement because their constituents were without money, yet had bills to pay and groceries to buy. The union had no choice but to accept an offer that it did not like.

Research on GRIT has accumulated more slowly primarily because it is so logistically difficult to simulate in a laboratory (Lindskold, 1983). Although some of the specific recommendations made by GRIT are still empirically questionable (Lindskold, 1978; Parks & Komorita, in press), overall it seems to be effective at inducing agreement when there is no time pressure. In that sense, LOA and GRIT can be seen as complementary negotiation strategies, in that the appropriate strategy to use can be determined by presence or absence of time pressure.

Both LOA and GRIT share the assumption that at least one participant in the negotiation will come away with less than he or she had hoped to get. There is a second school of thought that states that it is possible for all parties to meet their negotiating goals. This is known as *integrative bargaining* (Pruitt, 1981). The goal under integrative bargaining is to identify a creative solution to the conflict that will meet the needs of all concerned. For example, negotiators might add resources to the situation. Let's say that you and a woman are negotiating the sale of a car. She wants to sell it for $1000, but you want to pay only $750. She could add to the deal by including a car stereo that she no longer needs. If you will give her $1000, she will give you the car and the stereo. Presuming that the stereo is of interest to you, you'll both come away with a sense of satisfaction: She got the money that she wanted, and you got the car plus another item that you had not anticipated receiving. This is how integrative bargaining works. There are many other techniques for achieving an integrative agreement; they are clearly explained in Pruitt (1981).

In comparison to the compromise approaches, research shows that participants in integrative negotiation tend to be more satisfied with the outcomes and have positive feelings about their opponent, whereas compromise negotiators tend to be dissatisfied with outcomes and often harbor feelings of resentment toward the opponent (Pruitt, 1981; Sillars, 1981). Be aware that integrative bargaining can be difficult to apply, particularly if the negotiators lack the ability to detect creative solutions or if additional resources are not available. Nonetheless, one would do well to attempt to find an integrative solution whenever one is negotiating.

Mediation

We mentioned earlier that a stalemate occurs when negotiators cannot reach agreement. How can the stalemate be broken? A common technique is to bring in a third party who is knowledgeable about the dispute and skilled at dispute resolution. Such a person is called a *mediator.* There are mediators for many different types of conflict. Some are experts at labor-management conflict, some at international conflict, and some at two-person (often marital) conflict.

There are a number of goals that the mediator wants to accomplish: earn the trust of the disputants; manage any hostilities that exist between the disputants; devise a solution to the conflict; and win support for the solution. There are many different tactics that a mediator can use to achieve these goals, far more than we can present here, although a complete summary can be found in Wall and Lynn (1993). Some examples will suffice.

A common tactic for controlling hostility is to separate the parties and prohibit face-to-face communication. The mediator becomes an information pipeline through which all messages pass. By doing this, the mediator eliminates the problem of insults and name-calling and ensures that all transmitted information is task oriented. The mediator may also serve as a sounding board and allow disputants to vent their anger and frustration at him or her rather than at the opponent. In order to devise a solution to the conflict, the mediator collects a considerable amount of information not only by talking with each disputant but also by researching the history of the conflict and studying the available resources. Finally, the mediator can help win acceptance of the solution by helping disputants prepare for any negative reactions from the disputants' constituents, perhaps by bearing the blame for any unpopular concessions.

Carnevale (1986) has developed a model that predicts when mediators will use certain types of tactics. He argues that selection of tactics is determined by the mediator's concern that the disputants achieve their goals and by the extent to which the mediator believes a mutually satisfactory agreement is attainable ("common ground"). For example, a mediator is predicted to use an integrative bargaining approach if he or she is highly concerned about the disputants and believes that an integrative agreement is likely. By contrast, the mediator who doesn't care about the disputants and

TABLE 8.2   Predictions from Carnevale's (1986) Model of Mediator Behavior

Perceived likelihood of agreement	Mediator concern for disputant success	Predicted strategy of mediator
High	High	Integration: Mediator will search for integrative solution.
High	Low	Inaction: Mediator will do nothing.
Low	High	Compensation: Mediator will provide rewards for concessions.
Low	Low	Pressure: Mediator will force concessions via threat.

sees little common ground is predicted to exert pressure, perhaps through threat of force or sanctions, on the disputants to make concessions. The complete set of predictions is shown in Table 8.2. This model has considerable empirical support (see Pruitt & Carnevale, 1993), although it is not without its critics, who are primarily concerned with how "common ground" is measured (van de Vliert, 1992).

A common error that occurs in real-world disputes is the automatic summoning of a mediator whenever there is a stalemate. In fact, simply being stalemated does not guarantee that a mediator can solve the problem. For example, a mediator will be relatively ineffective if the disputants do not desire third-party intervention (Hiltrop, 1989). Thus, we do not want to force a mediator onto stalemated negotiators; rather, the negotiators need to believe that the mediator is needed. Related to this is the fact that mediators are fairly ineffective when the disputants have no overarching reason to settle the conflict (Touval & Zartman, 1985). A stalemate is a negative state of affairs only when it produces negative outcomes. Stalemated labor-management strike negotiations produce negative outcomes because both sides lose money as the strike drags on. By contrast, if you and the woman cannot agree on a selling price for her used car, you can terminate the negotiations and neither of you will suffer. Mediation would thus be more likely to resolve the labor-management conflict than your conflict over the used car. Finally, mediation tends to be more effective when the conflict is moderate rather than intense (Pruitt, Peirce, McGillicuddy, Welton, & Castrianno, 1993), although there are certain tactics that a mediator can employ to improve the chances of resolving an intense conflict (Hiltrop, 1989; Zubek, Pruitt, Peirce, McGillicuddy, & Syna, 1992).

Mediation Versus Arbitration

Mediation is not the same thing as arbitration, although the two are often confused. Under arbitration, each disputant submits a solution to an independent judge (an arbitrator), who selects one of the solutions for implementation. Under mediation, the third party works with the disputants to devise a solution. Hence, under arbitration the third party functions purely as a decisionmaker, whereas under mediation, the third party is a facilitator. It is not clear which of these two third-party intervention methods is preferable to disputants. Evidence can be found in support of either method over the other (Heuer & Penrod, 1986; Houlden, LaTour, Walker, & Thibaut, 1978; Roehl & Cook, 1989). Pruitt and Carnevale (1993) suggest that preference for one intervention over the other is situation-specific. There is considerable evidence to support this notion. For example, it is known that arbitration is preferable when there is time pressure to reach agreement or when the disputed issues are complex (Sheppard, Blumenfeld-Jones, & Roth, 1989). By contrast, mediation is the preferred intervention when the disputants have an ongoing relationship that requires future co-operation (Lewicki & Sheppard, 1985).

Teamwork

Teamwork is a topic that is currently receiving considerable attention in the popular management books and magazines as well as from researchers. The notion of a "team" is a somewhat slippery concept; for many researchers, it is not clear how a team differs from a group. Some have tried to explain the difference in terms of factors such as depth of commitment, arguing that a group becomes a team only after its members develop a deep identification with the group (Katzenbach & Smith, 1993), although such distinctions have not been rigorously tested. We favor the approach taken by Guzzo and Dickson (1996), who, rather than deal with the nuances of team versus group, proposed a general definition of a work group as a distinct collection of interdependent individuals who are part of a larger system and who perform tasks that affect others involved in the system. This definition encompasses just about all of the various types of teams that have been described in the research literature, yet also describes the types of groups that we have been discussing throughout this book. To this end, then, the study of teamwork is really just the study of work group performance.

Some readers may wonder why the work group is being isolated as a separate entity for study, given that we know so much overall about group performance and productivity. The primary reason involves the work setting itself. The work setting differs so much from the laboratory setting that it is not clear whether, or to what extent, laboratory findings are immediately generalizable to the workplace (Ilgen, Major, Hollenbeck, & Sego, 1993). For example, the work group's efforts will likely have a real effect on other nongroup members and have attached to it real consequences if there is poor performance. The experimental group has to deal with none of this. Note that we are not saying these factors *definitely* affect the work group; our point is simply that the work environment differs enough from the laboratory that we should not automatically assume that the behavior of laboratory groups mimics the behavior of work groups.

A primary difficulty in conducting research on work groups is the assessment of "efficient performance." This is certainly not a problem that is limited to field research, but by carefully designing a laboratory task we can at least partially determine what it means to be efficient. In the field we almost never have this degree of control over the task. Unfortunately, team research has too often been hampered by poor or inappropriate outcome measurement (Baker & Salas, 1992; Ilgen et al., 1993), making it difficult for us to get a clear picture of how performance-effective such groups really are. Guzzo and Dickson (1996) suggest that effectiveness be determined by looking at group output, the consequences of the group experience for members, and the extent to which the experience has enhanced the team's performance capabilities.

Aspects of Work Groups

Research on work groups is fairly recent, so we do not know very much about them. Much of the available research has addressed the issue of group composition. The general school of thought is that work groups should be carefully, rather than randomly, assembled, but what factors should be considered in assembling the group? Researchers have concentrated most heavily on the topics of heterogeneity and cohesion. However, the findings from these studies have not been all that consistent. On the issue of heterogeneity, some studies have found it to be an important contributor to work group effectiveness (Bantel & Jackson, 1989; Magjuka & Baldwin, 1991), but others have found it to be irrelevant (Campion, Medsker, & Higgs, 1993). There is general agreement that cohesive groups are more effective than noncohesive groups, but the strength of the association between cohesion and performance is still being debated (Evans & Dion, 1991; Guzzo & Shea, 1992; Smith, Smith, Olian, Sims, O'Bannon, & Scully, 1994). The research does clearly support the idea that group productivity increases as group members become more familiar with one another (Dubnicki & Limburg, 1991; Goodman & Leyden, 1991), which suggests that once a work group is assembled, it should remain intact for a long period of time. This argument for reducing group member turnover also follows from our discussion of group formation in Chapter 2. Recall that new members of a group need to be socialized into the ways of the group. If a work group is continually having to socialize new members, productivity will likely suffer.

Some research has looked at behavior within work groups, but here contradictions also exist. For example, Pearson (1992) reported that work teams show reduced rates of accidents, absenteeism, and turnover relative to mere collections of individuals, but Cordery, Mueller, and Smith (1991) found *higher* rates of absenteeism and turnover within the work team, and Wall, Kemp, Jackson, and Clegg (1986) found no difference in turnover between a work team and more nominal groups. It has also been shown that team members like being part of a work team, but whether this enjoyment translates into better performance is not clear (Wall et al., 1986).

The effectiveness of teams may also be culture-bound, as research in more stratified societies has found such social stratification to be a barrier to team performance if members of different classes are joined in the same team (Song & Parry, 1997; Wiersma & Bird, 1993). However, it should be noted that group-oriented job training has been shown to be more effective in collectivist societies (e.g., Japan) than in individualistic societies like the United States (Earley, 1994), so the relationship between culture and work group performance is likely much more complex than it now seems.

Some Thoughts on Teamwork

More so than most on other group-related topics, many groups researchers seem to have an opinion on whether the study of work groups is necessary. Those who do not see teamwork as an important topic of study often point to the fact that some high-profile grouping efforts, such as quality circles, generally do not enhance performance (Steel, Jennings, & Lindsey, 1990), whereas others, such as autonomous work groups, vary widely in their ability to affect group productivity (Levine & D'Andrea Tyson, 1990; Smith & Comer, 1994). Such frustrations are understandable but also somewhat misplaced. Management is a very faddish enterprise, with many examples of practices being implemented before there had accumulated empirical support for the practice (Abrahamson, 1996). Although it is definitely frustrating to a researcher to see interventions being put into practice without support for those interventions, this can be addressed by working with managers to encourage restraint while data are being collected. The workplace offers groups researchers a set of interesting variables that cannot reasonably be captured in the laboratory, and we should continue to study these variables.

Organizational Culture

Over the last decade, the notion of organizational culture has exploded to become one of the hottest group-related topics in industrial psychology.

The concept originated in the early 1980s, during a time when many American businesses were struggling, yet industries in other countries, particularly Japan, were booming. In trying to determine why this was so, a number of mass-market management books appeared arguing that both Japanese companies (Ouchi, 1981) and successful American companies (Peters & Waterman, 1982) have defining sets of norms, beliefs, assumptions, and roles that affect behavior. The Peters and Waterman book in particular was enormously influential within the business community, remaining at the top of the *New York Times* bestseller list for close to two years. Empirical interest in organizational culture was spurred by Schein's (1985; see also Schein, 1990) work, in which he argued that a "culture" is not just a large-scale (national, ethnic) phenomenon but is in fact present in groups of all sizes.

Organizational culture researchers consider it to be one of the most basic factors in organizational behavior. For example, it has been shown to influence work performance (Marcoulides & Heck, 1993); leadership style (Schein, 1985); role conflict (van der Velde & Class, 1995); group member retention (Sheridan, 1992); resource allocation (Mannix, Neale, & Northcraft, 1995); ethical behavior (Victor & Cullen, 1988); cooperation (Chatman & Barsade, 1995); and styles of decisionmaking (Weatherly & Beach, 1996). A difficulty in conducting organizational culture research lies in the accurate assessment of the components of the culture. It is typically assessed by means of some type of questionnaire, of which there are many. The validity of some of these instruments has been established (Xenikou & Furnham, 1996), but there are many other questionnaires that are being used for which we do not yet have validity information, which is a troubling state of affairs. Indeed, some theorists have argued that traditional research strategies, such as the use of questionnaires, are not appropriate for studying organizational culture, and instead a more clinical case study-type approach, including such data collection methods as interviewing and passive observation, should be used (Schein, 1993).

Organizational culture is not a concept that has been universally accepted. In fact, it has many critics. For example, a distinction is made between organizational culture and *organizational climate,* which can be defined as the workers' general perceptions of, and feelings about, the organization's culture (Dennison, 1996). However, the distinction seems to many people to be a superficial one, and perhaps not even a useful one, as it is not clear how organizational climate differs from more well-established concepts such as job satisfaction (Glick, 1985). More generally, researchers have questioned the entire notion that an organization can have a culture. Hofstede, Neujien, Ohayv, and Sanders (1990) have argued that what is called an organization's "culture" really refers to the common daily practices that occur within the company, practices that are quite facile (as evidenced by the number of managerial self-help books that explain how to change one's corporate culture for the better. Note, by the way, that the authors of these books tend to be almost completely ignorant of psychological research). By contrast, "culture" at the national level refers primarily to shared, deeply held values that are difficult to change. Hence, to equate a company's environment with a national or ethnic culture is misleading. Along these lines, some researchers have suggested thinking of "organizational culture" not as a culture per se but rather as a description of how the employees perceive the work environment (James & James, 1989; Rentsch, 1990). These writers have argued that there are common features that workers focus on when thinking about the workplace (e.g., leader support, cooperativeness of coworkers) and that the interpretation of these factors is affected by the *general psychological climate* within the organization. This model clearly moves us away from notions of shared values and focuses more on individual perceptions of the group environment, but the concept of general psychological climate needs to be more clearly fleshed out before it can be a truly useful model.

Chapter Summary

Groups are a part of many facets of work life, and many group phenomena have relevance for the workplace. Such basic factors as leadership, equity, and conflict play an important role in the functioning of a workplace. What we have done in this chapter is explain how group-related factors interact with the work environment not only in terms of productivity but also in terms of worker satisfaction, perceptions of the workplace, and interactions with coworkers. We noted at the start of the chapter that the study of groups is growing within industrial/organizational psychology, and this research should produce a number of interesting and important findings in the next few years.

Chapter Nine

Juries

Perhaps no American group is more hotly debated today than the trial jury. In recent years, there have been a number of high-profile legal cases in which the actions of jurors have been questioned. Some cases, such as the O. J. Simpson murder trial, which involved complex testimony on DNA testing, have led scholars to suggest that lay juries are not capable of understanding scientific evidence. Other cases, like that in which an eighty-one-year-old woman successfully sued McDonald's for damages after she spilled hot coffee on herself, have provoked the argument that jurors cannot comprehend what constitutes a reasonable damage award and hence devise awards that are out of proportion with the damage (McDonald's was forced to pay the woman $2.9 million, ten times the cost of the woman's medical bills). Finally, there is real evidence of jurors being swayed by irrelevant, extralegal factors. The jury in the first murder trial of the teenage brothers Lyle and Eric Menendez, a case in which the brothers were accused of murdering their parents, returned a hung verdict (i.e., the jurors could not agree on guilt or innocence). Some jurors later confided that they could not believe that the brothers had killed their parents, simply because the boys looked like nice young men. The later admission by the brothers' lawyer that she had carefully planned the boys' daily wardrobe to convey exactly this image (the boys wore slacks and crewneck sweaters almost every day, and their hair was always neatly trimmed) lends credence to the notion that extralegal factors play a role in jury decisionmaking.

The general question of how juries go about reaching a verdict is somewhat empirically testable. We are legally prohibited from having contact with a sitting jury while deliberations are in progress, so it is impossible to observe the decision processes of real juries. However, it is possible to simulate a courtroom in the laboratory, and through this method of *mock trials* researchers have learned a substantial amount about how juries work. The purpose of this chapter is to present some of the most basic findings with regard to jury processes. The reader who is interested in a thorough discussion of social psychology in the courtroom should consult Hastie's (1990) excellent book.

Mock Jury Methodology

Let us begin by looking at how mock jury research is conducted. At its most basic, a group of subjects in a laboratory is given some information on a trial. Often this information is in the form of a videotape, but it may also be conveyed via written transcript. After conclusion of the trial, each subject records a personal belief as to what the verdict should be. The subjects then discuss the case and reach consensus as to a verdict. Given the limits on laboratory space and available subjects, mock juries rarely consist of twelve persons; they are usually of four to six persons.

The external validity of mock jury research is a subject of some debate. On the positive side, any subject who is a citizen of the United States and a registered voter can potentially serve on a jury; hence, studying potential jurors in a jury-type format presents a quite lifelike setting. Also, there is evidence that subjects find the mock jury task quite engaging and involving (Davis, 1992). However, there have also been some sharp criticisms of mock juries. Legal scholars have criticized staged trial reenactments, which feature actors rather than actual lawyers, judges, and defendants, as being poor representations of actual trial procedure primarily because the performances are too scripted and lack spontaneous questions, answers, and reactions (Davis, 1989; Lindsay, Wells, & O'Connor, 1989). This was definitely a problem in early jury research (see Gerbasi, Zuckerman, & Reis, 1977), but the relatively recent allowance of video cameras into the courtroom, as well as the professional production of reenacted trials by local bar associations (e.g., Davis, Stasson, Parks, Hulbert, Kameda, Zimmerman, & Ono, 1993) has given researchers access to films of real, or realistic, trials that can be used as stimuli, thus minimizing problems of artificiality.

Mock jury research has also been criticized because its findings have occasionally been abused. Both scholars (see Davis, 1989) and the legal community (see Saks & Hastie, 1978) have been guilty of overgeneralization of mock jury data, and social scientists have additionally been faulted for failing to actively assist justices in interpretation of research (Acker, 1990). Such concerns are certainly not limited to jury research—indeed, these charges can be leveled against any research domain that has real-world relevance. But society is likely more sensitive to these abuses when they pertain to the legal process, simply because the decisions that emerge from the courtroom are so fundamental and affect lives. At the very least, social scientists and litigators need to collaborate more closely to minimize the misrepresentation and misinterpretation of jury research.

Jury Decision Processes

How does a group of jurors combine individual preferences into a single verdict? This question has intrigued jury researchers for more than thirty years. A number of different models of the jury decision process have been proposed over the years, and they continue to be developed. In this section, we want to look at some of these models in some degree of detail.

Social Decision Schemes

Probably the oldest model of jury decisionmaking involves Davis's (1973, 1980) social decision scheme (or SDS) theory, which we first mentioned in Chapter 4. Social decision scheme theory is a mathematical model that uses the distribution of individual preferences and the group's decision to infer what decision rule was most likely being applied within the group. Its essence is the notion that every verdict has associated with it a probability of group advocation, given the distribution of individual preferences. The SDS analysis asks the question, What decision rule must the group have applied if the distribution of individual preferences led to this specific group verdict? To take a simple example, consider a jury within which the distribution of individual preferences is seven for guilt and five for innocence. The jury returns a verdict of "guilty." How was this decision reached? One possible rule that the jurors might have used is unanimity: Only advocate a verdict if all members agree to it. Given the fairly considerable initial disagreement within the group, it's not likely that they used this rule. Another possible rule is 2/3-majority: Advocate the verdict that two-thirds of the members prefer. In a twelve-person group, the 2/3 rule requires agreement among eight group members. The initial preference for guilt was close to, but not at, eight, so this rule probably was not used either. Yet another decision rule is simple majority: Advocate what more than half of the people prefer. You can see that more than half of all jurors favored guilt at the outset. Hence, we would conclude that this jury probably applied a simple majority rule to determine what verdict should be offered.

This, of course, is an idealized example in which no juror changes his or her preferences during deliberation. But we know that such change often does happen (Davis, Stasser, Spitzer, & Holt, 1976). Perhaps one of our four "innocence" jurors changed his or her preference to guilt, making the distribution eight to four, which now fits the 2/3-majority rule. To address this potential for change, variants of the basic SDS model have been designed that can measure such changes and incorporate them into the prediction (Crott & Werner, 1994; Crott, Werner, & Hoffmann, 1996; Kerr, 1981; Stasser & Davis, 1981).

An SDS analysis can be applied both within groups, to give us an idea as to how a specific group reached a decision, and across groups, to help us determine whether there is a decision rule that tends to be favored by groups. Analysis of jury decisions suggests that, regardless of assigned decision rule, juries tend to apply a 2/3-majority, otherwise hung, rule in reaching verdicts (Davis, Kerr, Atkin, Holt, & Meek, 1975). Descriptively, this rule dictates that the group advocate as the verdict the preference of two-thirds of all group members; if two-thirds consensus is not forthcoming, the jury should report that they are hung; that is, they officially cannot decide between guilt or innocence. A defendant for whom the jury hangs can legally be retried. (The original Menendez trial resulted in a hung jury.)

The SDS approach has been successfully applied only to criminal trials, in which jurors have a discrete number of options from which to choose. Attempts to use SDS to model the decisions of civil juries, in which the range of choice options is continuous, have not succeeded (Davis, 1996). To that end, researchers have begun trying to develop an SDS analogue for the continuous-choice case (Davis, 1996; Hinsz, 1990). Also note that SDS analysis does not capture the procedural factors by which juries move from individual preferences to consensus (Davis, Stasson, Ono, & Zimmerman, 1988). Later in this chapter, we discuss at length a number of factors that influence the jury process.

Information Integration Theory

A number of theories of jury process focus on how jurors use trial information to reach a verdict. A number of these models assume that information is combined in a mathematical style. That is, judgments are the end result of some mathematics-like combination of information, under which mathematical operations are performed on the information in order to integrate it. Information integration theory, which is one of the fundamental theories of social cognition, operates in just such a manner, and it has been applied to jury processes. First proposed by Anderson (1968b), information integration theory was originally used to describe how people use information to form impressions of others. The theory states that information is combined in a weighted-averaging fashion to determine the overall impression. For example, assume that we have four pieces of information about a man: He is punctual, likes children, is dishonest, and sings in his church choir. What is your impression of such a person? Information integration theory says that you will first assign a value to each piece of information. Let's say that, on a scale from +10 (best trait a person could have) to –10 (worst trait a person could have), you would rate these four traits as +1, +3, –9, and +1 respectively. The theory next predicts that you will average these four values and that the average will serve as your overall impression. Your average rating for this person is –4 / 4 = –1. In other words, your impression of this man would be slightly negative, even though three of his four qualities are good ones. This is because his one negative trait is very negative, but his three good qualities are only mildly positive.

It can be argued that the job of a criminal juror is to form a judgment about the defendant. Hence, application of information integration theory to the study of jury decision processes is appealing. The logic is that each juror forms an initial guilt/innocence judgment based on a subset of all information presented during the trial. During deliberation, additional facts are presented from other jurors that the individual factors into his or her overall impression, resulting in choice shifts, either toward polarization or moderation, depending on the prevailing tendency within the group (Kaplan, 1987). Expressions of opinion also affect jurors, in that jurors integrate the opinions of others into their own, producing shifts in preference (Boster, Hunter, & Hale, 1991). The group verdict is determined by the direction in which most jurors are shifting (Boster et al., 1991).

The information integration model has generally good empirical support from both studies of changes in juror preferences (Kaplan & Schersching, 1981; Moore & Gump, 1995) and studies of civil trial jury verdicts (Boster et al., 1991). However, some researchers have suggested that information integration is situation-specific. For example, MacCoun (1990) found information integration to be operating when the defendant was physically attractive but not when he or she was unattractive. Other researchers have argued that seemingly information-integrative jury processes are better described as examples of signal detection theory (Mowen & Linder, 1986), although to date this line of inquiry does not seem to have been investigated any further.

Deliberation Style

The jury's ultimate goal is to determine the truth behind a disputed event. In a civil trial, the severity of the punishment to be administered to the wrongdoer must also be determined. What strategies are available to the jurors to help them reach these goals? Hastie, Penrod, and Pennington (1983; see also Pennington & Hastie, 1990) have argued that two primary strategies exist. Both are related to the style with which jurors deliberate the case. Under an *evidence-driven* deliberation style, the focus of deliberation is on reconstruction of the sequence of events. Jurors attempt to arrange the evidence into a coherent story, and the purpose of discussion is to reach consensus regarding the proper sequence of events and the meaning of those events. Once a sequence and meaning have been defined, the jurors can then determine the most appropriate verdict. Thus, under an evidence-driven deliberation style, groups begin with the evidence and end with the verdict. By contrast, under a *verdict-driven* deliberation style, jurors begin by identifying the most-preferred verdict within the group. This may be done via straw polling, through which each juror makes public his or her personal verdict preference (Davis et al., 1988; Kerr & MacCoun, 1985). After this polling, jurors use the evidence to justify their preferences and to win converts from the opposing faction. No attempt is made to order the evidence in a coherent fashion. In a sense, then, the verdict-driven style is the opposite of the evidence-driven style: The jury begins with the verdict and ends with the evidence.

Hastie et al. (1983) found the two styles to be used equally often across juries, although they also observed a third class of juries for which no clear deliberation style was seen. In criminal trials, the two styles do not seem to produce differential rates of conviction (Hastie et al., 1983; Kerr & Mac-Coun, 1985; see also Davis, Kameda, Parks, Stasson, & Zimmerman, 1989); the impact seems to be more on deliberation time, depth of discussion, and individual juror reactions to the jury experience. However, there is some evidence to suggest that under certain conditions, the two styles can lead to different rates of culpability judgments in civil trials (Davis et al., 1993; Kameda, 1991). Many questions about deliberation style remain to be answered—for example, what leads a jury to adopt one style over the other?—and hopefully future research will help us answer those questions.

Procedural Influences on the Jury

The jury is supposed to be an impartial body, the members of which are to attend solely to the facts of the case. There are many steps that the court system takes to ensure that this impartiality is achieved. During the jury selection process, each side's legal team interviews the jury candidates, and each has a number of peremptory challenges which can be used to dismiss a potential juror. No explanation is needed; a potential juror who is challenged by either side is simply sent home. Most often, a jury candidate is dismissed because something that was said during the interview process suggested to at least one lawyer that the candidate was susceptible to bias. For example, consider a civil case in which an auto worker sues Ford Motor Company for workplace negligence. A jury candidate who is a member of the United Auto Workers union would likely be dismissed by Ford's lawyers because of the fear that the union member would be biased toward supporting a fellow auto worker. Again, Ford's lawyers do not have to express this fear; they can simply say that this person should not sit on the jury. Lest you think that juror dismissal could become a quite petty affair, keep in mind that each side is given only a small number of challenges, so in fact they must be used wisely.

Once the jury is seated, the judge can implement a number of interventions to help the jurors avoid factors that may bias them. For example, the judge may prohibit the jurors from reading the newspaper, watching television news programs, or discussing the case with others. If there is extreme concern about potential bias, the judge may sequester the jury and literally cut them off from the outside world. The sequestered jury might live in hotel rooms without televisions or radios, eat all of their meals in the hotel rooms, and be chauffeured between the hotel and courtroom. Sequestering a jury is not uncommon, particularly in high-profile cases like the O. J. Simpson trial.

Clearly, the judicial system tries hard to avoid juror bias. Yet there seem to be a number of court cases in which it is clear that the verdict was influenced by factors other than the evidence. How can this happen? Actually, the answer is quite simple: There are a host of factors associated with the trial process that influence the jury. In this section, we look at some of the major factors and explore how they affect the jury.

Expert Testimony

A common tactic in the courtroom is to have experts serve as witnesses. The experts can help clarify information, provide insight into causal factors, and so on. A psychologist can testify as to a defendant's mental state at the time of the crime; a forensics expert can explain the dynamics of a discharged bullet; a geneticist can explain the logic of DNA testing. Cognitive psychologists have even been called to testify on the flaws in eyewitness reports (Penrod, Fulero, & Cutler, 1995). An expert is a highly credible witness; hence, one would think that expert testimony would weigh heavily on the jury verdict. Individual preferences do seem to be influenced by experts, but experts seem to have less of an impact on jury verdicts (Spanos, Dubreuil, & Gwynn, 1991; Spanos, Gwynn, & Terrade, 1989). Further, it has been shown that strenuous cross-examination of the expert, particularly if it involves insinuations about the expert's reputation, can do serious damage to the expert's credibility (Kassin, Williams, & Saunders, 1990; Spanos et al., 1991).

It is not yet clear why experts do not have the impact on jury verdicts that we would expect them to have, but the implications of this research are disturbing in that experts do seem to serve an important legal function. For example, research has shown that lay jurors cannot reliably determine whether a defendant who pleads insanity really is mentally unbalanced (Whittemore & Ogloff, 1995). Further, insanity judgments are affected by the race of the defendant, with a black defendant being more likely to be judged insane than a white defendant (Poulson, 1990). Clearly, jurors in insanity-plea trials need input from a psychologist. What remains to be determined is how to make expert testimony more effective and more resistant to insinuation.

Judge Instructions

One aspect of the trial process is the judge's instructions to the jurors on how to perform their duties. If a piece of information is improperly introduced, the judge will tell jurors to disregard that information; at the end of the trial, the judge explains the decision task to jurors; juries that are hung may be told by the judge to continue deliberating. What impact, if any, does jury-judge interaction have on the jury decision?

There are two potential ways in which the judge may have a negative impact on the jury. First, telling jurors to disregard a piece of information may have the opposite effect of highlighting the information. Second, via end-of-trial instructions or interaction with a hung jury, the judge may inadvertently convey his or her own personal beliefs about what the verdict should be. Researchers have studied each of these potential sources of bias.

Inadmissible Information.   When a lawyer presents a piece of information that the opposing lawyer feels is inappropriate, the opposing lawyer will raise an objection. If the judge agrees that the information should not have been introduced, he or she will sustain the objection. A sustained objection has a dual impact on the trial: The lawyer must cease discussing the information, and the objectionable statement must be stricken from the legal record. Removing it from the written record is no problem, as the court reporter will simply not include the statement in his or her official report of the proceedings, but the information must also be removed from the jurors' mental record. Hence, the judge will tell jurors to ignore the objectionable statement. But do they really ignore it? And if they don't, what influence does objectionable information have on the verdict?

A well-established finding in cognitive psychology is that directed forgetting is difficult to accomplish (Golding & Hauselt, 1994), and this holds up in mock jury simulations as well, although eventual jury verdicts do not seem to be influenced by inadmissible evidence (Kerwin & Shaffer, 1994). Consistent with the notion that group discussion provides an error-checking function (Steiner, 1972), during deliberation jurors seem to correct individual preferences that have been influenced by objectionable information.

Judge Bias.   At the conclusion of the testimony portion of the trial, the judge will carefully instruct the jury about their duties, legal definitions, and appropriate procedure. Such instructions can be quite involved and are supposed to be neutral in tone. However, through their words and actions judges often convey their own feelings about the case, and jurors seem to be able to detect these feelings. Further, jurors seem to tailor their personal preferences to be consistent with the verdict that the judge is believed to favor (Hart, 1995).

If a jury reports that it is hung, but the judge feels that the jurors have not thoroughly evaluated all of the evidence, the judge has the option of returning the jury for further deliberation. This latter judicial intervention is called a "dynamite charge," and it is clear that jurors misinterpret it as a covert statement that the judge believes the defendant is guilty. Members of the minority faction, particularly those who favor acquittal, report feeling considerable pressure to change their preference after receiving a dynamite charge (Smith & Kassin, 1993).

Overall, the judge seems to be a prominent, though unintentional, biasing factor in the jury process. In particular, jurors seem to very attuned to any information that seems to reveal the judge's own beliefs about the case, and this perceived belief does play a part in the eventual jury verdict.

Administrative Factors

Because of the backlog of cases in the American court system, legal experts are continually looking for process modifications that can speed up the trial process without affecting the ability to determine the truth. A number of such modifications have been proposed and implemented. Unfortunately, there is evidence that at least some of these modifications have undesirable effects on the jury. In this section, we look at some of these process interventions.

Type of Verdict. The standard approach to a trial is to charge a defendant with violation of a specific law and to try that charge. If a defendant has been accused of multiple violations, a series of separate trials can quickly get cumbersome (not to mention expensive). Hence, a common legal procedure is to conduct a *joinder* trial, in which multiple charges are adjudicated at the same time, and a single jury is asked to make judgments about all of the possible violations.

Compared to the alternative, this is an efficient legal procedure, but joinder juries seem to behave differently than single-trial juries. In criminal cases, juries are generally more likely to convict as the number of joined charges increases (Davis, Tindale, Nagao, Hinsz, & Robertson, 1984; Kerr, Harmon, & Graves, 1982; Tanford & Penrod, 1982, 1984), although the conviction rate seems to be influenced by the order of charges, in that a conviction is more likely if the most serious charges are considered first rather than last (Davis et al., 1984; Nagao & Davis, 1980). Jurors seem to assume that a defendant who has been charged with a large number of violations *must* be guilty of something, whereas the person who has been accused of just a few crimes could easily be innocent. In fact, conviction is fairly unlikely in a single-trial case primarily because of the "leniency bias"—at the start of a trial, jurors tend to be biased toward acquittal, believing that it is better to free the guilty than convict the innocent (Mac-Coun & Kerr, 1988).

Civil trials offer a host of possible verdict types. In a civil trial, decisions have to be made regarding the causation of the damage, which party is liable, and size of damage award. In a civil case, a joined trial involves a single jury making all three of these decisions (in civil litigation, this is often called a "unitary" trial). Consistent with the criminal literature, civil juries are more likely to blame the defendant in a joined trial than in a single-charge trial (Horowitz & Bordens, 1990). Interestingly, this same study found that damage awards were less in the joined trial than in a single trial, suggesting that the joined civil trial is a double-edged sword: The defendant is more likely to be blamed, but less likely to be severely punished, for the negative events.

Information Aids.   Recognizing the limitations of memory and the large amount of information presented during the typical trial, judges have begun permitting the use of aids to help jurors accurately record and process information. For example, jurors may now take notes during the trial and ask questions of the judge during deliberation. Some legal professionals have objected to the use of notes and juror questions. Criticisms of note taking are that it is distracting to other jurors and slows down the trial whenever note takers cannot keep pace. Also, the content of the notes may be biased, in that the note taker may write down only information that supports his or her personal verdict preference. Juror questions are predicted by critics to be inappropriate, biased, and leading, and it is felt that unanswered questions lead jurors to draw inaccurate inferences. A very thorough study of notes and questions was conducted by Heuer and Penrod (1994). Their data refuted all of these criticisms. In fact, they found that juror questions were an effective aid to the group decisionmaking process. Further, they found that critics of notes and questions tended to be legal professionals who had never encountered them in the courtroom. Judges and attorneys who had been involved in cases in which jurors had taken notes and asked questions perceived them as useful juror aids.

Another information aid that has begun appearing in court is the showing of a videotape of the crime scene. Photographs of crime scenes have long been a part of trials, but the clarity of a two-dimensional picture can be affected by lighting, camera position, and perspective, as well as other factors. The dynamic nature of a videotape can give jurors a more realistic picture of the scene and help them draw more accurate conclusions about what happened. However, that same dynamic nature may make the tape too vivid (imagine seeing a photograph of a mutilated body as opposed to a videotape of that body), which could have a negative impact on jurors. Because this is such a recent innovation, there has been little research on the impact of crime scene videotapes, but what data do exist suggest that such tapes have a biasing effect. Specifically, jurors who were shown videotapes of a murder scene were later biased toward conviction and maintained lower standards of proof than were jurors who did not see the tape (Kassin & Garfield,

1991). Obviously more work is needed on the impact of crime scene video-tapes on juries, but it seems that they may do more harm than good.

Scientific Jury Selection

Earlier, we mentioned that social scientists have complained about the ignorance of behavioral research by the legal community. One aspect of the legal process in which such research has not been ignored is jury composition. The technique of scientific jury selection (SJS) involves the use of theory in such areas as attitudes, person perception, and information processing to identify jurors who will be maximally receptive to the client's case (Davis & Stasson, 1988; Penrod & Cutler, 1987). In effect, the goal of SJS is to construct a jury such that the probability of the desired verdict is maximized. There are currently many jury consulting firms that charge substantial fees for analyzing a case and making recommendations as to the "ideal" juror. The goals of SJS are persuasive, particularly within the legal community. Indeed, one criticism of Los Angeles County prosecutor Marcia Clark in the wake of the O. J. Simpson criminal trial was that she ignored SJS analyses, which suggested that black female jurors would be most likely to support Simpson—Simpson's jury contained seven black women.

The question of interest to the scientist is, does SJS really work? Is it true that a verdict can be reliably produced by matching the mix of juror personalities with the dynamics of the case? The initial series of studies of SJS, conducted in the mid-1970s, were quite negative, reporting empirical data that did not support SJS predictions and criticizing the ethicality of SJS (e.g., Saks, 1976; Zeisel & Diamond, 1978). However, a later computer simulation by Tindale and Nagao (1986) suggested that jury composition could actually have a quite substantial impact on the verdict. They showed that slight alterations, such as changing just one or two jurors or sampling from a different juror population (via a change of venue), could produce noticeable differences in conviction rates. The Tindale and Nagao study pointed out a need for further empirical study of SJS. Not too long after this study, Penrod (1990) conducted a very thorough field investigation of SJS, involving more than 350 jurors and four different types of trial (homicide, robbery, rape, and civil). Penrod collected a host of personal information from the jurors. He could not find any consistent connections between the personal information and preference for conviction, nor was there any evidence that certain types of people are more likely to favor conviction than others. Some advocates of SJS may argue for the importance of personality traits that Penrod did not assess, but overall it is hard to construct a valid argument for the continued use of scientific jury selection in light of his data.

Chapter Summary

In this chapter we have explored some of the issues that surround jury performance. Our focus was less on individual reactions to courtroom phenomena and more on how the jury as a collective responds to occurrences during the trial. We have looked at how mock jury research is conducted; how jurors combine individual preferences into a single verdict; and how various procedural factors can influence the verdict. We also discussed the use of scientific jury selection, which suggests that one can purposefully assemble a jury that will be maximally sympathetic to one's point of view. Overall, we have seen that the jury is a complex entity about which much is still puzzling.

Chapter Ten

Computer-Based Groups

The advent of sophisticated computer networking systems, which allow people in different rooms, cities, or countries to interact in real time and are inexpensive to operate, has made possible a host of innovations in business and academia. Now people at different sites can collaborate on projects without incurring the long delays that arise whenever work is sent through postal mail or the inhibition of communication that occurs whenever information is sent via fax. In effect, what has happened is that a new kind of group has been formed, one in which the primary (or perhaps only) mode of interaction is through the computer. Industry is quite positive about computer-based groups. Besides the advantage of easy multisite collaboration, these groups are also thought to reduce status differences and encourage participation from all group members, allow for greater processing of information, and improve the quality of group decisionmaking (Aiken, Vanjani, & Krosp, 1995; Campbell, 1990). Researchers have recognized the potential benefits of computer-based groups for at least twenty years (Zinn, 1977), but active study of the dynamics of such groups has taken place only over the last decade or so. Hence, there is much that we do not know about computer-based groups. In this chapter, we look at what we do know about such groups, focusing both on to what extent the research supports the beliefs about these groups and on identifying those elements of computer-based groups that have not yet been addressed. We also look at computer-simulated groups, which are programs that behave as if they were large collections of individuals.

Group Software

Networking is not possible without software to run the network. This software is called "groupware," and there are many different programs available. Currently, the most popular program is Notes, produced by Lotus. There are also several recently developed programs, such as Electronic Meeting Systems, or EMS (Valacich, Dennis, & Nunamaker, 1991); TeamFocus (El-Sherif & Tang, 1994); Computer-Mediated Meeting Management, or CM3 (Gavish, Gerdes, & Sridhar, 1995); Tools (Dufner, Hiltz, Johnson, & Czech, 1995); GroupForum (Aiken & Chrestman, 1995); and GUNGEN (Munemori & Nagasawa, 1996). No studies have yet compared the relative effectiveness of these programs. However, studies have identified the general features that any groupware package should have in order to be satisfying for users. We know that it should contain information management capabilities to help users deal with a potentially large number of messages (Novick & Walpole, 1990); employ a graphical, rather than text-based, interface (Ahern, 1993); and use gallery writing rather than poolwriting (Aiken, Vanjani, & Paolillo, 1996). If the group is to contain residents of foreign countries, the program should also provide automatic translation of messages into a person's native language (Aiken & Martin, 1994; Aiken, Martin, Paolillo, & Shirani, 1994).

Dynamics of Computer-Based Groups

How does a computer-based group compare to a face-to-face group in terms of the factors that we have been discussing throughout this book? Some commentators have argued that the computer-based group has its own unique context, one that can only be described through the use of complex models (Mantovani, 1996), whereas others have suggested that groups simply graft the existing social context onto the computer-based group; hence, any factors that exist in the face-to-face group will also be seen in the computer group (Zack & McKenney, 1995). Most research has taken a middle ground between these two positions, both looking for phenomena that are common to both types of groups and trying to identify factors that are unique to the computer-based group. The study of the dynamics of computer-based groups is of interest to not only psychologists. Computer scientists have begun urging groupware developers to take note of this research and to design groupware that can deal with the social dynamics of computer-based groups (Grudin, 1994). This suggests a potentially fruitful line of collaboration between group researchers and computer scientists.

There are a number of similarities between face-to-face and computer-based groups. For example, the biased sampling effect, which we described in Chapter 4 and which refers to the fact that groups tend to discuss commonly known information more heavily than they do unique information, also shows up in computer-based groups (Hightower & Sayeed, 1995;

Hollingshead, 1996), as does social loafing on cognitive tasks (Valacich, Dennis, & Nunamaker, 1992). However, there are a number of other phenomena that occur in face-to-face groups for which it is less clear whether they also occur in computer-based groups.

Status Differences

In our introduction to this chapter, we noted that advocates of computer-based groups believe that interaction via network minimizes the status differences that often influence group performance and encourages equal participation among all group members. (Note that some researchers have argued that this is an inappropriate prediction, one that reflects flawed theorizing about the nature of influence processes [Spears & Lea, 1994], although theirs seems to be a minority position.) Unfortunately, it is not at all clear whether such equalization actually occurs. Some researchers have observed equal rates of participation (Dubrovsky, Kiesler, & Sethna, 1991; Kiesler & Sproull, 1992; Siegel, Dubrovsky, Kiesler, & McGuire, 1986), but others have not (Hitchings & Cox, 1992; Mantovani, 1994; Silver, Cohen, & Crutchfield, 1994; Straus, 1996; Weisband, Schneider, & Connolly, 1995). The discrepancy between the two sets of findings may be due to subjects' use of cues that convey status. Because we can neither see nor hear other group members, computer-based interaction removes many of the typical social cues that we use to determine status, such as physical attractiveness and rate of speech (Kiesler, Siegel, & McGuire, 1984). However, it is possible that the network environment itself provides some other social information that is status oriented. For example, Hitchings and Cox (1992) found that status was conferred upon group members who typed quickly and demonstrated mastery of a computer keyboard. Also, it is known that men and women tend to use distinctly different, detectable styles in writing computer messages (Fulton, 1985; Savicki, Kelley, & Lingenfelter, 1996a, 1996b), and it may be that subjects in some of the studies used these style differences to determine gender-related status (although the question of whether gender is a biasing factor in computer interaction is still open to debate; see Herschel, Cooper, Smith, & Arrington, 1994, and Matheson, 1991, for opposing sets of data). Related to this issue of writing style, it has been shown that, as messages from a group member accumulate, other group members analyze the general style and content of the person's messages, and then use that analysis to form an impression of the message writer (Walther, 1992, 1993; Walther & Burgoon, 1992). This suggests that the likelihood of there being status differences within the computer-based group is directly related to the number of messages being sent. Finally, computer-based groups seem to be susceptible to a "first advocate effect," under which the first group member to publicly state a preference has a disproportionate amount of influence over the final group decision (McGuire, Kiesler, & Siegel, 1987; Weisband, 1992).

Deindividuation

In our discussions of social loafing and of social dilemmas, we saw that behavior is affected by the extent to which one's actions are readily identifiable by others. When our actions are not identifiable (i.e., we are anonymous), we are more likely to behave in negative ways. The phenomenon of *deindividuation* has been related to negative behavior by anonymous individuals. Deindividuation occurs when a person loses touch with his or her personal values and sense of personal responsibility and instead relies on the actions of other group members to determine how to behave (Diener, 1980). A primary factor in the loss of self-awareness is anonymity. If a person is anonymous, his or her actions cannot easily be evaluated by others—the person becomes a "face in the crowd." Losing touch with one's sense of values makes it more likely that one will behave in a negative way. Anonymity can occur without necessarily being a member of a large group. Wearing a disguise can also instill feelings of anonymity (Diener, Fraser, Beaman, & Kelem, 1976).

As we just noted, networks remove many of the normal cues that we use in social perception. In fact, enough cues are removed that feelings of anonymity can easily arise. If you have ever experienced a "chat room" on the Internet, you may have experienced this sense of anonymity. The only thing that identifies you is your e-mail address, which may not be based on your name. Others in the chat room cannot see or hear you and probably do not even know where in the country you are. In such a situation, some people feel free to say things that they would not say in face-to-face conversation. To what extent does a computer-based group invoke feelings of anonymity and deindividuation? Perhaps surprisingly, there is no clear evidence that deindividuation is a problem in such groups. Some studies have found it (Kiesler et al., 1984; Lea & Spears, 1991; Spears, Lea, & Lee, 1990), but others studies have actually reported a heightened sense of self-awareness among members of computer-based groups (Matheson & Zanna, 1988, 1989, 1990). Much of these differences may well be due to differing operational definitions of deindividuation. For example, in the Matheson and Zanna studies, deindividuation was assessed by using questionnaires that measure private and public self-awareness. By contrast, Lea, Spears, and colleagues determined whether deindividuation was occurring by asking subjects to what extent they felt anonymous and isolated from others. Although feelings of isolation can affect group member reactions to computerized groups (Taha & Calwell, 1993), it seems unlikely that feeling isolated would automatically make one less self-aware. In fact, self-attention theory, which we discussed in Chapter 3, would predict the reverse: Feeling isolated should make you *more* self-aware because the size of your subgroup is very small relative to the total number of group members. Overall, we cannot draw any firm conclusions regarding deindividuation in computer-based groups, but the operational definition that has been used in some studies seems questionable.

"Flaming"

One specific type of negative behavior that can occur in the context of a computer-based group is the making of uninhibited remarks. The making of such remarks is called "flaming," and as with deindividuation, the frequency of flaming cannot be clearly established. Some researchers argue that flaming rates are greatly exaggerated, and concerns about flaming are driven by stereotypes of the computer-group domain (Lea, O'Shea, Fung, & Spears, 1992). Other researchers have presented evidence of frequent and severe flaming within such groups (Dubrovsky et al., 1991; Kiesler & Sproull, 1992; Siegel et al., 1986). However, the bulk of the research evidence seems to support the former argument. In a meta-analysis of flaming studies, Walther, Anderson, and Park (1994) found the effect size for flaming to be only 0.02. Field data have shown that the majority (specifically, 58 percent) of e-mail users report never having been flamed; another 19 percent are not sure (Thompsen & Ahn, 1992). The conditions under which flaming occurs seem to be quite specific. Few flaming messages seem to be spontaneous; most are in response to an earlier flame (Hiltz, Turoff, & Johnson, 1989). Further, there seems to be a connection between flaming and personality, as extroverted individuals are more likely to flame than introverted individuals (Smolensky, Carmody, & Halcomb, 1990). Thus, although the potential is there for computer-based group members to be nasty to each other, in practice this does not seem to happen.

Conformity

We have discussed conformity pressure in a number of chapters. Can conformity pressure also be exerted within a computer-based group? The research suggests that conformity pressures diminish when interaction is over a computer network (Adrianson & Hjelmquist, 1991). Smilowitz, Compton, and Flint (1988) conducted a conformity experiment with computer-based groups in which they exactly followed Asch's original conformity paradigm (modified, of course, to work on a computer network). They found little evidence of conformity among group members; group members were quite careful to critique the judgments of others and were willing to express their criticisms. Although we certainly need more data on conformity within computer-based groups, it seems safe to assume that network-based interaction counteracts much conformity pressure.

Satisfaction

The final aspect of computer group dynamics that we want to address is the extent to which participants in computer-based groups are satisfied with the system. A number of studies have shown that people are less satisfied with working in computer groups than in face-to-face groups (Adrianson & Hjelmquist, 1991; Galegher & Kraut, 1994; Matheson & Zanna, 1990; Straus & McGrath, 1994). A number of possible explanations for why people are unenthusiastic exist: discomfort with a social setting that lacks social cues (Straus & McGrath, 1994); stress caused by the need to perform a familiar task in an unfamiliar way (Stone & Allen, 1990); and experiences with groupware that is not "user-friendly" (Dufner et al., 1995). Savicki et al. (1996a, 1996b) have reported a sex difference in satisfaction, with females being more positive about computer-based groups than males. Group size is also related to satisfaction, although it is not clear whether larger or smaller groups are the more satisfying (Aiken, Krosp, Shirani, & Martin, 1994; Dennis, Valacich, & Nunamaker, 1990; Valacich et al., 1992).

There may be an important qualification to the idea that computer-based groups are dissatisfying. Some data suggest that participants in computer brainstorming groups prefer network interaction to face-to-face brainstorming (Gallupe, Dennis, Cooper, Valacich, Bastianutti, & Nunamaker, 1992; Valacich & Schwenk, 1995), although this effect has not always been replicated (Aiken et al., 1994). We discuss computer-based brainstorming in our next section.

Summary

Although much work remains to be done on the dynamics of computer-based groups, we can already see that there are both similarities and differences between face-to-face and computer-based groups. For example, status differences arise in both types of groups, but conformity pressure does not. Direct comparisons of the two types of groups in terms of provision of a satisfying experience seem to favor the face-to-face group, with brainstorming groups being a possible exception.

An understanding of computer group dynamics is important, especially if we are concerned with group members liking the group environment. However, we also need to know if computer-based groups are more *productive* than face-to-face groups. Given the cost (both financially and logistically) of setting up a computer-based group, we should expect noticeable increases in productivity. If such increases are not forthcoming, then organizations should not invest in the groupware and hardware.

Computer Group Performance

How well do computer-based groups perform, relative to face-to-face groups? Direct comparisons of the two types of groups do not show a clear advantage to computer-based interaction (with the exception of brainstorming, to be discussed in the next section). Comparisons of the quality of performance show no difference between the two types of group (Archer, 1990; Finn, 1988; Harmon, Schneer, & Hoffman, 1995; Laughlin et al., 1995; Reid, Malinek, Stott, & Evans, 1996; Straus, 1996; Straus & McGrath, 1994), although this may be to some extent an artifact of experience with networks, in that subjects in these experiments are generally unfamiliar with the use of groupware. Studies of experienced users tend to find that computer-based interaction enhances some aspects of the group process (Finholt, Sproull, & Kiesler, 1990; Hollingshead, McGrath, & O'Connor, 1993; Kiesler & Sproull, 1992). Whether this enhancement translates into higher-quality performance is not clear, however. In fact, studies of computer-based negotiation suggest that negotiators perform more poorly (i.e., receive poorer outcomes) when negotiating over a network than face-to-face (Arunachalam & Dilla, 1995; Griffith & Northcraft, 1994).

A number of studies have focused on the performance process within computer groups. For example, computer-based groups require more time to complete a task than face-to-face groups (Green & Williges, 1995; Hollingshead & McGrath, 1995; Reid et al., 1996). This may be because of the novelty of the computer-group medium; novices need considerable time to learn and develop network interaction rules (Brashers, Adkins, & Meyers, 1994). Process also seems to be a function of age of the group, as computer-based groups in which the members expect future interaction have patterns of communication and influence that differ from those seen in both face-to-face groups and in short-term computer groups (Arrow, 1997; Walther, 1994).

Brainstorming

In terms of general group performance, then, there is not much support for the superiority of computer-based groups over face-to-face groups. There may, however, be *specific* types of tasks for which computer-based interaction is effective. One such task is brainstorming. Recall our discussion of brainstorming in Chapter 4. We said that the likely explanation for why brainstorming does not work involves production blocking, or the inability to both attend to others and generate ideas at the same time. Computer-based interaction provides a possible solution to the problem. Since all comments are written, it might be possible to store the comments of others in a file that can be accessed at a later time. Thus, a group member can develop and modify ideas while information from others comes in. The person can then review the messages at his or her leisure.

In fact, a large body of research has looked at exactly this issue, and it clearly supports the superiority of computer-based brainstorming, in that participants generate a large number of high-quality ideas (Dennis & Valacich, 1993; Gallupe, Bastianutti, & Cooper, 1991; Gallupe, Cooper, Grise, & Bastianutti, 1994; Gallupe et al., 1992; Petrovic & Krickl, 1994; Sainfort, Gustafson, Bosworth, & Hawkins, 1990; Valacich, Dennis, & Connolly, 1994; Valacich, Paranka, George, & Nunamaker, 1993). There are, however, some aspects of the computer-group setting that can impact the number of ideas generated. Group size seems to be an important factor, with the research showing that the rate of idea generation is directly related to group size (Dennis & Valacich, 1993, 1994; Dennis, Valacich, & Nunamaker 1990; Gallupe et al., 1992; Valacich et al., 1992; Valacich, Wheeler, Mennecke, & Wachter, 1995). Thus, we would want our electronic brainstorming group to be as large as possible. The quantity of ideas is also increased if the overall decision problem is broken down into a series of smaller components, with group members generating ideas for each component (Dennis, Valacich, Connolly, & Wynne, 1996). Idea generation also goes up when each group member is asked to keep track of the number of ideas he or she has generated (Paulus, Larey, Putman, Leggett, & Roland, 1996) or when group members receive feedback regarding their performance (Roy, Gauvin, & Limayen, 1996). The anonymity that is an inherent part of computer interaction can actually be beneficial for brainstorming, as it seems to make people more willing to offer criticisms (Jessup, Connolly, & Tansik, 1990). However, this same anonymity can also lead to social loafing, although loafing can be minimized by providing the group with a standard of performance against which they can compare their own rate of productivity (Shepherd, Briggs, Reinig, Yen, & Nunamaker, 1995).

Summary and Comment

The research is quite clear: With the exception of brainstorming, computer-based groups are not more productive than face-to-face groups. Despite this, problemsolving computer-based groups are currently quite popular in management (which, given the faddish nature of management, is perhaps not surprising—Abrahamson, 1996) and education (Anderson, 1996). There is certainly no harm in extensive reliance on such groups, since they are not any *less* productive than face-to-face groups, but given the (at least initial) cost of establishing computer-based groups, the net benefit to the organization is questionable. Brainstorming groups, which are clearly more effective than face-to-face groups, are again the exception to this, but it seems that the enthusiasm for using computer-based groups for solving problems should be tempered somewhat.

Simulated Groups

All of the groups that we have discussed so far contain real people. The role of the computer is to link these people and serve as a conduit for interaction. But another type of computer-based group is one in which the computer or some mathematical function, or set of functions, simulates the actions of a large number of other people. Such simulated groups are valuable research tools that can help researchers draw some conclusions about groups that, if composed of actual people, would be too large or too complex to be studied in either a laboratory or field setting. In this section, we look at some such simulated groups.

Note that simulation research is not intended as a substitute for empirical research. We do not assume that the "actions" of a simulated group perfectly represent how an actual group of people would behave in the same situation. Rather, simulated groups provide theoretical baselines that can be empirically tested. At some point, the groups researcher is going to have to go into the lab or field and collect data. Simulation also has implications for the planning of research, and these are discussed in the Methodological Appendix.

Jury Decisionmaking

In Chapter 9, we saw that the study of juries is quite difficult to undertake because we are prohibited from observing actual sitting juries. One way around this problem is to use mock juries. Other researchers have conducted simulations of the jury decisionmaking process. Some of these simulations have employed sophisticated computer algorithms that allow the researcher to manipulate a number of factors (e.g., the JUS program—Penrod & Hastie, 1980), whereas other simulations have involved development of mathematical functions with procedural factors as predictors and with the verdict as the dependent variable (e.g., Gelfand & Solomon, 1977; Klevorick, Rothschild, & Winship, 1984). Each of these approaches provides a convenient means of testing various trial factors. The predictions made by the model can then be empirically tested, using far fewer subjects than if the empirical study was exploratory in nature.

Simulation has also been crucial to the comparison of various jury sizes and decision rules. This research has shown that the differences in the rates of guilty verdicts between twelve-, nine-, and six-person juries and between unanimity-rule, 2/3-majority-rule, and majority-rule juries are negligible, perhaps as low as one discrepant verdict per every one thousand juries

(Davis, Bray, & Holt, 1977). Such comparisons of actual juries, if data were even available (and there is no guarantee that they would be), would be very difficult to make. Law reports from across the country, and across many years, would need to be read, and the information would need to be translated into a data base. The simulated juries provide a much more efficient way to estimate the effects of changing jury-legal parameters. Finally, note that one of the important studies of scientific jury selection, the Tindale and Nagao (1986) study that suggested that SJS might be of some value, was a simulation.

Group Decisionmaking

The more general processes of group discussion and problemsolving have also been the subject of considerable simulation work. Some of this work has employed highly flexible computer programs that let the researcher configure the group in a variety of ways. For example, two different computer programs have been developed by Garold Stasser to address elements of group discussion: DISCUSS, which examines the flow of information within a group (Stasser, 1988, 1992), and SPEAK, which addresses turn taking among speakers within a group (Stasser & Taylor, 1991). More recently, Larson (1997) has presented a different model of discussion. Research on group decision rules has also benefited from simulations of groups. Similar to the above-mentioned work on distributions of jury verdicts, this research has examined differences in distributions of group preferences as a function of various decision rules (Davis, Hulbert, & Au, 1996). These simulations involve hundreds of large groups; a comparable laboratory or field experiment could not be run in any reasonable amount of time.

Social Dilemmas

In Chapter 7, we discussed some laboratory research on social dilemmas. Of course, in the real world dilemmas usually involve far more than the eight or nine subjects that can fit into a laboratory. For example, there may be thousands of people who get their household water from a single water table. We also saw that social dilemma research is sometimes criticized for the artificiality of its research paradigms (e.g., playing for points). To that end, social dilemma researchers have begun using computer-simulated groups to estimate how people behave in social dilemmas that involve very large groups or in dilemmas in which the scenario is more realistic. Some researchers have simulated entire groups of people (Messick & Liebrand, 1993, 1995; Parks & Komorita, 1997), whereas others have developed programs with which a single subject can interact and which make the subject feel as if he or she is part of a larger collective (Fusco, Bell, Jorgenson, & Smith, 1991; Summers, 1996). For example, Robert Gifford and associates have created programs that can simulate a realistic resource dilemma (Gifford & Wells, 1991; Hine & Gifford, 1996, 1997). The subject role-plays a member of a resource-consuming group (e.g., fishermen, loggers), and he or she must both sample from the resource and try to make the resource last as long as possible. The computer simulates the behaviors of the other "group members," and the researcher can determine how these "others" will behave.

Other Simulated Aspects of Groups

A number of other group phenomena have been simulated as well. For example, researchers have developed computer models of group formation (Billard & Pasquale, 1993; Platt, 1992), influence (Nowak, Szamrej, & Latané, 1990), status effects (Ridgeway & Balkwell, 1997), perceptions of ingroup and outgroup members (Linville, Fischer, & Salovey, 1989), and conformity processes (McGarty, Turner, Hogg, David, & Wetherell, 1992), to name a few. The advent of powerful desktop computers has provided groups researchers with an important new methodological tool, one that will likely see increasing use in the years to come.

Chapter Summary

Our goal in this chapter was to introduce the reader to the study of groups in which the computer plays a role. The bulk of the chapter was devoted to research on real groups that interact over a computer network. We saw that, with the exception of brainstorming groups, the productivity of computer-based groups is not enhanced relative to face-to-face groups. We also looked at the research on "groups" that have been simulated by a computer program or mathematical function. Such groups can help the researcher complete necessary exploratory work, saving subjects for the testing of formal predictions and theories.

Chapter Eleven

Unique Groups

An emerging emphasis in groups research is a focus on very particular groups that perform specific, unusual tasks in a sharply defined environment. The environment contains features that the typical social group does not encounter (e.g., extreme danger, huge audiences), and the tasks are not ones that we would ask a "normal" group to perform (e.g., perform a tracheotomy). What impact does a unique task and/or setting have on these groups? In this chapter, we want to look at some of these unique groups. Specifically, we want to focus on four types of groups, all of which are being heavily studied: flight crews, military groups, hospital teams, and sports teams.

Military Groups

Perhaps no single institution is more heavily dependent upon the group as the modern military. As military equipment and procedures become increasingly complex, the need for effective group performance has become ever stronger (Salas, Bowers, & Cannon-Bowers, 1995). Over the past ten to fifteen years, military personnel have taken an increasing interest in some aspects of groups research. In this section, we review some of the topics that are of interest to the military.

Coordination

Coordination of effort among the members of a troop is essential. There is almost no room for wasted effort or duplication, particularly during combat. For that reason, researchers of military teams have studied the issue of coordination in detail, with the emphasis being on the training of coordination (Prince & Salas, 1993). Some military theorists assume that coordination is a function of group member familiarity, predicting that groups with members that know each other and each other's abilities will be better at coordinating effort than will groups with members that are strangers. However, research refutes this notion. Groups that have undergone coordination training more efficiently perform tasks than do untrained, yet familiar, groups (Leedom & Simon, 1995).

Training, then, is clearly necessary for effective coordination of group member effort. But how should this training be conducted? Coordination training is most effective when the training program has been constructed with group member input; that is, trainees have been asked for which aspects of interpersonal coordination they most need instruction, and the program responds to those needs (Bowers, Morgan, Salas, & Prince, 1993). One reason that such input is important is that accurate, objective assessment of the importance of various behaviors is difficult (Bowers, Baker, & Salas, 1994). The training should also address interdependent thinking, in that trainees should be taught to focus on both the performance of specific tasks and the integration of their tasks with the actions of other group members (Shaud, 1989). The program should also provide ample opportunities for trainees to practice coordination, as this practice seems to be a reliable indicator of the impact of the training (Leedom & Simon, 1995).

Cohesion

Cohesion is a topic of great interest to the military, so much so that the United States Army has developed a program called COHORT (COHesion, Operational Readiness, and Training), which is directed toward keeping units together despite the myriad of personnel transfers that are so common within the armed forces. Cohesion does seem to have some effect on soldier morale. A soldier in a cohesive unit has a strong sense of personal well-being (O'Brien, 1993), as well as a high level of trust in his or her fellow soldiers and superiors (Gal, 1986). However, COHORT is partially predicated on the beliefs that cohesion improves group performance and inhibits group member breakdown during times of stress, assumptions that are being debated in the research literature (Swets & Bjork, 1990; Zaccaro, Gualtieri, & Minionis, 1995). Curiously, the army has acknowledged this lack of empirical support, yet still promotes the global benefits of improving cohesion (Kirkland, 1987). Given the military's continued interest in cohesion, a stronger program of research on the effects of cohesion on performance is certainly warranted, particularly given the recent advances in sociometric measurement that may help to accurately assess cohesion within the military unit (Lucius & Kuhnert, 1997).

Leadership

Not surprisingly, leadership is also a topic of interest to the military. For many years, the focus of armed forces leadership research was almost entirely on leader selection and the development of psychometric instruments for identifying the most-qualified officer candidates. This research continues, although scientists are now also beginning to study the dynamics of leader-subordinate interaction within military groups. For example, some researchers have looked at how leader prototypes affect officer-subordinate interaction. It seems that military superiors and subordinates maintain different leader prototypes. Officers emphasize conformity when thinking about an ideal leader; subordinates place more emphasis on intelligence and athleticism (Atwater & Yammarino, 1993), although they may also be concerned with conformity (Polley & Eid, 1994).

A key finding that is emerging from the research on military leadership is that, as in the private sector, subordinate performance is affected by the leader's degree of support. In fact, leader supportiveness seems to be a better predictor of soldier performance motivation than is peer support (Weiner, 1990), which contradicts one of the basic assumptions behind unit cohesion: that performance can be enhanced by developing a cohesive unit. The issue of leader support has led to a number of studies of the effectiveness of transformational leadership in the military. Some interesting, and perhaps surprising, data have emerged from these studies. For example, the data consistently show that transformational officers are perceived as being very effective leaders (Atwater & Yammarino, 1993; Deluga, 1991), but actual soldier performance is not significantly better under transformational leadership than under transactional leadership (Deluga, 1991).

Military scholars are also concerned with the training of officers in decisionmaking. Given the complex systems with which military leaders must now work, formal training in decisionmaking theory is now seen as necessary (Rouse, Cannon-Bowers, & Salas, 1992). The United States Military Academy has developed a leadership training procedure called The Intellectual Procedure that has as one of its goals the development of complex decisionmaking ability. Data suggest that it is an effective program, one that might be adapted to civilian settings (McNally, Gerras, & Bullis, 1996).

Flight Crews: Groups in the Cockpit

A Boeing 757 lies at the bottom of the ocean with 187 passengers and crew inside. The plane left the Dominican Republic in February 1996 with a load of German vacationers. Minutes later, the plane plunged into the ocean, into shark-infested waters. There were no survivors. More than 7,000 feet down on the ocean's floor, the National Transportation and Safety Board (NTSB) recovered the plane's flight recorder. It seems that a cockpit instrument was not working. The captain knew it but took off anyway. Everyone on board paid the price. The higher the plane went, the faster the faulty instrument had indicated that the plane was going. The crew erroneously continued to slow the plane down—until it dropped from the sky.

In 1972, British European Airlines' (BEA; later to become British Airways) younger pilots were fighting for better pay, and they were prepared to disrupt flights to get it. This possibility enraged some senior pilots, including Stanley Key. Key was a decorated World War II pilot and training captain, but some junior pilots found him brusque and overbearing. On June 18, 1972, Key had a furious argument with a junior pilot and was still angry one hour later when he left to pilot a flight to Brussels. Two minutes after takeoff, the plane crashed into a field killing all onboard. Investigators later found that the plane's "droops" (flaps on the front of wings) had been pushed up too early and that the crew had overridden the mechanical warning system. Hateful graffiti was also scribbled on the back of Key's seat: "Key must go. Where? Down the drain," and, ironically, "When Stanley Key dies, who will be God's next representative in B.E.A.?"

Flight crews are another type of unique group. How do flight crews interact? What types of dynamics exist in the cockpit? The outcomes of these interactions are of great and real consequence to us all, as the above two examples illustrate. This is even more apparent when one realizes that forty years ago, more than 50 percent of all plane accidents were due to mechanical failures. Today, more than 66 percent can be traced back to the flight crew in some way. A greater understanding of groups may help lead us to an increased understanding of cockpit dynamics.

Crew Resource Management

As you might guess, an interest in crew dynamics has been of concern to many commercial airlines, as well as the military, over the years. The term Crew Resource Management, or CRM, has come to be used to describe this interest. CRM includes a recognition of those persons in the cockpit (e.g., pilot, copilot) and those persons who are essential for successful flying not directly in the cockpit (e.g., flight controllers, flight attendants); each of these persons are viewed as part of a team (Lauber, 1994). It focuses on crew-level, as well as individual-level, training and operations (Barker, Clothier, Woody, & McKinney, 1996; Guzzo & Dickson, 1996; Helmreich & Foushee, 1993). Research on CRM has been undertaken by commercial airlines, as well as the military, and even space flights (e.g., Barker et al., 1996; Chute & Weiner, 1995; Neville, Bisson, French, & Boll, 1994; Sandal, Vaernes, & Ursin, 1995). Cohesion, communication, and decisionmaking have been among the topics of focus for CRM researchers.

Cohesion.   Group *cohesion* is a topic that has already come up several times in this book (e.g., Chapter 2). Cohesion has proven to be one of the most significant variables in determining flight crew success. It relates to the interpersonal closeness felt among the crew members as well as their time together. Interestingly, in the commercial airline industry, any given flight crew probably works together for, at most, four days. Indeed, many crews are together for only part of one day. Because of this, training is considered critical. A type of training used in CRM is called Line-Oriented Flight Training, or LOFT. LOFT is a broad category that encompasses flight simulations that are conducted for several purposes (e.g., to qualify as a pilot, for training, etc.). Butler (1993) proposed that LOFT is an important training method that greatly reinforces CRM concepts. This particular type of training is called CRM LOFT, and it includes simulations of real-life situations involving problemsolving and crew communication that may occur during actual flights (Weiner, Kanki, & Helmreich, 1993). CRM LOFT is not carried out with the intention of strengthening the bonds between any particular set of crew members (since as we mentioned crews are sometimes together for only a short time) but with the intention of making members more effective within any flight crew they happen to find themselves.

The process of fostering cohesion among flight crews is also facilitated by having them engage in preflight briefings; during this meeting, the captain can explicitly lay out his or her expectations for the crew, and the crew can voice any questions or concerns that it might have concerning the goals of the flight or interactions among crew members (Ginnett, 1993). A good deal of research has shown that greater cohesion exists among crews that have undergone preflight briefings (e.g., Salas, Bowers, & Cannon-Bowers, 1995). Foushee, Lauber, Baetge, and Acomb (1986) found that newly formed crews may communicate less effectively and are more likely to have accidents than are crews who have been together for at least a short time. Because of this, Hackman (1993) recommended a modification of flight crew scheduling in order to keep flight crews together for longer periods of time (there is currently some resistance to this among commercial flight crews because it reduces flexibility in travel). The U.S. Army has been using schedules that keep crews together for longer periods of time, what they have called "battle-rostering" (Leedom & Simon, 1995). The underlying purpose of battle-rostering is to increase crew members' familiarity and to increase the predictability of behaviors within a team setting (Prince & Salas, 1993).

Communication and Decisionmaking.   As we already alluded to, effective *communication* and *decisionmaking* of crew members is important to the success of any flight. It is interesting to speculate whether better communication among crew members could have avoided the tragedies that were described at the beginning of this section (cockpit voice recordings were unavailable in those flights). Once again, training appears to be key. In the context of CRM, communication training has focused on crew members being polite but assertive, on participative and active listening, and on providing concise feedback (Orlady & Foushee, 1987). Effective communication is almost universally recognized as critical to successful flight crew performance. Training has focused on coordinating the communication between crew members (e.g., Skogstad, Dyregrov, & Hellesoy, 1995; Stout, Salas, & Carson, 1994). For example, when crew members must act interdependently to perform effectively, such things as providing information before it is needed, planning, asking for input, and stepping in to help others were all related to increased crew effectiveness and to fewer errors (Urban, Bowers, & Monday, 1995).

One particularly important variable that has been studied with regard to flight crew effectiveness is communication between the crew and cockpit when the crew (e.g., flight attendants) has a question about safety and must decide whether or not to take the information it has to the cockpit. This is exemplified by a situation in 1982 when Air Florida flight 90 crashed into the Potomac River in Washington, D.C., shortly after takeoff due to ice forming on the wings; the lone surviving flight attendant (and the few surviving passengers) said they noticed snow on the wings, but no one brought it to the attention of the cockpit. Chute and Weiner (1995) have found that at times flight attendants can be reluctant to come forward because of self-doubts about the accuracy and importance of the information or because of fear of dismissal or rebuke by the pilots (see also Skogstad et al., 1995).

In many ways, flight crews are thus like many other decisionmaking groups (see Chapter 4). Things that are detrimental to any group decision, such as groupthink and other factors, can become particularly insidious when one is flying a jumbo jet with more than 600 passengers onboard. Flight crews are similar to many previous groups that we have talked about in that they must determine what the situation is, assess available options, and choose among them. However, there is at least one important way that flight crews differ from most of the other decisionmaking groups that we have discussed previously. Crew decisionmaking is hierarchical decisionmaking: Each member of the crew contributes his or her knowledge and opinions, but the captain has the final say in the decision (we mention a similar dynamic in our discussion of hospital teams). A final interesting feature of flight crews is that a great deal of expertise is necessary in order to make effective decisions, and each crew member fulfills important and unique roles. Flight crews members are therefore perhaps more heterogeneous than many other decisionmaking groups (Orasanu, 1993).

Summary of Flight Crews

Flight crews are another very important and somewhat unique group. Although forty years ago about 50 percent of aircraft accidents were traced to mechanical failures, today about 66 percent are traced to the flight crews in some way. The dynamics of flight crew interactions obviously have extremely important, and unfortunately sometimes tragic, consequences. CRM has been developed to try to foster smoother interactions among crew members. Cohesion, communication, and decisionmaking have been some variables of central focus within this approach. By studying flight crews, researchers may capitalize on some unique and intriguing opportunities to study group processes.

Hospital Teams

Fans of the television show *ER* regularly see groups at work. Each patient who is brought to the emergency room is attended to by a team of doctors, nurses, and aides, who must coordinate their actions carefully and make critical decisions quickly, confidently, and accurately. One would think that such extremely stressful conditions would have a negative impact on the individual group members and on the group itself; this is certainly suggested in the television show. What is it really like to be part of a hospital team? What impact does working in a life-and-death environment have on group performance? In this section, we take a look at some research on hospital teams. Many of the phenomena that we have discussed in earlier chapters are of considerable concern to those in the medical profession. In particular, the medical community is concerned about stress and satisfaction, roles, interpersonal conflict, and group composition. We examine each of these issues in turn.

Stress

Environmentally induced stress is a major factor that affects hospital teams. This is probably not too surprising. However, it is also the case that the stress is not constant across situations; rather, particular medical situations impose higher levels of stress than do others. In particular, stress seems to be highest among hospital teams that work with seriously ill (especially terminally ill) children (Cunning, 1976; Harper, 1993; Patenaude, Szymanski, & Rappaport, 1979; Raimbault, 1991) or with patients who suffer from debilitating, incurable diseases (Koin, 1989). Interpersonal support within the team is important for helping group members deal with this stress (Harper, 1993; Peiro, Gonzalez-Roma, & Ramos, 1992).

Roles

Hospital teams can have considerable problems with status and role definition. In regard to status, physicians tend to prefer that the team be stratified, with nurses taking a subordinate role to doctors, whereas nurses prefer that status differences be eliminated (Campbell-Heider & Pollock, 1987). This issue of stratification is important because failure to include nurses in the decisionmaking process has been clearly connected to poor team performance (Abramson, 1989; Ellis & Miller, 1993). Whether a group member is a trainee or full-fledged staff member is also important, as team members are generally less willing to work with trainees than with staff (Stahelski & Tsukuda, 1990). Disturbingly, within-group status may affect ethical behavior. A large-scale study of 665 medical students has shown that students who witnessed unethical behavior within their teams were themselves likely to commit an unethical act (Feudtner, Christakis, & Christakis, 1994). The two major reasons given for such behavior were fear of a negative evaluation and the belief that the student's low within-team status compelled him or her to behave as high-status team members were behaving.

Role definition can also be a problem within the hospital group. Often, there is considerable ambiguity regarding who is to perform what tasks and who has authority to act independently (Drinka & Streim, 1994; Peiro et al., 1992). The most immediate problem resulting from role ambiguity is inadequate coordination of behaviors within the group. Sometimes the same action is independently performed by different group members, whereas other actions may not be performed at all (Berteotti & Seibold, 1994).

Interpersonal Conflict

Conflict between members of a hospital team can have a substantial impact on team performance. In fact, it has been argued that lack of effective conflict resolution techniques presents a major obstacle to effective hospital team performance (Abramson, 1989; McMahan, Hoffman, & McGee, 1994; Muthny, 1989; Zeiss & Steffen, 1996). Much of the conflict is rooted in the strict hierarchy that is found in most hospital teams. Earlier in this chapter, we saw that a hierarchy can cause problems within a flight crew when a captain refuses to listen to advice from the copilot or engineer. Similarly, conflict within the hospital group often arises when a physician ignores input from a nurse (Campbell-Heider & Pollock, 1987; McMahan et al., 1994). Some theorists have suggested that physician-nurse conflict can be minimized through assertiveness training for nurses (Ellis & Miller, 1993). Conflict can also have detrimental effects on individual group members in terms of their satisfaction with the group and willingness to stay in the group. In particular, personality clashes between group members seem to be quite stress inducing (Muthny, 1989; Sessa, 1996). Interestingly, hospital team members are better able to deal with professional conflict, which arises whenever there is disagreement about such issues as proper treatment or diagnosis, than with personal conflict; it does not seem to be as stress inducing as is personal conflict (Sessa, 1996).

Group Composition

Considerable attention has been paid to how to best assemble a hospital team. There is general agreement that teams need to be composed of professionals from a number of different areas of expertise, so that a broad range of skills and knowledge bases are present within the group (Cowley, Swanson, Chapman, Kitik, & Mackay, 1994; Cox, 1995; Waite, Harker, & Messerman, 1994; Zeiss & Steffen, 1996). Besides the obvious benefits to the patient of a group with such a broad skill base, such composed teams (often called "interdisciplinary health care teams," or IHTs, in the medical literature) have additional beneficial qualities. For example, their organization tends to be linear rather than hierarchical (Zeiss & Steffen, 1996), and we have seen that hierarchical organization can instigate a variety of problems. Interdisciplinary team members also closely attend to the coordination of actions within the team (Zeiss & Steffen, 1996).

These teams are not without their problems. The relatively high turnover rate within the health care profession can keep the IHT in a continual state of transition and waste valuable resources (Drinka, 1994). A group that is too diverse runs the risk of having members who cannot communicate with each other, in that technical terms that are used in one discipline may not be known by members of another discipline, or members of different professions may describe the same phenomenon with different words (Faulkner, 1985). So, for example, when a physician mentions that a patient has a history of myocardial infarction, a social worker might not realize the physician means that the patient has had heart attacks in the past.

The Role of Education

In a sharply critical review of the literature on hospital teams, McMahan et al. (1994) argued that hospital group dynamics have long been recognized as important within the nursing profession but have been virtually ignored by medical scholars. This ignorance may be rooted in the nature of medical school education and its authoritative and rigid structure. The idea that medical education works against teamwork is not a new one (see Vinet, 1974), and an analysis of residency training by Weinholtz (1991) provides support for the notion. He found residency training to be authoritative and hierarchical, with residents having little contact with nurses and allied health professionals, people who are necessary members of hospital teams. Programs do exist to prepare medical students for teamwork (Bair & Greenspan, 1986; Orgren, Weiler, & Higby, 1989), but there seems to be little data on their effectiveness. Given the problem areas that we have identified in our discussion of hospital groups, it certainly seems that medical schools would want to include course work on group dynamics and performance as part of their curriculum.

Sports Teams: There's No Place
Like Home . . . Or Is There?

When it comes to sports teams, one can readily see that many of the topics we have already discussed in this book have great applicability—such issues as group performance and decisionmaking (Chapter 4), social motivation losses and gains (Chapter 6), and leadership (Chapter 8). In this section of the chapter, we focus on two interrelated issues: the "home field advantage" and the "home field disadvantage." Studying sports teams within this context is interesting because not only are the teams themselves groups but the audiences are, too. The influences of spectators on team athletic performance, and possible reasons for it, underlie our discussion.

Home Field Advantage

In organized professional sports in the United States, much is made about the *home field advantage*. As an example, it has become part of the lexicon of sports broadcasters to make reference to such things as "gaining home field advantage for the play-offs" or "maintaining that home court edge." Some professional sports teams (e.g., football teams) are actually rewarded for a good regular season record by being allowed to play their play-off games at home; the teams with the best records get to play at home throughout the play-offs as long as they are not eliminated. Perhaps since the early stages of athletic competition, players, coaches, and fans have subscribed to the belief that home teams play better than visiting teams. However, it was not until relatively recently that psychologists and other researchers began to document the home field advantage empirically. Is the home field advantage for real? The answer to this question, at least initially, was an emphatic "yes."

One of the first major studies on home field advantage was conducted by Schwartz and Barsky (1977). These researchers examined the outcomes of more than 1,880 professional baseball, 182 professional football, and 910 collegiate football games during 1971 and 542 professional hockey games from the 1971–1972 season. The home field advantage was found to exist in each of the sports that were studied. In particular, the home teams won more often than visiting teams in professional baseball (53 percent of the time), professional football (55 percent of the time), collegiate football (59 percent of the time), and professional hockey (53 percent of the time). Similar support for the home field advantage was also obtained by several other researchers (e.g., Edwards, 1979; Edwards & Archambault, 1989; Pollard, 1986; Irving & Goldstein, 1990). Moreover, research has demonstrated that the home field advantage is generalizable across many diverse sports and levels of competition, such as in college basketball (Snyder & Purdy, 1985; Varca, 1980), alpine skiing (Bray & Carron, 1993), junior ice hockey (Agnew & Carron, 1994), minor league baseball (Courneya & Carron, 1991), women's collegiate basketball and field hockey (Gayton, Mutrie, & Hearns, 1987), and Olympic performances (Leonard, 1989).

Courneya and Carron (1992) conducted the most recent review of the home field advantage literature. These investigators concluded that the home field advantage is a real and measurable phenomenon and that college and professional teams do not significantly differ in their degree of home field advantage. However, the magnitude of the home field advantage may differ by type of sport. Their review found that the home field advantage seems to be greatest for soccer, basketball, and hockey. The home field advantage seems to be least strong in baseball (which is consistent with Schwartz and Barsky [1977]). As an overall summary statement, then, it does appear that home teams do have an advantage over visiting teams. But why might this be the case? That is, what is the mechanism that produces the home field advantage? Several possible mechanisms have been proposed. We discuss some of the primary ones in the following section. After that, we describe how the notion of home field advantage has not gone unchallenged. Some researchers have proposed that playing at home can actually be disadvantageous under certain conditions.

Possible Mechanisms Underlying the Home Field Advantage

Because the home field advantage has been so well documented, several researchers have begun to attempt to ascertain why it occurs. In fact, there might be many factors that are responsible for the effect.

Supportive Home Audience. One of the first factors that had been proposed as a mechanism that produces the home field advantage effect is a *supportive home audience* (Cox, 1990; Schwartz & Barsky, 1977; see also Iso-Ahola & Hatfield, 1986; Taylor & Lanni, 1981). The notion here is that the partisan home crowd enhances the home team member's motivation and performance. There is a good deal of research that supports this general argument. For example, Mizruchi (1985) found that social support by home fans was one of the main determinants of the home advantage and that there may be a number of more specific variables that determine the magnitude of this effect. Mizruchi's study of twenty-three professional basketball teams during the 1981–1982 season found that such things as the proportion of attendance in the home team's arena, the tradition of the franchise, and number of years in the location can affect the home field advantage; the larger the proportion of filled to empty seats, the longer the history of success of the franchise, and the longer the team had been in a particular city, the stronger was the home field advantage. All of these things, as you might imagine, seem to foster a supportive home environment.

Research on crowd density additionally supports these arguments. For example, Pollard (1986) found a positive relationship between crowd density (the actual number of spectators relative to the number of available seats in the stadium) and team performance in professional baseball. Agnew and Carron (1994) found a similar result in their investigation of junior hockey teams. Interestingly, in both of these studies, absolute crowd size did not matter as much. It thus appears that more filled seats gives a greater impression of fan support than does the actual number of people who show up to watch. A further analysis of professional baseball teams bolsters the argument that home teams may benefit from home fans' support by suggesting that the home field advantage is even stronger for teams who play in domed stadiums than in open-air stadiums (e.g., Horn, 1988)—what might be called the "dome field" advantage. It is interesting to note that playing in enclosed arenas may be responsible for the fact that the home field advantage in general is stronger in sports like professional basketball (which are played indoors) than in baseball (which is normally played outdoors). The increased home field advantage for teams that play indoors, and for indoor sports in general, may be due to the ability of enclosed arenas to hold more noise and give a greater impression of a supportive audience.

Disruptive Visiting Audience.   There is a flip side to this argument, however. Some theorists believe that the home field advantage is not so much the result of supportive home audiences but the result of a *disruptive visiting audience.* In other words, it is argued that playing games in a nonsupportive environment for the visiting team (a supportive environment for the home team) interferes with the visiting team's performance, while leaving the home team's performance relatively unaffected. In an interesting test of this proposal, Greer (1983) studied college basketball games and assessed the effects of sustained (fifteen or more seconds) spectator protests (e.g., booing). Specifically, Greer examined both home and away players' reactions during these "postbooing" periods—things such as scoring, turnovers, and fouls. Although subsequent to crowd protests there were slight improvements in the performance indicators of home teams (e.g., more scoring and fewer fouls), there were more significant decreases in the performance indicators for visiting teams (e.g., less scoring and more fouls). In short, crowd reactions seemed to inhibit the performances of visiting teams.

Silva and Andrew (1987) obtained analogous results in another study of college basketball. These authors demonstrated that away teams perform more poorly in terms of committing more fouls, turnovers, and a variety of other indices, such as scoring percentage. Also interesting about this study was that Silva and Andrew had previously obtained a variety of ratings made by coaches on what a good, average, and poor performance would look like. For example, coaches said that a field goal (scoring) percentage of 51.4 percent was good, one of 49.2 percent was average, and one of 46.0 percent was poor (these ratings were obtained by averaging across several coaches). On almost all measures, performances of visiting teams generally fell into the "poor" category; also noteworthy was that performances of home teams generally fell into the "average" category. As a result, Silva and Andrew concluded that the home advantage is due more to the crowd's impairing effect on the visiting team than it is due to the crowd's facilitating effect on the home team (cf. Bar-Tal & Kubzansky, 1987).

Other Factors.   It is worth mentioning that other, nonaudience factors have also been proposed to account for the home field advantage. Some of these factors include stadium familiarity, travel, biased officiating, and game rules. For example, the potential impact of *stadium familiarity* seems intuitive. Knowing all of the little nuances of your own ballpark (e.g., the potentially uncertain caroms off the "green monster" at Boston's Fenway Park) may favor the home team more than the visiting team—since home team players who practice there and who play more games there during the season would be better able to learn all of the little intricacies. Moreover, teams have been known to select players who fit their ballpark. For example, the New York Yankees have been famous over the years for selecting left-handed power hitters who can better take advantage of the short right-field wall at their stadium. Familiarity with the playing environment does not seem to totally account for the home advantage, however. For instance, we saw earlier that the home advantage effect is weakest in baseball and strongest in sports like basketball and hockey. Because professional baseball stadiums are not of standardized size and dimensions, familiarity with one's home field would seem to be particularly important. In contrast, all professional basketball and hockey arenas are of the same size and dimensions no matter where they are, and thus one might expect familiarity with one's arena to be less of an issue in these sports. But exactly the opposite appears to be the case.

The impact of *travel* has also been proposed to account for the home field advantage. There is mixed support for this argument. Several researchers have argued that travel cannot account for the home field advantage (e.g., Courneya & Carron, 1991; Edwards & Archambault, 1989; Pollard, 1986). However, it is possible that whether travel affects home performance may depend on whether teams are traveling east or west. For example, in a study of professional basketball teams, it was found that when West Coast teams traveled east for games, they scored more points and won more games than did home teams; it was argued that most games are played at about 9:00 P.M., which is 6:00 P.M. on a West Coaster's internal clock—a peak performance time (Steenland & Deppens, 1997). However, when East Coast teams travel west, the games are played at 12:00 A.M. according to an East Coaster's internal clock, a less generous time for performing. Overall, the effect of travel on home field advantage is difficult to evaluate at this point.

Even more difficult to evaluate is whether *biased officiating* is part of the home field advantage. Some evidence does suggest that officials' calls do tend to favor the home team (e.g., Greer, 1983; Lehman & Reifman, 1987). However, it should be noted that an official's decision may also be interpreted as an audience-related factor, since the decision itself may be influenced by the crowd.

Finally, the *game rules* may contribute to the home advantage. For example, in baseball and softball, the home team bats last (if needed). This gives the home team the final opportunity to strategize in a way that may allow them to win the game in the bottom of the last inning. In one study that directly tested this possibility, however, Courneya and Carron (1990) found that this particular rule did not have much impact on the ultimate outcome of the games. Thus, although each of the "other factors" that we have mentioned in this section can potentially have an impact on determining the magnitude of the home field advantage, certainly more research is needed on whether and when they affect actual game outcomes and how they interact with audience variables.

Home Field Disadvantage

Although much research has found that home teams generally perform better than visiting teams, there may actually be circumstances that lead to a reversal of this effect—what has come to be known as the *home field disadvantage*. In particular, Baumeister and Steinhilber (1984) found that in certain "defining moments" home teams tend to do more poorly. These researchers argued that when a team is close to a highly desired goal (e.g., redefining themselves as "champions"), then an increased self-focus and self-attention associated with a supportive audience may be detrimental to performance. According to Baumeister and Steinhilber, there are two mechanisms that may produce the home field disadvantage effect: (1) increased self-focus may distract one from cues or information that is necessary for optimal performance (e.g., the first baseman who is busy imagining himself in a World Series victory parade may misjudge a ball thrown to him); and

(2) increased self-attention may cause one to disrupt the execution of well-learned or automatic responses (e.g., the first baseman who begins to monitor all of the minute leg and arm muscle movements as he sets to receive the throw from second may alter the skillful execution of this task and make an error; see also Baumeister, 1984; Baumeister, Hamilton, & Tice, 1985; Baumeister & Showers, 1986).

To assess their hypotheses, Baumeister and Steinhilber (1984) examined the outcomes of baseball World Series from 1924 to 1982. They found that the home teams were victorious a little over 60 percent of the time in the first two games of the series, replicating the home field advantage effect that we described previously. However, and here is the important point, when the last game was considered, the *visiting team* was more likely to be the winner; the visiting team won about 59 percent of final games. This is in stark contrast to the home field advantage. Perhaps even more to the point, Baumeister and Steinhilber also looked at series that went the full seven games (best out of seven determines the World Series winner). Here, the home field disadvantage was even more striking. Home teams won only a little over 38 percent of seventh and final games. It was argued that these seventh games would produce the greatest amount of self-focus and self-attention, and under these conditions it seems to be the visiting team that has the advantage with a 62 percent likelihood of winning. Baumeister and Steinhilber also replicated these results in a second study using National Basketball Championships.

If there is a home field disadvantage, at least under certain conditions, why is this so? Similar to the home field advantage, researchers have attempted to address whether the home field disadvantage is due to the visiting team exhibiting improved performance or to the home team exhibiting impaired performance. As we alluded to above, Baumeister and Steinhilber (1984) proposed that it was because of impaired home team performances, what has come to be known as "choking under pressure" or the "championship choke" (see also Baumeister, 1984; Baumeister & Showers, 1986; Heaton & Sigall, 1989; Leith, 1988). To support their contention, Baumeister and Steinhilber compared the fielding errors from games 1 and 2 with the errors committed in game 7. They found that the visiting team displayed a slight tendency to commit fewer errors in the final game. However, more importantly, in support of the notion of choking under pressure, they found that home teams committed significantly more errors in the final game, which is consistent with an increased self-focus and self-attention for home teams playing in front of supportive audiences. Heaton and Sigall conducted some additional analyses of Baumeister and Steinhilber's data and further found that within the final games, home teams also have trouble maintaining the lead when ahead or gaining the lead when behind. For example, when scoring first in the seventh game, home teams held the lead only about

30 percent of the time; when they fell behind in the seventh game, home teams were able to gain the lead about only 25 percent of the time.

The home field disadvantage effect has not gone without its own challenges, however. For example, some researchers have questioned the generalizability and validity of the home field disadvantage. In particular, Courneya and Carron (1992) were critical of the Baumeister and Steinhilber (1984) and Heaton and Sigall (1989) data and noted that these data sets included only a relatively small number of games. Moreover, it is unclear how much the effect would generalize to other sports. In this regard, for example, Gayton, Matthews, and Nickless (1987) did not find a home field disadvantage in National Hockey League Championships (cf. Wright, Jackson, Christie, McGuire, & Wright, 1991). Perhaps even more to the point, Schlenker, Phillips, Boniecki, and Schlenker (1995a, 1995b) updated the Baumeister and Steinhilber data set by including World Series played in the decade following the Baumeister and Steinhilber analysis and found that the home field disadvantage was no longer present. Schlenker et al. found that home teams win about equally often early as late in the World Series.

There is an additionally intriguing aspect to Schlenker et al.'s (1995a, 1995b) analyses. Recall that Baumeister and Steinhilber (1984) proposed that the "championship choke" was due to the home team members focusing on a redefinition of themselves as champions in front of supportive audiences (e.g., having disruptive fantasies of success). However, Schlenker et al. proposed that when there is some evidence for the home team doing poorly, it is not because of thoughts about success. When choking does occur, it is associated with the anticipation of an important failure, not the distractions of possible success as suggested by Baumeister and Steinhilber. To support their arguments, for example, Schlenker et al. (1995a) found that home teams commit more errors in decisive games only after the team falls behind. It is noteworthy that this latter analysis is also consistent with some social facilitation and social loafing research in which expectations of failure have been shown to lead to impaired performance when one is under public scrutiny (e.g., Sanna, 1992; Sanna & Mark, 1995; Sanna & Pusecker, 1994; Sanna & Shotland, 1990), as was discussed in Chapters 5 and 6. In short, the interesting phenomenon of home field disadvantage will likely remain of interest to group researchers into the foreseeable future and may be fueled by some controversy over when and why it might occur (see also Baumeister, 1995; Benjafield, Liddell & Benjafield, 1989; Lewis & Linder, 1997).

Summary of Home Field Advantage and Disadvantage

The home field advantage and disadvantage are two related phenomena that have been of interest to group researchers. This setting is particularly interesting not only because the sports teams themselves can be considered a group but also because so can the audience. The home field advantage does seem to be a real and measurable phenomenon. We discussed several possible reasons why it might occur. The possibility of a home field disadvantage presents an interesting flip side to the home field advantage. It appears that the home field disadvantage may occur under certain circumstances. Whether the home field disadvantage is due to thoughts about possible success or to thoughts about possible failure is still an open question. These issues should continue to intrigue group researchers into the foreseeable future.

Sports Fans as Groups: Affiliating and Dissociating with Teams

There is another interesting dynamic that occurs with sports groups—one with a focus on the fans. Not only can supportive audiences influence the performances of their teams, as we saw in our discussion of the home field advantage and disadvantage, but the sports fans themselves often try to manipulate perceived associations with sports teams in order to try to maintain or restore a favorable impression of themselves. That people like to maintain favorable impressions, or *self-presentation,* has been described in Chapter 5. As a fan, if you can make it known that you have some kind of connection with a positively viewed team, then the argument is that by association, you may be viewed positively as well. This type of self-presentation is known as an *indirect tactic,* since it involves presenting information that is not directly about you but merely about your associations (e.g., Cialdini, 1989; Cialdini & Richardson, 1980; Richardson & Cialdini, 1981). Indirect tactics contrast with more *direct tactics* of self-presentation, in which people provide information that is directly about themselves in order to try to look good (e.g., "Did I ever tell you how great a social psychologist I am?"). We focus on how sports fans as a group may use these indirect tactics of self-presentation in order to try to manipulate the associations between themselves and their teams.

Basking in Reflected Glory

There is ample anecdotal evidence that sports fans try to manipulate the associations between themselves and their teams (see Photo 11.1). Most of us can think of times when we noticed someone or perhaps even ourselves publicly trumpeting a connection with a successful sports team. (By the way, as it happens, one of your authors has a framed Sports Illustrated cover of his beloved 1996 World Champion New York Yankees hanging in his office, and the other has a framed Sports Illustrated cover of his favorite 1997 World Champion Detroit Red Wings hanging in his office.) The strategy of *basking in reflected glory,* or *BIRGing* (the BIRG referring to Basking In Reflected Glory), or just *basking* for short, is exactly this. When basking, people are trying to

PHOTO 11.1   Basking in the reflected glory of favorite sports teams (photo by Collin Evans).

make sure to emphasize a strong connection between themselves and a successful sports team. The logic of it all is that if a sports team is viewed positively (e.g., like a champion) and you can make it known that you have a connection with that team, then by association, you may be viewed positively as well (e.g., you are also a "champion"). Note that this is true even though you are not in any way responsible for the team's successful outcome; for example, although one of your authors had dreams of playing center field for the New York Yankees as a child, he does not now currently play for the Yankees, nor for that matter, has he had time to attend a Yankee game in person to root his team on during the past decade.

In the first empirical examinations of basking, Cialdini, Borden, Thorne, Walker, Freeman, and Sloan (1976) conducted a series of studies. In a first study, the tendency of college students to bask by displaying connections with their home university was assessed. To do this, Cialdini et al. recorded three types of data on Mondays in introductory psychology courses during the 1973 college football season: (1) the number of students in class; (2) the number of students wearing apparel (e.g., hats, sweatshirts, etc.) designating their home school; and (3) the number of students wearing apparel designating other schools. This was done at several universities that had highly ranked football programs at that time. It was predicted that students would be more likely to display publicly an affiliation with their university when the school's football team had been successful the previous weekend than when it was not. This is exactly what was found. The success of the school's football team the previous Saturday predicted students' selection of apparel the following Monday. Students were more likely to wear something that alerted others to the connection with their university after wins than after losses or ties. Another interesting finding was that the degree of basking was greater the more soundly the home team beat their opponent. The greater the win, the more students trumpeted their associations.

Cialdini et al. (1976) also provided more direct support for a self-presentation interpretation of basking using a slightly different methodology. Here, it was reasoned that students would be more likely to use the pronoun "we" to describe a recent win and "non-we" pronouns, such as "they," to describe a recent loss. By using "we," people would be connecting themselves with their team—as in "We won," or "We're #1." (Anyone who has watched a college football game has probably seem this happen.) By contrast, using the pronoun "they," for example, would involve a distancing from the team—as in "They lost." To test this possibility, Cialdini et al. telephoned students and asked them to describe a recent football game. As predicted, students were in fact more likely to use "we" after wins, and "they" after losses. Moreover, this effect was even stronger for students who were given false failure feedback before being asked to describe the game. That is, some students were first told that they did poorly on a preliminary test of campus knowledge, whereas others were told they did well. Cialdini et al. argued that the tendency to bask was even stronger among those who experienced a preliminary failure, since their self-esteem may have been damaged and they thus would try to bask in order to restore their self-esteem. A number of additional studies have since replicated and extended Cialdini et al.'s initial work on basking (Burger, 1985; Cialdini & Richardson, 1980; Hirt, Zillman, Erickson, & Kennedy, 1992; Kimble & Cooper, 1992; Lee, 1985; Sloan, 1989).

Cutting Off Reflected Failure

In our discussion of basking, we alluded to the fact that not only do people like to associate themselves with a positively viewed team but they also prefer to dissociate themselves from a negatively viewed team. For example, students used "We won" but "They lost" to describe a win and loss, respectively. This latter strategy of dissociating oneself from a negatively

viewed team has come to be known as *cutting off reflected failure,* or
CORFing (the CORF referring to Cutting Off Reflected Failure). Snyder,
Lassegard, and Ford (1986) were among the first researchers to test directly
the notion of CORFing. These researchers asked participants to complete a
cognitive task after which they presented them with bogus feedback about
their performances; some participants were told they did well, some poorly,
and others were given no feedback as a control condition. After receiving
the feedback, participants were given the opportunity to take and wear
badges that identified their group membership. Consistent with the notion
of CORFing, participants were more reluctant to take badges and wear
them after receiving negative feedback because in these cases they attempted to distance themselves from an unsuccessful group (cf. Brown,
Collins, & Schmidt, 1988). Moreover, in support of basking, participants
were more willing to take and wear the badges displaying their affiliation
after their received success feedback. Thus, not only do people appear to
bask in the reflected glory of their teams but they also appear to try to distance themselves from the reflected failure of their teams. Each of these may
be part of the sports fan's strategy for self-image maintenance.

Blasting and Other Indirect Tactics

It has been theorized that both basking and CORFing may be used to foster
a sense of group membership and social identity (e.g., Cialdini & Richardson, 1980), two topics that we discussed previously in Chapter 2. However,
it is worth noting that in addition to basking and CORFing, other indirect
tactics of self-presentation have been identified. One of these is known as
blasting (Cialdini, 1989; Cialdini & Richardson, 1980). Blasting involves
denigrating a person or group in order to boost one's own self-esteem. For
example, by derogating outgroup members, a person may acquire the perception that he or she is better than the outgroup. In a demonstration of
this, Cialdini and Richardson (1980) asked university students to first complete a bogus creativity test. After this test, students were given either negative feedback (i.e., they were described as being low in creativity) or were
given no feedback. Students were then asked to rate a *rival* university. Consistent with the notion of blasting, participants gave more negative evaluations of the rival school after suffering damage to their own self-esteem (after receiving the preliminary negative feedback). Blasting may also have an
even more insidious nature, showing itself as prejudice and discrimination.
Basking, CORFing, and blasting are some indirect tactics of self-image
management that have been directly applied to sports fans. There are other
indirect tactics that have been identified as well (e.g., see Cialdini, 1989, for
a review); however, these have not yet been applied directly to fan behaviors. The variety of contexts and mechanisms by which these strategies

work (see also Cialdini & DeNicholas, 1989; Finch & Cialdini, 1989; Harrison, Struthers, & Moore, 1988) should remain important issues for researchers interested in the behaviors of sports fan groups.

Summary of Sports Fans' Affiliations with Teams

Basking and CORFing are two prominent ways in which sports fans can use indirect self-presentation strategies to attempt to maintain a positive self-image. Basking involves a fan increasing his or her association with a positively viewed team, whereas CORFing involves a fan decreasing his or her association with a negatively viewed team. Each of these tactics may have implications for a fan's sense of group membership and social identity. In addition, there are other indirect self-presentation strategies, such as blasting, that may also be used by sports fans and others that have not as yet been applied directly to sports fan behaviors. Sports fans as groups affiliating and dissociating with their teams represent another interesting dynamic that occurs with sports groups.

Chapter Summary

In this chapter, we have discussed some very specific kinds of groups. Such groups function in special environments and engage in unique kinds of tasks. Specifically, we looked at military groups, flight crews, hospital groups, and sports-related groups. We saw that all of these groups have some features that are common to many kinds of groups but that each also has some unique characteristics.

This chapter, along with the chapters on work groups, juries, and computer-based groups, demonstrates the breadth of issues that are addressed by groups researchers and the impact that groups research can have on some segments of society. Finally, it should be clear that research on the group is important in both the theoretical and applied sense and is of interest to people from a wide variety of disciplines.

Chapter Twelve

Future Directions in Group Research

We have covered a considerable range of topics in this book. We have tried to concentrate on topics for which the scientific community has accumulated a sizable amount of data. However, there are a number of other, newer issues in group research that are still largely in the conceptual stage of development. In this final chapter, we want to introduce some of these "new" issues, as well as some aspects of group research that we feel require attention. These are topics that will likely draw much research attention in the future.

The Dynamic Nature of Groups

There are many theories about aspects of groups that contain time as a component. That is, these theories argue that groups change over time, and this element of change is a factor in the phenomenon of interest. Some examples of such theories are situational leadership theory (Hersey & Blanchard, 1982), which argues that groups in different stages of development (or "maturity") need different types of leaders; the attraction-selection-attrition (or ASA) model of group performance (Katz, 1982; Schneider, 1987), which suggests that groups become more homogeneous, and thus less flexible and creative, as they mature; and the goal/expectation theory of cooperation (Pruitt & Kimmel, 1977), which argues that, upon entering into a situation of social interdependence, group members maintain a short-term focus regarding outcomes, but as time goes on, members change their focus from short-term to long-term, which then leads to increased rates of cooperation.

Dynamical theories of group processes tend to be well received by the scientific community perhaps because time-based changes in groups seem intuitively logical. Most of us can think of group experiences that we have had in which the group has "naturally" altered over time, and many other group variables clearly must have some connection to time (e.g., cohesion). However, data that are directed toward the actual testing of dynamic group theories are sparse. This is undoubtedly due in some part to the logistic difficulties in conducting longitudinal group research. The time-based processes that these theories address unfold over a long period of time, much longer than a laboratory group could reasonably expect to be kept intact. Hence, research on dynamic factors needs to be conducted with real groups. However, there are many difficulties associated with conducting field research on groups, not the least of which is gaining access to such groups. (See the Methodological Appendix for an expanded discussion of field research.) In addition to the logistic issues, it is also the case that social psychologists have historically favored static theories of behavior, under which isolated actions, independent of context, are modeled, over dynamic theories, which address behaviors within larger systems (McGrath, 1988; Messick & Liebrand, 1997). Messick and Liebrand (1997) argue strongly that researchers who are interested in generalization of their results to real-world issues need to consider the role of dynamics. An intervention that seems likely to be effective from a static point of view may not look so good from the dynamic viewpoint. As an example, they describe the provision of rewards for cooperative behavior. Static theories suggest that such an intervention will immediately increase the frequency of cooperation, but over time these rewards may produce an upward shift in the reference point that a person uses to evaluate outcomes, which ultimately would lead to the bonus losing its attractiveness and motivational properties.

There is increasing evidence, however, that longitudinal research on groups is growing in popularity. Methodologically, researchers have begun developing data collection techniques that circumvent the need for subjects to be continually observed by the experimenter. These methods require subjects to maintain daily diaries in which they record their actions at either regular (Robinson, 1988) or randomly selected (Marco & Suls, 1993) intervals. Philosophically, theorists are beginning to demonstrate how a dynamic systems approach can be integrated into social-psychological research (Vallacher & Nowak, 1997). Given these developments, it seems likely that studies of groups over time will appear with increasing frequency in the near future.

Group Information Processing

By now, students of decisionmaking processes have documented a host of judgmental biases and inaccuracies that are committed by individuals and by groups. As we discussed in Chapter 4, the question of whether groups are more, or less, accurate judges than isolated individuals has a long history in social psychology. However, the number of studies that have directly compared individuals against groups is surprisingly small. In conducting a comprehensive review of the literature, Kerr, MacCoun, and Kramer (1996) found less than thirty studies that made such comparisons, and the structures of the studies, in terms of factors like decision task and experimental procedure, differed so widely that Kerr et al. were unable to conduct any kind of statistical aggregation analysis (e.g., meta-analysis) that would combine results across studies and allow for general conclusions to be drawn. Instead, Kerr et al. relied on social decision scheme analysis (SDS) to demonstrate that, depending on a variety of factors, groups can be either more or less biased than individuals.

In conducting this analysis, Kerr et al. demonstrated how little is known about how group members use and aggregate information. In fact, they argued that this issue is one of the most fundamental in the field of group research. Related to this, Hinsz, Tindale, and Vollrath (1997) have demonstrated how groups can be conceived of, and studied as, information processors, much as individual information processing phenomena are studied by cognitive psychologists. Hinsz et al. describe a number of ways in which theoretical perspectives from cognitive psychology and human communications research could be applied to the study of group processes. Some of these approaches have already been initiated. For example, research is emerging on collective mental models (e.g., Klimoski & Mohammed, 1994; Wegner, Erber, & Raymond, 1991; Weick & Roberts, 1993) and group-level learning (Argote, 1993; Liang, Moreland, & Argote, 1995) that is drawing on cognitive psychological theories of mental processes. It seems, then, that a focus on the collective use of information and the strengthening of connections between cognitive psychology and group research will only increase in the future.

Groups and Social Cognition

Social psychologists are increasingly concerned about a gap that seems to be forming between group researchers and researchers of social cognition. Although there are many reasons why such a gap would be of concern, a primary reason is that researchers in each interest area can draw upon the other to gain insights. On the social cognitive side, theorists have argued that the research is losing its "social" component, focusing strictly on cognitive processes (e.g., memory) at the expense of the social context in which it occurs (Ickes & Gonzalez, 1994; Levine, Resnick, & Higgins, 1993). On the groups side, the argument is that social cognitive processes may well influence the means by which groups use information and make decisions. For example, Hinsz et al. (1997) argue for the importance of emotion and affect in group processes because these factors have been clearly identified as influences on individual information processing (see Bodenhausen, Kramer, & Susser, 1994, and Gannon, Skowronski, & Betz, 1994, for examples). The few studies on emotion in groups that have been conducted support Hinsz et al.'s assertion. Brandstatter and Hoggatt (1982) demonstrated that emotion can have an impact on the success of two-person negotiation, in that agreements were reached more quickly when negotiators were in positive moods as opposed to negative moods. In a series of studies, George (1989, 1990, 1991; George & Bettenhausen, 1990; George & James, 1993; George & Jones, 1996) has found mood to be connected to a host of group-related workplace behaviors. To cite just a couple of examples, she found that individuals with the same mood temperament (i.e., the mood the person is typically in—good or bad) tended to work together and that withdrawal from the group was less common when the prevailing mood within the group was positive or when the group leader's mood was generally positive. There also seems to be a connection between prevailing mood and performance, as sales clerks within negative-mood work groups tended to engage in few positive customer-related acts.

George's work clearly demonstrates the value of combining social cognitive research with group research. There are many other social-cognitive variables that might also interplay with group processes. For example, researchers have begun studying the effects of group discussion on attributions (Wittenbaum & Stasser, 1995; Wright, Luus, & Christie, 1990), the impact of group membership on the self-concept (Trafimow, Triandis, & Goto, 1991; Triandis, 1989), relationships between person perception and social interdependence (Pendry & Macrae, 1994), and the influence of schematic information processing on conflict resolution (Pinkley, 1990).

Electronic Performance Monitoring

Organizations are increasingly using electronic performance monitoring to oversee the performance of workers. Typically, such monitoring involves electronic recording of the worker's performance at random intervals, followed by a supervisor's reviewing of the recording. An important question to ask is, does electronic monitoring affect work performance? The electronic monitor can be conceived of as a type of audience, in that it allows other members of the organization to eventually observe an individual's performance. We saw in Chapter 5 that the presence of an audience can influence individual behavior via social facilitation, and in fact, research on electronic performance monitoring suggests that it also produces facilitation effects—talented workers tend to work faster, and untalented workers slower, when their performances are electronically monitored (Aiello &

Kolb, 1995). Further, workers who are electronically monitored experience high levels of stress from the monitoring (Aiello & Kolb, 1995; DiTecco, Cwitco, Arsenault, & Andre, 1992; Nebeker & Tatum, 1993; Smith, Carayon, Sanders, Lim, & LeGrande, 1992). These studies suggest some interesting follow-up questions, particularly regarding the role of evaluation in social facilitation, that could both help clear up some of the controversies surrounding social facilitation that we discussed in Chapter 5 and help gain additional insight into the influences on work group behavior.

Evaluation of Group
Improvement Interventions

A theme that echoes fairly loudly throughout this book is the notion that groups really do not perform that well, given the amount of resources that are at group members' disposal. It is certainly important to document shortcomings of the group, but it is also important to address the question of how to improve groups. This is hardly a novel idea; as we noted in Chapter 8, a number of supposedly performance-enhancing interventions and approaches, particularly in the management realm, have been advocated over the years, but these interventions and approaches have almost invariably been shown to not work as advertised. Unfortunately, what seems to happen after the negative results come in is wholesale abandonment of the intervention. A prominent example of this is the quality circle. As we mentioned in Chapter 8, research really does not support the quality circle as an effective group decisionmaking tool. Perhaps as a result, companies have largely abandoned the quality circle in favor of other approaches (e.g., Total Quality Management). Unfortunately, what is not clear from the research is whether quality circles have failed because they are inherently flawed or because they have been improperly implemented by organizations (e.g., Tang, Tollison, & Whiteside, 1991). If the former is the case, then it may well be appropriate to abandon the quality circle, but if the latter is true, then the quality circle is being rejected before it gets a fair chance.

Program evaluation is a systematic approach to the determination of whether some program is functioning as it should. A proper program evaluation involves both evaluation of the various components of the program and revision of those elements of the program that do not seem to "work" (Sechrest & Figueredo, 1993). What typically has been the practice of researchers, however, is to conduct the evaluation and leave the revision to others, often those for whom the evaluation was conducted. However, Sechrest and Figueredo (1993) argue that such revisions are usually not conducted, resulting in continued use of flawed programs or abandonment of a program that could work well if modified. Those researchers who are interested in group improvement would do well to adopt a more formal program evaluative approach to the study of group interventions.

Concluding Thoughts

The goal of this book is to provide an introduction to the field of group research. By no means should it be considered a complete, all-inclusive reference work. Rather, we view it as a sourcebook that can provide a starting point for anyone who is interested in some aspect of group performance or interaction within groups. We have also tried to demonstrate the vitality and broad applicability of group research and to identify connections between academic fields that previously were not apparent. Although group research is no longer as strongly concentrated within social psychology as it once was, we feel that, if anything, it is a more popular field of inquiry now than it ever has been, and we hope that we have conveyed that enthusiasm.

Appendix:
Methodological Issues
in Groups Research

The purpose of this appendix is to give the reader a feel for how groups researchers collect and analyze data. Relative to individual-based research, groups research is often quite difficult to conduct, both in terms of procedure and analysis. Further, groups research has too often been conducted in a sloppy manner (Gigone & Hastie, 1997), so an understanding of the methodological and analytical issues underlying the research is important. Our discussion is largely nontechnical, although it presumes that the reader has had undergraduate introductory courses in statistics and methodology.

Procedural Issues in Groups Research

It is difficult to execute a groups study. Some of the difficulties are inherent in the nature of groups research itself, while other problems are peculiar to particular research questions within the groups field. In this section, we review many of the factors that a groups researcher must consider during the design of an experiment. These are certainly not all of the potential snags that one can run into, but rather they are the most common ones.

Subjects

In a groups study, the *group,* not the individual, is typically the unit of analysis. What this means is that at some point, we are going to assess and analyze some collectively produced variable. If we are studying group decisionmaking, for example, we may or may not care what each group member's personal preference is, but we definitely need to know what those members *as a group* advocate. The problem is that when we recruit study subjects, we are recruiting individual group members, and so we need more than one subject to get just one piece of data. If we are going to design a

209

study that has any statistical power whatsoever, we are going to need a fairly large number of groups. The end result is that groups research is very draining on a pool of study participants.

Consider this simple example. Let's say you have a 2 x 2 between-subjects design, which means that you have four possible combinations of treatments, and a subject is going to experience just one of those combinations. You want to study individual decisionmaking, so the person is the unit of analysis, and each person is one data point. You'd like to have 15 replications per cell. That means you need a total of 4 x 15 = 60 data points. If each person is a data point, then this translates into a need for 60 subjects to complete your study.

Now let's say you want to repeat the study, except now you want to research group decisionmaking. Specifically, you want to study four-person groups. You again want 15 replications, so you'll need a total of 60 data points. However, now the group is the unit of analysis. In other words, in your study it takes four persons to produce one data point. How many subjects do you need now? The answer is, you need 60 data points x 4 persons per point = 240 subjects, which is four times as many people as you needed to conduct your study of individuals.

It can be seen that to conduct a study that contains just the statistically bare minimum number of replications, one is going to need a quite large number of participants. This need for large numbers of subjects can make it difficult for the researcher at a small college, or for the graduate student who has only limited access to a subject pool, to conduct groups research. Hence, before embarking on a groups research program, a researcher needs to make sure that he or she has regular access to a large number of study subjects.

Simulation

Some groups researchers have suggested that the problem of small subject pools can be circumvented by making use of mathematical and computer simulations of groups (Davis & Kerr, 1986). We talked in Chapter 10 about simulated groups as a particular kind of research topic and explored the kinds of conclusions that can be drawn from studies of simulated groups. A more technical variant of the basic simulated group is a simulated group that has been created by means of "bootstrapping." Bootstrapping involves random assemblage of a large number of groups from a pool of individuals (Efron & Gong, 1983). The individuals may be either real or hypothetical, and sampling is done with replacement. For example, assume that you have individual preference data for 120 people. What you can do is treat them as a single 120-member subject pool. You can randomly select six people from this pool, aggregate their preferences in some fashion to produce a single group decision, and return the six to the pool. With replacement, there are a huge number of possible six-person groups that you can assemble (well over

500 million). Thus, you can repeat this process a large number of times (say, 1000), and you will end up with normative data regarding what the distribution of group preferences would look like if a large number of randomly assembled groups were all using the same particular decision process.

Laboratory Space

Groups research also places demands on laboratory size. Individual research can be conducted in rooms that are little more than cubicles, but a groups study requires a room that can offer comfortable seating to a number of people. If some kind of analysis of group interaction is desired, then the room must also be equipped with audio or video recording equipment. Further, the equipment needs to be discreetly placed, as having a microphone or video camera in plain sight can make group members self-conscious and may inhibit their responses. Discreet placing of a camera is often accomplished by means of a one-way mirror, while a microphone may be located at the side of the room, under a table, or suspended from the ceiling. Some researchers who do not have access to a large laboratory instead use a classroom as the research site, but such factors as windows and hall noise can affect the construct validity of the study by distracting subjects.

It is important for the researcher to actually test whether the laboratory can accommodate the number of people in the group. One of your authors once wanted to do a study of six-person groups, but the only room to which he had access was fairly small. However, he was able to fit six desks in the room, and so he assumed that the lab space would work. What he failed to recognize was that he had gotten the desks in the room by lining them up right next to each other, and he had grossly underestimated how much additional space people would need for leg room, arm movements, and so on. After his first group of six seated themselves and shifted the desks to accommodate their arms and legs, there was literally no floor space left for him to enter the room, so that session had to be aborted (with all of the students receiving credit for participation). In the second session, he told group members that they could not move the desks. He now had space in which to walk around, but after about ten minutes two people complained that they were so uncomfortable that it was impossible for them to work. He stopped that session and in fact terminated the experiment. Had he simply asked six people to sit in the lab before he started the study, he would have discovered that the room was not large enough, and he would not have wasted the time of twelve students (and himself).

Field Research

We have noted in many places throughout this book the difficulty of conducting research on actual groups. For example, we are legally prohibited from observing an actual jury. Many other groups, such as boards of directors, are typically quite hesitant to allow outside observers, often out of fear that the observer will obtain privileged information. Some types of groups, such as flight crews and hospital teams, must be studied in the field, but in general groups research has been typified by the laboratory experiment. Given that there are a large number of variables that can influence real, but not laboratory, groups (e.g., incentives, ramifications of a poor decision), this inability to work in the field has been unfortunate.

Field work that has been done has often been the result of a fortuitous set of circumstances rather than careful planning on the part of the experimenter. For example, Plott and Levine (1978) demonstrated that the mere ordering of items on an agenda can influence the eventual outcome of a group decision by studying a group of flying enthusiasts who were going to purchase a new airplane and were considering a number of different models. Plott happened to be a member of this club, and he had the power to decide the order in which pairs of airplanes would be considered. Even what is probably the most famous groups field study, the Robbers Cave study of groups of boys at a summer camp (Sherif, Harvey, White, Hood, & Sherif, 1961), was less of a true field study than it seems. The researchers did not simply take advantage of a summer camp population: Each of the boys had been carefully selected by the experimenters to ensure that the group contained a particular mix of personalities, backgrounds, and abilities. Hence, Robbers Cave was less a study of real groups and more a study of concocted groups in a realistic setting.

It is fairly common for field researchers to use as real groups a class of students. Such a group has assembled more or less at random and is a group in which real incentives exist. For example, Michaelsen, Watson, and Black (1989) constructed task-oriented subgroups out of a class of business students and gave the subgroups weekly assignments to complete. Such groups are certainly subject to some of the real-world influences that groups face, but the classroom approach suffers from a number of serious methodological problems, most notably lack of an independent control group against which the task groups can be compared (Tindale & Larson, 1992). A more promising approach to the use of classes as real groups has recently been developed by McGrath (1993). He and his colleagues have created a classroom paradigm that retains many of the features of real groups and that is conducted as a typical class is conducted, yet it allows for systematic comparison of subgroups who have experienced different types of interventions and for the examination of changes across time within subgroups.

Statistical Issues in Groups Research

A groups study can be challenging to execute, and the analysis of the data can be tricky as well. This applies both to how we define the data points and to the actual statistical techniques that we use. In this section, we look at some of the analytical issues.

Data Coding

Usually there is no question as to what constitutes a piece of data. Group members may choose one specific option from many possible options, provide a numerical estimate of some quantity, or perform some task at a level or rate that is easily measured. But what if we are interested in group interaction? How can we measure and analyze group process? This is a tricky question that has not really been answered to the satisfaction of many groups researchers.

The conversion of group process information into analyzable data is known as coding. This process usually involves two steps: identification of a coding scheme for conversion of the data, and application of that scheme by outside individuals. It is the first part, identification of the coding scheme, that remains troubling to many groups researchers. Sometimes the scheme is a simple one: Listen to an audiotaped group discussion and count how many times group members mention Topic X, for example. But more often the coding scheme requires us to interpret some statement or action, and it is this interpretive aspect of coding that has been so controversial.

Imagine that you are watching a videotape of a group discussion. You notice that, in the middle of making a point, the speaker suddenly shifts her body so that she is close to the person on her left. Why did she do this? Was this body movement an attempt to win the approval of the person on her left (by getting physically close to that person), or were the speaker's legs starting to fall asleep? What about the person who gestures while talking? Are those gestures serving a specific purpose? How about tone of voice, rate of speech, and loudness of speech? Many group process researchers feel that such nonverbal actions are an important part of group process, but how do we analyze such actions? This question has long intrigued groups researchers. The first attempt to develop a coding scheme for the analysis of the nonverbal part of group interaction was undertaken by Bales (1950), who developed a scheme called interaction process analysis (IPA). Basically, Bales argued that all actions undertaken within a group serve one of two purposes: moving the group toward task completion (Bales called this *instrumental* concern) or maintaining the interrelationships between group members (*expressive* concern). He further argued that an action has one of two valences: positive/active or negative/passive. He combined these two features (purpose and valence) to come up with four different types of behaviors: positive-expressive, negative-expressive, active-instrumental, and passive-instrumental. He then used these four types to develop a coding system of twelve categories that could be used to interpret every action that occurs within a group. These categories are shown in Table A.1.

TABLE A.1   Bales's (1950) Interaction Process Analysis (IPA) Coding System

Valence/Function	Instrumental	Expressive
Positive/active	Gives suggestion	Shows solidarity
	Gives opinion	Shows tension release
	Gives orientation	Agrees
Negative/passive	Asks for suggestion	Shows antagonism
	Asks for opinion	Shows tension
	Asks for opinion	Disagrees

On the face of it, the IPA system is quite easy to use. One simply observes an action within a group and determines to which of the twelve categories it belongs. (Bales assumed that the categories were mutually exclusive and exhaustive.) And in fact, IPA was a popular research tool throughout the 1950s and much of the 1960s. However, it has also been criticized on many grounds. Some critics feel that the categories are much too general and that the system relies too heavily on the interpretive skills of the researcher (McGrath, 1984). For example, consider the statement "Are you sure about that?" This could be interpreted either as an indication of disagreement ("I don't think you're right") or as a request for orientation ("Could you explain why you think this?"). The IPA system forces the researcher to place this statement into just one category, but it is going to be up to the researcher to decide whether the speaker's intent was disagreement or orientation. This problem alone is severe enough that IPA is no longer a commonly used tool for interaction coding. In addition, IPA now seems to be theoretically questionable, as recent empirical analyses have been largely unable to reproduce the twelve categories (Allen, Comerford, & Ruhe, 1989).

Despite the problems with IPA, researchers who are interested in group interaction processes continue to search for a useful coding scheme. Many have been developed of late. Bales himself revised IPA into a more detailed coding system called SYMLOG (Bales & Cohen, 1979). This system is much more detailed but also extremely complex, and to date it has not been used as heavily as might be expected. Many other coding systems exist that have not yet received enough research attention for us to be able to evaluate their worth. These include TEMPO (Futoran, Kelly, & McGrath, 1989), speech act classification schemes (Wish, D'Andrade, & Goodnow, 1980), verbal response mode analysis (VRM) (Stiles, 1978), pattern variable coding (PVC) (Mabry, 1975), and RELCOM (Fisher & Drecksel, 1983). Note that all of these systems require the researcher to do some kind of interpretation of interaction. Because it is the interpretive aspect of the systems that causes concern for some theorists, the researcher who uses any of these needs to be prepared to defend his or her use of the system.

Regardless of whether we are using an interpretation-based coding scheme, such as those just described, or a simple counting of the frequencies with which various topics are mentioned, it is necessary to have naive experimental assistants, who are unaware of the purpose of the study, do the actual coding. These people are known as *blind coders;* by being unaware of the study's goals they are objective about whether a questionable piece of data (i.e., a piece of data that may or may not belong in the final data set) should be included for analysis. Coders need to receive extensive training with the coding system, even if they are to just count statements. Two blind coders should each independently code the entire data set, and then we can compare each coder's data set against the other to see if they coded the data points in the same ways. Consider again the statement "Are you sure about that?" What we need to know is, did each coder interpret this statement in the same way? If so, then there is no question how we should treat that piece of data, but if the coders disagree, then we must make a decision about what to do with the data point. We hope that there is little, or no, disagreement between coders.

We can actually measure the extent to which the coders agree with each other by obtaining a numerical estimate of the *reliability* of the coders. Reliability is measured on a scale from 0 to 1.00, with zero meaning that there was absolutely no agreement between the two coders (i.e., there was not one data point that was interpreted in the same way by the two coders), and one indicating perfect agreement (i.e., every single data point was interpreted the same way by both coders). We wouldn't expect to see a reliability of 1.00, but a value in the 0.90s is certainly reasonable, and in fact is often the norm. If our reliability is in this range, then we can just discard any data point that was interpreted in different ways by our two coders (there will be very few) and keep the rest. A reliability below about 0.80 is cause for serious concern because it suggests that there is a fair amount of disagreement between our two coders. If the reliability value is still fairly large, we may want to bring in a third coder, but if the reliability is quite bad, then we have probably either done a poor job of training the coders or have used a poor coding scheme. In either situation, the best thing to do is rectify the problem and start over with a new pair of coders.

Data Analysis

We of course must to do some kind of formal analysis of the data. But what techniques should we use? In many situations, standard inferential statistics (analysis of variance, regression) will suffice, but there are a number of groups problems that cannot easily be analyzed with such statistics. For these problems, theorists have developed some special analytical techniques. Our review serves simply as an introduction. If you would like to use any of these techniques in your own research, you should seek out the references that we cite in order to gain a complete understanding of how they work.

Qualitative Analysis.   Qualitative analysis is a tool for analyzing the content of interactions. It is commonly used in anthropology to analyze things like differences in conversational patterns between various cultural subgroups. However, it can also be applied to the study of within-group interaction. Qualitative analysis involves description of patterns within the discourse by means of coding statements into various categories. So, for example, we might look to see if group members make a greater number of group-maintenance statements during periods of within-group conflict than when there is no conflict. Qualitative analysis is often a quite laborious strategy to use. The initial work of developing the code categories can be very difficult, and then one must read and classify a potentially huge number of statements, depending on how many groups are being studied, the length and depth of conversations, and so on. There are now, however, a large number of computer programs that can simplify qualitative analysis (see Weitzman & Miles, 1995, for a summary of these programs), so this is not as great a concern as it once was, but the analysis can still be quite demanding even after use of a computer program. There is also concern among some researchers about the subjective nature of qualitative analysis, in that the researcher (or, more accurately, blind coders) must decide into which category a statement should be placed. It is beyond our scope to evaluate this argument, but Miller and Dingwall (1997) cover this issue in detail. If you would like to know more about qualitative analysis, an excellent sourcebook is Miles and Huberman (1994).

Pseudogroup and Hierarchical Analysis.   There are many groups questions for which the researcher might like to use a basic inferential test, such as ANOVA, but should not because one or more assumptions have been violated. For example, one might be interested in how the experience of group membership affects individual preferences or beliefs. The problem is that discussion of the issue within the group will likely render the individual preferences nonindependent of one another, which violates the ANOVA requirement of independence of observations. How can we handle this problem? Myers, DiCecco, and Lorch (1981) have devised a technique in which group member preferences are compared against preferences of individuals who have not participated in a group. We cannot simply analyze such data with a traditional ANOVA, with "group membership" being treated as an independent variable, because the data points in the "group" condition will not be independent of one another. Instead, Myers et al. have derived a "pseudogroup" F-ratio statistic for which the error term and degrees of freedom have been adjusted to account for the nonindependence within the "group" condition. The pseudogroup analysis is ideally suited for designs in which the number of individuals in the "individual" condition (N) is a multiple of the number of groups in the "group" condition (g). When N is not evenly divisible by g, Myers et al. suggest using a "quasi-F" statistic, which is a variant of the pseudogroup F-ratio.

Kenny and La Voie (1985) have taken a slightly different approach and advocate a hierarchical analysis technique that involves assessing both individual- and group-level correlations between variables and testing these correlations for evidence of nonindependence. If there is variance at both the individual and group levels (which there often will be), we can then derive some adjusted correlations for each level that account for there being variance at the other level. These adjusted correlations can then be directly compared against each other to give us an indication of how strong a particular relationship is at both the individual and group levels.

Note that each technique is designed for just those situations in which individual-level data is collected from members of an interacting group. They are not applicable to situations in which individual efforts are aggregated into a single group product.

Social Relations Modeling. Social relations modeling is a fairly complex statistical technique for producing theoretical "networks" of interrelations between members of a group. These networks provide a picture of which members most heavily interact with which other members, the frequency of interaction being reflected in coefficients that are assigned to each path in the network—the larger the coefficient, the more frequent the interaction between the two people who are connected by the path. The technique is based in part on cluster analysis, which is a method for identifying subgroups of individuals such that each member of the subgroup responded in a similar way to a stimulus, but the response that characterizes that subgroup differs from that seen in other subgroups (Arabie & Hubert, 1992). Network analysis is particularly useful for the study of group interaction and communication networks, although it has many other potential applications, such as to the study of influence patterns (Mizruchi, 1994). A good nontechnical introduction to the technique is provided by Scott (1992); researchers who plan to use network analysis as their regular mode of analysis will prefer Wasserman and Faust (1994).

References

Abrahamson, E. (1996). Management fashion. *Academy of Management Review, 21,* 254–285.

Abramson, J.S. (1989). Making teams work. *Social Work with Groups, 12,* 45–63.

Acker, J.R. (1990). Social science in Supreme Court criminal cases and briefs: The actual and potential contribution of social scientists as amici curaie. *Law and Human Behavior, 14,* 25–42.

Adams, J.S. (1963). Toward an understanding of inequity. *Journal of Abnormal and Social Psychology, 67,* 422–436.

Adams, J.S. (1965). Inequity in social exchange. *Advances in Experimental Social Psychology, 2,* 267–299.

Adams, J.S., & Jacobsen, P.R. (1964). Effects of wage inequities on work quality. *Journal of Abnormal and Social Psychology, 69,* 19–25.

Adrianson, L., & Hjelmquist, E. (1991). Group processes in face-to-face and computer-mediated communication. *Behaviour and Information Technology, 10,* 281–296.

Agnew, G.A., & Carron, A.V. (1994). Crowd effects and the home advantage. *International Journal of Sport Psychology, 25,* 53–62.

Ahern, T.C. (1993). The effect of a graphic interface on participation, interaction, and student achievement in a computer-mediated small-group discussion. *Journal of Educational Computing Research, 9,* 535–548.

Aiello, J.R., & Kolb, K.J. (1995). Electronic performance monitoring and social context: Impact on productivity and stress. *Journal of Applied Psychology, 80,* 339–353.

Aiken, M.W., & Chrestman, M. (1995). Electronic meeting systems. *Journal for Quality and Participation, 18,* 98–101.

Aiken, M.W., Krosp, J., Shirani, A.I., & Martin, J.S. (1994). Electronic brainstorming in small and large groups. *Information and Management, 27,* 141–149.

Aiken, M.W., & Martin, J.S. (1994). Enhancing business communication with group decision support systems. *Bulletin of the Association for Business Communication, 57*(3), 24–26.

Aiken, M.W., Martin, J.S., Paolillo, J.G.P., & Shirani, A.I. (1994). A group decision support system for multilingual groups. *Information and Management, 26,* 155–161.

Aiken, M.W., Vanjani, M., & Krosp, J. (1995). Group decision support systems. *Review of Business, 16*(3), 38–42.

Aiken, M.W., Vanjani, M., & Paolillo, J.G.P. (1996). A comparison of two electronic idea generation techniques. *Information and Management, 30,* 91–99.

Allen, W.R., Comerford, R.A., & Ruhe, J.A. (1989). Factor analytic study of Bales' Interaction Process Analysis. *Educational and Psychological Measurement, 49,* 701–707.

Allison, S.T., McQueen, L.R., & Schaerfl, L.M. (1992). Social decision making processes and the equal partitionment of shared resources. *Journal of Experimental Social Psychology, 28,* 23–42.

Allison, S.T., & Messick, D.M. (1985). Effects of experience on performance in a replenishable resource trap. *Journal of Personality and Social Psychology, 49,* 943–948.

Allison, S.T., & Messick, D.M. (1990). Social decision heuristics in the use of shared resources. *Journal of Behavioral Decision Making, 3,* 195–204.

Allport, F.H. (1920). The influence of the group upon association and thought. *Journal of Experimental Psychology, 3,* 159–182.

Allport, F.H. (1924). *Social psychology.* Boston: Houghton Mifflin.

Anderson, M.D. (1996). Using computer conferencing and electronic mail to facilitate group projects. *Journal of Educational Technology and Systems, 24,* 113–127.

Anderson, N.H. (1968a). Likableness ratings of 555 personality-trait words. *Journal of Social Psychology, 9,* 272–279.

Anderson, N.H. (1968b). A simple model for information integration. In R.P. Abelson, E. Aronson, W.J. McGuire, T.M. Newcomb, M.J. Rosenberg, & P.H. Tannenbaum (Eds.), *Theories of cognitive consistency* (pp. 731–743). Chicago: Rand McNally.

Anthony, T., Cooper, C., & Mullen, B. (1992). Cross-racial facial identification: A social cognitive integration. *Personality and Social Psychology Bulletin, 18,* 296–301.

Arabie, P., & Hubert, L.J. (1992). Combinatorial data analysis. *Annual Review of Psychology, 43,* 169–203.

Archer, N.P. (1990). A comparison of computer conferences with face-to-face meetings for small group business decisions. *Behaviour and Information Technology, 9,* 307–317.

Argote, L. (1993). Group and organizational learning curves: Individual, system, and environmental components. *British Journal of Social Psychology, 32,* 31–52.

Arkin, R.M., & Burger, J.M. (1980). Effects of unit relation tendencies on interpersonal attraction. *Social Psychology Quarterly, 43,* 380–391.

Aronson, E., & Linder, D. (1965). Gain and loss of esteem as determinants of interpersonal attractiveness. *Journal of Experimental Social Psychology, 1,* 156–171.

Arrow, H. (1997). Stability, bistability, and instability in small group influence patterns. *Journal of Personality and Social Psychology, 72,* 75–85.

Arunachalam, V., & Dilla, W.N. (1995). Judgment accuracy and outcomes in negotiation: A causal modeling analysis of decision-aiding effects. *Organizational Behavior and Human Decision Processes, 61,* 289–304.

Asch, S.E. (1951). Effects of group pressure upon the modification and distortion of judgments. In H. Guetzkow (Ed.), *Groups, leadership, and men* (pp. 177–190). Pittsburgh, PA: Carnegie Press.

Atwater, L.E., & Yammarino, F.J. (1993). Personal attributes as predictors of superiors' and subordinates' perceptions of military academy leadership. *Human Relations, 46,* 645–668.

Austin, W., McGinn, N.C., & Susmilch, C. (1980). Internal standards revisited: The effects of social comparisons and expectancies on judgments of fairness and satisfaction. *Journal of Experimental Social Psychology, 16,* 426–441.

Axelrod, R. (1984). *The evolution of cooperation.* New York: Basic Books.

Ayman, R., Chemers, M.M., & Fiedler, F. (1995). The contingency model of leadership effectiveness: Its level of analysis. *Leadership Quarterly, 6,* 147–167.

Bair, J.P., & Greenspan, B.K. (1986). TEAMS: Teamwork training for interns, residents, and nurses. *Hospital and Community Psychiatry, 37,* 633–635.

Baird, J.E. (1977). *The dynamics of organizational communication.* New York: Harper & Row.

Baker, D.P., & Salas, E. (1992). Principles for measuring teamwork skills. *Human Factors, 34,* 469–475.

Bales, R.F. (1950). *Interaction process analysis.* Cambridge, MA: Addison-Wesley.

Bales, R.F., & Cohen, S.P. (1979). *SYMLOG: A system for the multilevel observation of groups.* New York: Free Press.

Bandura, A. (1986). *Social foundations of thought and action.* Englewood Cliffs, NJ: Prentice-Hall.

Bantel, K.A., & Jackson, S.E. (1989). Top management and innovations in banking: Does composition of the top teams make a difference? *Strategic Management Journal, 10,* 107–124.

Barker, J.M., Clothier, C.C., Woody, J.R., & McKinney, E.H. (1996). Crew resource management: A simulator study comparing fixed versus formed aircrew. *Aviation, Space, and Environment Medicine, 67,* 3–7.

Barnes, S., & Greller, L.M. (1994). Computer-mediated communication in the organization. *Communication Education, 43,* 129–142.

Baron, J.N., & Pfeffer, J. (1994). The social psychology of organizations and inequality. *Social Psychology Quarterly, 57,* 190–209.

Baron, R.S. (1986). Distraction-conflict theory: Progress and problems. *Advances in Experimental Social Psychology, 19,* 1–40.

Baron, R.S., Moore, D.L., & Sanders, G.S. (1978). Distraction as a source of drive in social facilitation research. *Journal of Personality and Social Psychology, 36,* 816–824.

Bar-Tal, Y., & Kubzansky, P.E. (1987). Resident advantage as social role performance. *British Journal of Psychology, 26,* 147–154.

Bartis, S., Szymanski, K., & Harkins, S.G. (1988). Evaluation and performance: A two-edged knife. *Personality and Social Psychology Bulletin, 14,* 242–251.

Bass, B.M. (1985). Leadership: Good, better, best. *Organizational Dynamics, 14,* 26–40.

Bat-Chava, Y. (1994). Group identity and self-esteem of deaf adults. *Personality and Social Psychology Bulletin, 20,* 494–502.

Baumeister, R.F. (1982). A self-presentational view of social phenomena. *Psychological Bulletin, 91,* 3–26.

Baumeister, R.F. (1984). Choking under pressure: Self-consciousness and paradoxical effects of incentives on skillful performance. *Journal of Personality and Social Psychology, 46,* 610–620.

Baumeister, R.F. (1995). Disputing the effects of championship pressures and home audiences. *Journal of Personality and Social Psychology, 68,* 644–648.

Baumeister, R.F., Hamilton, J.C., & Tice, D.M. (1985). Public versus private expectancy of success: Confidence booster or performance pressure? *Journal of Personality and Social Psychology, 48,* 1447–1457.

Baumeister, R.F., & Showers, C.J. (1986). A review of paradoxical performance effects: Choking under pressure in sports and mental tests. *European Journal of Social Psychology, 16,* 361–383.

Baumeister, R.F., & Steinhilber, A. (1984). Paradoxical effects of supportive audiences on performance under pressure: The home field disadvantage in sports championships. *Journal of Personality and Social Psychology, 47,* 85–93.

Beatty, M.J., & Payne, S.K. (1983). Speech anxiety as a multiplicative function of size of audience and social desirability. *Perceptual and Motor Skills, 56,* 792–794.

Bell, P.A., Petersen, T.R., & Hautaluoma, J.E. (1989). The effect of punishment probability on overconsumption and stealing in a simulated commons. *Journal of Applied Social Psychology, 19,* 1483–1495.

Benjafield, J., Liddell, W.W., & Benjafield, I. (1989). Is there a home field disadvantage in professional sports championships? *Social Behavior and Personality, 17,* 45–50.

Berger, J., Webster, M., Ridgeway, C., & Rosenholtz, S.J. (1986). Status cues, expectations, and behavior. *Advances in Group Processes, 3,* 1–22.

Bernstein, M., & Crosby, F.J. (1980). An empirical investigation of relative deprivation theory. *Journal of Experimental Social Psychology, 16,* 442–456.

Bernthal, P.R., & Insko, C.A. (1993). Cohesiveness without groupthink: The interactive effects of social and task cohesion. *Group and Organization Management, 18,* 66–87.

Berteotti, C.R., & Seibold, D.R. (1994). Coordination and role-definition problems in health-care teams: A hospice case study. In L.R. Frey (Ed.), *Group communication in context* (pp. 107–131). Hillsdale, NJ: Erlbaum.

Billard, E.A., & Pasquale, J.C. (1993). Effects of delayed communication in dynamic group formation. *IEEE Transactions on Systems, Man, and Cybernetics, 23,* 1265–1275.

Blank, T.O. (1980). Observer and incentive effects on word association responding. *Personality and Social Psychology Bulletin, 6,* 267–272.

Bodenhausen, G.V., Kramer, G.P., & Susser, K. (1994). Happiness and stereotypic thinking in social judgment. *Journal of Personality and Social Psychology, 66,* 621–632.

Bond, C.F. (1982). Social facilitation: A self-presentational view. *Journal of Personality and Social Psychology, 42,* 1042–1050.

Bond, C.F., & Titus, L.J. (1983). Social facilitation: A meta-analysis of 241 studies. *Psychological Bulletin, 94,* 265–292.

Bornstein, G. (1992). The free-rider problem in intergroup conflicts over step-level and continuous public goods. *Journal of Personality and Social Psychology, 62,* 597–606.

Bornstein, G., & Rapoport, A. (1988). Intergroup competition for the provision of step-level public goods: Effects of preplay communication. *European Journal of Social Psychology, 18,* 125–144.

Bornstein, G., Rapoport, A., Kerpel, L., & Katz, T. (1989). Within- and between-group communication in intergroup competition for public goods. *Journal of Experimental Social Psychology, 25,* 422–436.

Boster, F.J., Hunter, J.E., & Hale, J.L. (1991). An information-processing model of jury decision making. *Communication Research, 18,* 524–547.

Bowers, C.A., Baker, D.P., & Salas, E. (1994). Measuring the importance of teamwork: The reliability and validity of job/task analysis indices for team-training design. *Military Psychology, 6,* 205–214.

Bowers, C.A., Morgan, B.B., Salas, E., & Prince, C. (1993). Assessment of coordination demand for aircrew coordination training. *Military Psychology, 5,* 95–112.

Brandstatter, H., & Hoggatt, A.C. (1982). The influence of social emotions on bargaining outcomes in a bilateral monopoly game. In H. Brandstatter, J.H. Davis, & G. Stocker-Kreichgauer (Eds.), *Group decision making* (pp. 279–294). London: Academic Press.

Brandstatter, V., Ellemers, N., Gaviria, E., Giosue, F., Huguet, P., Kroon, M., Morchain, P., Pujal, M., Rubini, M., Mugny, G., & Perez, J.A. (1991). Indirect majority and minority influence: An exploratory study. *European Journal of Social Psychology, 21,* 199–211.

Brashers, D.E., Adkins, M., & Meyers, R.A. (1994). Argumentation and computer-mediated group decision-making. In L.R. Frey (Ed.), *Group communication in context* (pp. 263–282). Hillsdale, NJ: Erlbaum.

Braver, S.L., & Wilson, L.A. (1986). Choices in social dilemmas: Effects of communication within subgroups. *Journal of Conflict Resolution, 30,* 51–62.

Bray, S.R., & Carron, A.V. (1993). The home advantage in alpine skiing. *Australian Journal of Science and Medicine in Sport, 25,* 76–81.

Brewer, M.B. (1979). Ingroup bias in the minimal intergroup situation: A cognitive-motivational analysis. *Psychological Bulletin, 86,* 207–324.

Brewer, M.B. (1981). Ethnocentrism and its role in interpersonal trust. In M.B. Brewer & B.E. Collins (Eds.), *Scientific inquiry in the social sciences* (pp. 345–360). New York: Jossey-Bass.

Brewer, M.B., & Kramer, R.M. (1986). Choice behavior in social dilemmas: Effects of social identity, group size, and decision framing. *Journal of Personality and Social Psychology, 50,* 543–549.

Brewer, M.B., & Miller, N. (1996). *Intergroup relations.* Pacific Grove, CA: Brooks/Cole.

Brickner, M.A., Harkins, S.G., & Ostrom, T.M. (1986). Effects of personal involvement: Thought-provoking implications for social loafing. *Journal of Personality and Social Psychology, 51,* 763–769.

Brockner, J., & Wiesenfeld, B.M. (1996). An integrative framework for explaining reactions to decisions: Interactive effects of outcomes and procedures. *Psychological Bulletin, 120,* 189–208.

Brodwin, D.R., & Bourgeois, L.J. (1984). Five steps to strategic action. In G. Carroll & D. Vogel (Eds.), *Strategy and organization* (pp. 167–181). Boston: Pitman.

Brown, J.D., Collins, R.L., & Schmidt, G.W. (1988). Self-esteem and direct versus indirect forms of self-enhancement. *Journal of Personality and Social Psychology, 55,* 445–453.

Brown, R. (1965). *Social psychology.* New York: Free Press.

Burden, C.A., Miller, K.E., & Boozer, A.E. (1996). Tough enough: Gang membership. In D. Capuzzi & D.R. Gross (Eds.), *Youth at risk* (pp. 283–306). Alexandria, VA: American Counseling Association.

Burger, J.M. (1985). Temporal effects on attributions for academic performances and reflected-glory basking. *Social Psychology Quarterly, 48,* 330–336.

Butler, R.E. (1993). LOFT: Full-mission simulations crew resource management training. In E.L. Weiner, B.G. Kanki, & R.L. Helmreich (Eds.), *Cockpit resource management* (pp. 231–259). San Francisco: Academic Press.

Buunk, B.P., Collins, R.L., Taylor, S.E., Van Yperen, N., & Dakof, G.A. (1990). The affective consequences of social comparison: Either direction has its ups and downs. *Journal of Personality and Social Psychology, 59,* 1238–1249.

Cacioppo, J.T., Rourke, P., Tassinary, L., Marshall-Goodall, B., & Baron, R.S. (1990). Rudimentary physiological effects of mere observation. *Psychophysiology, 27,* 177–186.

Callan, V.J. (1993). Subordinate-manager communication in different sex dyads: Consequences for job satisfaction. *Journal of Occupational and Organizational Psychology, 66,* 13–27.

Callaway, M.R., & Esser, J.K. (1984). Groupthink: Effects of cohesiveness and problem-solving on group decision making. *Social Behavior and Personality, 12,* 157–164.

Callaway, M.R., Marriott, R.G., & Esser, J.K. (1985). Effects of dominance on group decision making: Toward a stress reduction explanation of groupthink. *Journal of Personality and Social Psychology, 49,* 949–952.

Campbell, T.L. (1990). Technology update: Group decision support systems. *Journal of Accountancy, 170,* 47–50.

Campbell-Heider, N., & Pollock, D. (1987). Barriers to physician-nurse collegiality: An anthropological perspective. *Social Science and Medicine, 25,* 421–425.

Campion, M.A., Medsker, G.J., & Higgs, A.C. (1993). Relations between work group characteristics and effectiveness: Implications for designing effective work groups. *Personnel Psychology, 46,* 823–850.

Carnevale, P.J. (1986). Strategic choice in mediation. *Negotiation Journal, 2,* 41–56.

Carver, C.S. (1979). A cybernetic model of self-attention processes. *Journal of Personality and Social Psychology, 37,* 1251–1281.

Carver, C.S., & Scheier, M.F. (1981a). The self-attention induced feedback loop and social facilitation. *Journal of Experimental Social Psychology, 17,* 545–556.

Carver, C.S., & Scheier, M.F. (1981b). *Attention and self-regulation: A control-theory approach to human behavior.* New York: Springer-Verlag.

Carver, C.S., & Scheier, M.F. (1990). Origins and functions of positive and negative affect: A control process view. *Psychological Review, 97,* 19–35.

Chapman, J.C. (1991). The impact of socially projected group composition on behavior in a commons dilemma: A self-attention perspective. *Current Psychology Research and Reviews, 10,* 183–198.

Chatman, J.A., & Barsade, S.G. (1995). Personality, organizational culture, and cooperation: Evidence from a business simulation. *Administrative Science Quarterly, 40,* 423–443.

Chute, R.D., & Weiner, E.L. (1995). Cockpit-cabin communication: I. A tale of two cultures. *International Journal of Aviation Psychology, 5,* 257–276.

Chute, R.D., & Weiner, E.L. (1997). Cockpit-cabin communication: II. Shall we tell the pilots? *International Journal of Aviation Psychology, 6,* 211–231.

Cialdini, R.B. (1989). Indirect tactics of image management: Beyond basking. In R. Giacalone & P. Rosenfeld (Eds.), *Impression management in the organization* (pp. 45–56), Hillsdale, NJ: Erlbaum.

Cialdini, R.B. (1993). *Influence: Science and practice* (3d ed.). New York: Harper Collins.

Cialdini, R.B., Borden, R.J., Thorne, A., Walker, M.R., Freeman, S., & Sloan, L.R. (1976). Basking in reflected glory: Three (football) field studies. *Journal of Personality and Social Psychology, 34,* 366–375.

Cialdini, R.B., & DeNicholas, M.E. (1989). Self-presentation by association. *Journal of Personality and Social Psychology, 57,* 626–631.

Cialdini, R.B., & Richardson, K.D. (1980). Two indirect tactics of image management: Basking and blasting. *Journal of Personality and Social Psychology, 39,* 406–415.

Clampitt, P.G., & Downs, C.W. (1993). Employee perceptions of the relationship between communication and productivity: A field study. *Journal of Business Communication, 30,* 5–28.

Clark, R.D. III (1990). Minority influence: The role of argument refutation of the majority position and social support for the minority position. *European Journal of Social Psychology, 20,* 489–497.

Clark, R.D. III (1994). The role of censorship in minority influence. *European Journal of Social Psychology, 24,* 331–338.

Collins, R.L. (1996). For better or worse: The impact of upward comparisons on self-evaluation. *Psychological Bulletin, 119,* 51–69.

Cook, T.D., Crosby, F.J., & Hennigan, K.M. (1977). The construct validity of relative deprivation. In J.M. Suls & R.L. Miller (Eds.), *Social comparison processes* (pp. 307–336). Washington, DC: Hemisphere.

Cordery, J.L., Mueller, W.S., & Smith, L.M. (1991). Attitudinal and behavioral effects of autonomous group working: A longitudinal field study. *Academy of Management Journal, 34,* 464–476.

Cota, A.A., Evans, C.R., Dion, K.L., Kilik, L., & Longman, R.S. (1995). The structure of group cohesion. *Personality and Social Psychology Bulletin, 21,* 572–580.

Cottrell, N.B. (1968). Performance in the presence of other human beings: Mere presence and affiliation effects. In E.C. Simmel, R.A. Hoppe, & G.A. Milton (Eds.), *Social facilitation and imitative behavior* (pp. 91–110). Boston: Allyn and Bacon.

Cottrell, N.B. (1972). Social facilitation. In C.G. McClintock (Ed.), *Experimental social psychology* (pp. 185–236). New York: Holt, Rinehart, & Winston.

Cottrell, N.B., Wack, D.L., Sekerak, G.J., & Rittle, R.H. (1968). Social facilitation of dominant responses by the presence of an audience and the mere presence of others. *Journal of Personality and Social Psychology, 9,* 245–250.

Courneya, K.S., & Carron, A.V. (1990). Batting first versus last: Implications for the home advantage. *Journal of Sport and Exercise Psychology, 12,* 312–316.

Courneya, K.S., & Carron, A.V. (1991). Effects of travel and length of home stand/road trip on the home advantage. *Journal of Sport and Exercise Psychology, 13,* 42–49.

Courneya, K.S., & Carron, A.V. (1992). The home advantage in sport competitions: A literature review. *Journal of Sport and Exercise Psychology, 14,* 13–27.

Cowley, R.S., Swanson, B., Chapman, P., Kitik, B.A., & Mackay, L.E. (1994). The role of rehabilitation in the intensive care unit. *Journal of Head Trauma Rehabilitation, 9,* 32–42.

Cox, A.W. (1995). Nursing. In B.A. Thyer & N.P. Kropf (Eds.), *Developmental disabilities* (pp. 93–103). Cambridge, MA: Brookline Books.

Cox, R.H. (1990). *Sport psychology: Concepts and applications* (2d ed.). Dubuque, IA: Brown.

Crano, W.D. (1994). Context, comparison, and change: Methodological and theoretical contributions to a theory of minority (and majority) influence. In A. Mucchi-Faina, S. Moscovici, & A. Maass (Eds.), *On minority influence* (pp. 17–46). Chicago: Nelson-Hall.

Crano, W.D., & Hannula-Bral, K.A. (1994). Context/categorization model of social influence: Minority and majority influence in the formation of a novel response norm. *Journal of Experimental Social Psychology, 30*, 247–276.

Crocker, J., & Luhtanen, R. (1990). Collective self-esteem and ingroup bias. *Journal of Personality and Social Psychology, 58*, 60–67.

Crocker, J., & Major, B. (1989). Social stigma and self-esteem: The self-protecting properties of stigma. *Psychological Review, 96*, 608–630.

Cronshaw, S.F., & Lord, R.G. (1987). Effects of categorization, attribution, and encoding processes on leadership perceptions. *Journal of Applied Psychology, 72*, 97–106.

Crosby, F.J. (1976). A model of egoistic relative deprivation. *Psychological Review, 83*, 85–113.

Crosby, F.J. (1982). *Relative deprivation and working women.* New York: Oxford University Press.

Crosby, F.J., Muehrer, P., & Loewenstein, G. (1986). Relative deprivation and explanation: Models and concepts. In J.M. Olson, C.P. Herman, & M.P. Zanna (Eds.), *The Ontario symposium: Relative deprivation and social comparison* (Vol. 4, pp. 17–32). Hillsdale, NJ: Erlbaum.

Crott, H.W., Szilvas, K., & Zuber, J.A. (1991). Group decision, choice shift, and polarization in consulting, political, and local political scenarios: An experimental investigation and theoretical analysis. *Organizational Behavior and Human Decision Processes, 49*, 22–41.

Crott, H.W., & Werner, J. (1994). The norm-information-distance model: A stochastic approach to preference change in group interaction. *Journal of Experimental Social Psychology, 30*, 68–95.

Crott, H.W., Werner, J., & Hoffmann, C. (1996). A probabilistic model of opinion change considering distance between alternatives: An application to mock jury data. In E.H. Witte & J.H. Davis (Eds.), *Understanding group behavior* (Vol. 1, pp. 15–33). Mahwah, NJ: Erlbaum.

Crott, H.W., Zuber, J.A., & Schermer, T. (1986). Social decision schemes and choice shift: An analysis of group decisions among bets. *Journal of Experimental Social Psychology, 22*, 1–21.

Cunning, J.E. (1976). Emotional aspects of head trauma in children. *Rehabilitation Literature, 37*, 335–339.

Dalkey, N.C. (1969). The Delphi method: An experimental study of group opinion. Technical report #RM-5888PR, Rand Corporation.

Dansereau, F., Graen, G., & Haga, W.J. (1975). A vertical dyad linkage approach to leadership within formal organizations: A longitudinal investigation of the role making process. *Organizational Behavior and Human Performance, 13*, 46–78.

Darley, J.M., & Latané, B. (1968). Bystander intervention in emergencies: Diffusion of responsibility. *Journal of Personality and Social Psychology, 8*, 377–383.

Davis, J.H. (1969). *Group performance.* Reading, MA: Addison-Wesley.

Davis, J.H. (1973). Group decision and social interaction: A theory of social decision schemes. *Psychological Review, 80,* 97–125.

Davis, J.H. (1980). Group decision and procedural justice. In M. Fishbein (Ed.), *Progress in social psychology* (pp. 157–229). Hillsdale, NJ: Erlbaum.

Davis, J.H. (1989). Psychology and law: The last 15 years. *Journal of Applied Social Psychology, 19,* 199–230.

Davis, J.H. (1992). Some compelling intuitions about group consensus decisions, theoretical and empirical research, and interpersonal aggregation phenomena: Selected examples, 1950–1990. *Organizational Behavior and Human Decision Processes, 52,* 3–38.

Davis, J.H. (1996). Group decision making and quantitative judgments: A consensus model. In E. Witte & J.H. Davis (Eds.), *Understanding group behavior* (Vol. 1, pp. 35–60). Hillsdale, NJ: Erlbaum.

Davis, J.H., Bray, R.M., & Holt, R.W. (1977). The empirical study of decision processes in juries: A critical review. In J.L. Tapp & F.J. Levine (Eds.), *Law, justice, and the individual in society* (pp. 345–360). New York: Holt, Rinehart, and Winston.

Davis, J.H., Hulbert, L.G., & Au, W.T. (1996). Procedural influence on group decision making: The case of straw polls—observation and simulation. In R.Y. Hirokawa & M.S. Poole (Eds.), *Communication and group decision making* (2d ed., pp. 384–425). Beverly Hills, CA: Sage.

Davis, J.H., Kameda, T., Parks, C.D., Stasson, M.F., & Zimmerman, S.K. (1989). Some social mechanics of group decision making: The distribution of opinion, polling sequence, and implications for consensus. *Journal of Personality and Social Psychology, 57,* 1000–1012.

Davis, J.H., & Kerr, N.L. (1986). Thought experiments and the problem of sparse data in small-group performance research. In P.S. Goodman and Associates (Eds.), *Designing effective work groups* (pp. 305–349). San Francisco: Jossey-Bass.

Davis, J.H., Kerr, N.L., Atkin, R.S., Holt, R., & Meek, D. (1975). The decision processes of 6- and 12-person juries assigned unanimous and 2/3 majority rules. *Journal of Personality and Social Psychology, 32,* 1–14.

Davis, J.H., Stasser, G., Spitzer, C.E., & Holt, R. (1976). Changes in group members' decision preferences during discussion: An illustration with mock juries. *Journal of Personality and Social Psychology, 34,* 1177–1187.

Davis, J.H., & Stasson, M.F. (1988). Small group performance: Past and present research trends. *Advances in Group Processes, 5,* 245–277.

Davis, J.H., Stasson, M.F., Ono, K., & Zimmerman, S.K. (1988). Effects of straw polls on group decision making: Sequential voting pattern, timing, and local majorities. *Journal of Personality and Social Psychology, 55,* 918–926.

Davis, J.H., Stasson, M.F., Parks, C.D., Hulbert, L.G., Kameda, T., Zimmerman, S.K., & Ono, K. (1993). Quantitative decisions by groups and individuals: Voting procedures and monetary awards by mock civil juries. *Journal of Experimental Social Psychology, 29,* 326–346.

Davis, J.H., Tindale, R.S., Nagao, D.H., Hinsz, V.B., & Robertson, B. (1984). Order effects in multiple decisions by groups: A demonstration with mock juries and trial procedures. *Journal of Personality and Social Psychology, 47,* 1003–1012.

Dawes, R.M. (1988). *Rational choice in an uncertain world*. San Diego: Harcourt Brace Jovanovich.

Dawes, R.M. (1990). Social dilemmas, economic self-interest, and evolutionary theory. In D.R. Brown & J.E.K. Smith (Eds.), *Frontiers of mathematical psychology* (pp. 53–79). New York: Springer-Verlag.

Dawes, R.M., Orbell, J.M., Simmons, R.T., & van de Kragt, A.J.C. (1986). Organizing groups for collective action. *American Political Science Review, 80,* 1171–1185.

Deaux, K., Reid, A., Mizrahi, K., & Ethier, K.A. (1995). Parameters of social identity. *Journal of Personality and Social Psychology, 68,* 280–291.

de Dreu, C.K.W., & de Vries, N.K. (1993). Numerical support, information processing, and attitude change. *European Journal of Social Psychology, 23,* 647–662.

Delbecq, A.L., Van de Ven, A.H., & Gustafson, D.H. (1975). *Group techniques for program planning*. Glencoe, IL: Scott, Foresman.

Deluga, R.J. (1991). The relationship of leader and subordinate influencing activity in naval environments. *Military Psychology, 3,* 25–39.

Dennis, A.R., & Valacich, J.S. (1993). Computer brainstorms: More heads are better than one. *Journal of Applied Psychology, 78,* 531–537.

Dennis, A.R., & Valacich, J.S. (1994). Group, sub-group, and nominal group idea generation: New rules for a new media? *Journal of Management, 20,* 723–736.

Dennis, A.R., Valacich, J.S., Connolly, T., & Wynne, B.E. (1996). Process structuring in electronic brainstorming. *Information Systems Research, 7,* 268–277.

Dennis, A.R., Valacich, J.S., & Nunamaker, J.F. (1990). An experimental investigation of the effects of group size in an electronic meeting environment. *IEEE Transactions on Systems, Man, and Cybernetics, 20,* 1049–1057.

Dennison, D.R. (1996). What is the difference between organizational culture and organizational climate? A native's point of view on a decade of paradigm wars. *Academy of Management Review, 21,* 619–654.

Diehl, M., & Stroebe, W. (1987). Productivity loss in brainstorming groups: Toward the solution of a riddle. *Journal of Personality and Social Psychology, 53,* 497–509.

Diehl, M., & Stroebe, W. (1990). Productivity loss in idea-generating groups: Tracking down the blocking effect. *Journal of Personality and Social Psychology, 61,* 392–403.

Diener, E. (1980). Deindividuation: The absence of self-awareness and self-regulation in group members. In P.B. Paulus (Ed.), *Psychology of group influence* (pp. 209–242). Hillsdale, NJ: Erlbaum.

Diener, E., Fraser, S.C., Beaman, A.L., & Kelem, Z.R.T. (1976). Effects of deindividuation variables on stealing among Halloween trick-or-treaters. *Journal of Personality and Social Psychology, 33,* 178–183.

Dienesch, R.M., & Liden, R.C. (1986). Leader-member exchange model of leadership: A critique and further development. *Academy of Management Review, 11,* 618–634.

Dipboye, R.L., Smith, C.S., & Howell, W.C. (1994). *Understanding industrial and organizational psychology*. Fort Worth: Harcourt Brace.

DiTecco, D., Cwitco, G., Arsenault, A., & Andre, M. (1992). Operator stress and monitoring practices. *Applied Ergonomics, 23,* 29–34.

Downs, G.W., Rocke, D.M., & Siverson, R.M. (1985). Arms races and cooperation. *World Politics, 38,* 118–146.

Drinka, T.J.K. (1994). Interdisciplinary geriatric teams: Approaches to conflict as indicators of potential to model teamwork. *Educational Gerontology, 20,* 87–103.

Drinka, T.J.K., & Streim, J.E. (1994). Case studies from purgatory: Maladaptive behavior within geriatrics health care teams. *Gerontologist, 34,* 541–547.

Dubnicki, C. & Limburg, W.J. (1991). How do healthcare teams measure up? *Healthcare Forum, 34*(5), 10–11.

Dubrovsky, V.J., Kiesler, S., & Sethna, B.N. (1991). The equalization phenomenon: Status effects in computer-mediated and face-to-face decision-making groups. *Human-Computer Interaction, 6,* 119–146.

Dufner, D., Hiltz, S.R., Johnson, K., & Czech, R. (1995). Distributed group support: The effects of voting tools on group perceptions of media richness. *Group Decision and Negotiation, 4,* 235–250.

Dunnette, M.D., Campbell, J., & Jaastad, K. (1963). The effect of group participation on brainstorming effectiveness for two industrial samples. *Journal of Applied Psychology, 47,* 30–37.

Duval, S., & Wicklund, R.A. (1972). *A theory of objective self-awareness.* New York: Academic Press.

Earley, P.C. (1994). Self or group? Cultural effects of training on self-efficacy and performance. *Administrative Science Quarterly, 39,* 89–117.

Easterbrook, J.A. (1959). The effect of emotion on cue utilization and the organization of behavior. *Psychological Review, 66,* 183–201.

Edwards, J. (1979). The home-field advantage. In J.H. Goldstein (Ed.), *Sports, games, and play: Social and psychological viewpoints* (1st ed., pp. 409–438). Hillsdale, NJ: Erlbaum.

Edwards, J., & Archambault, D. (1989). The home-field advantage. In J.H. Goldstein (Ed.), *Sports, games, and play: Social and psychological viewpoints* (2d ed., pp. 333–370). Hillsdale, NJ: Erlbaum.

Efron, B., & Gong, G. (1983). A leisurely look at the bootstrap, the jackknife, and cross-validation. *American Statistician, 37,* 36–48.

Ellis, B.H., & Miller, K.I. (1993). The role of assertiveness, personal control, and participation in the prediction of nurse burnout. *Journal of Applied Communication Research, 21,* 327–342.

El-Sherif, H.H., & Tang, V.W. (1994). TeamFocus—electronic brainstorming. *Training and Management Development Methods, 8,* 5.25–5.33.

Esser, J.K., & Lindoerfer, J.S. (1989). Groupthink and the space shuttle Challenger accident: Toward a quantitative case analysis. *Journal of Behavioral Decision Making, 2,* 167–177.

Evans, C.R., & Dion, K.L. (1991). Group cohesion and performance: A meta-analysis. *Small Group Research, 22,* 175–186.

Fairhurst, G.T. (1993). The leader-member exchange patterns of women leaders in industry: A discourse analysis. *Communication Monographs, 60,* 321–351.

Faulkner, A.O. (1985). Interdisciplinary health care teams: An educational approach. *Gerontology and Geriatrics Education, 5,* 29–39.

Festinger, L. (1954). A theory of social comparison processes. *Human Relations, 7,* 117–140.

Feudtner, C., Christakis, D.A., & Christakis, N.A. (1994). Do clinical clerks suffer ethical erosion? Students' perceptions of their ethical environment and personal development. *Academic Medicine, 69*, 670–679.

Fiedler, F.E. (1967). *A theory of leadership effectiveness.* New York: McGraw-Hill.

Finch, J.F., & Cialdini, R.B. (1989). Another indirect tactic of (self-) image management: Boosting. *Personality and Social Psychology Bulletin, 15*, 222–232.

Finholt, T., Sproull, L.C., & Kiesler, S. (1990). Communication and performance in ad hoc task groups. In J. Galegher, R.E. Kraut, & C. Egido (Eds.), *Intellectual teamwork* (pp. 291–325). Hillsdale, NJ: Erlbaum.

Finn, T.A. (1988). Process and structure in computer-mediated group communication. In B.D. Ruben (Ed.), *Information and behavior* (Vol. 2, pp. 167–193). New Brunswick, NJ: Transaction Publishers.

Fisher, B.A., & Drecksel, G.L. (1983). A cyclical model of developing relationships: A study of relational control interaction. *Communication Monographs, 50*, 66–78.

Folger, R. (1986a). A referent cognitions theory of relative deprivation. In J.M. Olson, C.P. Herman, & M.P. Zanna (Eds.), *The Ontario symposium: Relative deprivation and social comparison* (Vol. 4, pp. 33–55). Hillsdale, NJ: Erlbaum.

Folger, R. (1986b). Rethinking equity theory: A referent cognitions model. In H.W. Bierhoff, R.L. Cohen, & J. Greenberg (Eds.), *Justice in social relations* (pp. 145–162). New York: Plenum.

Folger, R., & Martin, C. (1986). Relative deprivation and referent cognitions: Distributive and procedural justice effects. *Journal of Experimental Social Psychology, 22*, 531–546.

Folger, R., Rosenfield, D., & Martin, C. (1983). Relative deprivation and procedural justifications. *Journal of Personality and Social Psychology, 45*, 268–273.

Folger, R., Rosenfield, D., Rheaume, K., & Martin, C. (1983). Relative deprivation and referent cognitions. *Journal of Experimental Social Psychology, 19*, 172–184.

Folger, R., Rosenfield, D., & Robinson, T. (1983). Relative deprivation and procedural justifications. *Journal of Personality and Social Psychology, 45*, 268–273.

Foti, R.J., & Luch, C.H. (1992). The influence of individual differences on the perception and categorization of leaders. *Leadership Quarterly, 3*, 55–66.

Foushee, H.C., Lauber, J.K., Baetge, M.M., & Acomb, D.B. (1986). Crew performance as a function of exposure to high-density, short-haul duty cycles. *NASA Technical Memo, 88322.* Moffett Field, CA: NASA-AMES Research Center.

Fulton, M.A. (1985). A research model for studying the gender/power aspects of human-computer interaction. *International Journal of Man-Machine Studies, 23*, 369–382.

Fusco, M.E., Bell, P.A., Jorgenson, M.D., & Smith, J.M. (1991). Using a computer to study the commons dilemma. *Simulation and Gaming, 22*, 67–74.

Futoran, G.C., Kelly, J.R., & McGrath, J.E. (1989). TEMPO: A time-based system for analysis of group interaction process. *Basic and Applied Social Psychology, 10*, 211–232.

Gabbert, B., Johnson, D.W., & Johnson, R.T. (1986). Cooperative learning, group-to-individual transfer, process gain, and the acquisition of cognitive reasoning strategies. *Journal of Psychology, 120*, 265–278.

Gabrenya, W.K., Latané, B., & Wang, Y. (1983). Social loafing in cross-cultural perspective: Chinese and Taiwan. *Journal of Cross-Cultural Psychology, 14*, 368–384.

Gaffie, B. (1992). The processes of minority influence in an ideological confrontation. *Political Psychology, 13*, 407–427.

Gaines, J.H. (1980). Upward communication in industry: An experiment. *Human Relations, 33*, 929–942.

Gal, R. (1986). Unit morale: From a theoretical puzzle to an empirical illustration: An Israeli example. *Journal of Applied Social Psychology, 16*, 549–564.

Galegher, J., & Kraut, R.E. (1994). Computer-mediated communication for intellectual teamwork: An experiment in group writing. *Management Sciences, 5*, 110–138.

Gallupe, R.B., Bastianutti, L.M., & Cooper, W.H. (1991). Unblocking brainstorms. *Journal of Applied Psychology, 76*, 137–142.

Gallupe, R.B., Cooper, W.H., Grise, M.L., & Bastianutti, L.M. (1994). Blocking electronic brainstorms. *Journal of Applied Psychology, 79*, 77–86.

Gallupe, R.B., Dennis, A.R, Cooper, W.H., Valacich, J.S., Bastianutti, L.M., & Nunamaker, J.F. (1992). Group size and electronic brainstorming. *Academy of Management Journal, 35*, 350–369.

Gannon, K.M., Skowronski, J.J., & Betz, A.L. (1994). Depressive diligence in social information processing: Implications for order effects in impressions and for social memory. *Social Cognition, 12*, 263–280.

Garlick, R., & Mongeau, P.A. (1993). Argument quality and group member status as determinants of attitudinal minority influence. *Western Journal of Communication, 57*, 289–308.

Gavish, B., Gerdes, J., & Sridhar, S. (1995). CM3: A distributed group decision support system. *IIE Transactions, 27*, 722–733.

Gayton, W.F., Matthews, G.R., & Nickless, C.J. (1987). The home disadvantage in sports championships: Does it exist in hockey? *Journal of Sport Psychology, 9*, 183–185.

Gayton, W.F., Mutrie, S.A., & Hearns, J.F. (1987). Home advantage: Does it exist in women's sports? *Perceptual and Motor Skills, 65*, 653–654.

Geen, R.G. (1979). Effects of being observed on learning following success and failure experiences. *Motivation and Emotion, 3*, 355–371.

Geen, R.G. (1980). The effects of being observed on performance. In P.B. Paulus (Ed.), *Psychology of group influence* (pp. 61–97). Hillsdale, NJ: Erlbaum.

Geen, R.G. (1981). Evaluation apprehension and social facilitation: A reply to Sanders. *Journal of Experimental Social Psychology, 17*, 252–256.

Geen, R.G. (1989). Alternative conceptions of social facilitation. In P.B. Paulus (Ed.), *Psychology of group influence* (2d ed., pp. 15–51). Hillsdale, NJ: Erlbaum.

Geen, R.G. (1991). Social motivation. *Annual Review of Psychology, 42*, 377–399.

Geen, R.G., & Gange, J.J. (1977). Drive theory of social facilitation: Twelve years of theory and research. *Psychological Bulletin, 84*, 1267–1288.

Gelfand, A.E., & Solomon, H. (1977). Considerations in building jury behavior models and in comparing jury schemes: An argument in favor of twelve-member juries. *Jurimetrics Journal, 17*, 292–313.

George, J.M. (1989). Mood and absence. *Journal of Applied Psychology, 74*, 317–324.

George, J.M. (1990). Personality, affect, and behavior in groups. *Journal of Applied Psychology, 75*, 107–116.

George, J.M. (1991). State or trait: Effects of positive mood on prosocial behaviors at work. *Journal of Applied Psychology, 76*, 299–307.

George, J.M., & Bettenhausen, K. (1990). Understanding prosocial behavior, sales performance, and turnover: A group-level analysis in a service context. *Journal of Applied Psychology, 75*, 698–709.

George, J.M., & James, L.R. (1993). Personality, affect, and behavior in groups revisited: Comment on aggregation, levels of analysis, and a recent application of within and between analysis. *Journal of Applied Psychology, 78*, 798–804.

George, J.M., & Jones, G.R. (1996). The experience of work and turnover intentions: Interactive effects of value attainment, job satisfaction, and positive mood. *Journal of Applied Psychology, 81*, 318–325.

Gerard, H.B. (1985). When and how the minority prevails. In S. Moscovici, G. Mugny, & E. van Avermaet (Eds.), *Perspectives in minority influence* (pp. 171–186). Cambridge: Cambridge University Press.

Gerard, H.B., Wilhelmy, R.A., & Conolly, E.S. (1968). Conformity and group size. *Journal of Personality and Social Psychology, 8*, 79–82.

Gerbasi, K.C., Zuckerman, M., & Reis, H.T. (1977). Justice needs a new blindfold: A review of mock jury research. *Psychological Bulletin, 84*, 323–345.

Geurts, S.A., Buunk, B.P., & Schaufeli, W.B. (1994). Social comparisons and absenteeism: A structural modeling approach. *Journal of Applied Social Psychology, 24*, 1871–1890.

Gifford, R., & Wells, L. (1991). FISH: A commons dilemma simulation. *Behavior Research Methods, Instrumentation, and Computers, 23*, 437–441.

Gigone, D., & Hastie, R. (1993). The common knowledge effect: Information sharing and group judgment. *Journal of Personality and Social Psychology, 65*, 959–974.

Gigone, D., & Hastie, R. (1997). Proper analysis of the accuracy of group judgments. *Psychological Bulletin, 121*, 149–167.

Ginnett, R.C. (1993). Crews as groups: Their formation and their leadership. In E.L. Weiner, B.G. Kanki, & R.L. Helmreich (Eds.), *Cockpit resource management* (pp. 71–98). San Francisco: Academic Press.

Glaser, A.N. (1982). Drive theory of social facilitation: A critical reappraisal. *British Journal of Social Psychology, 21*, 265–282.

Glick, W.H. (1985). Conceptualizing and measuring organizational and psychological climate: Pitfalls in multilevel research. *Academy of Management Review, 10*, 601–616.

Goethals, G.R., & Darley, J.M. (1987). Social comparison theory: Self-evaluation and group life. In B. Mullen & G.R. Goethals (Eds.), *Theories of group behavior* (pp. 21–48). New York: Springer-Verlag.

Goethals, G.R., & Zanna, M.P. (1979). The role of social comparison in choice shifts. *Journal of Personality and Social Psychology, 37*, 1469–1476.

Golding, J.M., & Hauselt, J. (1994). When instructions to forget become instructions to remember. *Personality and Social Psychology Bulletin, 20*, 178–183.

Good, K.J. (1973). Social facilitation: Effects of performance anticipation, evaluation, and response competition on free associations. *Journal of Personality and Social Psychology, 28*, 270–275.

Goodman, P.S., Friedman, A. (1971). An examination of Adams theory of inequity. *Administrative Science Quarterly, 16,* 271–288.

Goodman, P.S., & Leyden, D.P. (1991). Familiarity and group productivity. *Journal of Applied Psychology, 76,* 578–586.

Graen, G.B., & Schiemann, W. (1978). Leader-member agreement: A vertical dyad linkage approach. *Journal of Applied Psychology, 63,* 206–212.

Graen, G.B., & Uhl-Bien, M. (1995). Relationship-based approach to leadership: Development of leader-member exchange (LMX) theory of leadership over 25 years: Applying a multi-level multi-domain perspective. *Leadership Quarterly, 6,* 219–247.

Green, C.A., & Williges, R.C. (1995). Evaluation of alternate media used with a groupware editor in a simulated telecommunications environment. *Human Factors, 37,* 283–289.

Green, T.B. (1975). An empirical analysis of nominal and interacting groups. *Academy of Management Journal, 18,* 67–73.

Greenberg, J. (1980). Attentional focus and locus of performance causality as determinants of equity behavior. *Journal of Personality and Social Psychology, 38,* 579–585.

Greenwald, A.G., Pratkanis, A.R., Leippe, M.R., & Baumgardner, M.H. (1986). Under what conditions does theory obstruct research progress? *Psychological Review, 93,* 216–229.

Greer, D.L. (1983). Spectator booing and the home advantage: A study of social influence in the basketball arena. *Social Psychology Quarterly, 46,* 252–261.

Griffith, T.L., Fichman, M., & Moreland, R.L. (1989). Social loafing and social facilitation: An empirical test of the cognitive-motivational model of performance. *Basic and Applied Social Psychology, 10,* 253–271.

Griffith, T.L., & Northcraft, G.B. (1994). Distinguishing between the forest and the trees: Media, features, and methodology in electronic communication research. *Organization Science, 5,* 272–285.

Groff, B.D., Baron, R.S., & Moore, D.L. (1983). Distraction, attentional conflict, and drivelike behavior. *Journal of Experimental Social Psychology, 19,* 359–380.

Grudin, J. (1994). Groupware and social dynamics: Eight challenges for developers. *Communications of the ACM, 37,* 92–105.

Guerin, B. (1983). Social facilitation and social monitoring: A test of three models. *British Journal of Social Psychology, 22,* 203–214.

Guerin, B. (1993). *Social facilitation.* Cambridge: Cambridge University Press.

Guerin, B., & Innes, J.M. (1982). Social facilitation and social monitoring: A new look at Zajonc's mere presence hypothesis. *British Journal of Social Psychology, 21,* 7–18.

Guzzo, R.A., & Dickson, M.W. (1996). Teams in organizations: Research on performance and effectiveness. *Annual Review of Psychology, 47,* 307–338.

Guzzo, R.A., & Shea, G.P. (1992). Group performance and intergroup relations in organizations. In M.D. Dunnette & L.M. Hough (Eds.), *Handbook of industrial and organizational psychology* (2d ed., Vol. 3, pp. 269–313). Palo Alto, CA: Consulting Psychologists Press.

Hackman, J.R. (1993). Teams, leaders, and organizations: New directions for crew-oriented flight training. In E.L. Weiner, B.G. Kanki, & R.L. Helmreich (Eds.), *Cockpit resource management* (pp. 47–70). San Francisco: Academic Press.

Hardin, G. (1968). The tragedy of the commons. *Science, 162,* 1243–1248.

Harkins, S.G. (1987). Social loafing and social facilitation. *Journal of Experimental Social Psychology, 23,* 1–18.

Harkins, S.G., & Jackson, J.M. (1985). The role of evaluation in eliminating social loafing. *Personality and Social Psychology Bulletin, 11,* 457–465.

Harkins, S.G., Latané, B., & Williams, K. (1980). Social loafing: Allocating effort or taking it easy? *Journal of Experimental Social Psychology, 16,* 457–465.

Harkins, S.G., & Petty, R.E. (1982). Effects of task difficulty and task uniqueness on social loafing. *Journal of Personality and Social Psychology, 43,* 1214–1229.

Harkins, S.G., & Szymanski, K. (1987). Social loafing and social facilitation: New wine in old bottles. *Review of Personality and Social Psychology, 9,* 167–188.

Harkins, S.G., & Szymanski, K. (1988). Social loafing and self-evaluation with an objective standard. *Journal of Experimental Social Psychology, 24,* 354–365.

Harkins, S.G., & Szymanski, K. (1989). Social loafing and group evaluation. *Journal of Personality and Social Psychology, 56,* 934–941.

Harmon, J., Schneer, J.A., & Hoffman, L.R. (1995). Electronic meetings and established decision groups: Audioconferencing effects on performance and structural stability. *Organizational Behavior and Human Decision Processes, 61,* 138–147.

Harper, B.C. (1993). Staff support. In A. Armstrong-Dailey & S.Z. Goltzer (Eds.), *Hospice care for children* (pp. 184–197). New York: Oxford University Press.

Harrison, A.A., Struthers, N.J., & Moore, M. (1988). On the conjunction of national holidays and reported birthdates: One more path to reflected glory? *Social Psychology Quarterly, 51,* 365–370.

Hart, A.J. (1995). Naturally occurring expectation effects. *Journal of Personality and Social Psychology, 68,* 109–115.

Hastie, R. (1990). *Inside the juror.* Cambridge, MA: Harvard University Press.

Hastie, R., Penrod, S.D., & Pennington, N. (1983). *Inside the jury.* Cambridge, MA: Harvard University Press.

Hater, J.J., & Bass, B.M. (1988). Supervisors' evaluations and subordinates' perceptions of transformational and transactional leadership. *Journal of Applied Psychology, 73,* 695–702.

Heaton, A.W., & Sigall, H. (1989). The "championship choke" revisited: The role of fear of acquiring a negative identity. *Journal of Applied Social Psychology, 19,* 1019–1033.

Heinemann, G.D., Farrell, M.P., & Schmitt, M.H. (1994). Groupthink theory and research: Implications for decision making in geriatric health care teams. *Educational Gerontology, 20,* 71–85.

Helgeson, V.S., & Mickelson, K.D. (1995). Motives for social comparison. *Personality and Social Psychology Bulletin, 21,* 1200–1209.

Helmreich, R.L., & Foushee, H.C. (1993). Why crew resource management? Empirical and theoretical bases of human factors training in aviation. In E.L. Weiner, B.G. Kanki, & R.L. Helmreich (Eds.), *Cockpit resource management* (pp. 3–45). San Francisco: Academic Press.

Hemphill, K.J., & Lehman, D.R. (1991). Social comparisons and their affective consequences: The importance of comparison dimension and individual difference variables. *Journal of Social and Clinical Psychology, 10,* 372–394.

Henchy, T., & Glass, D.C. (1968). Evaluation apprehension and the social facilitation of dominant and subordinate responses. *Journal of Personality and Social Psychology, 10,* 446–454.

Hepworth, J.T., & West, S.G. (1988). Lynchings and the economy: A time-series reanalysis of Hovland and Sears (1940). *Journal of Personality and Social Psychology, 55,* 239–247.

Herschel, R.T., Cooper, T.R., Smith, L.F., & Arrington, L. (1994). Exploring numerical proportions in a unique context: The group support systems meeting environment. *Sex Roles, 31,* 99–123.

Hersey, P., & Blanchard, K.H. (1982). *Management of organizational behavior* (2d ed.). Englewood Cliffs, NJ: Prentice-Hall.

Heuer, L.B., & Penrod, S.D. (1986). Procedural preference as a function of conflict intensity. *Journal of Personality and Social Psychology, 51,* 700–710.

Heuer, L.B., & Penrod, S.D. (1994). Juror notetaking and question asking during trials: A national field experiment. *Law and Human Behavior, 18,* 121–150.

Hightower, R., & Sayeed, L. (1995). The impact of computer-mediated communication systems on biased group discussion. *Computers in Human Behavior, 11,* 33–44.

Hiltrop, J.M. (1989). Factors associated with successful labor mediation. In K. Kressel & D.G. Pruitt (Eds.), *Mediation research* (pp. 241–262). San Francisco: Jossey-Bass.

Hiltz, S.R., Turoff, M., & Johnson, K. (1989). Experiments in group decision making 3: Disinhibition, deindividuation, and group process in pen name and real name computer references. *Decision Support Systems, 5,* 217–232.

Hine, D.W., & Gifford, R. (1996). Individual restraint and group efficiency in commons dilemmas: The effects of two types of environmental uncertainty. *Journal of Applied Social Psychology, 26,* 993–1009.

Hine, D.W., & Gifford, R. (1997). What harvesters really think about in commons dilemma situations: A grounded theory analysis. *Canadian Journal of Behavioural Science, 29,* 180–194.

Hinkle, S., & Schopler, J. (1986). Bias in the evaluation of in-group and out-group performance. In S. Worchel & W.G. Austin (Eds.), *Psychology of intergroup relations* (2d ed., pp. 196–212). Chicago: Nelson-Hall.

Hinsz, V.B. (1990). Cognitive and consensus processes in group recognition memory performance. *Journal of Personality and Social Psychology, 61,* 705–718.

Hinsz, V.B., Tindale, R.S., & Vollrath, D.A. (1997). The emerging conceptualization of groups as information processors. *Psychological Bulletin, 121,* 43–64.

Hirt, E.R., Zillman, D., Erickson, G.A., & Kennedy, C. (1992). Costs and benefits of allegiance: Changes in fans' self-ascribed competencies after team victory versus defeat. *Journal of Personality and Social Psychology, 63,* 724–738.

Hitchings, G., & Cox, S. (1992). Generating ideas using randomized search methods: A method of managed convergence. *Management Decision, 30*(8), 58–61.

Hofstede, G., Neujien, B., Ohayv, D.D., & Sanders, G. (1990). Measuring organizational cultures: A qualitative/quantitative study across twenty cases. *Administrative Science Quarterly, 35,* 286–316.

Hollingshead, A.B. (1996). The rank-order effect in group decision making. *Organizational Behavior and Human Decision Processes, 68,* 181–193.

236 References

Hollingshead, A.B., & McGrath, J.E. (1995). Computer-assisted groups: A critical review of the empirical research. In R.A. Guzzo & E. Salas (Eds.), *Team effectiveness and decision making in organizations* (pp. 46–78). San Francisco: Jossey-Bass.

Hollingshead, A.B., McGrath, J.E., & O'Connor, K.M. (1993). Group task performance and communication technology: A longitudinal study of computer-mediated versus face-to-face work groups. *Small Group Research, 24,* 307–333.

Horn, J.C. (1988, October). Dome-inating the game. *Psychology Today,* 20.

Horowitz, I.A., & Bordens, K.S. (1990). An experimental investigation of procedural issues in complex tort trials. *Law and Human Behavior, 14,* 269–285.

Houlden, P., LaTour, S., Walker, L., & Thibaut, J. (1978). Preference for modes of dispute resolution as a function of process and decision control. *Journal of Experimental Social Psychology, 14,* 13–30.

Hoyle, R.H., & Crawford, A.M. (1994). Use of individual-level data to investigate group phenomena: Issues and strategies. *Small Group Research, 25,* 464–485.

Hull, C.L. (1943). *Principles of behavior: An introduction to behavior theory.* New York: Appleton-Crofts.

Hume, S. (1990a). BK franchisees pan ad theme. *Advertising Age, 61*(5), 3, 55.

Hume, S. (1990b). Burger King tinkers with "break the rules." *Advertising Age, 61*(37), 3, 85.

Hume, S. (1991). BK brakes the "rules." *Advertising Age, 62*(9), 1, 50.

Ickes, W., & Gonzalez, R. (1994). "Social" cognition and social cognition: From the subjective to the intersubjective. *Small Group Research, 25,* 294–315.

Ilgen, D.R., Major, D.A., Hollenbeck, J.R., & Sego, D.J. (1993). Team research in the 1990s. In M.M. Chemers & R. Ayman (Eds.), *Leadership theory and research* (pp. 245–270). San Diego: Academic Press.

Ingham, A.G., Levinger, G., Graves, J., & Peckham, V. (1974). The Ringelmann effect: Studies of group size and group performance. *Journal of Experimental Social Psychology, 10,* 371–384.

Innes, J.M., & Young, R.F. (1975). The effect of the presence of an audience, evaluation apprehension, and objective self-awareness on learning. *Journal of Experimental Social Psychology, 11,* 35–42.

Irving, P.G., & Goldstein, S.R. (1990). Effect of home-field advantage on peak performance of baseball pitchers. *Journal of Sport Behavior, 13,* 23–27.

Isaac, R.M., & Walker, J.M. (1988a). Communication and free-riding behavior: The voluntary contribution mechanism. *Economic Inquiry, 6,* 585–607.

Isaac, R.M., & Walker, J.M. (1988b). Group size effects in public goods provision: The voluntary contributions mechanism. *Quarterly Journal of Economics, 53,* 179–199.

Iso-Ahola, S.E., & Hatfield, B. (1986). *Psychology of sports: A social psychological approach.* Dubuque, IA: Brown.

Jackson, J.M. (1986). In defense of social impact theory: Comment on Mullen. *Journal of Personality and Social Psychology, 50,* 511–513.

Jackson, J.M. (1987). Social impact theory: A social forces model of influence. In B. Mullen & G.R. Goethals (Eds.), *Theories of group behavior* (pp. 111–124). New York: Springer-Verlag.

Jackson, J.M., & Latané, B. (1981). All alone in front of all those people: Stage fright as a function of number and type of co-performers and audience. *Journal of Personality and Social Psychology, 40,* 73–85.

Jackson, J.M., & Latané, B. (1987). Strength and number of solicitors and the urge toward altruism. *Personality and Social Psychology Bulletin, 7,* 415–422.

Jackson, J.M., & Williams, K.D. (1985). Social loafing on difficult tasks: Working collectively can improve performance. *Journal of Personality and Social Psychology, 49,* 937–942.

Jago, A.G., & Ragan, J.W. (1986). The trouble with Leader Match is that it doesn't match Fiedler's contingency model. *Journal of Applied Psychology, 71,* 555–559.

James, L.A., & James, L.R. (1989). Integrating work environment perceptions: Explorations in the measurement of meaning. *Journal of Applied Psychology, 74,* 739–751.

Janis, I.L. (1982). *Groupthink: Psychological studies of policy decisions and fiascoes.* Boston: Houghton Mifflin.

Jessup, L.M., Connolly, T., & Tansik, D.A. (1990). Toward a theory of automated group work: The deindividuating effects of anonymity. *Small Group Research, 21,* 333–348.

Johnson, D.W., Johnson, R.T., Ortiz, A.E., & Stanne, M. (1991). The impact of positive goal and resource interdependence on achievement, interaction, and attitudes. *Journal of General Psychology, 118,* 341–347.

Judd, C.M., Ryan, C.S., & Park, B. (1991). Accuracy in the judgment of in-group and out-group variability. *Journal of Personality and Social Psychology, 61,* 366–379.

Kahneman, D., & Tversky, A. (1982). The simulation heuristic. In D. Kahneman, P. Slovic, & A. Tversky (Eds.), *Judgment under uncertainty* (pp. 201–209). New York: Cambridge University Press.

Kameda, T. (1991). Procedural influence in small-group decision making: Deliberation style and assigned decision rule. *Journal of Personality and Social Psychology, 61,* 245–256.

Kaplan, M.F. (1987). The influencing process in group decision making. *Review of Personality and Social Psychology, 8,* 189–212.

Kaplan, M.F. (1989). Task, situational, and personal determinants of influence processes in group decision making. *Advances in Group Processes, 6,* 87–105.

Kaplan, M.F., & Schersching, C. (1981). Juror deliberation: An information integration analysis. In B.D. Sales (Ed.), *The trial process* (pp. 120–134). New York: Plenum.

Karau, S.J., & Williams, K.D. (1993). Social loafing: A meta-analytic review and theoretical integration. *Journal of Personality and Social Psychology, 65,* 681–706.

Kassin, S.M., & Garfield, D.A. (1991). Blood and guts: General and trial-specific effects of videotaped crime scenes on mock jurors. *Journal of Applied Social Psychology, 21,* 1459–1472.

Kassin, S.M., Williams, L.N., & Saunders, C.L. (1990). Dirty tricks of cross-examination: The influence of conjectural evidence on the jury. *Law and Human Behavior, 14,* 373–384.

Katz, R. (1982). The effects of group longevity on project communication and performance. *Administrative Science Quarterly, 27,* 81–104.

Katzenbach, J.R., & Smith, D.K. (1993). The discipline of teams. *Harvard Business Review, 71,* 111–120.

Kenney, R.A., Blascovich, J., & Shaver, P.R. (1994). Implicit leadership theories: Prototypes for new leaders. *Basic and Applied Social Psychology, 15,* 409–437.

Kenny, D.A., & La Voie, L. (1985). Separating individual and group effects. *Journal of Personality and Social Psychology, 48,* 339–348.

Kerr, N.L. (1981). Social transition schemes: Charting the group's road to agreement. *Journal of Personality and Social Psychology, 41,* 684–702.

Kerr, N.L. (1983). Motivation losses in small groups: A social dilemma analysis. *Journal of Personality and Social Psychology, 45,* 819–828.

Kerr, N.L. (1989). Illusions of efficacy: The effects of group size on perceived efficacy in social dilemmas. *Journal of Experimental Social Psychology, 25,* 287–313.

Kerr, N.L. (1992). Efficacy as a causal and moderating variable in social dilemmas. In W.B.G. Liebrand, D.M. Messick, & H.A.M. Wilke (Eds.), *Social dilemmas* (pp. 59–80). New York: Pergamon Press.

Kerr, N.L., & Bruun, S.E. (1981). Ringelmann revisited: Alternative explanations for the social loafing effect. *Personality and Social Psychology Bulletin, 7,* 224–231.

Kerr, N.L., & Bruun, S.E. (1983). Dispensability of member effort and group motivation losses: Free-rider effects. *Journal of Personality and Social Psychology, 44,* 78–94.

Kerr, N.L., Harmon, D.L., & Graves, J.K. (1982). Independence of multiple verdicts by jurors and juries. *Journal of Applied Social Psychology, 12,* 12–29.

Kerr, N.L., & MacCoun, R.J. (1985). The effects of jury size and polling method on the process and products of jury deliberation. *Journal of Personality and Social Psychology, 48,* 349–363.

Kerr, N.L., MacCoun, R.J., & Kramer, G.P. (1996). Bias in judgment: Comparing individuals and groups. *Psychological Review, 103,* 687–719.

Kerwin, J., & Shaffer, D.R. (1994). Mock jurors versus mock juries: The role of deliberations in reactions to inadmissable testimony. *Personality and Social Psychology Bulletin, 20,* 153–162.

Kiesler, S., Siegel, J., & McGuire, T.W. (1984). Social psychological aspects of computer-mediated communication. *American Psychologist, 39,* 1123–1134.

Kiesler, S., & Sproull, L. (1992). Group decision making and communication technology. *Organizational Behavior and Human Decision Processes, 52,* 96–123.

Kimble, C.E., & Cooper, B.P. (1992). Association and dissociation by football fans. *Perceptual and Motor Skills, 75,* 303–309.

Kirkland, F.R. (1987). *Unit manning system field evaluation* (Tech. Rep. No. 5) (WRAIR Publication No. UM415.3U54). Washington, DC: Walter Reed Army Institute for Research.

Klevorick, A.K., Rothschild, M., & Winship, C. (1984). Information processing and jury decisionmaking. *Journal of Public Economics, 23,* 245–278.

Klimoski, R., & Mohammed, S. (1994). Team mental model: Construct or metaphor? *Journal of Management, 20,* 403–437.

Knowles, E.S. (1978). The gravity of crowding: Application of social physics to the effects of others. In A. Baum & Y. Epstein (Eds.), *Human response to crowding* (pp. 183–218). Hillsdale, NJ: Erlbaum.

Knowles, E.S. (1983). Social physics and the effects of others: Tests of the effects of audience size and distance on social judgments and behavior. *Journal of Personality and Social Psychology, 45,* 1263–1279.

Knowles, E.S. (1989). Spatial behavior of individuals in groups. In P.B. Paulus (Ed.), *Psychology of group influence* (2d ed., pp. 53–86). Hillsdale, NJ: Erlbaum.

Knowles, E.S., Kreuser, B., Haas, S., Hyde, M., & Schuchart, G.E. (1976). Group size and the extension of personal space boundaries. *Journal of Personality and Social Psychology, 33,* 647–654.

Koin, D. (1989). The effects of caregiver stress on physical health status. In E. Light & B.D. Lebowitz (Eds.), *Alzheimer's disease treatment and family stress* (pp. 310–320). Rockville, MD: U.S. Dept. of Health and Human Services.

Komorita, S.S., & Carnevale, P.J. (1992). Motivational arousal vs. decision framing in social dilemmas. In W.B.G. Liebrand, D.M. Messick, & H.A.M. Wilke (Eds.), *Social dilemmas* (pp. 209–224). Tarrytown, NY: Pergamon Press.

Komorita, S.S., Chan, D.K.S., & Parks, C.D. (1993). The effects of reward structure and reciprocity in social dilemmas. *Journal of Experimental Social Psychology, 29,* 252–267.

Komorita, S.S., Hilty, J.A., & Parks, C.D. (1991). Reciprocity and cooperation in social dilemmas. *Journal of Conflict Resolution, 35,* 494–518.

Komorita, S.S., & Parks, C.D. (1995). Interpersonal relations: Mixed-motive interaction. *Annual Review of Psychology, 46,* 183–207.

Komorita, S.S., & Parks, C.D. (1996). *Social dilemmas.* Boulder: Westview Press.

Komorita, S.S., Parks, C.D., & Hulbert, L.G. (1992). Reciprocity and the induction of cooperation in social dilemmas. *Journal of Personality and Social Psychology, 62,* 607–617.

Kozakai, T., Moscovici, S., & Personnaz, B. (1994). Contrary effects of group cohesiveness in minority influence: Intergroup categorization of the source and levels of influence. *European Journal of Social Psychology, 24,* 713–718.

Kramer, R.M., & Brewer, M.B. (1984). Effects of group identity on resource use in a simulated commons dilemma. *Journal of Personality and Social Psychology, 46,* 1044–1057.

Kramer, R.M., McClintock, C.G., & Messick, D.M. (1986). Social values and cooperative response to a simulated resource conservation crisis. *Journal of Personality, 54,* 576–592.

Kramer, R.M., & Messick, D.M. (1995). *Negotiation as a social process.* Thousand Oaks, CA: Sage.

Kravitz, D.A., & Martin, B. (1986). Ringelmann rediscovered: The original article. *Journal of Personality and Social Psychology, 50,* 936–941.

Krosnick, J.A., Boninger, D.S., Chuang, Y.C., Berent, M.K., & Carnot, C.G. (1993). Attitude strength: One construct or many related constructs? *Journal of Personality and Social Psychology, 65,* 1132–1151.

Lamm, H., & Trommsdorf, G. (1973). Group versus individual performance on tasks requiring ideational proficiency (brainstorming): A review. *European Journal of Social Psychology, 3,* 361–388.

Landler, M. (1990). Tempers are sizzling over Burger King's new ads. *Business Week,* Feb. 12, 33.

Larey, T.S., & Paulus, P.B. (1995). Social comparison and goal setting in brainstorming groups. *Journal of Applied Social Psychology, 25,* 1579–1596.

Larson, J.R. (1997). Modeling the entry of shared and unshared information into group discussion: A review and BASIC language computer program. *Small Group Research, 28,* 454–479.

Larson, J.R., Christensen, C., Abbott, A.S., & Franz, T.M. (1996). Diagnosing groups: Charting the flow of information in medical decision-making teams. *Journal of Personality and Social Psychology, 71,* 315–330.

Latané, B. (1981). The psychology of social impact. *American Psychologist, 36,* 343–356.

Latané, B. (1986). Responsibility and effort in organizations. In P.S. Goodman and Associates (Eds.), *Designing effective work groups* (pp. 277–304). San Francisco: Jossey-Bass.

Latané, B., & Darley, J.M. (1970). *The unresponsive bystander: Why doesn't he help?* New York: Appleton-Century-Crofts.

Latané, B., Liu, J.H., Nowak, A., Bonevento, M., & Zheng, L. (1995). Distance matters: Physical space and social impact. *Personality and Social Psychology Bulletin, 8,* 795–805.

Latané, B., & Nida, S. (1980). Social impact theory and group influence: A social engineering perspective. In P.B. Paulus (Ed.), *Psychology of group influence* (pp. 3–34). Hillsdale, NJ: Erlbaum.

Latané, B., Williams, K., & Harkins, S. (1979). Many hands make light the work: The causes and consequences of social loafing. *Journal of Personality and Social Psychology, 37,* 822–832.

Latané, B., & Wolf, S. (1981). The social impact of majorities and minorities. *Psychological Review, 88,* 438–453.

Lauber, J.K. (1994). Forward. In E.L. Weiner, B.G. Kanki, & R.L. Helmreich (Eds.), *Cockpit resource management* (pp. xv–xvii). San Francisco: Academic Press.

Laughlin, P.R. (1980). Social combination processes of cooperative problem-solving groups on verbal intellective tasks. In M. Fishbein (Ed.), *Progress in social psychology* (pp. 127–156). Hillsdale, NJ: Erlbaum.

Laughlin, P.R., & Barth, J.M. (1981). Group-to-individual and individual-to-group problem-solving transfer. *Journal of Personality and Social Psychology, 41,* 1087–1093.

Laughlin, P.R., Chandler, J.S., Shupe, E.I., Magley, V.J., & Hulbert, L.G. (1995). Generality of a theory of collective induction: Face-to-face and computer-mediated interaction, amount of potential information, and group versus member choice of evidence. *Organizational Behavior and Human Decision Processes, 63,* 98–111.

Laughlin, P.R., & Ellis, A.L. (1986). Demonstrability and social combination processes on mathematical intellective tasks. *Journal of Experimental Social Psychology, 22,* 177–189.

Laughlin, P.R., & Hollingshead, A.B. (1995). A theory of collective induction. *Organizational Behavior and Human Decision Processes, 61,* 94–107.

Laughlin, P.R., & Sweeney, J.D. (1977). Individual-to-group and group-to-individual transfer in problem solving. *Journal of Experimental Psychology: Human Learning and Memory, 3,* 246–254.

Laughlin, P.R., VanderStoep, S.W., & Hollingshead, A.B. (1991). Collective versus individual induction: Recognition of truth, rejection of error, and collective information processing. *Journal of Personality and Social Psychology, 61,* 50–67.

Lawler, E.E., & O'Gara, P.W. (1967). Effects of inequity produced by underpayment on work output, work quality, and attitudes toward work. *Journal of Applied Psychology, 51,* 39–45.

Lea, M., O'Shea, T., Fung, P., & Spears, R. (1992). "Flaming" in computer-mediated communication: Observations, explanations, implications. In M. Lea (Ed.), *Contexts of computer-mediated communication* (pp. 89–112). London: Harvester Wheatsheaf.

Lea, M., & Spears, R. (1991). Computer-mediated communication, de-individuation and group decision-making. *International Journal of Man-Machine Studies, 34,* 283–301.

Leana, C.R. (1985). A partial test of Janis' groupthink model: Effects of group cohesiveness and leader behavior on defective decision making. *Journal of Management, 11,* 5–17.

Leary, M.R., Rogers, P.A., Canfield, R.W., & Coe, C. (1986). Boredom in interpersonal encounters: Antecedents and social implications. *Journal of Personality and Social Psychology, 51,* 968–975.

Lee, F. (1993). Being polite and keeping MUM: How bad news is communicated in organizational hierarchies. *Journal of Applied Social Psychology, 23,* 1124–1149.

Lee, M.J. (1985). Self-esteem and social identity in basketball fans: A closer look at basking-in-reflected glory. *Journal of Sport Behavior, 8,* 210–223.

Leedom, D.K., & Simon, R. (1995). Improving team coordination: A case for behavior-based training. *Military Psychology, 7,* 109–122.

Legrenzi, P., Butera, F., Mugny, G., Perez, J.A. (1991). Majority and minority influence in inductive reasoning: A preliminary study. *European Journal of Social Psychology, 21,* 359–363.

Lehman, D.R., & Reifman, A. (1987). Spectator influence on basketball officiating. *Journal of Social Psychology, 127,* 673–675.

Leith, L.M. (1988). Choking in sports: Are we our own worst enemies? *International Journal of Sport Psychology, 19,* 59–64.

Leonard, W.M. (1989). The "home advantage": The case of modern Olympiads. *Journal of Sport Behavior, 12,* 227–241.

Levine, D.I., & D'Andrea Tyson, L. (1990). Participation, productivity, and the firm's environment. In A.S. Blinder (Ed.), *Paying for productivity* (pp. 183–237). Washington, DC: Brookings Institution.

Levine, J.M., & Moreland, R.L. (1987). Social comparison and outcome evaluation in group contexts. In J.C. Masters & W.P. Smith (Eds.), *Social comparison, social justice, and relative deprivation* (pp. 90–120). Hillsdale, NJ: Erlbaum.

Levine, J.M., Resnick, L.B., & Higgins, E.T. (1993). Social foundations of cognition. *Annual Review of Psychology, 44,* 585–612.

Lewicki, R.J., & Sheppard, B.H. (1985). Choosing how to intervene: Factors affecting the use of process and outcome control in third party dispute resolution. *Journal of Occupational Behavior, 6,* 49–64.

Lewin, K. (1948). *Resolving social conflict.* New York: Harper.

Lewin, K. (1951). *Field theory and social science.* New York: Harper.

Lewis, B.P., & Linder, D.E. (1997). Thinking about choking? Attentional processes and paradoxical performance. *Personality and Social Psychology Bulletin, 23,* 973–944.

Liang, D.W., Moreland, R.L., & Argote, L. (1995). Group versus individual training and group performance: The mediating effects of transactive memory. *Personality and Social Psychology Bulletin, 21,* 384–393.

Liden, R.C., & Graen, G.B. (1980). Generalizability of the vertical dyad linkage model of leadership. *Academy of Management Journal, 23*, 451–465.

Liden, R.C., Wayne, S.J., & Stilwell, D. (1993). A longitudinal study on the early development of leader-member exchanges. *Journal of Applied Psychology, 78*, 662–674.

Liebrand, W.B.G. (1984). The effect of social motives, communication, and group size on behaviour in an N-person multi-stage mixed-motive game. *European Journal of Social Psychology, 14*, 239–264.

Likert, R. (1961). *New patterns of management.* New York: McGraw-Hill.

Lindsay, R.C.L., Wells, G.L., & O'Connor, F.J. (1989). Mock-juror belief of accurate and inaccurate eyewitnesses: A replication and extension. *Law and Human Behavior, 13*, 333–339.

Lindskold, S. (1978). Trust development, the GRIT proposal, and the effects of conciliatory acts on conflict and cooperation. *Psychological Bulletin, 85*, 772–793.

Lindskold, S. (1983). Conflict and conciliation with groups and individuals. In H.H. Blumberg, A.P. Hare, V. Kent, & M. Davies (Eds.), *Small groups and social interaction* (Vol. 2, pp. 95–100). New York: Wiley and Sons.

Linville, P.W., Fischer, G.W., & Salovey, P. (1989). Perceived distributions of the characteristics of in-group and out-group members: Empirical evidence and a computer simulation. *Journal of Personality and Social Psychology, 57*, 165–188.

Locke, E.A., & Latham, G.P. (1990). *A theory of goal-setting and task performance.* Englewood Cliffs, NJ: Prentice-Hall.

Lord, R.G. (1985). An information processing approach to social perceptions, leadership, and behavioral measurement. *Research in Organizational Behavior, 7*, 87–128.

Lord, R.G., Foti, R.J., & DeVader, C.L. (1984). A test of leadership categorization theory: Internal structure, information processing, and leadership perceptions. *Organizational Behavior and Human Performance, 34*, 343–378.

Lord, R.G., & Hohenfeld, J.A. (1979). Longitudinal field assessment of equity effects on the performance of major league baseball players. *Journal of Applied Psychology, 64*, 19–26.

Lorge, I., & Solomon, H. (1955). Two models of group behavior in the solution of Eureka-type problems. *Psychometrika, 20*, 139–148.

Lortie-Lussier, M., Lemieux, S., & Godbout, L. (1989). Reports of a public manifestation: Their impact according to minority influence theory. *Journal of Social Psychology, 129*, 285–295.

Lott, A.J., Lott, B.E., Reed, T., & Crow, T. (1970). Personality-trait descriptions of differentially liked persons. *Journal of Personality and Social Psychology, 16*, 284–290.

Lucius, R.H., & Kuhnert, K.W. (1997). Using sociometry to predict team performance in the work place. *Journal of Psychology, 131*, 21–32.

Lydon, J.E., Jamieson, D.W., & Zanna, M.P. (1988). Interpersonal similarity and the social and intellectual dimensions of first impressions. *Social Cognition, 6*, 269–286.

Mabry, E.A. (1975). Exploratory analysis of a developmental model for task-oriented small groups. *Human Communication Research, 2*, 66–74.

MacCoun, R.J. (1990). The emergence of extralegal bias during jury deliberation. *Criminal Justice and Behavior, 17,* 303–314.

MacCoun, R.J., & Kerr, N.L. (1988). Asymmetric influence in mock jury deliberation: Juror's bias for leniency. *Journal of Personality and Social Psychology, 54,* 21–33.

Mackie, D.M. (1987). Systematic and nonsystematic processing of majority and minority persuasive communications. *Journal of Personality and Social Psychology, 53,* 41–52.

Magjuka, R.J., & Baldwin, T.T. (1991). Team-based employee involvement programs: Effects of design and administration. *Personnel Psychology, 44,* 793–812.

Mannix, E.A., Neale, M.A., & Northcraft, G.B. (1995). Equity, equality, or need? The effects of organizational culture on the allocation of benefits and burdens. *Organizational Behavior and Human Decision Processes, 63,* 276–286.

Manstead, A.S.R., & Semin, G.R. (1980). Social facilitation effects: Mere enhancement of dominant responses? *British Journal of Social Psychology, 19,* 119–136.

Mantovani, G. (1994). Is computer-mediated communication intrinsically apt to enhance democracy in organizations? *Human Relations, 47,* 45–62.

Mantovani, G. (1996). Social context in HCI: A new framework for mental models. *Cognitive Science, 20,* 237–269.

Marchi, S. (1997). Psychology research for environmental policy. *Canadian Journal of Behavioural Science, 29,* 224–226.

Marco, C.A., & Suls, J. (1993). Daily stress and the trajectory of mood: Spillover, response assimilation, contrast, and chronic negative affectivity. *Journal of Personality and Social Psychology, 64,* 1053–1063.

Marcoulides, G.A., & Heck, R.H. (1993). Organizational culture and performance: Proposing and testing a model. *Organization Science, 4,* 209–225.

Mark, M.M., & Folger, R. (1984). Responses to relative deprivation: A conceptual framework. *Review of Personality and Social Psychology, 5,* 192–218.

Markus, H. (1978). The effect of mere presence on social facilitation: An unobtrusive test. *Journal of Experimental Social Psychology, 14,* 257–261.

Markus, H. (1981). The drive for integration: Some comments. *Journal of Experimental Social Psychology, 17,* 257–261.

Markus, H., & Nurius, P. (1986). Possible selves. *American Psychologist, 41,* 954–969.

Marquart, D.I. (1955). Group problem-solving. *Journal of Social Psychology, 41,* 103–113.

Martin, L.L., Ward, W., Achee, J.W., & Wyer, R.S. (1993). Mood as input: People have to interpret the motivational implications of their moods. *Journal of Personality and Social Psychology, 64,* 317–326.

Martin, R. (1988). Minority influence and "trivial" social categorization. *European Journal of Social Psychology, 18,* 465–470.

Martin, R. (1992). The effects of ingroup-outgroup membership on minority influence when group membership is determined by a trivial categorization. *Social Behavior and Personality, 20,* 131–141.

Marwell, G., & Ames, R.E. (1979). Experiments on the provision of public goods I: Resources, interest, group size, and the free-rider problem. *American Journal of Sociology, 84,* 1335–1360.

Mason, R.O. (1969). A dialectical approach to strategic planning. *Management Science, 15,* B403-B414.

Matheson, K. (1991). Social cues in computer-mediated negotiations: Gender makes a difference. *Computers in Human Behavior, 7,* 137–145.

Matheson, K., & Zanna, M.P. (1988). The impact of computer-mediated communication on self-awareness. *Computers in Human Behavior, 4,* 221–233.

Matheson, K., & Zanna, M.P. (1989). Persuasion as a function of self-awareness in computer-mediated communication. *Social Behaviour, 4,* 99–111.

Matheson, K., & Zanna, M.P. (1990). Computer-mediated communications: The focus is on me. *Social Science Computer Review, 8,* 1–12.

Maznevski, M.L. (1994). Understanding our differences: Performance in decision-making groups with diverse members. *Human Relations, 47,* 531–552.

McGarty, C., Turner, J.C., Hogg, M.A., David, B., & Wetherell, M.S. (1992). Group polarization as conformity to the prototypical group member. *British Journal of Social Psychology, 31,* 1–19.

McGrath, J.E. (1984). *Groups: Interaction and performance.* Englewood Cliffs, NJ: Prentice Hall.

McGrath, J.E. (1988). The place of time in social psychology. In J.E. McGrath (Ed.), *The social psychology of time* (pp. 7–20). Newbury Park, CA: Sage.

McGrath, J.E. (1993). The JEMCO workshop: Description of a longitudinal study. *Small Group Research, 24,* 285–306.

McGuire, T.W., Kiesler, S., & Siegel, J. (1987). Group and computer-mediated discussion effects in risk decision making. *Journal of Personality and Social Psychology, 52,* 917–930.

McMahan, E.M., Hoffman, K., & McGee, G.W. (1994). Physician-nurse relationships in clinical settings: A review and critique of the literature, 1966–1992. *Medical Care Review, 51,* 83–112.

McNally, J.A., Gerras, S.J., & Bullis, C.R. (1996). Teaching leadership at the U.S. military academy at West Point. *Journal of Applied Behavioral Science, 32,* 175–188.

Messe, L., Hymes, R., & MacCoun, R. (1986). Group categorization and distributive justice decisions. In H. Bierhoff, R. Cohen, & J. Greenberg (Eds.), *Justice and social relations* (pp. 227–248). New York: Plenum Press.

Messick, D.M. (1973). To join or not to join: An approach to the unionization decision. *Organizational Behavior and Human Performance, 10,* 145–156.

Messick, D.M., Allison, S.T., & Samuelson, C.D. (1988). Framing and communication effects on group members' responses to environmental and social uncertainty. In S. Maital (Ed.), *Applied Behavioural Economics* (Vol. 2, pp. 677–700). Brighton: Wheatsheaf Books.

Messick, D.M., & Brewer, M.B. (1983). Solving social dilemmas: A review. *Review of Personality and Social Psychology, 4,* 11–44.

Messick, D.M., & Liebrand, W.B.G. (1993). Computer simulations of the relation between individual heuristics and global cooperation in prisoners dilemmas. *Social Science Computer Review, 11,* 301–312.

Messick, D.M., & Liebrand, W.B.G. (1995). Individual heuristics and the dynamics of cooperation in large groups. *Psychological Review, 102,* 131–145.

Messick, D.M., & Liebrand, W.B.G. (1997). Levels of analysis and the explanation of the costs and benefits of cooperation. *Personality and Social Psychology Review, 1,* 129–139.

Messick, D.M., & Sentis, K.P. (1979). Fairness and preference. *Journal of Experimental Social Psychology, 15*, 418–434.

Messick, D.M., Wilke, H., Brewer, M.B., Kramer, R.M., Zemke, P.E., & Lui, L. (1983). Individual adaptations and structural change as solutions to social dilemmas. *Journal of Personality and Social Psychology, 44*, 294–309.

Michaelsen, L.K., Watson, W.E., & Black, R.H. (1989). A realistic test of individual versus group consensus decision making. *Journal of Applied Psychology, 74*, 834–839.

Miles, J.A., & Greenberg, J. (1993). Using punishment threats to attenuate social loafing effects among swimmers. *Organizational Behavior and Human Decision Processes, 56*, 246–265.

Miles, M.B., & Huberman, A.M. (1994). *Qualitative data analysis* (2d ed.). Beverly Hills, CA: Sage.

Milgram, S., Bickman, L., & Berkowitz, L. (1969). Note on the drawing power of crowds of different size. *Journal of Personality and Social Psychology, 13*, 79–82.

Miller, G., & Dingwall, R. (1997). *Context and method in qualitative research.* Beverly Hills, CA: Sage.

Milsap, R.E., & Taylor, R. (1996). Latent variable models in the investigation of discrimination: Theory and practice. *Journal of Management, 22*, 653–673.

Miranda, S.M. (1994). Avoidance of groupthink: Meeting management using group support systems. *Small Group Research, 25*, 105–136.

Mishra, J. (1990). Managing the grapevine. *Public Personnel Management, 19*, 213–228.

Mishra, P.K., & Das, B.K. (1983). Group size and helping behavior: A comprehensive review. *Perspectives in Psychological Researches, 6*, 60–64.

Mitroff, I.I. (1982). Dialectic squared: A fundamental difference in perception of the meanings of some key concepts in social science. *Decision Sciences, 13*, 222–224.

Mizruchi, M.S. (1985). Local sports teams and the celebration of community: A comparative analysis of the home advantage. *Sociological Quarterly, 26*, 507–518.

Mizruchi, M.S. (1994). Social network analysis: Recent achievements and current controversies. *Acta Sociologica, 37*, 329–343.

Molm, L.D. (1986). Gender, power, and legitimization: A test of three theories. *American Journal of Sociology, 91*, 1156–1186.

Mook, D.G. (1983). In defense of external invalidity. *American Psychologist, 38*, 379–387.

Moore, P.J., & Gump, B.B. (1995). Information integration in juror decision making. *Journal of Applied Social Psychology, 25*, 2158–2179.

Moorhead, G., Ference, R., & Neck, C.P. (1991). Group decision fiascoes continue: Space shuttle Challenger and a revised groupthink framework. *Human Relations, 44*, 539–550.

Moorhead, G., & Montanari, J.R. (1986). An empirical investigation of the groupthink phenomenon. *Human Relations, 39*, 399–410.

Moreland, R.L., Hogg, M.A., & Hains, S.C. (1994). Back to the future: Social psychological research on groups. *Journal of Experimental Social Psychology, 30*, 527–555.

Moscovici, S. (1980). Toward a theory of conversion behavior. *Advances in Experimental Social Psychology, 13,* 309–329.

Moscovici, S., & Paicheler, G. (1983). Minority or majority influences: Social change, compliance, and conversion. In H.H. Blumberg, A.P. Hare, V. Kent, & M. Davies (Eds.), *Small groups and social interaction* (Vol. 1, pp. 215–224). New York: Wiley.

Mowen, J.C., & Linder, D.E. (1986). Discretionary aspects of jury decision making. In H.R. Arkes & K.R. Hammond (Eds.), *Judgment and decision making* (pp. 593–612). Cambridge: Cambridge University Press.

Mucchi-Faina, A. (1987). Mouvement social et conversion. In S. Moscovici & G. Mugny (Eds.), *Psychologie de la conversion* (pp. 82–93). Cousset, France: Delval.

Mucchi-Faina, A. (1994). Minority influence: The effects of social status of an inclusive versus exclusive group. *European Journal of Social Psychology, 24,* 679–692.

Mucchi-Faina, A., Maass, A., & Volpato, C. (1991). Social influence: The role of originality. *European Journal of Social Psychology, 21,* 183–197.

Mullen, B. (1983). Operationalizing the effect of the group on the individual: A self-attention perspective. *Journal of Experimental Social Psychology, 19,* 295–322.

Mullen, B. (1985). Strength and immediacy of sources: A meta-analytic evaluation of the forgotten elements of social impact theory. *Journal of Personality and Social Psychology, 48,* 1458–1466.

Mullen, B. (1986a). Atrocity as a function of lynch mob composition: A self-attention perspective. *Personality and Social Psychology Bulletin, 12,* 187–197.

Mullen, B. (1986b). Stuttering, audience size, and the Other-Total Ratio: A self-attention perspective. *Journal of Applied Social Psychology, 16,* 139–149.

Mullen, B. (1986c). Effects of strength and immediacy in group contexts: Reply to Jackson. *Journal of Personality and Social Psychology, 50,* 514–516.

Mullen, B. (1987). Self-attention theory: The effects of group composition on the individual. In B. Mullen & G.R. Goethals (Eds.), *Theories of group behavior* (pp. 125–146). New York: Springer-Verlag.

Mullen, B., & Baumeister, R.F. (1987). Group effects on self-attention and performance: Social loafing, social facilitation, and social impairment. *Review of Personality and Social Psychology, 9,* 189–206.

Mullen, B., & Hu, L. (1989). Perceptions of ingroup and outgroup variability: A meta-analytic integration. *Basic and Applied Social Psychology, 10,* 233–252.

Mullen, B., Johnson, C., & Salas, E. (1991). Productivity loss in brainstorming groups: A meta-analytic integration. *Basic and Applied Social Psychology, 12,* 3–24.

Mullen, B., Johnson, D.A., & Drake, S.D. (1987). Organizational productivity as a function of group composition: A self-attention perspective. *Journal of Social Psychology, 127,* 143–150.

Munemori, J., & Nagasawa, Y. (1996). GUNGEN: Groupware for a new idea generation support system. *Information and Software Technology, 38,* 213–220.

Muthny, F.A. (1989). Job strains and job satisfaction of dialysis nurses. *Psychotherapy and Psychosomatics, 51,* 150–155.

Myers, J.L., DiCecco, J.V., & Lorch, R.F. Jr. (1981). Group dynamics and individual performances: Pseudogroup and quasi-F analyses. *Journal of Personality and Social Psychology, 40,* 86–98.

Nagao, D.H., & Davis, J.H. (1980). The effects of prior experience on mock juror case judgments. *Social Psychology Quarterly, 43,* 190–199.

Nebeker, D.M., & Tatum, C. (1993). The effects of computer monitoring, standards, and rewards on work performance, job satisfaction, and stress. *Journal of Applied Social Psychology, 23,* 508–536.

Neck, C.P., & Moorhead, G. (1995). Groupthink remodeled: The importance of leadership, time pressure, and methodical decision-making procedures. *Human Relations, 48,* 537–557.

Nemeth, C.J. (1986). Differential contributions of majority and minority influence. *Psychological Review, 93,* 23–32.

Nemeth, C.J., & Kwan, J. (1985). Originality of word associations as a function of majority and minority influence. *Social Psychology Quarterly, 48,* 277–282.

Nemeth, C.J., & Kwan, J.L. (1987). Minority influence, divergent thinking and detection of correct solutions. *Journal of Applied Social Psychology, 17,* 788–799.

Nemeth, C.J., Mayseless, O., Sherman, J., & Brown, Y. (1990). Exposure to dissent and recall of information. *Journal of Personality and Social Psychology, 58,* 429–437.

Nemeth, C.J., Mosier, K., & Chiles, C. (1992). When convergent thought improves performance: Majority versus minority influence. *Personality and Social Psychology Bulletin, 18,* 139–144.

Nemeth, C.J., & Wachtler, J. (1983). Creative problem solving as a result of majority and minority influence. *European Journal of Social Psychology, 13,* 45–55.

Neville, K.J., Bisson, R.U., French, J., & Boll, P.A. (1994). Subjective fatigue of C-141 aircrews during Operation Desert Storm. *Human Factors, 36,* 339–349.

Nisbett, R.E., & Ross, L. (1980). *Human inference.* Englewood Cliffs, NJ: Prentice-Hall.

Nisbett, R.E., & Wilson, T.D. (1977). The halo effect: Evidence for unconscious alteration of judgments. *Journal of Personality and Social Psychology, 35,* 250–256.

Noel, J.G., Wann, D.L., & Branscombe, N.R. (1995). Peripheral ingroup membership status and public negativity toward outgroups. *Journal of Personality and Social Psychology, 68,* 127–137.

Novick, D.G., & Walpole, J. (1990). Enhancing the efficiency of multiparty interaction through computer mediation. *Interacting with Computers, 2,* 229–246.

Nowak, A., Szamrej, J., & Latané, B. (1990). From private attitude to public opinion: A dynamic theory of social impact. *Psychological Review, 97,* 362–376.

O'Brien, S. (1993). Morale and the inner life in the armed forces. *Therapeutic Communities, 14,* 285–296.

Offermann, L.R., Kennedy, J.K., & Wirtz, P.W. (1994). Implicit leadership theories: Content, structure, and generalizability. *Leadership Quarterly, 5,* 43–58.

Olson, J.M., & Hafer, C.L. (1996). Affect, motivation, and cognition in relative deprivation research. In R.M. Sorrentino & E.T. Higgins (Eds.), *Handbook of motivation and cognition* (Vol. 3, pp. 85–117). New York: Guilford Press.

Olson, M. (1965). *The logic of collective action.* Cambridge, MA: Harvard University Press.

Orasanu, J.M. (1993). Decision making in the cockpit. In E.L. Weiner, B.G. Kanki, & R.L. Helmreich (Eds.), *Cockpit resource management* (pp. 137–172). San Francisco: Academic Press.

Orbell, J.M., & Dawes, R.M. (1981). Social dilemmas. In G. Stephenson & J.H. Davis (Eds.), *Progress in applied social psychology* (Vol. 1, pp. 37–66). Chichester: Wiley.

Orbell, J.M., & Dawes, R.M. (1991). A "cognitive miser" theory of cooperators' advantage. *American Political Science Review, 85,* 515–528.

Orbell, J.M., van de Kragt, A.J.C., & Dawes, R.M. (1988). Explaining discussion-induced cooperation. *Journal of Personality and Social Psychology, 54,* 811–819.

O'Reilly, C.A. III (1978). The intentional distortion of information in organizational communication: A laboratory and field approach. *Human Relations, 31,* 173–193.

Orgren, R.A., Weiler, P.G., & Higby, H.R. (1989). Multidisciplinary training in geriatric health care for preclinical students. *Gerontology and Geriatrics Education, 10,* 13–21.

Orlady, H.W., & Foushee, H.C. (1987). *Proceedings of the NASA/MAC workshop on cockpit resource management.* Moffett Field, CA: NASA-Ames Research Center.

Osborn, A.F. (1957). *Applied imagination.* New York: Scribner's.

Osgood, C.E. (1962). *An alternative to war or surrender.* Urbana: University of Illinois Press.

Ouchi, W.G. (1981). *Theory Z: How American business can meet the Japanese challenge.* Reading, MA: Addison-Wesley.

Papastamou, S., & Mugny, G. (1990). Synchronic consistency and psychologization in minority influence. *European Journal of Social Psychology, 20,* 85–98.

Park, W.W. (1990). A review of research on groupthink. *Journal of Behavioral Decision Making, 3,* 229–245.

Parks, C.D. (1994). The predictive ability of social values in resource dilemmas and public goods games. *Personality and Social Psychology Bulletin, 20,* 431–438.

Parks, C.D., & Cowlin, R. (1995). Group discussion as affected by number of alternatives and by a time limit. *Organizational Behavior and Human Decision Processes, 62,* 267–275.

Parks, C.D., & Cowlin, R.A. (1996). Acceptance of uncommon information into group discussion when that information is or is not demonstrable. *Organizational Behavior and Human Decision Processes, 66,* 307–315.

Parks, C.D., & Hulbert, L.G. (1995). High- and low-trusters' responses to fear in a payoff matrix. *Journal of Conflict Resolution, 39,* 718–730.

Parks, C.D., & Komorita, S.S. (1997). Reciprocal strategies for large groups. *Personality and Social Psychology Review, 1,* 314–326.

Parks, C.D., & Komorita, S.S. (in press). Reciprocity research and its implications for the negotiation process. *Negotiation Journal.*

Patenaude, A.F., Szymanski, L., & Rappaport, J. (1979). Psychological costs of bone marrow transplantation in children. *American Journal of Orthopsychiatry, 49,* 409–422.

Paulus, P.B. (1983). Group influence on individual task performance. In P.B. Paulus (Ed.), *Basic group processes* (pp. 97–120). New York: Springer-Verlag.

Paulus, P.B., & Dzindolet, M.T. (1993). Social influence processes in group brainstorming. *Journal of Personality and Social Psychology, 64,* 575–586.

Paulus, P.B., Dzindolet, M.T., Poletes, G., & Camacho, L.M. (1993). Perception of performance in group brainstorming: The illusion of group effectivity. *Personality and Social Psychology Bulletin, 19*, 73–89.

Paulus, P.B., Larey, T.S., Putman, V.L., Leggett, K.L., & Roland, E.J. (1996). Social influence processes in computer brainstorming. *Basic and Applied Social Psychology, 18*, 3–14.

Paulus, P.B., & Murdoch, P. (1971). Anticipated evaluation and audience presence in the enhancement of dominant responses. *Journal of Experimental Social Psychology, 7*, 280–291.

Pearson, C.A.L. (1992). Autonomous workgroups: An evaluation at an industrial site. *Human Relations, 45*, 905–936.

Peiro, J.M., Gonzalez-Roma, V., & Ramos, J. (1992). The influence of work-team climate on role stress, tension, satisfaction and leadership perceptions. *European Review of Applied Psychology, 42*, 49–58.

Pendry, L.F., & Macrae, C.N. (1994). Stereotypes and mental life: The case of the motivated but thwarted tactician. *Journal of Experimental Social Psychology, 30*, 303–325.

Pennington, N., & Hastie, R. (1990). Practical implications of psychological research on juror and jury decision making. *Personality and Social Psychology Bulletin, 16*, 90–105.

Penrod, S.D. (1990). Predictors of jury decision making in criminal and civil cases: A field experiment. *Forensic Reports, 3*, 261–277.

Penrod, S.D., & Cutler, B.L. (1987). Assessing the competence of juries. In I.B. Weiner & A.K. Hess (Eds.), *Handbook of forensic psychology* (pp. 293–318). New York: Wiley and Sons.

Penrod, S.D., Fulero, S.M., & Cutler, B.L. (1995). Expert psychological testimony on eyewitness reliability before and after Daubert: The state of the law and the science. *Behavioral Sciences and the Law, 13*, 229–259.

Penrod, S.D., & Hastie, R. (1980). A computer simulation of jury decision making. *Psychological Review, 87*, 133–159.

Perez, J.A., & Mugny, G. (1987). Paradoxical effects of categorization in minority influence: When being an outgroup is an advantage. *European Journal of Social Psychology, 17*, 157–169.

Peters, L.H., Hartke, D.D., & Pohlmann, J.T. (1985). Fiedler's contingency theory of leadership: An application of the meta-analysis procedures of Schmidt and Hunter. *Psychological Bulletin, 97*, 274–285.

Peters, T.J., & Waterman, R.H. (1982). *In search of excellence.* New York: Harper and Row.

Peterson, R.S., & Nemeth, C.J. (1996). Focus versus flexibility: Majority and minority influence can both improve performance. *Personality and Social Psychology Bulletin, 22*, 14–23.

Petrovic, O., & Krickl, O. (1994). Traditionally moderated versus computer-supported brainstorming: A comparative study. *Information and Management, 27*, 233–243.

Pettigrew, T.F. (1978). Three issues in ethnicity: Boundaries, deprivations, and perceptions. In J.M. Yinger & S.J. Cutler (Eds.), *Major social issues* (pp. 25–49). New York: Free Press.

Petty, R.E., & Cacioppo, J.T. (1981). *Attitudes and persuasion.* Dubuque, IA: William C. Brown.

Petty, R.E., Harkins, S.G., & Williams, K.D. (1980). The effects of group diffusion of cognitive effort on attitudes: An information-processing view. *Journal of Personality and Social Psychology, 38*, 81–92.

Petty, R.E., Harkins, S.G., Williams, K.D., & Latané, B. (1977). The effects of group size on cognitive effort and evaluation. *Personality and Social Psychology Bulletin, 3*, 579–582.

Phillips, A.S., & Bedian, A.G. (1994). Leader-follower exchange quality: The role of personal and interpersonal attributes. *Academy of Management Journal, 37*, 990–1001.

Phillips, J.S., & Lord, R.G. (1982). Schematic information processing and perceptions of leadership in problem-solving groups. *Journal of Applied Psychology, 67*, 486–492.

Phinney, J.S. (1991). Ethnic identity and self-esteem: A review and integration. *Hispanic Journal of Behavioral Sciences, 13*, 193–208.

Pinkley, R.L. (1990). Dimensions of conflict frame. *Journal of Applied Psychology, 75*, 117–126.

Platow, M.J., O'Connell, A., Shave, R., & Hanning, P. (1995). Social evaluation and unfair allocators in interpersonal and intergroup situations. *British Journal of Social Psychology, 14*, 234–242.

Platt, M.B. (1992). The effects of selection rules on group composition and selection outcome. *Journal of Social Behavior and Personality, 7*, 59–77.

Plott, C.R., & Levine, M.E. (1978). A model of agenda influence on committee decisions. *American Economic Review, 68*, 146–160.

Podsakoff, P.M., MacKenzie, S.B., Moorman, R.H., & Fetter, R. (1990). Transformational leader behaviors and their effects on followers' trust in leader, satisfaction, and organizational citizenship behaviors. *Leadership Quarterly, 1*, 107–142.

Pollard, R. (1986). Home advantage in soccer: A retrospective analysis. *Journal of Sport Sciences, 4*, 237–248.

Polley, R.B., & Eid, J. (1994). First among equals: Leaders, peers, and choice. *Journal of Group Psychotherapy, Psychodrama and Sociometry, 47*, 59–76.

Poulson, R.L. (1990). Mock juror attribution of criminal responsibility: Effects of race and the Guilty But Mentally Ill (GBMI) verdict option. *Journal of Applied Social Psychology, 20*, 1596–1611.

Price, K.H. (1987). Decision responsibility, task responsibility, identifiability, and social loafing. *Organizational Behavior and Human Decision Processes, 40*, 330–345.

Prince, C., & Salas, E. (1993). Training and research for teamwork in the military aircrew. In E.L. Weiner, B.G. Kanki, & R.L. Helmreich (Eds.), *Cockpit resource management* (pp. 337–366). San Diego: Academic Press.

Pritchard, R.D. (1969). Equity theory: A review and critique. *Organizational Behavior and Human Performance, 4*, 176–211.

Pritchard, R.D., Dunnette, M.D., & Jorgenson, D.O. (1972). Effects of perceived equity and inequity on worker performance and satisfaction. *Journal of Applied Psychology Monograph, 56*, 75–94.

Pruitt, D.G. (1971). Choice shifts in group discussion: An introductory review. *Journal of Personality and Social Psychology, 20*, 339–360.

Pruitt, D.G. (1981). *Negotiation behavior.* New York: Academic Press.

Pruitt, D.G., & Carnevale, P.J. (1993). *Negotiation in social conflict.* Pacific Grove, CA: Brooks Cole.

Pruitt, D.G., & Kimmel, M.J. (1977). Twenty years of experimental gaming: Critique, synthesis, and suggestions for the future. *Annual Review of Psychology, 28*, 363–392.

Pruitt, D.G., Peirce, R.S., McGillicuddy, N.B., Welton, G.L., & Castrianno, L.M. (1993). Long-term success in mediation. *Law and Human Behavior, 17*, 313–330.

Raimbault, G. (1991). The seriously ill child: Management of family and medical surroundings. In D. Papadatou & C. Papadatos (Eds.), *Children and death* (pp. 177–187). New York: Hemisphere Publishing.

Rajecki, D.W., Ickes, W., Corcoran, C., & Lenerz, K. (1977). Social facilitation of human performance: Mere presence effects. *Journal of Social Psychology, 102*, 297–310.

Rapoport, Am. (1987). Research paradigms and expected utility models for the provision of step-level public goods. *Psychological Review, 94*, 74–83.

Rapoport, Am. (1988). Provision of step-level public goods: Effects of inequality in resources. *Journal of Personality and Social Psychology, 54*, 432–440.

Rapoport, Am., & Bornstein, G. (1989). Solving public good problems in competition between equal and unequal size groups. *Journal of Conflict Resolution, 33*, 460–479.

Rapoport, Am., Bornstein, G., & Erev, I. (1989). Intergroup competition for public goods: Effects of unequal resources and relative group size. *Journal of Personality and Social Psychology, 56*, 748–756.

Rapoport, Am., & Eshed-Levy, D. (1989). Provision of step-level public goods: Effects of greed and fear of being gypped. *Organizational Behavior and Human Decision Processes, 44*, 325–344.

Rapoport, An., & Chammah, A.M. (1965). *Prisoner's dilemma.* Ann Arbor, MI: University of Michigan Press.

Reid, F.J.M., Malinek, V., Stott, C.J.T., & Evans, J. St.B.T. (1996). The messaging threshold in computer-mediated communication. *Ergonomics, 39*, 1017–1037.

Rentsch, J.R. (1990). Climate and culture: Interaction and qualitative differences in organizational meanings. *Journal of Applied Psychology, 75*, 668–681.

Restle, F., & Davis, J.H. (1962). Success and speed of problem solving by individuals and groups. *Psychological Review, 69*, 520–536.

Rice, R.W. (1978). Construct validity of the least preferred coworker (LPC) score. *Psychological Bulletin, 85*, 1199–1237.

Richardson, K.D., & Cialdini, R.B. (1981). Basking and blasting: Tactics of indirect self-presentation. In J.T. Tedeschi (Ed.), *Impression management theory and social psychological research* (pp. 41–53). New York: Academic Press.

Ridgeway, C.L., & Balkwell, J.W. (1997). Group processes and the diffusion of status beliefs. *Social Psychology Quarterly, 60*, 14–31.

Ringelmann, M. (1913). Recherches sur les moteurs animés: Travail de l'homme. *Annales de l'Institut National Agronomique, 12*, 1–40.

Robinson, J.P. (1988). Time-diary evidence about the social psychology of everyday life. In J.E. McGrath (Ed.), *The social psychology of time* (pp. 134–150). Newbury Park, CA: Sage.

Roehl, J.A., & Cook, R.F. (1989). Mediation in interpersonal disputes: Effectiveness and limitations. In K. Kressel & D.G. Pruitt (Eds.), *Mediation behavior* (pp. 31–52). San Francisco: Jossey-Bass.

Roese, N.J. (1994). The functional basis of counterfactual thinking. *Journal of Personality and Social Psychology, 66,* 805–818.

Rohrbaugh, J. (1979). Improving the quality of group judgment: Social judgment analysis and the Delphi technique. *Organizational Behavior and Human Performance, 24,* 73–92.

Rosenbaum, M.E. (1986). The repulsion hypothesis: On the nondevelopment of relationships. *Journal of Personality and Social Psychology, 51,* 1156–1166.

Rosenthal, R. (1984). *Meta-analytic procedures for social research.* Beverly Hills, CA: Sage.

Rouse, W.B., Cannon-Bowers, J.A., & Salas, E. (1992). The role of mental models in team performance in complex systems. *IEEE Transactions on Systems, Man, and Cybernetics, 22,* 1296–1308.

Roy, M.C., Gauvin, S., & Limayen, M. (1996). Electronic group brainstorming: The role of feedback on productivity. *Small Group Research, 27,* 215–225.

Rugs, D., & Kaplan, M.F. (1993). Effectiveness of informational and normative influences in group decision making depends on group interactive goal. *British Journal of Social Psychology, 32,* 147–158.

Rush, M.C., Thomas, J.C., & Lord, R.G. (1977). Implicit leadership theory: A potential threat to the internal validity of leader behavior questionnaires. *Organizational Behavior and Human Performance, 20,* 93–110.

Rutte, C.G., & Wilke, H.A.M. (1985). Preference for decision structures in a social dilemma situation. *European Journal of Social Psychology, 15,* 367–370.

Rutte, C.G., Wilke, H.A.M., & Messick, D.M. (1987). Scarcity or abundance caused by people or the environment as determinants of behavior in the resource dilemma. *Journal of Experimental Social Psychology, 23,* 208–216.

Sainfort, F.C., Gustafson, D.H., Bosworth, K., & Hawkins, R.P. (1990). Decision support system effectiveness: Conceptual framework and empirical evaluation. *Organizational Behavior and Human Decision Processes, 45,* 232–252.

Saks, M. (1976). The limits of Scientific Jury Selection: Ethical and empirical. *Jurimetrics Journal, 17,* 3–22.

Saks, M., & Hastie, R. (1978). *Social psychology in court.* Princeton, NJ: Van Nostrand-Reinhold.

Salas, E., Bowers, C.A., & Cannon-Bowers, J.A. (1995). Military team research: 10 years of progress. *Military Psychology, 7,* 55–75.

Samuelson, C.D. (1991). Perceived task difficulty, causal attributions, and preferences for structural change in resource dilemmas. *Personality and Social Psychology Bulletin, 17,* 181–187.

Samuelson, C.D., & Messick, D.M. (1986a). Alternative structural solutions to resource dilemmas. *Organizational Behavior and Human Decision Processes, 37,* 139–155.

Samuelson, C.D., & Messick, D.M. (1986b). Inequities in access to and use of shared resources in social dilemmas. *Journal of Personality and Social Psychology, 51,* 960–967.

Samuelson, C.D., Messick, D.M., Rutte, C.G., & Wilke, H. (1984). Individual and structural solutions to resource dilemmas in two cultures. *Journal of Personality and Social Psychology, 47,* 94–104.

Sandal, G.M., Vaernes, R., & Ursin, H. (1995). Interpersonal relations during simulated space missions. *Aviation, Space, and Environmental Medicine, 66,* 617–624.

Sanders, G.S. (1981). Driven by distraction: An integrative review of social facilitation theory and research. *Journal of Experimental Social Psychology, 17,* 227–251.

Sanders, G.S. (1984). Self-presentation and drive in social facilitation. *Journal of Experimental Social Psychology, 20,* 312–322.

Sanders, G.S., & Baron, R.S. (1975). The motivating effects of distraction on task performance. *Journal of Personality and Social Psychology, 32,* 956–963.

Sanders, G.S., Baron, R.S., & Moore, D.L. (1978). Distraction and social comparison as mediators of social facilitation effects. *Journal of Experimental Social Psychology, 14,* 291–303.

Sanna, L.J. (1992). Self-efficacy theory: Implications for social facilitation and social loafing. *Journal of Personality and Social Psychology, 62,* 774–786.

Sanna, L.J. (1996a). Defensive pessimism, optimism, and simulating alternatives: Some ups and downs of counterfactual thinking. *Journal of Personality and Social Psychology, 71,* 1020–1036.

Sanna, L.J. (1996b). Group productivity: An attributional analysis of free-rider, sucker, and social compensation effects. Unpublished manuscript.

Sanna, L.J., & Mark, M.M. (1991, June). *Potential mediators of social loafing: A structural model.* Paper presented at the third annual convention of the American Psychological Society, Washington, DC.

Sanna, L.J., & Mark, M.M. (1995). Self-handicapping, expected evaluation, and performance: Accentuating the positive and attenuating the negative. *Organizational Behavior and Human Decision Processes, 64,* 84–102.

Sanna, L.J., & Parks, C.D. (1997). Group research trends in social and organizational psychology: Whatever happened to intragroup research? *Psychological Science, 8,* 261–267.

Sanna, L.J., & Pusecker, P.A. (1994). Self-efficacy, valence of self-evaluation, and performance. *Personality and Social Psychology Bulletin, 20,* 82–92.

Sanna, L.J., & Shotland, R.L. (1990). Valence of anticipated evaluation and social facilitation. *Journal of Experimental Social Psychology, 26,* 82–92.

Sanna, L.J., Turley, K.J., & Mark, M.M. (1996). Expected evaluation, goals, and performance: Mood as input. *Personality and Social Psychology Bulletin, 22,* 323–335.

Savicki, V., Kelley, M., & Lingenfelter, D. (1996a). Gender, group composition, and task type in small task groups using computer-mediated communication. *Computers in Human Behavior, 12,* 549–565.

Savicki, V., Kelley, M., & Lingenfelter, D. (1996b). Gender and group composition in small task groups using computer-mediated communication. *Computers in Human Behavior, 12,* 209–224.

Scandura, T.A., & Graen, G.B. (1984). Moderating effects of initial leader-member exchange status on the effects of a leadership intervention. *Journal of Applied Psychology, 69,* 428–436.

Schein, E.H. (1985). *Organizational culture and leadership*. San Francisco: Jossey-Bass.

Schein, E.H. (1990). Organizational culture. *American Psychologist, 45*, 109–119.

Schein, E.H. (1993). Legitimating clinical research in the study of organizational culture. *Journal of Counseling and Development, 71*, 703–708.

Schlenker, B.R. (1980). *Impression management: The self-concept, social identity, and interpersonal relations*. Belmont, CA: Brooks/Cole.

Schlenker, B.R., & Bonoma, T.V. (1978). Fun and games: The validity of games for the study of conflict. *Journal of Conflict Resolution, 22*, 7–38.

Schlenker, B.R., Phillips, S.T., Boniecki, K.A., & Schlenker, D.R. (1995a). Championship pressures: Choking or triumphing in one's own territory? *Journal of Personality and Social Psychology, 68*, 632–643.

Schlenker, B.R., Phillips, S.T., Boniecki, K.A., & Schlenker, D.R. (1995b). Where is the choke? *Journal of Personality and Social Psychology, 68*, 649–652.

Schmitt, B.H., Gilovich, T., Goore, N., & Joseph, L. (1986). Mere presence and social facilitation: One more time. *Journal of Experimental Social Psychology, 22*, 242–248.

Schmitt, D.R., & Marwell, G. (1972). Withdrawal and reward allocation as responses to inequity. *Journal of Experimental Social Psychology, 8*, 207–221.

Schneider, B. (1987). The people make the place. *Personnel Psychology, 40*, 437–453.

Schriesheim, C.A., Bannister, B.D., & Money, W.H. (1979). Psychometric properties of the LPC scale: An extension of Rice's review. *Academy of Management Review, 4*, 287–290.

Schriesheim, C.A., Tepper, B.J., & Tetrault, L.A. (1994). Least preferred co-worker score, situational control, and leadership effectiveness: A meta-analysis of contingency model performance predictions. *Journal of Applied Psychology, 79*, 561–573.

Schwartz, A.E. (1994). Group decision-making. *CPA Journal, 64*(8), 60–63.

Schwartz, B., & Barsky, S.F. (1977). The home advantage. *Social Forces, 55*, 641–661.

Schweiger, D.M., Sandberg, W.R., & Ragan, J.W. (1986). Group approaches for improving strategic decision making: A comparative analysis of dialectical inquiry, devil's advocacy, and consensus. *Academy of Management Journal, 29*, 51–71.

Schweiger, D.M., Sandberg, W.R., & Rechner, P.L. (1989). Experiential effects of dialectical inquiry, devil's advocacy, and consensus approaches to strategic decision making. *Academy of Management Journal, 32*, 745–772.

Schwenk, C.R. (1990). Effects of devil's advocacy and dialectical inquiry on decision making: A meta-analysis. *Organizational Behavior and Human Decision Processes, 47*, 161–176.

Schwenk, C.R., & Cosier, R.A. (1993). Effects of consensus and devil's advocacy on strategic decision-making. *Journal of Applied Social Psychology, 23*, 126–139.

Schwenk, C.R., & Valacich, J.S. (1994). Effects of devil's advocacy and dialectical inquiry on individuals versus groups. *Organizational Behavior and Human Decision Processes, 59*, 210–222.

Scott, J. (1992). *Social network analysis: A handbook*. Newbury Park, CA: Sage.

Sechrest, L., & Figueredo, A.J. (1993). Program evaluation. *Annual Review of Psychology, 44*, 645–674.

Sedikides, C., & Jackson, J.M. (1990). Social impact theory: A field test of source strength, source immediacy, and number of targets. *Basic and Applied Social Psychology, 11*, 273–281.

Sedikides, C., & Strube, M.J (1995). The multiply motivated self. *Personality and Social Psychology Bulletin, 21*, 1330–1335.

Sedikides, C., & Strube, M.J (1997). Self-evaluation: To thine own self be good, to thine own self be sure, to thine own self be true, and to thine own self be better. *Advances in Experimental Social Psychology, 29*, 209–269.

Sessa, V.I. (1996). Using perspective taking to manage conflict and affect in teams. *Journal of Applied Behavioral Science, 32*, 101–115.

Seta, J.J., & Hassan, R.K. (1980). Awareness of prior success or failure: A critical factor in task performance. *Journal of Personality and Social Psychology, 39*, 70–76.

Shaud, J.A. (1989). Aircraft coordination training in the U.S. Air Force Air Training Command. *Aviation, Space, and Environmental Medicine, 60*, 601–602.

Shaw, M.E. (1932). Comparison of individuals and small groups in the rational solution of complex problems. *American Journal of Psychology, 44*, 491–504.

Shepherd, M.M., Briggs, R.O., Reinig, B.A., Yen, J., & Nunamaker, J.F. (1995). Invoking social comparison to improve electronic brainstorming: Beyond anonymity. *Journal of Management Information Systems, 12*(3), 155–170.

Sheppard, B.H., Blumenfeld-Jones, K., & Roth, J. (1989). Informal thirdpartyship: Studies of everyday conflict intervention. In K. Kressel & D.G. Pruitt (Eds.), *Mediation research* (pp. 166–189). San Francisco: Jossey-Bass.

Shepperd, J.A. (1993). Productivity loss in performance groups: A motivation analysis. *Psychological Bulletin, 113*, 67–81.

Shepperd, J.A., & Wright, R.A. (1989). Individual contribution to a collective effort: An incentive analysis. *Personality and Social Psychology Bulletin, 15*, 141–149.

Sheridan, J.E. (1992). Organizational culture and employee retention. *Academy of Management Journal, 35*, 1036–1056.

Sherif, M., Harvey, O.J., White, B.J., Hood, W.R., & Sherif, C. (1961). *Intergroup conflict and cooperation: The Robbers Cave experiment*. Norman, OK: Institute of Group Relations.

Shirakashi, S. (1985). Social loafing of Japanese students. *Hiroshima Forum for Psychology, 10*, 35–40.

Siegel, J., Dubrovsky, V.J., Kiesler, S., & McGuire, T.W. (1986). Group processes in computer-mediated communication. *Organizational Behavior and Human Decision Processes, 37*, 157–187.

Siegel, S., & Fouraker, L.E. (1960). *Bargaining and group decision making*. New York: McGraw-Hill.

Sillars, A.L. (1981). Attributions and interpersonal conflict resolution. In J.H. Harvey, W. Ickes, & R.F. Kidd (Eds.), *New directions in attribution research* (Vol. 3, pp. 279–305). Hillsdale, NJ: Erlbaum.

Silva, J.M., & Andrew, J.A. (1987). An analysis of game location and basketball performance in the Atlantic Coast Conference. *International Journal of Sport Psychology, 18*, 188–204.

Silver, S.D., Cohen, B.P., & Crutchfield, J.H. (1994). Status differentiation and information exchange in face-to-face and computer-mediated idea generation. *Social Psychology Quarterly, 57*, 108–123.

Simpson, J.A., & Harris, B.A. (1994). Interpersonal attraction. In A.L. Weber & J.H. Harvey (Eds.), *Perspectives on close relationships* (pp. 45–66). Boston: Allyn & Bacon.

Singh, R., & Singh, R.P. (1989). Job specificity as a deterrent to social loafing. *Indian Council of Social Science Research*, 36, 27–39.

Skogstad, A., Dyregrov, A., & Hellesoy, O.H. (1995). Cockpit-cabin crew interaction: Satisfaction with communication and information exchange. *Aviation, Space, and Environmental Medicine*, 66, 841–848.

Sloan, L.R. (1989). The motives of sports fans. In J.H. Goldstein (Ed.), *Sports, games, and play: Social and psychological viewpoints* (2d ed., pp. 175–240). Hillsdale, NJ: Erlbaum.

Smilowitz, M., Compton, D.C., & Flint, L. (1988). The effects of computer-mediated communication on an individual's judgment: A study based on the methods of Asch's social influence experiment. *Computers in Human Behavior*, 4, 311–321.

Smith, C., & Comer, D. (1994). Self-organization in small groups: A study of group effectiveness within non-equilibrium conditions. *Human Relations*, 47, 553–581.

Smith, H.J., & Tyler, T.R. (1997). Choosing the right pond: The impact of group membership on self-esteem and group-oriented behaviors. *Journal of Experimental Social Psychology*, 33, 146–170.

Smith, K.A., Smith, K.G., Olian, J.D., Sims, H.P., O'Bannon, D.P., & Scully, J. (1994). Top management team demography and process: The role of social integration and communication. *Administrative Science Quarterly*, 39, 412–438.

Smith, M.J., Carayon, P., Sanders, K.J., Lim, S.Y., & LeGrande, D. (1992). Employee stress and health complaints in jobs with and without electronic performance monitoring. *Applied Ergonomics*, 23, 17–28.

Smith, V.L., & Kassin, S.M. (1993). Effects of the dynamite charge on the deliberations of deadlocked mock juries. *Law and Human Behavior*, 17, 625–643.

Smoke, W.H., & Zajonc, R.B. (1962). On the reliability of group judgments and decision. In J.H. Criswell, H. Solomon, & P. Suppes (Eds.), *Mathematical models in small group processes* (pp. 322–333). Stanford: Stanford University Press.

Smolensky, M.W., Carmody, M.A., & Halcomb, C.G. (1990). The influence of task type, group structure and extroversion on uninhibited speech in computer-mediated communication. *Computers in Human Behavior*, 6, 261–272.

Snyder, C.R., Lassegard, M.A., & Ford, C.E. (1986). Distancing after group success and failure: Basking in reflected glory and cutting off reflected failure. *Journal of Personality and Social Psychology*, 51, 382–388.

Snyder, E.E., & Purdy, D.A. (1985). The home advantage in collegiate basketball. *Sociology of Sport Journal*, 2, 352–356.

Song, X.M., & Parry, M.E. (1997). Teamwork barriers in Japanese high-technology firms: The sociocultural differences between R&D and marketing managers. *Journal of Product Innovation Management*, 14, 356–371.

Spanos, N.P., Dubreuil, S.C., & Gwynn, M.I. (1991). The effects of expert testimony concerning rape on the verdicts and beliefs of mock jurors. *Imagination, Cognition, and Personality*, 11, 37–51.

Spanos, N.P., Gwynn, M.I., & Terrade, K. (1989). Effects on mock jurors of experts favorable and unfavorable toward hypnotically elicited eyewitness testimony. *Journal of Applied Psychology*, 74, 922–926.

Spears, R., & Lea, M. (1994). Panacea or panopticon? The hidden power in computer-mediated communication. *Communication Research, 21*, 427–459.

Spears, R., Lea, M., & Lee, S. (1990). De-individuation and group polarization in computer-mediated communication. *British Journal of Social Psychology, 29*, 121–134.

Spence, K.W. (1956). *Behavior theory and conditioning.* New Haven: Yale University Press.

Stahelski, A.J., & Tsukuda, R.A. (1990). Predictors of cooperation in health care teams. *Small Group Research, 21*, 220–233.

Stasser, G. (1988). Computer simulation as a research tool: The DISCUSS model of group decision making. *Journal of Experimental Social Psychology, 24*, 393–422.

Stasser, G. (1992). Information salience and the discovery of hidden profiles by decision-making groups: A "thought experiment." *Organizational Behavior and Human Decision Processes, 52*, 156–181.

Stasser, G., & Davis, J.H. (1981). Group decision making and social influence: A social interaction sequence model. *Psychological Review, 88*, 523–551.

Stasser, G., & Stewart, D. (1992). Discovery of hidden profiles by decision-making groups: Solving a problem versus making a judgment. *Journal of Personality and Social Psychology, 63*, 426–434.

Stasser, G., & Taylor, L.A. (1991). Speaking turns in face-to-face discussions. *Journal of Personality and Social Psychology, 60*, 675–684.

Stasser, G., Taylor, L.A., & Hanna, C. (1989). Information sampling in structured and unstructured discussions of three- and six-person groups. *Journal of Personality and Social Psychology, 57*, 67–78.

Stasser, G., & Titus, W. (1985). Pooling of unshared information in group decision making: Biased information sampling during discussion. *Journal of Personality and Social Psychology, 48*, 1467–1478.

Stasser, G., & Titus, W. (1987). Effects of information load and percentage of shared information on the dissemination of unshared information during group discussion. *Journal of Personality and Social Psychology, 53*, 81–93.

Stasson, M.F., & Hawkes, W.G. (1995). Effect of group performance on subsequent individual performance: Does influence generalize beyond the issues discussed by the group? *Psychological Science, 6*, 305–307.

Stasson, M.F., Kameda, T., Parks, C.D., Zimmerman, S.K., & Davis, J.H. (1991). Effects of assigned group consensus requirement on group problem solving and group members' learning. *Social Psychology Quarterly, 54*, 25–35.

Steel, R.P., Jennings, K.R., & Lindsey, J.T. (1990). Quality circle problem solving and common cents: Evaluating study findings from a United States federal mint. *Journal of Applied Behavioral Science, 26*, 361–382.

Steenland, K., & Deppens, J.A. (1997). Effect of travel and rest on performance of professional basketball players. *Sleep, 20*, 366.

Steil, J.M., & Hay, J.L. (1997). Social comparison in the workplace: A study of 60 dual-career couples. *Personality and Social Psychology Bulletin, 23*, 427–438.

Steiner, I.D. (1966). Models for inferring relationships between group size and potential group productivity. *Behavioral Science, 11*, 273–283.

Steiner, I.D. (1972). *Group process and productivity.* New York: Academic Press.

Steiner, I.D. (1974). Whatever happened to the group in social psychology? *Journal of Experimental Social Psychology, 10,* 93–108.

Steiner, I.D. (1983). Whatever happened to the touted revival of the group? In H.H. Blumberg, A.P. Hare, V. Kent, & M. Davies (Eds.), *Small groups and social interaction* (Vol. 2, pp. 539–548). Chichester: Wiley and Sons.

Steiner, I.D. (1986). Paradigms and groups. *Advances in Experimental Social Psychology, 19,* 251–289.

Steiner, I.D., & Rajaratnam, N. (1961). A model for the comparison of individual and group performance scores. *Behavioral Science, 6,* 142–147.

Stern, P.C. (1976). Effect of incentives and education on resource conservation decisions in a simulated commons dilemma. *Journal of Personality and Social Psychology, 34,* 1285–1292.

Stiles, W.B. (1978). Verbal response modes and dimensions of interpersonal roles: A method of discourse analysis. *Journal of Personality and Social Psychology, 36,* 693–703.

Stone, W.S., & Allen, M.W. (1990). Assessing the impact of new communication technologies on organizational dynamics. *Consultation, 9,* 229–240.

Stouffer, S.A., Suchman, E.A., DeVinney, L.C., Star, S.A., & Williams, R.M. (1949). *The American soldier.* New York: Wiley.

Stout, R.J., Salas, E., & Carson, R. (1994). Individual task proficiency and team process: What's important for team functioning? *Military Psychology, 6,* 177–192.

Straus, S.G. (1996). Getting a clue: The effects of communication media and information distribution on participation and performance in computer-mediated and face-to-face groups. *Small Group Research, 27,* 115–142.

Straus, S.G., & McGrath, J.E. (1994). Does the medium matter? The interaction of task type and technology on group performance and member reactions. *Journal of Applied Psychology, 79,* 87–97.

Stroebe, W., Diehl, M., & Abakoumkin, G. (1992). The illusion of group effectivity. *Personality and Social Psychology Bulletin, 18,* 643–650.

Stroebe, W., & Frey, B.S. (1982). Self-interest and collective action: The economics and psychology of public goods. *British Journal of Social Psychology, 21,* 121–137.

Strube, M.J, & Garcia, J.E. (1981). A meta-analytic investigation of Fiedler's contingency model of leader effectiveness. *Psychological Bulletin, 90,* 307–321.

Strube, M.J, Miles, M.E., & Finch, W.H. (1981). The social facilitation of a simple task: Field tests of alternative explanations. *Personality and Social Psychology Bulletin, 7,* 701–707.

Suls, J., & Wills, T.A. (1981). *Social comparison.* Hillsdale, NJ: Erlbaum.

Summers, C. (1996). Multimedia environmental decision making simulation. *Behavior Research Methods, Instruments, and Computers, 28,* 598–602.

Swets, J.A., & Bjork, R.A. (1990). Enhancing human performance: An evaluation of "New Age" techniques considered by the U.S. Army. *Psychological Science, 1,* 85–96.

Szymanski, K., & Harkins, S.G. (1987). Social loafing and self-evaluation with a social standard. *Journal of Personality and Social Psychology, 53,* 891–897.

Szymanski, K., & Harkins, S.G. (1992). Self-evaluation and creativity. *Personality and Social Psychology Bulletin, 18,* 259–265.

Szymanski, K., & Harkins, S.G. (1993). The effect of experimenter evaluation on self-evaluation within the social loafing paradigm. *Journal of Experimental Social Psychology, 29,* 268–286.

Taha, L.H., & Calwell, B.S. (1993). Social isolation and integration in electronic environments. *Behaviour and Information Technology, 12,* 276–283.

Tajfel, H. (1982). *Social identity and intergroup relations.* Cambridge: Cambridge University Press.

Tajfel, H., & Turner, J.C. (1986). The social identity theory of intergroup behavior. In S. Worchel & W.G. Austin (Eds.), *Psychology of intergroup relations* (2d ed., pp. 7–24). Chicago: Nelson-Hall.

Tanford, S., & Penrod, S. (1982). Biases in trials involving defendants charged with multiple offenses. *Journal of Applied Social Psychology, 12,* 453–480.

Tanford, S., & Penrod, S. (1984). Social inference processes in juror judgments of multiple-offense trials. *Journal of Personality and Social Psychology, 47,* 749–765.

Tang, T.L., Tollison, P.S., & Whiteside, H.D. (1991). Managers' attendance and the effectiveness of small work groups: The case of quality circles. *Journal of Social Psychology, 131,* 335–344.

Taylor, D.W., Berry, P.C., & Block, C.H. (1958). Does group participation when using brain storming facilitate or inhibit creative thinking? *Administrative Science Quarterly, 3,* 23–47.

Taylor, D.W., & Faust, W.L. (1952). Twenty questions: Efficiency in problem-solving as a function of size of group. *Journal of Experimental Psychology, 44,* 360–368.

Taylor, R.B., & Lanni, J.C. (1981). Territorial dominance: The influence of the resident advantage in triadic decision making. *Journal of Personality and Social Psychology, 41,* 909–915.

Taylor, S.E., & Brown, J.D. (1988). Illusion and well-being: A social psychological perspective on mental health. *Psychological Bulletin, 116,* 193–210.

Taylor, S.E., & Lobel, M. (1989). Social comparison activity under threat: Downward evaluation and upward contacts. *Psychological Review, 96,* 569–575.

Taylor, S.E., Neter, E., & Wayment, H.A. (1995). Self-evaluation processes. *Personality and Social Psychology Bulletin, 21,* 1278–1287.

Taylor, S.E., Wayment, H.A., & Carrillo, M. (1996). Social comparison, self-regulation, and motivation. In R.M. Sorrentino & E.T. Higgins (Eds.), *Handbook of motivation and cognition* (Vol. 3, pp. 3–27). New York: Guilford Press.

Tesser, A. (1988). Toward a self-evaluation maintenance model of social behavior. *Advances in Experimental Social Psychology, 21,* 181–227.

Tesser, A., & Rosen, S. (1975). The reluctance to transmit bad news. *Advances in Experimental Social Psychology, 8,* 192–232.

Tetlock, P.E. (1979). Identifying victims of groupthink from public statements of decision makers. *Journal of Personality and Social Psychology, 37,* 1314–1324.

Thaima, S., & Woods, M.F. (1984). A systematic small group approach to creativity and innovation: A case study. *R & D Management, 14,* 25–35.

't Hart, P. (1991). Irving L. Janis' Victims of Groupthink. *Political Psychology, 12,* 247–278.

Thibaut, J.W., & Kelley, H.H. (1959). *The social psychology of groups.* New York: Wiley.

Thomas, E.J., & Fink, C.F. (1961). Models of group problem solving. *Journal of Abnormal and Social Psychology, 68,* 53–63.

Thompsen, P.A., & Ahn, D. (1992). To be or not to be: An exploration of e-prime, copula deletion, and flaming in electronic mail. *Et Cetera, 49,* 146–164.

Tindale, R.S., Davis, J.H., Vollrath, D.A., Nagao, D.H., & Hinsz, V.B. (1990). Asymmetrical social influence in freely interacting groups: A test of three models. *Journal of Personality and Social Psychology, 58,* 438–449.

Tindale, R.S., & Larson, J.R. (1992). Assembly bonus effect or typical group performance? A comment on Michaelsen, Watson, and Black (1989). *Journal of Applied Psychology, 77,* 102–105.

Tindale, R.S., & Nagao, D.H. (1986). An assessment of the potential of "Scientific Jury Selection": A "thought experiment" approach. *Organizational Behavior and Human Decision Processes, 37,* 409–425.

Touval, S., & Zartman, I.W. (1985). *International mediation in theory and practice.* Boulder: Westview Press.

Trafimow, D., Triandis, H.C., & Goto, S.G. (1991). Some tests of the distinction between the private self and the collective self. *Journal of Personality and Social Psychology, 60,* 649–655.

Triandis, H.C. (1989). The self and social behavior in differing cultural contexts. *Psychological Review, 96,* 506–520.

Triandis, H.C., McCusker, C., & Hui, C.H. (1990). Multimethod probes of individualism and collectivism. *Journal of Personality and Social Psychology, 59,* 1006–1020.

Triplett, N. (1898). The dynamogenic factors in pacemaking and competition. *American Journal of Psychology, 9,* 507–533.

Trope, Y. (1983). Self-assessment in achievement behavior. In J.M. Suls & A.G. Carver (Eds.), *Psychological perspectives on the self* (Vol. 2, pp. 93–122). Hillsdale, NJ: Erlbaum.

Trost, M.R., Maass, A., & Kenrick, D.T. (1992). Minority influence: Personal relevance biases cognitive processes and reverses private acceptance. *Journal of Experimental Social Psychology, 28,* 234–254.

Turner, J.C., & Killian, L.M. (1987). *Collective behavior* (3d ed.). Englewood Cliffs, NJ: Prentice-Hall.

Turner, J.C., Oakes, P.J., Haslam, S.A., & McGarty, C. (1994). Self and collective: Cognition and social context. *Personality and Social Psychology Bulletin, 20,* 454–463.

Turner, M.E., Pratkanis, A.R., Probasco, P., & Leve, C. (1992). Threat, cohesion, and group effectiveness: Testing a social identity maintenance perspective on groupthink. *Journal of Personality and Social Psychology, 63,* 781–796.

Tyler, T.R., Degoey, P., & Smith, H.J. (1996). Understanding why the justice of group procedures matters. *Journal of Personality and Social Psychology, 70,* 913–930.

Tyler, T.R., & Lind, E.A. (1992). A relational model of authority in groups. *Advances in Experimental Social Psychology, 25,* 115–191.

Tyler, T.R., & Sears, D.O. (1977). Coming to like obnoxious people when we must live with them. *Journal of Personality and Social Psychology, 35,* 200–211.

Urban, J.M., Bowers, C.A., & Monday, S.D. (1995). Workload, team structure, and communication in team performance. *Military Psychology, 7,* 123–139.

Valacich, J.S., Dennis, A.R., & Connolly, T. (1994). Idea generation in computer-based groups: A new ending to an old story. *Organizational Behavior and Human Decision Processes, 57*, 448–467.

Valacich, J.S., Dennis, A.R., & Nunamaker, J.F. (1991). Electronic meeting support: The GroupSystems concept. *International Journal of Man-Machine Studies, 34*, 261–282.

Valacich, J.S., Dennis, A.R., & Nunamaker, J.F. (1992). Group size and anonymity effects on computer-mediated idea generation. *Small Group Research, 23*, 49–73.

Valacich, J.S., Paranka, D., George, J.F., & Nunamaker, J.F. (1993). Communication concurrency and the new media: A new dimension for media richness. *Communication Research, 20*, 249–276.

Valacich, J.S., & Schwenk, C. (1995). Devil's advocacy and dialectical inquiry effects on face-to-face and computer-mediated group decision making. *Organizational Behavior and Human Decision Processes, 63*, 158–173.

Valacich, J.S., Wheeler, B.C., Mennecke, B.E., & Wachter, R. (1995). The effects of numerical and logical group size on computer-mediated idea generation. *Organizational Behavior and Human Decision Processes, 62*, 318–329.

Vallacher, R.R., & Nowak, A. (1997). The emergence of dynamical social psychology. *Psychological Inquiry, 8*, 73–99.

van de Kragt, A.J.C., Dawes, R.M., Orbell, J.M., Braver, S.R., & Wilson, L.A. (1986). Doing well and doing good as ways of resolving social dilemmas. In H.A.M. Wilke, D.M. Messick, & C.G. Rutte (Eds.), *Experimental social dilemmas* (pp. 177–203). Frankfurt: Lang.

van de Kragt, A.J.C., Orbell, J.M., & Dawes, R.M. (1983). The minimal contributing set as a solution to public good problems. *American Political Science Review, 77*, 112–122.

van den Bos, K., Lind, E.A., Vermunt, R., & Wilke, H.A.M. (1997). How do I judge my outcome when I do not know the outcome of others? The psychology of the fair process effect. *Journal of Personality and Social Psychology, 72*, 1034–1046.

van den Bos, K., Vermunt, R., & Wilke, H.A.M. (1997). Procedural and distributive justice: What is fair depends more on what comes first than on what comes next. *Journal of Personality and Social Psychology, 72*, 95–104.

van der Velde, M., & Class, M.D. (1995). The relationship of role conflict and ambiguity to organizational culture. In S.L. Sauter & L.R. Murphy (Eds.), *Organizational risk factors for job stress* (pp. 53–59). Washington, DC: American Psychological Association.

Van de Ven, A.H. (1974). *Group decision-making effectiveness.* Kent, OH: Kent State University Press.

Van de Ven, A.H., & Delbecq, A.L. (1971). Nominal versus interacting group process for committee decisionmaking effectiveness. *Academy of Management Journal, 14*, 203–212.

van de Vliert, E. (1992). Questions about the strategic choice model of mediation. *Negotiation Journal, 8*, 379–386.

van Dijk, E., & Wilke, H.A.M. (1994). Asymmetry of wealth and public good provision. *Social Psychology Quarterly, 57*, 352–359.

van Lange, P.A.M., Liebrand, W.P.G., Messick, D.M., & Wilke, H.A.M. (1992). Introduction and literature review. In W.B.G. Liebrand, D.M. Messick, & H.A.M. Wilke (Eds.), *Social dilemmas* (pp. 3–28). Tarrytown, NY: Pergamon Press.

Varca, P.E. (1980). An analysis of home and away game performance of male college basketball teams. *Journal of Sport Psychology, 2,* 245–257.

Victor, B., & Cullen, J.B. (1988). The organizational bases of ethical work climates. *Administrative Science Quarterly, 33,* 101–125.

Vinet, A. (1974). Medical education and team work. *Vie Medicale au Canada Français, 3,* 63–66.

Volpato, C., Maass, A., Mucchi-Faina, A., & Vitti, E. (1990). Minority influence and social categorization. *European Journal of Social Psychology, 20,* 119–132.

Waite, M.S., Harker, J.O., & Messerman, L.I. (1994). Interdisciplinary team training and diversity: Problems, concepts, and strategies. *Gerontology and Geriatrics Education, 15,* 65–82.

Wall, J.A. Jr., & Lynn, A. (1993). Mediation: A Current review. *Journal of Conflict Resolution, 37,* 160–194.

Wall, T.D., Kemp, N.J., Jackson, P.R., & Clegg, C.W. (1986). Outcomes of autonomous workgroups: A long-term field experiment. *Academy of Management Journal, 29,* 280–304.

Wallach, M.A., Kogan, N., & Bem, D.J. (1962). Group influence on individual risk taking. *Journal of Abnormal and Social Psychology, 65,* 75–86.

Walster, E., Berscheid, E., & Walster, G.W. (1973). New directions in equity research. *Journal of Personality and Social Psychology, 25,* 151–176.

Walther, J.B. (1992). Interpersonal effects in computer-mediated interaction: A relational perspective. *Communication Research, 19,* 52–90.

Walther, J.B. (1993). Impression development in computer-mediated interaction. *Western Journal of Communication, 57,* 381–398.

Walther, J.B. (1994). Anticipated ongoing interaction versus channel effects on relational communication in computer-mediated interaction. *Human Communication Research, 20,* 473–501.

Walther, J.B., Anderson, J.F., & Park, D.W. (1994). Interpersonal effects in computer-mediated interaction: A meta-analysis of social and antisocial communication. *Communication Research, 21,* 460–487.

Walther, J.B., & Burgoon, J.K. (1992). Relational communication in computer-mediated interaction. *Human Communication Research, 19,* 50–88.

Wasserman, S., & Faust, K. (1994). *Social network analysis: Methods and applications.* New York: Cambridge University Press.

Wayne, S.J., & Ferris, G.R. (1990). Influence tactics, affect, and exchange quality in supervisor-subordinate interactions: A laboratory experiment and field study. *Journal of Applied Psychology, 75,* 487–499.

Weatherly, K.A., & Beach, L.R. (1996). Organizational culture and decision making. In L.R. Beach (Ed.), *Decision making in the workplace* (pp. 117–132). Mahwah, NJ: Erlbaum.

Wegner, D.M., Erber, R., & Raymond, P. (1991). Transactive memory in close relationships. *Journal of Personality and Social Psychology, 61,* 923–929.

Weick, K.E., & Roberts, K.H. (1993). Collective mind in organizations: Heedful interrelating in the cockpit. *Administrative Science Quarterly, 38,* 357–381.

Weiner, E.L., Kanki, B.G., & Helmreich, R.L. (Eds.) (1993). *Cockpit resource management.* San Francisco: Academic Press.

Weiner, H.R. (1990). Group-level and individual-level mediators of the relationship between soldier satisfaction with social support and performance motivation. *Military Psychology, 2*, 21–32.

Weinholtz, D. (1991). The socialization of physicians during attending rounds: A study of team learning among medical students. *Qualitative Health Research, 1*, 152–177.

Weisband, S.P. (1992). Group discussion and first advocacy effects in computer-mediated and face-to-face decision making groups. *Organizational Behavior and Human Decision Processes, 53*, 352–380.

Weisband, S.P., Schneider, S.K., & Connolly, T. (1995). Computer-mediated communication and social information: Status salience and status differences. *Academy of Management Journal, 38*, 1124–1151.

Weitzman, E.A., & Miles, M.B. (1995). *Computer programs for qualitative data analysis*. Beverly Hills, CA: Sage.

White, P.H., Kjelgaard, M.M., & Harkins, S.G. (1995). Testing the contribution of self-evaluation to goal-setting effects. *Journal of Personality and Social Psychology, 69*, 69–79.

White, R.K. (1977). Misperceptions in the Arab-Israeli conflict. *Journal of Social Issues, 33*, 190–221.

Whittemore, K.E., & Ogloff, J.R.P. (1995). Factors that influence jury decision making: Disposition instructions and mental state at the time of the trial. *Law and Human Behavior, 19*, 283–303.

Wiersma, M.F., & Bird, A. (1993). Organizational demography in Japanese firms: Group heterogeneity, individual dissimilarity, and top management team turnover. *Academy of Management Journal, 36*, 996–1025.

Williams, K.B., & Williams, K.D. (1983). Social inhibition and asking for help: The effects of number, strength, and immediacy of potential help givers. *Journal of Personality and Social Psychology, 44*, 67–77.

Williams, K.D., Harkins, S., & Latané, B. (1981). Identifiability as a deterrent to social loafing: Two cheering experiments. *Journal of Personality and Social Psychology, 40*, 303–311.

Williams, K.D., & Karau, S.J. (1993). Social loafing and social compensation: The effects of expectations of co-worker performance. *Journal of Personality and Social Psychology, 61*, 570–581.

Williams, K.D., & Sommer, K.L. (1997). Social ostracism by coworkers: Does rejection lead to loafing or compensation? *Personality and Social Psychology Bulletin, 23*, 693–706.

Williams, K.D., & Williams, K.B. (1989). Impact of source strength on two compliance techniques. *Basic and Applied Social Psychology, 10*, 149–159.

Wills, T.A. (1981). Downward comparison principles in social psychology. *Psychological Bulletin, 90*, 245–271.

Winters, P. (1987). BK enters Ayer era: Ayer, JWT face challenges. *Advertising Age, 58*(43), 1, 103–104.

Wish, M., D'Andrade, R.G., & Goodnow, J.E. (1980). Dimensions of interpersonal communication: Structures for speech acts and bipolar scales. *Journal of Personality and Social Psychology, 39*, 848–860.

Wolf, S., & Bugaj, A.M. (1990). The social impact of courtroom witnesses. *Social Behavior, 5*, 1–13.

Wolf, S., & Latané, B. (1981). If laboratory research doesn't square with you, then Qube it: The potential of interactive TV for social psychological research. *Personality and Social Psychology Bulletin, 7*, 344–352.

Wolf, S., & Latané, B. (1983). Majority and minority influence on restaurant preferences. *Journal of Personality and Social Psychology, 45*, 282–292.

Wood, J.V. (1989). Theory and research concerning social comparisons of personal attributes. *Psychological Bulletin, 106*, 231–248.

Wood, W., Lundgren, S., Ouellette, J.A., Busceme, S., & Blackstone, T. (1994). Minority influence: A meta-analytic review of social influence processes. *Psychological Bulletin, 115*, 323–345.

Worringham, C.J., & Messick, D.M. (1983). Social facilitation of running: An unobtrusive study. *Journal of Social Psychology, 121*, 23–29.

Wright, E.F., Jackson, W., Christie, S.D., McGuire, G.R., & Wright, R.D. (1991). The home-course disadvantage in golf championships: Further evidence for the undermining effect of supportive audiences on performance under pressure. *Journal of Sport Behavior, 14*, 51–60.

Wright, E.F., Luus, C.A., & Christie, S.D. (1990). Does group discussion facilitate the use of consensus information in making causal attributions? *Journal of Personality and Social Psychology, 59*, 261–269.

Xenikou, A., & Furnham, A. (1996). A correlational and factor analytic study of four questionnaire measures of organizational culture. *Human Relations, 49*, 349–371.

Yamagishi, T. (1986). The structural goal/expectation theory of cooperation in social dilemmas. *Advances in Group Processes, 3*, 51–87.

Yamagishi, T. (1988). Seriousness of social dilemmas and the provision of a sanctioning system. *Social Psychology Quarterly, 51*, 32–42.

Yamagishi, T., & Sato, K. (1986). Motivational bases of the public goods problem. *Journal of Personality and Social Psychology, 50*, 67–73.

Yamaguchi, S., Okamoto, K., & Oka, T. (1985). Effects of coactor's presence: Social loafing and social facilitation. *Japanese Psychological Research, 27*, 215–222.

Zaccaro, S.J. (1984). Social loafing: The role of task attractiveness. *Personality and Social Psychology Bulletin, 10*, 99–106.

Zaccaro, S.J., Gualtieri, J., & Minionis, D. (1995). Task cohesion as a facilitator of team decision making under temporal urgency. *Military Psychology, 7*, 77–93.

Zack, M.H., & McKenney, J.L. (1995). Social context and interaction in ongoing computer-supported management groups: Electronic communication and changing organizational forms. *Organization Science, 6*, 394–422.

Zahn, G.L. (1991). Face-to-face communication in an office setting. *Communication Research, 18*, 737–754.

Zajonc, R.B. (1965). Social facilitation. *Science, 149*, 269–274.

Zajonc, R.B. (1968). Attitudinal effects of mere exposure. *Journal of Personality and Social Psychology*, Monograph Supplement Pt. 2, 1–29.

Zajonc, R.B. (1980). Compresence. In P.B. Paulus (Ed.), *Psychology of group influence* (pp. 35–60). Hillsdale, NJ: Erlbaum.

Zajonc, R.B., Heingartner, A., & Herman, E.M. (1969). Social enhancement and impairment of performance in the cockroach. *Journal of Personality and Social Psychology, 13,* 83–92.

Zeisel, H., & Diamond, S. (1978). The effect of peremptory challenges on jury and verdict: An experiment in a federal district court. *Stanford Law Review, 30,* 491–531.

Zeiss, A.M., & Steffen, A.M. (1996). Interdisciplinary health care teams: The basic unit of geriatric care. In L.L. Carstensen, B.A. Edelstein, & L. Dornbrand (Eds.), *The practical handbook of clinical gerontology* (pp. 423–450). Thousand Oaks, CA: Sage.

Zinn, K.L. (1977). Computer facilitation of communication within professional communities. *Behavioral Research Methods and Instrumentation, 9,* 96–107.

Zubek, J.M., Pruitt, D.G., Peirce, R.S., McGillicuddy, N.B., & Syna, H. (1992). Disputant and mediator behaviors affecting short-term success in mediation. *Journal of Conflict Resolution, 36,* 546–572.

Zuber, J.A., Crott, H.W., & Werner, J. (1992). Choice shift and group polarization: An analysis of the status of arguments and social decision schemes. *Journal of Personality and Social Psychology, 62,* 50–61.

Index

Abakoumkin, G., 48
Abbott, A.S., 51
Abrahamson, E., 153, 176
Abramson, J.S., 188
Achee, J.W., 89
Acker, J.R., 158
Acomb, D.B.,185
Adams, J.S., 4, 132, 134
Adkins, M., 175
Adrianson, L., 173–174
Agnew, G.A., 191–192
Ahern, T.C., 170
Ahn, D., 173
Aiello, J.R., 206–207
Aiken, M.W., 169–170, 174
Allen, M.W., 174
Allen, W.R.,214
Allison, S.T., 119–121
Allport, F.H., 62–63
Ames, R.E., 108
Anderson, J.F., 173
Anderson, M.D., 176
Anderson, N.H., 11, 160
Andre, M., 207
Andrew, J.A., 193
Anthony, T., 18
Arabie, P., 217
Archambault, D., 191, 193
Archer, N.P., 175
Argote, L., 205
Arkin, R.M., 12
Aronson, E., 10
Arousal
    mere presence and performance,
        65–67
    evaluation expectations, 64–69, 73
    social facilitation and, 64–65
    social impact and, 27–28

Arrington, L., 171
Arrow, H., 175
Arsenault, A., 207
Arunachalam, V., 175
Asch, S.E., 25, 173
Atkin, R.S., 160
Atwater, L.E., 183
Au, W.T., 178
Audiences
    evaluation apprehension and, 67–69
    distraction/conflict and, 69–70
    home field advantage/disadvantage,
        190–197
    social influence, 29
    social facilitation and, 61–62
Austin, W., 140
Axelrod, R., 101
Ayman, R., 4, 128

Baetge, M.M., 185
Bair, J.P., 189
Baird, J.E., 16
Baker, D.P., 152, 182
Baldwin, T.T., 152
Bales, R.F. 50, 213–214
Balkwell, J.W., 179
Bandura, A., 74, 105
Bannister, B.D., 128
Bantel, K.A., 152
Barker, J.M., 184
Barnes, S., 56
Baron, J.N., 67, 144
Baron, R.S., 3, 69–70, 76–77
Barsade, S.G.,154
Barsky, S.F.,190–191
Bar-Tal, Y.,193
Barth, J.M., 20
Bartis, S., 88

Basking in reflected glory, 197–199
  group membership and, 11
  other tactics and, 200–201
Bass, B.M., 131
Bastianutti, L.M., 49, 174, 176
Bat-Clava, Y., 19
Baumeister, R.F., 72, 97, 194–196
Beach, L.R.,154
Beaman, A.L., 172
Beatty, M.J., 22, 27
Bedian, A.G., 130
Bell, P.A., 122, 179
Bem, D.J., 146
Benjafield, I., 196
Benjafield, J., 196
Berent, M.K., 41
Berger, J., 2, 14
Berkowitz, L., 25
Bernstein, M., 137
Bernthal, P.R., 55
Berry, P.C., 47
Berscheid, E.,132
Berteotti, C.R.,188
Bettenhausen, K., 206
Betz, A.L., 206
Bickman, L., 25
Billard, E.A.,179
Bird, A., 153
Bisson, R.U., 184
Bjork, R.A., 182
Black, R.H., 212
Blackstone, T., 37
Blanchard, K.H., 203
Blank, T.O., 76
Blascovich, J., 130–131
Block, C.H., 47
Blumenfeld-Jones, K., 151
Bodenhausen, G.V., 206
Boll, P.A., 184
Bond, C.F., 62, 68, 72–73
Bonevento, M., 27
Boniecki, K.A., 196
Boninger, D.S., 41
Bonoma, T.V., 102
Boozer, A.E., 11
Borden, R.J., 11, 198–199
Bordens, K.S., 166

Bornstein, G., 106–107, 110, 112–113
Boster, F.J., 161
Bosworth, K., 176
Bourgeois, L.J., 49
Bowers, C.A., 181–182, 185–186
Brainstorming, 47–48, 175–176
Brandstatter, H.,206
Brandstatter, V., 38
Branscombe, N.R., 19
Brashers, D.E., 175
Braver, S.L., 106, 109
Bray, R.M., 178
Bray, S.R., 191
Brewer, M.B., 2, 18, 110, 113, 115,
  117–119, 122–123
Brickner, M.A., 82, 88
Briggs, R.O., 176
Brockner, J., 135, 140
Brodwin, D.R., 49
Brown, J.D., 143, 200
Brown, R., 146
Brown, Y., 38
Bruun, S.E., 82, 86, 91–92, 105–108
Bugaj, A.M., 27
Bullis, C.R.,183
Burden, C.A., 11
Burger, J.M., 12, 199
Burgoon, J.K., 171
Busceme, S., 37
Butera, F., 38
Butler, R.E., 185
Buunk, B.P., 144–145

Cacioppo, J.T., 67, 88
Callan, V.J., 16
Callaway, M.R., 55–56
Calwell, B.S., 172
Camacho, L.M., 48
Campbell, J., 47
Campbell, T.L., 169
Campbell-Heider, N., 188
Campion, M.A., 152
Canfield, R.W., 11
Cannon-Bowers, J.A., 181, 183, 185
Carayon, P., 207
Carmody, M.A., 173
Carnevale, P.J., 4, 109, 147, 149–151

Carnot, C.G., 41
Carrillo, M., 144
Carron, A.V., 191–194, 196
Carson, R., 186
Carver, C.S., 28, 71–73, 89
Castrianno, L.M., 150
Chammah, A., 101
Chan, D.K.S., 101
Chandler, J.S., 58–59, 175
Chapman, J.C., 30
Chapman, P., 189
Chatman, J.A., 154
Chemers, M.M., 4, 128
Chiles, C., 38
Chrestman, M., 170
Christakis, D.A., 188
Christakis, N.A., 188
Christensen, C., 51
Christie, S.D., 196, 206
Chuang, Y.C., 41
Chute, R.D., 184, 186
Cialdini, R.B., 11, 21, 197–201
Clampitt, P.G., 16
Clark, R.D., 40
Class, M.D., 154
Clegg, C.W., 153
Clothier, C.C., 184
Coe, C., 11
Cohen, B.P., 171
Cohen, S.P., 214
Cohesion
    flight crews, 184–185
    group membership and, 15
    groupthink, 55
    military groups, 182
Collins, R.L., 143, 145, 200
Comer, D., 153
Comerford, R.A., 214
Compton, D.C., 173
Computers in groups
    deindividuation and flaming,
        172–173
    performance, 175–176
    status differences, 171–172
    simulations, 210–211
Connolly, T., 171, 176
Conolly, E.S., 25

Conversion model, 36–37
Cook, R.F., 151
Cook, T.D., 137
Cooper, C., 18
Cooper, B.P., 199
Cooper, T.R., 171
Cooper, W.H., 49, 174, 176
Cooperation
    social compensation, 94–96
    social dilemmas, 109–112
Corcoran, C., 67
Cordery, J.L., 153
Cosier, R.A., 50
Cota, A.A., 15
Cottrell, N.B., 3, 67–68
Courneya, K.S., 191, 193–194, 196
Cowley, R.S., 189
Cowlin, R.A., 51
Cox, A.W., 189
Cox, R.H., 191
Cox, S., 171
Crano, W.D., 2, 39
Crawford, A.M., 20
Crocker, J., 19
Cronshaw, S.F., 130
Crosby, F.J., 137–138
Crott, H.W., 53, 159
Crow, T., 11
Crutchfield, J.H., 171
Cullen, J.B., 154
Cunning, J.E., 187
Cutler, B.L., 163, 167
Cwitco, G., 207
Czech, R., 170, 174

D'Andrade, R.G., 214
D'Andrea Tyson, L., 153
Dakof, G.A., 145
Dalkey, N.C., 48
Dansereau, F., 129
Darley, J.M., 25–26, 144
Das, B.K., 22, 26
David, B., 179
Davis, J.H., 4, 20, 35, 52–53, 86,
        158–160, 162, 165, 167, 178, 210
Dawes, R.M., 106–111, 122
Deaux, K., 18

Decisionmaking, 45–59
  conflict, 49–50
  context/categorization, 39
  Delphi and nominal, 48–49
  discussion, 46–51
  objective/consensus model, 37–39
de Dreu, C.K.W., 38
Degoey, P., 19
Delbecq, A.L., 49
Deluga, R.J., 183
DeNicholas, M.E., 201
Dennis, A.R., 170–171, 174, 176
Dennison, D.R., 154
Deppens, J.A., 194
DeVader, C.L., 130
DeVinney, L.C., 136
de Vries, N.K., 38
Diamond, S., 167
DiCecco, J.V., 216–217
Dickson, M.W., 151–152, 184
Diehl, M., 3, 47–48
Diener, E., 4, 172
Dienesch, R.M., 130
Dilla, W.N., 175
Dingwall, R., 216
Dion, K.L., 15, 152
Dipboye, R.L., 127
DiTecco, D., 207
Downs, C.W., 102
Downs, G.W., 16
Drake, S.D., 30
Drecksel, G.L., 214
Drinka, T.J.K., 188–189
Drive, 62–65
  attentional overload, 76–77
  mere presence, 65–67
  distraction and, 69–71
  evaluation apprehension,
    67–69
Dubnicki, C., 152
Dubreuil, S.C., 163
Dubrovsky, V.D., 171, 173
Dufner, D., 170, 174
Dunnette, M.D., 47, 135
Duval, S., 71–72
Dyregrov, A., 186
Dzindolet, M.T., 48

Earley, P.C., 153
Easterbrook, J.A., 76
Edwards, J., 191, 193
Efron, B., 210
Eid, J., 183
El-Sherif, H.H., 170
Ellemers, N., 38
Ellis, A.L., 39, 56–57
Ellis, B.H., 188
Equity
  free riders and suckers, 90–94
  work and, 131–135
Erber, R., 205
Erev, I., 106–107, 112
Erickson, G.A., 199
Eshed-Levy, D., 107, 111
Esser, J.K., 55–56
Ethier, K.A., 18
Evans, C.R., 15, 152
Evans, J.St.B.T., 175
Expectations
  social dilemmas and, 105–107
  social facilitation and, 72, 74–75
  social loafing and, 96–97

Fairhurst, G.T., 130
Farrell, M.P., 56
Faulkner, A.O., 189
Faust, K., 217
Faust, W.L., 45
Ference, R., 56
Ferris, G.R., 18
Festinger, L., 142–143
Fetter, R., 131
Feudtner, C., 188
Fichman, M., 97
Fiedler, F.E., 4, 128–129
Figueredo, A.J., 207
Finch, J.F., 201
Finch, W.H., 68
Finholt, T., 175
Finn, T.A., 175
Fischer, G.W., 179
Fisher, B.A., 214
Flight crews, 183–187
  cohesion and, 184–185
Flint, L., 173

Folger, R., 4, 137–142
Ford, C.E., 11, 200
Foti, R.J., 130
Fouraker, L.E., 147
Foushee, H.C., 184–186
Franz, T.M., 51
Fraser, S.C., 172
Freeman, S., 11, 198–199
Free riders
  performance and, 90–93
  social dilemmas, 107–109
French, J., 184
Frey, B.S., 108
Friedman, A., 135
Fulero, S.M., 163
Fulton, M.A., 171
Fung, P., 4, 173
Furnham, A., 154
Fusco, M.E., 179
Futoran, G.C., 50, 214

Gabbert, B., 20
Gabrenya, W.K., 82
Gaffie, B., 40
Gaines, J.H., 16
Gal, R., 182
Galegher, J., 174
Gallupe, R.B., 49, 174, 176
Gange, J.J., 65
Gannon, K.M., 206
Garcia, J.E., 129
Garfield, D.A., 166
Garlick, R., 40
Gauvin, S., 176
Gaviria, E., 38
Gavish, B., 170
Gayton, W.F., 191, 196
Geen, R.G., 62, 65, 69–71, 74, 76–77, 97
Gelfand, A.E., 177
George, J.F., 176, 206
Gerard, H.B., 25, 37
Gerbasi, K.C., 158
Gerdes, J., 170
Gerras, S.J., 183
Geurts, S.A., 144
Gifford, R., 179

Gigone, D., 51, 209
Gilovich, T., 66
Ginnett, R.C., 185
Giosue, F., 38
Glaser, A.N., 71
Glass, D.C., 68
Glick, W.H., 154
Goals
  membership in groups and, 10
  social loafing and, 88–89
Godbout, L., 41
Goethals, G.R., 144, 146
Golding, J.M., 164
Goldstein, S.R., 191
Gong, G., 210
Gonzalez, R., 205
Gonzalez-Roma, V., 187–188
Good, K.J., 74
Goodman, P.S., 135, 152
Goodnow, J.E., 214
Goore, N., 66
Goto, S., 206
Graen, G.B., 17, 129–130
Graves, J.K., 83, 165
Green, C.A., 175
Green, T.B., 49
Greenberg, J., 88, 140
Greenspan, B.K., 189
Greer, D.L., 192, 194
Greller, L.M., 56
Griffith, T.L., 97, 175
Grise, M.L., 176
Groff, B.D., 69–70
Group-to-individual transfer, 19–20
Groupthink, 54–56, 145–146
Grudin, J., 170
Gualtieri, J., 182
Guerin, B., 62, 66–68, 77
Gump, B.B., 161
Gustafson, D.H., 49, 176
Guzzo, R.A., 151–152, 184
Gwynn, M.I., 163

Hackman, J.R., 185
Hafer, C.L., 142
Haga, W.J., 129
Hains, S.C., 1

Halcomb, C.G., 173
Hale, J.L., 161
Hamilton, J.L., 195
Hanna, C., 51
Hanning, P., 135
Hannula-Bral, K.A., 39
Hardin, G., 113
Harker, J.O., 189
Harkins, S.G., 3, 26–27, 82–83, 85–89, 91, 95–96, 145
Harmon, D.L., 165
Harmon, J., 175
Harper, B.C., 187
Harris, B.A., 2, 12
Harrison, A.A., 201
Hart, A.J., 164
Hartke, D.D., 129
Harvey, O.J., 212
Haslam, S.A., 2, 18
Hass, S., 31
Hassan, R.K., 74
Hastie, R., 33, 51, 158, 161–162, 177, 209
Hater, J.J., 131
Hatfield, B., 191
Hauselt, J., 164
Hautaluoma, J.E., 122
Hawkes, W.G., 20
Hawkins, R.P., 176
Hay, J.L., 144
Hearns, J.F., 191
Heaton, A.W., 195–196
Heck, R.H., 154
Heinemann, G.D., 56
Heingartner, A., 65–66
Helgeson, V.S., 144
Hellesoy, O.H., 186
Helmreich, R.L., 184–185
Hemphill, K.J., 145
Henchy, T., 68
Hennigan, K.M., 137
Hepworth, J.T., 112
Herman, E.M., 65–66
Herschel, R.T., 171
Hersey, P., 203
Heuer, L.B., 151, 166
Higby, H.R., 189

Higgins, E.T., 205
Higgs, A.C., 152
Hightower, R., 170
Hiltrop, J.M., 150
Hilty, J.A., 101
Hiltz, S.R., 170, 173–174
Hine, D.W., 179
Hinkle, S., 18
Hinsz, V.B., 35, 160, 165, 205–206
Hirt, E.R., 199
Hitchings, G., 171
Hjelmquist, E., 173–174
Hoffman, K., 188–189
Hoffman, L.R., 175
Hoffmann, C., 159
Hofstede, G., 154
Hogg, M.A., 1, 179
Hoggatt, A.C., 206
Hohenfeld, J.A., 135
Hollenbeck, J.R., 152
Hollingshead, A.B., 58–59, 171, 175
Holt, R.W., 159–160, 178
Home field advantage, 190–194
Home field disadvantage, 194–196
Hood, W.R., 212
Horn, J.C., 192
Horowitz, I.A., 166
Hospital teams, 187–189
Houlden, P., 151
Howell, W.C., 127
Hoyle, R.H., 20
Hu, L., 18
Huberman, A.M., 216
Hubert, L.J., 217
Huguet, P., 38
Hui, C.H., 17
Hulbert, L.G., 53, 58–59, 101–102, 107, 123, 158, 162, 175, 178
Hull, C.L., 64
Hume, S., 54
Hunter, J.E., 161
Hyde, M., 31
Hymes, R., 17

Ickes, W., 67, 205
Ilgen, D.R., 152
Ingham, A.G., 83

Innes, J.M., 67
Insko, C.A., 55
Irving, P.G., 191
Isaac, R.M., 108–109
Iso-Ahola, S.E., 191

Jaastad, K., 47
Jackson, J.M., 4, 22, 26–28, 30, 82,
    86–87, 95, 97, 145
Jackson, P.R., 153
Jackson, S.E., 152
Jackson, W., 196
Jacobsen, P.R., 134
Jago, A.G., 128
James, L.A., 155
James, L.R., 155, 206
Jamieson, D.W., 11
Janis, I.L., 3, 54, 145
Jennings, K.R., 153
Jessup, L.M., 176
Johnson, C., 47
Johnson, D.A., 30
Johnson, D.W., 20
Johnson, K., 170, 173–174
Johnson, R.T., 20
Jones, G.R., 206
Jorgenson, D.O., 179
Jorgenson, M.D., 135
Joseph, L., 66
Judd, C.M., 18
Juries
    computers and, 177–178
    deliberation, 161–163
    mock, 158–159
    selection, 167–168
    social decision schemes, 159–161
    social influence model, 34–35

Kahneman, D., 138
Kameda, T., 20, 53, 158, 162
Kanki, B.G., 185
Kaplan, M.F., 4, 39, 161
Karau, S.J., 4, 82, 94–97, 145
Kassin, S.M., 163, 165–166
Katz, R., 203
Katz, T., 112
Katzenbach, J.R., 151

Kelem, Z.R.T., 172
Kelley, H.H., 2, 11–13, 36
Kelley, M., 171, 174
Kelly, J.R., 50, 214
Kemp, N.J., 153
Kennedy, C., 131
Kennedy, J.K., 199
Kenney, R.A., 130–131
Kenny, D.A., 217
Kenrick, D.T., 38
Kerpel, L., 112
Kerr, N.L., 4, 82, 86, 91–94, 105–110,
    145, 159–160, 162, 165, 205, 210
Kerwin, J., 164
Kiesler, S., 171–173, 175
Kilik, L., 15
Killian, L.M., 13
Kimble, C.E., 199
Kimmel, M.J., 203
Kirkland, F.R., 182
Kitik, B.A., 189
Kjelgaard, M.M., 88–89
Klevorick, A.K., 177
Klimoski, R., 205
Knowles, E.S., 2, 31–33
Kogan, N., 146
Koin, D., 187
Kolb, K.J., 206–207
Komorita, S.S., 4, 100–102, 107, 109,
    114, 123, 148, 178
Kozakai, T., 40
Kramer, G.P., 206
Kramer, R.M., 113, 115, 117–119,
    123, 147, 205
Kraut, R.E., 174
Kravitz, D.A., 82
Kreuser, B., 31
Krickl, O., 176
Kroon, M., 38
Krosnick, J.A., 41
Krosp, J., 169, 174
Kubzansky, P.E., 193
Kuhnert, K.W., 182
Kwan, J.L., 38

Lamm, H., 47
Landler, M., 54–55

Lanni, J.C., 191
Larey, T.S., 48, 176
Larson, J.R., 51, 178, 212
Lassegard, N.A., 11, 200
Latane, B., 2–3, 22–27, 82–83, 85–86, 93, 179
Latham, G.P., 88
Latour, S., 151
Lauber, J.K., 184–185
Laughlin, P.R., 20, 39, 52, 56–59, 175
Lavoie, L., 217
Lawler, E.E., 134
Lea, M., 4, 171–173
Leadership
    military, 182–183
    prototypes, 130–131
    work and, 127–131
Leana, C.R., 55
Leary, M.R., 11
Lee, F., 16
Lee, M.J., 199
Lee, S., 172
Leedom, D.K., 182, 185
Leggett, K.L., 176
LeGrande, D., 207
Legrenzi, P., 38
Lehman, D.R., 145, 194
Leith, L.M., 195
Lemieux, S., 41
Lenerz, K., 67
Leonard, W.M., 190
Leve, C., 55–56
Levine, D.I., 153
Levine, J.M., 144, 205
Levine, M.E., 212
Levinger, G., 83
Lewicki, R.J., 151
Lewis, B.P., 196
Leyden, D.P., 152
Liang, D.W., 205
Liddell, W.W., 196
Liden, R.C., 130
Liebrand, W.B.G., 102, 110, 120–121, 178, 204
Likert, R., 16
Lim, S.Y., 207
Limayen, M., 176

Limburg, W.J., 152
Lind, E.A., 19, 142
Linder, D.E., 10, 161, 196
Lindoerfer, J.S., 56
Lindsay, R.C.L., 158
Lindsey, J.T., 153
Lindskold, S., 148
Lingenfelter, D., 171, 174
Linville, P.W., 179
Liu, J.H., 27
Lobel, M., 143
Locke, E.A., 88
Loewenstein, G., 137
Longman, R.S., 15
Lorch, R.F., 216–217
Lord, R.G., 130, 135
Lorge, I., 46, 51
Lortie-Lussier, M., 41
Lott, A.J., 11
Lott, B.E., 11
Luch, C.H., 130
Lucius, R.H., 182
Luhtanen, R., 19
Lui, L., 113, 115, 117–119
Lundgren, S., 37
Luus, C.A., 206
Lydon, J.E., 11
Lynn, A., 149

MacCoun, R.J., 17, 161–162, 165, 205
MacKenzie, S.B., 131
McClintock, C.G., 123
McCusker, C., 17
McGarty, C., 2, 18, 179
McGee, G.W., 188–189
McGillicuddy, N.B., 150
McGinn, N.C., 140
McGrath, J.E., 3, 49–50, 174–175, 204, 212, 214
McGuire, G.R., 196
McGuire, T.W., 171–173
McKenney, J.L., 170
McKinney, E.H., 184
McMahan, E.M., 188–189
McNally, J.A., 183
McQueen, L.R., 120
Maass, A., 38, 40

Mabry, E.A., 214
Mackay, L.E., 189
Mackie, D.M., 37
Macrae, C.N., 206
Magjuka, R.J., 152
Magley, V.J., 58–59, 175
Major, B., 19
Major, D.A., 152
Malinek, V., 175
Mannix, E.A., 154
Manstead, A.S.R., 71, 76–77
Mantovani, G., 170–171
Marchi, S., 123
Marco, C.A., 204
Marcoulides, G.A., 154
Mark, M.M., 75, 85, 88–90, 137–139, 142, 196
Markus, H.R., 67, 70, 143
Marquardt, D.I., 46
Marriott, R.G., 56
Marshall-Goodall, B.S., 67
Martin, B., 82
Martin, C., 140–141
Martin, J.S., 170, 174
Martin, L.L., 89
Martin, R., 40
Marwell, G., 108, 135
Mason, R.O., 49
Matheson, K.A., 171–172, 174
Matthews, G.R., 196
Mayseless, O., 38
Maznevski, M.L., 16
Medsker, G.J., 152
Meek, D., 160
Membership in groups, 9–12
  cost/benefit ratio, 11
  development, 10–12,
  similarity, 11–12
Mennecke, B.E., 176
Messe, L., 17
Messerman, L.I., 189
Messick, D.M., 68, 102, 105, 110, 113, 115–123, 147, 178, 204
Meyers, R.A., 175
Michaelsen, L.K., 212
Mickelson, K.D., 144
Miles, J.A., 88

Miles, M.B., 216
Miles, M.E., 68
Milgram, S., 25
Miller, G., 216
Miller, K.E., 11
Miller, K.I., 188
Miller, N., 18
Milsap, R.E., 135
Minionis, D., 182
Miranda, S.M., 56
Mishra, J., 17
Mishra, P.K., 22, 26
Mitroff, I.I., 50
Mizrahi, K., 18
Mizruchi, M.S., 191, 217
Mohammed, S., 205
Molm, L.D., 14
Monday, S.D., 186
Money, W.H., 128
Mongeau, P.A., 40
Montanari, J.R., 56
Mook, D.G., 102
Moore, D.L., 69–70
Moore, M., 201
Moore, P.J., 161
Moorhead, G., 56
Moormann, R.H., 131
Morchain, P., 38
Moreland, R.L., 1, 97, 144, 205
Morgan, B.B., 182
Moscovici, S., 36–37, 40
Mosier, K., 38
Mowen, J.C., 161
Mucchi-Faina, A., 38–40
Muehrer, P., 137
Mueller, W.S., 153
Mugny, G., 38, 40
Mullen, B., 2, 18, 27–30, 47, 97
Munemori, J., 170
Murdoch, P., 68
Muthny, F.A., 188
Mutrie, S.A., 191
Myers, J.L., 216–217

Nagao, D.H., 35, 165, 167, 178
Nagasawa, Y., 170
Neale, M.A., 154

Nebeker, D.M., 207
Neck, C.P., 56
Negotiation, 146–151
Nemeth, C.J., 37–38
Neter, E., 143
Neujien, B., 154
Neville, K.J., 184
Nickless, C.J., 196
Nida, S., 25
Nisbett, R.E., 15, 143
Noel, J.G., 19
Norms and group membership, 13
Northcraft, G.B., 154, 175
Novick, D.G., 170
Nowak, A., 27, 179, 204
Nunamaker, J.F., 170–171, 174, 176
Nurius, P., 143

O'Bannon, D.P., 152
O'Brien, S., 182
O'Connell, A., 135
O'Connor, F.J., 158
O'Connor, K.M., 175
O'Gara, P.W., 134
O'Reilly, C.A., 16
O'shea, T., 4, 173
Oakes, P.J., 2, 18
Offermann, L.R., 131
Ogloff, J.R.P., 163
Ohayv, D.D., 154
Oka, T., 96
Okamoto, K., 96
Olian, J.D., 152
Olson, J.M., 142
Olson, M., 90, 105
Ono, K., 53, 158, 160, 162
Orasanu, J.M., 186
Orbell, J.M., 106–111, 122
Organizations
    culture at work, 153–155
    industrial-organizational
        psychology, 1–2, 127, 146–147
Orgren, R.A., 189
Orlady, H.W., 186
Ortiz, A.E., 20
Osborn, A.F., 46
Osgood, C.E., 147

Ostrom, T., 82, 88
Other-total ratio, 28–29
    audiences, 29
    social influence and, 29–30
    productivity, 30
Ouchi, W.G., 154
Ouellette, J.A., 37

Paicheler, G., 37
Paolillo, J.G.P., 170
Papastamou, S., 40
Paranka, D., 176
Park, B., 18
Park, D.W., 173
Park, W.W., 55–56
Parks, C.D., 1, 4, 20, 51, 53, 100–102,
        107, 109, 114, 123, 127, 146,
        148, 158, 162, 178
Parry, M.E., 153
Pasquale, J.C., 179
Patenaude, A.F., 187
Paulus, P.B., 48, 68, 97, 176
Payne, S.K., 22, 27
Pearson, C.A.L., 153
Peckham, V., 83
Peirce, R.S., 150
Peiro, J.M., 187–188
Pendry, L.F., 206
Pennington, N., 161–162
Penrod, S.D., 2, 33–35, 151, 161–163,
        165–167, 177
Perez, J.A., 38, 40
Personnaz, B., 40
Peters, L.H., 129
Peters, T.J., 154
Peterson, R.S., 37–38
Peterson, T.R., 122
Petrovic, O., 176
Pettigrew, T.F., 112
Petty, R.E., 82, 85, 88, 91
Pfeffer, J., 144
Phillips, A.S., 130
Phillips, S.T., 196
Phinney, J.S., 18
Pinkley, R.L., 206
Platow, M.J., 135
Platt, M.B., 179

Plott, C.E., 212
Podsakoff, P.M., 131
Pohlmann, J.T., 129
Poletes, G., 48
Pollard, R., 191–193
Polley, R.B., 183
Pollock, D., 188
Poulson, R.L., 163
Pratkanis, A., 55–56
Price, K.R., 88
Prince, C., 181–182, 185
Pritchard, R.D., 135
Probasco, P., 55–56
Pruitt, D.G., 4, 146–151, 203
Public goods, 102–105, 112–113
Pujal, M., 38
Purdy, D.A., 191
Pusecker, P.A., 74–75, 87, 97, 196
Putnam, V.L., 176

Ragan, J.W., 50, 128
Raimbault, G., 187
Rajaratnam, N., 46, 52
Rajecki, D.W., 67
Ramos, J., 187–188
Rapoport, Am., 106–108, 110–112
Rapoport, An., 101
Rappaport, J., 187
Raymond, P., 205
Rechner, P.L., 50
Reed, T., 11
Reid, A., 18
Reid, F.J.M., 175
Reifman, A., 194
Reinig, B.A., 176
Reis, H.T., 158
Relative deprivation
   referent cognitions, 138–142
   work and, 135–142
Rentsch, J.R., 155
Resnick, L.B., 205
Rheaume, K., 141
Rice, R.W., 128
Richardson, K.D., 197, 199–200
Ridgeway, C.L., 2, 14, 179
Ringelmann, M., 82–83
Rittle, R.H., 68

Roberts, K.H., 205
Robertson, B., 165
Robinson, J.P., 204
Robinson, T., 141
Rocke, D.M., 102
Roehl, J.A., 151
Roese, N., 145
Rogers, P.A., 11
Rohrbaugh, J., 49
Roland, E.J., 176
Rosen, S., 16
Rosenbaum, M.E., 12
Rosenfield, D., 141
Rosenholtz, S.J., 2, 14
Rosenthal, R., 29
Ross, L., 143
Roth, J., 151
Rothschild, M., 177
Rourke, P.A., 67
Rouse, W.B., 183
Roy, M.C., 176
Rubini, M., 38
Rugs, D., 39
Ruhe, J.A., 214
Rush, M.C., 130
Rutte, C.G., 116–117, 119
Ryan, C.S., 18

Sainfort, F.C., 176
Saks, M., 158, 167
Salas, E., 47, 152, 181–183, 185–186
Salovey, P., 179
Samuelson, C.D., 116–119, 121
Sandal, G.M., 184
Sandberg, W.R., 50
Sanders, G.S., 69–70, 76, 154
Sanders, K.J., 207
Sanna, L.J., 1, 27, 74–75, 85, 87–90,
   97, 127, 145–146, 196
Sato, K., 111
Saunders, C.L., 163
Savicki, V., 171, 174
Sayeed, L., 170
Scandura, T.A., 17, 130
Schaerfl, L.M., 120
Schaufeli, W.B., 144
Scheier, M.F., 28, 71–73, 89

Schein, E.A., 154

Schermer, T., 53

Schersching, C., 4, 161

Schiemann, W., 130

Schlenker, B.R., 72, 102, 196

Schlenker, D.R., 196

Schmidt, G.W., 200

Schmitt, B.H., 66

Schmitt, D.R., 135

Schmitt, M.H., 56

Schneer, J.A., 175

Schneider, B., 203

Schneider, S.K., 171

Schopler, J., 18

Schreisheim, C.A., 128–129

Schuchart, G.E., 31

Schwartz, A.E., 127

Schwartz, B., 190–191

Schweiger, D.M., 50

Schwenk, C.R., 50, 174

Scott, J., 217

Scully, J., 152

Sears, D.O., 12

Sechrest, L., 207

Sedikides, C., 27, 143

Sego, D.J., 152

Seibold, D.R., 188

Sekerak, G.J., 68

Self-efficacy
   performance and, 74–75, 96–97
   social dilemmas, 105–106

Self-perceptions, 18–19

Self-presentation
   basking in reflected glory, 197
   home-field advantage, 194–196
   performance, 72–74

Semin, G.R., 71, 76–77

Sentis, K.P., 120

Sessa, V.I., 188–189

Seta, J.J., 74

Sethna, B.N., 171

Shaffer, D.R., 164

Shaud, J.A., 182

Shave, R., 135

Shaver, P.R., 130–131

Shaw, M.E., 45

Shea, G.P., 152

Shepherd, M.M., 176

Sheppard, B.H., 151

Shepperd, J.A., 88, 93, 97

Sheridan, J.E., 154

Sherif, C., 212

Sherif, M., 212

Sherman, J., 38

Shirakashi, S., 82

Shirani, A.I., 170, 174

Shotland, R.L., 74–75, 196

Showers, C.J., 195

Shupe, E.I., 58–59, 175

Siegel, J., 171–173

Siegel, S., 147

Sigall, H., 195–196

Sillars, A.L., 149

Silva, J.M., 193

Silver, S.D., 171

Simmons, R.T., 110–111

Simon, R., 182, 185

Simpson, J.A., 2, 12

Sims, H.P., 152

Singh, R., 22

Singh, R.P., 22

Siverson, R.M., 102

Skogstad, A., 186

Skowronski, J.J., 206

Sloan, L.R., 11, 198–199

Smilowitz, M., 173

Smith, C., 153

Smith, C.S., 127

Smith, D.K., 151

Smith, H.J., 19

Smith, J.M., 179

Smith, K.A., 152

Smith, K.G., 152

Smith, L.F., 171

Smith, L.M., 153

Smith, M.J., 207

Smith, V.L., 165

Smolensky, M.W., 173

Snyder, C.R., 11, 200

Snyder, E.E., 191

Social comparison
   direction, 145
   distraction/conflict, 69–70
   membership in groups and, 12–13

social loafing and, 86–88
work and, 142–146
Social compensation, 94–96
Social dilemmas
computer-based, 178–179
conformity, 116
cooperation, 105–109
performance and, 90–94
prisoners dilemma, 100–102
resource dilemma, 113–115
Social facilitation, 61–77
audiences and coactors, 61–62
drive theory, 64–65
evaluation, 67–69, 73, 74–75
mere presence, 65–67
self-efficacy, 74–75
Social impact, 22–28
diffusion of responsibility, 26
multiplicative and divisive, 22–24
social loafing, 26–27
Social influence
informational, 36–37
social impact, 25
Social influence model, 33–35
juries, 34
Social loafing, 82–89
evaluation and, 86–88
goals, 88–89
identifiability, 83–86
social impact, 26–27
Social physics, 31–33
crowding and, 33
Solomon, H., 46, 51, 177
Sommer, K.L., 95
Song, X.M., 153
Spanos, N.P., 163
Spears, R., 4, 171–173
Spence, K.W., 64
Spitzer, C.E., 159
Sproull, L., 171, 173, 175
Sridhar, S., 170
Stahelski, A.J., 188
Stanne, M., 20
Star, S.A., 136
Stasser, G., 3, 50–51, 159, 178, 206
Stasson, M.F., 20, 53, 158, 160, 162, 167

Status, 13–15
hospital teams, 187–189
Steel, R.P., 153
Steenland, K., 194
Steffen, A.M., 188–189
Steil, J.M., 144
Steiner, I.D., 1, 46, 52, 80–84, 164
Steinhilber, A., 194–196
Stern, P.C., 121
Stewart, D., 51
Stiles, W.B., 214
Stilwell, D., 130
Stone, W.S., 174
Stott, C.J.T., 175
Stouffer, S.A., 136
Stout, R.J., 186
Straus, S.G., 171, 174–175
Streim, J.E., 188
Stroebe, W., 3, 47–48, 108
Strube, M.J, 68, 129, 143
Struthers, N.J., 201
Suchman, E.A., 136
Sucker effect, 90–94, 108–109
Suls, J.M., 142, 204
Summers, C., 179
Susmilch, C., 140
Susser, K., 206
Swanson, B., 189
Sweeney, J.D., 20
Swets, J.A., 182
Syna, H., 150
Szamrej, J., 179
Szilvas, K., 53
Szymanski, K., 87–88, 96
Szymanski, L., 187

Taha, L.H., 172
Tajfel, H., 2, 17–19, 144
Tanford, S., 2, 33–35, 165
Tang, T.L., 207
Tang, V.W., 170
Tansik, D.A., 176
Tasks
difficulty and social facilitation, 62–64
intellective and judgmental, 56–59
resources, 79–82

typology, 81
Tassinary, L.G., 67
Tatum, C., 207
Taylor, D.W., 46–47
Taylor, L.A., 51, 178
Taylor, R., 135
Taylor, R.B., 191
Taylor, S.E., 143–145
Teamwork, 151–153
Tepper, B.J., 129
Terrade, K., 163
Tesser, A., 16, 143, 145
Tetlock, P.E., 55
Tetreault, L.A., 129
Thaima, S., 48
't Hart, P., 56
Thibaut, J.W., 2, 11–13, 36, 151
Thomas, J.C., 130
Thompsen, P.A., 173
Thorne, A., 11, 198–199
Tice, D.M., 195
Tindale, R.S., 35, 165, 167, 178, 205–206, 212
Titus, L.J., 62, 68
Titus, W., 3, 51
Tolleson, P.S., 207
Touval, S., 150
Trafimow, D., 206
Triandis, H.C., 17–18, 206
Triplett, N., 61, 63
Trommsdorf, G., 47
Trope, Y., 143
Trost, M.R., 38
Tsukuda, R.A., 188
Turley, K.J., 89–90
Turner, J.C., 2, 13, 17–19, 144, 179
Turner, M.E., 55–56
Turoff, M., 173
Tversky, A., 138
Tyler, T.R., 12, 19

Uhl-Bien, M., 129
Urban, J.M., 186
Ursin, H., 184

Vaernes, R., 184
Valacich, J.S., 50, 170–171, 174, 176

Vallacher, R.R., 204
VanderStoep, S.W., 58
van de Kragt, A.J.C., 106, 109–111
van de Vliert, E., 150
van den Bos, K., 140, 142
van der Velde, M., 154
van Dijk, E., 135
van Lange, P.A.M., 102
Van de Ven, A.H., 49
Van Yperen, N., 145
Vanjani, M., 169–170
Varca, P.E., 191
Vermunt, R., 140, 142
Victor, B., 154
Vinet, A., 189
Vitti, E., 40
Vollrath, D.A., 35, 205–206
Volpato, C., 38, 40

Wachter, R., 176
Wachtler, J., 38
Wack, D.L., 68
Waite, M.S., 189
Walker, J.M., 108–109
Walker, L., 151
Walker, M.R., 11, 198–199
Wall, J.W., 149
Wall, T.D., 153
Wallach, M.A., 146
Walpole, J., 170
Walster, E., 132
Walster, G.W., 132
Walther, J.B., 171, 173, 175
Wang, Y., 82
Wann, D.L., 19
Ward, W., 89
Wasserman, S., 217
Waterman, R.H., 154
Watson, W.E., 212
Wayment, H.A., 143–144
Wayne, S.J., 18, 130
Weatherly, K.A., 154
Webster, M., 2, 14
Wegner, D.M., 205
Weick, K.E., 205
Weiler, P.G., 189
Weiner, E.L., 184–186

Weiner, H.R., 183
Weinholtz, D., 189
Weisband, S.P., 171–172
Weitzman, E.A., 216
Wells, G.L., 158
Wells, J., 179
Welton, G.L., 150
Werner, J., 53, 159
West, S.G., 112
Wetherell, M.S., 179
Wheeler, B.C., 176
White, B.J., 212
White, P.H., 88–89
White, R.K., 112
Whiteside, H.D., 207
Whittemore, K.E., 163
Wicklund, R.A., 71–72
Wiersma, M.E., 153
Wilhemy, R.A., 25
Wilke, H.A.M., 102, 113, 115–119, 135, 140, 142
Williams, K.B., 22, 26
Williams, K.D., 3–4, 22, 26, 82–83, 85–86, 94–97, 145
Williams, L.N., 163
Williams, R.M., 136
Williges, R.C., 175
Wills, T.A., 19, 142–143
Wilson, L.A., 106, 109
Wilson, T.D., 15
Winship, C., 177
Winters, P., 54–55
Wirtz, P.W., 131
Wisenfield, B.M., 135, 140
Wish, M., 214
Wittenbaum, G.M., 206
Wolf, S., 22, 25, 27

Wood, J.V., 143
Wood, W., 37
Woods, M.F., 48
Woody, J.R., 184
Worringham, C.J., 68
Wright, E.F., 196, 206
Wright, R.A., 88
Wright, R.D., 196
Wyer, R.S., 89
Wynne, B.E., 176

Xenikou, A., 154

Yamagishi, T., 4, 109, 111–112, 122
Yamaguchi, S., 96
Yammarino, F.J., 183
Yen, J., 176
Young, R.F., 67

Zaccaro, S.J., 82, 88, 182
Zack, M.H., 170
Zahn, G.L., 16
Zajonc, R.B., 3, 12, 64–68
Zanna, M.P., 11, 146, 172, 174
Zartman, I.W., 150
Zeisel, H., 167
Zeiss, A.M., 188–189
Zemke, P.E., 113, 115, 117–119
Zheng, L., 27
Zillman, D., 199
Zimmerman, S.K., 20, 53, 158, 160, 162
Zinn, K.L., 169
Zubek, J.M., 150
Zuber, J.A., 53
Zuckerman, M., 158